"In recent years, interest in work and age has grown considerably. Zacher and Rudolph provide a definitive volume on the topi~ *h~* ~dd~~~~~~ *h~* k~~ ~h~ll~~~~~ of today and suggests the advancements neede set of leading scholars share their expertise or practical issues making the book an essential and professionals alike."

—**Tammy D. Allen, Ph.D.**, *Di*
Department of P.

"Zacher and Rudolph have assembled top intellectuals in the study of workplace aging in *Age and Work: Advances in Theory, Methods, and Practice* to push theory, research, and practice to the next level. There is something for everyone here. For researchers, this far-reaching volume suggests new perspectives on well-worn theories and presents practical methodological insights. Practitioners will better understand the aging workforce. It promises to be required reading for anyone interested in workplace aging."

—**Margaret E. Beier, Ph.D.**, *Professor in the Department of Psychological Sciences, Rice University*

"Research on work and aging has exploded in the past couple of decades. *Age and Work* is the perfect gateway to this literature and an excellent resource for those wanting to grasp the complexities and implications of workforce aging. With its emphasis on theory, methods, and practice, it will be of interest to seasoned researchers as well as newcomers to this field."

—**Prashant Bordia, Ph.D.**, *Professor of Management, Australian National University*

"This book excels in promoting age from supporting act as a standard control variable to chief character. The long-standing call to take time and process more seriously is expertly answered from multiple perspectives in the well-curated collection of chapters. Researchers and practitioners from every field in work and organizational psychology will find that considering age more fully offers amazing conceptual insights and new avenues for effective interventions."

—**Gudela Grote, Ph.D.**, *Professor of Work and Organizational Psychology, ETH Zurich*

"This comprehensive book offers up-to-date knowledge and innovative ideas regarding the role of age and aging in the workplace. Written by leading experts in the field, it is a valuable resource for scholars and practitioners interested in understanding and addressing the consequences of demographic change."

—**Kène Henkens, Ph.D.**, *Head of the Theme Group on Work & Retirement at Netherlands Interdisciplinary Demographic Institute (NIDI); Chair in Sociology of Retirement at the University of Amsterdam; Professor of Ageing, Retirement and the Life Course at the University Medical Center Groningen*

"This book presents an impressive set of chapters from some of the leading researchers on the topic of age in the workplace. Beyond an integrative review of the current state of knowledge in theory, methods, and practical applications, the book presents key advances, novel ideas, and directions for future research. Overall, the book makes a strong case for paying more attention to the role age plays in the workplace and how researchers and practitioners can address this challenge and opportunity."

—**Andreas Hirschi, Ph.D.**, *Professor of Work and Organizational Psychology, University of Bern*

AGE AND WORK

The edited volume *Age and Work: Advances in Theory, Methods, and Practice* presents a systematic collection of key advances in theory, methods, and practice regarding age(ing) and work. This cutting-edge collection breaks new ground by developing novel and useful theory, explaining underutilized but important methodological approaches, and suggesting original practical applications of emerging research topics.

The book begins with a prologue by the World Health Organization's unit head for aging and health, an introduction on the topic by the editors, and an overview of past, current, and future workforce age trends. Subsequently, the first main section outlines theoretical advances regarding alternative age constructs (e.g., subjective age), intersectionality of age with gender and social class, paradoxical age-related actions, generational identity, and integration of lifespan theories. The second section presents methodological advances regarding behavioral assessment, age at the team and organizational levels, longitudinal and diary methods, experiments and interventions, qualitative methods, and the use of archival data. The third section covers practical advances regarding age and job crafting, knowledge exchange, the work/nonwork interface, healthy aging, and absenteeism and presenteeism, and organizational meta-strategies for younger and older workers. The book concludes with an epilogue by an eminent scholar in age and work.

Written in a scientific yet accessible manner, the book offers a valuable resource for undergraduate and graduate students, academics in the fields of psychology and business, as well as practitioners working in the areas of human resource management and organizational development.

Hannes Zacher is Professor of Work and Organizational Psychology at Leipzig University, Germany. His research program focuses on aging at work and career development, occupational health and wellbeing, proactive and adaptive employee behaviors, and environmental sustainability in organizations.

Cort W. Rudolph is Associate Professor of Industrial and Organizational Psychology at Saint Louis University, USA. His research program focuses on a variety of issues related to the aging workforce, including applications of lifespan development theories, wellbeing and work-longevity, and ageism.

SIOP Organizational Frontiers Series

Series Editors

Angelo DeNisi
Tulane University, USA

Kevin Murphy
University of Limerick, Ireland

Editorial Board

Derek R. Avery
Wake Forest University, USA

Jill Ellingson
University of Kansas, USA

Franco Fraccaroli
University of Trento, Italy

Susan Jackson
Rutgers University, USA

Paul Sparrow
Lancaster University, UK

Hannes Zacher
Leipzig University, Germany

Jing Zhou
Rice University, USA

The Organizational Frontiers Series is sponsored by the Society for Industrial and Organizational Psychology (SIOP). Launched in 1983 to make scientific contributions accessible to the field, the series publishes books addressing emerging theoretical developments, fundamental and translational research, and theory-driven practice in the field of Industrial-Organizational Psychology and related organizational science disciplines including organizational behavior, human resource management, and labor and industrial relations.

Books in this series aim to inform readers of significant advances in research; challenge the research and practice community to develop and adapt new ideas; and promote the use of scientific knowledge in the solution of public policy issues and increased organizational effectiveness.

The Series originated in the hope that it would facilitate continuous learning and spur research curiosity about organizational phenomena on the part of both scientists and practitioners.

The Society for Industrial and Organizational Psychology is an international professional association with an annual membership of more than 8,000 industrial-organizational (I-O) psychologists who study and apply scientific principles to the workplace. I-O psychologists serve as trusted partners to business, offering strategically focused and scientifically rigorous solutions for a number of workplace issues. SIOP's mission is to enhance human well-being and performance in organizational and work settings by promoting the science, practice, and teaching of I-O psychology. For more information about SIOP, please visit www.siop.org.

For more information about this series, please visit www.routledge.com/SIOP-Organizational-Frontiers-Series/book-series/SIOP

AGE AND WORK

Advances in Theory, Methods, and Practice

Edited by Hannes Zacher and Cort W. Rudolph

Routledge
Taylor & Francis Group
NEW YORK AND LONDON

SOCIETY for
INDUSTRIAL and
ORGANIZATIONAL
PSYCHOLOGY
ORGANIZATIONAL FRONTIERS SERIES

Cover image: © Getty Images

First published 2022
by Routledge
605 Third Avenue, New York, NY 10158

and by Routledge
4 Park Square, Milton Park, Abingdon, Oxon, OX14 4RN

Routledge is an imprint of the Taylor & Francis Group, an informa business

Library of Congress Cataloging-in-Publication Data
A catalog record for this title has been requested

ISBN: 9780367545543 (hbk)
ISBN: 9780367545536 (pbk)
ISBN: 9781003089674 (ebk)

DOI: 10.4324/9781003089674

Typeset in Bembo
by Apex CoVantage, LLC

To Benjamin and Lily
Hannes Zacher

To Amy and Grier
Cort W. Rudolph

CONTENTS

FIGURES

TABLES

EDITOR BIOGRAPHIES

Hannes Zacher is a professor of work and organizational psychology at Leipzig University. He earned his Ph.D. from the University of Giessen and subsequently worked in academic positions in Australia and the Netherlands. In his research program, he investigates aging at work and career development, occupational health and well-being, proactive and adaptive behavior, and environmental sustainability in organizations. Across these research agendas, he employs multiple methodologies, including longitudinal and experience sampling studies. His research is well supported through competitive grants and industry funding. He has published over 160 articles in peer-reviewed journals and serves on a number of international journal editorial boards.

Cort W. Rudolph is an associate professor of industrial and organizational psychology at Saint Louis University. He earned his Ph.D. from Wayne State University. His research focuses broadly on issues associated with age(ing) at work, including a focus on leadership, occupational health and well-being, proactive and adaptive behavior, and careers and career development. Cort's research employs complex longitudinal methodologies that allow for the modeling of dynamic inter- and intra-individual variability. His research is supported through both grants and industry funding, and he has published over 70 articles in peer-reviewed journals and serves as an editor for—and editorial board member of— several international journals.

CONTRIBUTOR BIOGRAPHIES

Daniela M. Andrei is a senior research fellow at Curtin University where she coordinates the research stream on "Organizations and the Mature Workforce" within the Centre for Excellence in Population Ageing Research. She completed her PhD in Romania and worked in academic positions in both Romania and Australia. Daniela's research interests revolve around work design, with a focus on the multilevel antecedents of work design; its consequences for performance, well-being, and safety; and its role in supporting successful aging at work. Daniela's research has been published in journals such as *Journal of Applied Psychology*, *Journal of Vocational Behavior*, and *Safety Science*.

Boris B. Baltes is Associate Provost for Faculty Affairs and Professor of Psychology at Wayne State University. His major research interests include examining biases in performance appraisal, age and workplace issues, and the area of work–family conflict. His work has appeared in many journals, including the *Journal of Applied Psychology*, the *Journal of Management*, and the *Journal of Organizational Behavior*. He has been an associate editor for the *Journal of Organizational Behavior* and a guest editor for the *Journal of Business and Psychology* and is on the editorial boards of various journals. He is also a fellow of the Society for Industrial/ Organizational Psychology.

Janet L. Barnes-Farrell is an industrial-organizational psychologist and Professor of Psychological Sciences at the University of Connecticut, USA. She is also an investigator with the Center for the Promotion of Health in the New England Workplace (CPH-NEW), a national Center of Excellence on Total Worker Health. Dr. Barnes-Farrell has been conducting research on issues related to our aging workforce for over 40 years; her published work addresses topics ranging from age discrimination to retirement decision processes. Her current research centers on psychosocial aspects of work and aging, with special emphasis on the work-life concerns of older workers.

Julia L. Beckel, M.S., is a doctoral student in industrial-organizational psychology with a concentration in occupational health psychology at Colorado State University. Her current research primarily concerns the health and safety of vulnerable populations in the workplace, work design, and cognitive aging. Prior to her graduate studies, Julia worked for the Federal Aviation Administration where she assisted in the development and implementation of a variety of research projects related to personnel selection and assessment, training, and stress management for air traffic control personnel.

Grant M. Brady is Assistant Professor of management at California State University East Bay in the College of Business and Economics. Dr. Brady's research interests are in improving the workplace for employees, and, more specifically, he focuses on aging at work, employee well-being, and organizational staffing processes. He is particularly interested in how organizations can support employees working effectively across the lifespan, including what factors facilitate and hinder working effectively later in one's career. Dr. Brady's research has been presented at national conferences and published in several peer-reviewed journals and book chapters.

Anne Burmeister is Assistant Professor HRM at Rotterdam School of Management. She obtained her PhD in work and organizational psychology from Leuphana University Lüneburg (Germany) and spent two years as a postdoc in work and organizational psychology at University of Bern (Switzerland). Before her PhD, she worked as a strategy consultant for Boston Consulting Group, where she built expertise on strategy and people and organization topics in various industries. Her research on knowledge transfer processes and social interactions at work with a focus on aging and age-diverse workforces contributes to the more effective management of knowledge and diversity in organizations.

David M. Cadiz is a faculty member in the School of Business at Portland State University. Dr. Cadiz's research focuses on the influence of diversity in the workplace and is influenced by his applied work experiences in the healthcare, training, and technology industries. Specifically, he investigates multiple aspects of the aging workforce, the intersection of behavioral health and work, and developing interventions to effectively address workplace diversity issues. He has coauthored several peer-reviewed articles and book chapters related to these topics and frequently presents at academic and professional conferences. He is on the editorial board of *Work, Aging and Retirement*.

David P. Costanza is Associate Professor of organizational sciences and of psychology at The George Washington University and a Senior Consortium Fellow with the US Army Research Institute. He earned his bachelor's degree from the University of Virginia and his master's and doctorate degrees from George Mason University. His research, teaching, and consulting are in the areas of organizational processes, generational differences, leadership, organizational decline, and organizational culture as well as statistics and research methods. His work has been published in journals including the *Journal of Business and Psychology*, *Personnel Psychology*, *Journal of Vocational Behavior*, and *Work, Aging and Retirement*.

Jürgen Deller is a professor of psychology at Leuphana University Lüneburg, Germany. He is also the research director of the Silver Workers Research Institute in Berlin and delegate to the ISO Technical Committee "Ageing Societies." He earned his PhD from Helmut Schmidt University, Hamburg. Following university education, he joined the corporate headquarters of Daimler-Benz, Stuttgart and worked with Daimler Chrysler Services (debis) AG, Berlin, as the senior HR manager until 1999. His research program includes organizational management of the demographic change, international human resources management, and the labor market integration of refugees. He has published over 120 articles and book chapters.

Caitlin A. Demsky is Associate Professor of Management in the School of Business Administration at Oakland University in Rochester, Michigan, USA. She earned her PhD in industrial-organizational psychology with a concentration in occupational health psychology from Portland State University. Her research program explores employee stress and the intersection between the work and nonwork domains, with a focus on recovery from work demands, work–life balance, and workplace mistreatment. Her research has been recognized in national and international media outlets, including Newsweek, Forbes, and ABC News, and she serves on the editorial board of several international journals.

Laura Dietz is a research assistant and doctoral candidate of work and organizational psychology at the University of Hohenheim. During her master's studies, she participated in a predoctoral program to gain her first experience in the academic world. Her research focuses on aging and age diversity at work, workplace friendship, and knowledge transfer.

Yanran Fang is an Assistant Professor of the Department of Leadership and Organizational Management in the School of Management, Zhejiang University. She earned her PhD from Sun Yat-sen University, and has worked as a postdoctoral associate at the University of Florida. In her research programs, she investigates employee career development and well-being, migrant worker adaptation and retention, as well as leadership and team processes. She has employed various research methods to answer research questions in these areas, including social network analysis, multilevel modeling, and structural equation modeling.

Ulrike Fasbender is Professor of business and organizational psychology at the University of Hohenheim. She received her PhD from Leuphana University Lüneburg. Ulrike is passionate about research on work and aging, including career development over the lifespan, managing age diversity, and intergroup and workplace relationships. Her research has been published in a wide range of journals, such as *Personnel Psychology* and the *Journal of Applied Psychology*. Moreover, Ulrike is Associate Editor of the *Journal of Occupational and Organizational Psychology* and on the editorial boards of *Work, Aging and Retirement*; the *Journal of Vocational Behavior*; and the *Journal of Organizational Behavior*.

Lisa M. Finkelstein (PhD, Tulane University, 1996) is Professor of social-I/O psychology at Northern Illinois University (NIU), where she has served on the faculty for 25 years. Her scholarship is primarily in the areas of age stereotyping, metastereotyping, and discrimination, stigma in the workplace, mentoring, high potential identification, and humor at work. Lisa serves on several editorial boards and has served the Society for Industrial and Organizational Psychology (SIOP) as a member of the executive board, conference chair, and program chair. She won the 2016 SIOP Distinguished Contributions to Service Award, is a fellow of SIOP, and has received recognition at NIU for her teaching and mentoring.

Gwenith G. Fisher is Associate Professor in the Department of Psychology at Colorado State University, Adjunct Associate Professor in the Colorado School of Public Health, and Affiliate Investigator with the Centre of Excellence in Population Ageing Research. She received a PhD and MA in Psychology from Bowling Green State University and a BA from Penn State University. Her research examines individual and work factors related to worker health, well-being, and retirement, including cognitive functioning. She is President-Elect for the Society for Occupational Health Psychology, directs the CSU Occupational Health Psychology program, and serves on the editorial board of multiple journals.

Fabiola H. Gerpott is Professor of Leadership at WHU–Otto Beisheim School of Management in Germany. She graduated from a double PhD program in business administration and organizational psychology from Jacobs University Bremen and Vrije Universiteit Amsterdam. In her research program, she blends management science, social psychology, and communication research. Identifying as an interdisciplinary researcher with a passion for behavior-focused research, she publishes in top-tier journals in different fields. Her mission is to create, teach, and communicate evidence to shape more inclusive workplaces.

Kilian Hampel is a research associate and doctoral candidate at the Future of Work Lab at the University of Konstanz, Germany. He completed a double degree master program at the University of Konstanz and Universitat Pompeu Fabra Barcelona, Spain. In his research, he focuses on aging at work, the digital transformation of the workplace, as well as new work environments and remote work.

Guido Hertel is chair of organizational and business psychology at the University of Münster, Germany. His research addresses emerging trends and challenges in organizations, including digitalization of work, demographic changes and aging populations, integration of refugees, and synergy effects in collaborations. His work is published widely in top-ranked journals, such as the *Journal of Applied Psychology, Journal of Management, Journal of Organizational Behavior, Journal of Personality and Social Psychology*, and *Psychological Bulletin*, and he serves as both the editor and a member of editorial boards. In addition to his academic activities, Guido works as speaker and consultant for organizations. For more information, see *www.uni-muenster.de/OWMS/*

Sabine Hommelhoff is a senior researcher at the Institute of Psychology at Friedrich-Alexander University Erlangen-Nürnberg (FAU), where she completed her postdoctoral qualification (Habilitation) in the field of work and organizational psychology. She earned her doctoral degree from Technical University Munich in the field of consumer behavior and has worked for several years in the corporate sector. In her research, she focuses on workplace relationships and aging at work.

Ruth Kanfer is a Professor of work and organizational psychology and Director of the Work Science Center at the Georgia Institute of Technology. She is a leading scholar in work motivation and engagement, job search and reemployment, and learning across the lifespan. Her current interests focus on workforce aging, reskilling, and postpandemic work design. She has published over 125 articles and chapters and four edited books and is coauthor of *Ageless Talent: Enhancing the Performance and Well-Being of Your Age-Diverse Workforce*. She is a Fellow of the Academy of Management, the American Psychological Association, and the Association for Psychological Sciences.

Tine Köhler is Associate Professor for international management at the University of Melbourne, Australia. Dr. Köhler's research focuses on global teamwork and research methods and statistics. Her main research interests include cross-cultural management, cross-cultural communication and coordination, group processes, qualitative research methods, research design, meta-analysis, and regression. She received her prediploma (undergraduate degree) from the Philipps-University Marburg in Germany and her MA and PhD degrees from George Mason University in the US. She is currently Incoming Co-Editor-in-Chief at Organizational Research Methods (ORM) and previously held Associate Editor roles at ORM and Academy of Management Learning and Education.

Dorien T. A. M. Kooij is Professor of human resource studies at the Department of Human Resource Studies of Tilburg University, the Netherlands. Her research focuses on aging at work, in particular on HR practices for older workers, on how work motivation changes with aging, on future time perspective, and on job crafting. She has published in international peer-reviewed journals such as the *Journal of Applied Psychology*, the *Journal of Organizational Behavior*, *Work & Stress*, and *Psychology and Aging*.

Florian Kunze is Professor for organizational studies and head of the Future of Work Lab at the University of Konstanz, Germany. Before, he was Assistant Professor at the University of St. Gallen, Switzerland, where he also completed his dissertation in 2010. His research revolves around managing the demographic change in organizations, the digitalization of the workplace, and effective leadership behaviors in teams and companies.

Nale Lehmann-Willenbrock is Professor of industrial/organizational psychology at the University of Hamburg. Previously, she was Associate Professor at the University of Amsterdam and assistant professor at VU University Amsterdam. She holds a PhD from Technische Universität Braunschweig. She studies team processes, workplace meetings, leader–follower dynamics, and methodological advances for understanding emergent behavioral patterns in workplace interactions. Her work is supported by grants and industry funding and has been published in the *Academy of Management Journal*, the *Journal of Applied Psychology*, the *Journal of Organizational Behavior*, and the *Leadership Quarterly*, among others. She currently serves as Associate Editor for *Small Group Research*.

Ignacio Madero-Cabib is an assistant professor of sociology and public health at Pontificia Universidad Católica de Chile. Dr. Madero-Cabib serves as a deputy director of the Millennium Nucleus for the Study of the Life Course and Vulnerability (http://mliv.cl) and as an associate researcher at the Centre for Social Conflict and Cohesion Studies (https://coes.cl). His research, published in several leading life course and aging journals, focuses on the impact of cumulative advantages and disadvantages on vulnerability among older people.

Justin Marcus is an assistant professor of management and strategy at the College of Administrative Sciences and Economics of Koç University, in Istanbul, Turkey. He received a BA and a BS from the University of Nebraska–Lincoln, and an MS and PhD from the University of Central Florida. His research interests include substantive topics in cross-cultural management and workplace prejudice/diversity with a concerted focus on work and aging. His work has been published in numerous top scientific journals such as the *Journal of World Business*, the *Journal of Vocational Behavior*, the *Journal of Organizational Behavior*, and the *Journal of Cross-Cultural Psychology*.

Sharon K. Parker is an ARC Laureate Fellow, a John Curtin Distinguished Professor, and Director of the Centre for Transformative Work Design at Curtin University. She is a recipient of the ARC's Kathleen Fitzpatrick Award, and the Academy of Management OB Division Mentoring Award. Her research focuses on work design, employee performance and development, and proactive behavior. She has published more than 150 internationally refereed articles, including publications in top-tier journals, and her research has been cited more than 25,000 times. She has attracted competitive research funding worth over $40,000,000 and was named among the world's most influential social scientists.

Rachel S. Rauvola is Assistant Professor of industrial & organizational psychology at DePaul University. She received her BA from Macalester College and her MS and PhD from Saint Louis University. Her research focuses on occupational health as it relates to aging, trauma, and marginalization, promoting attention to the intersections among diversity, equity, health, and work in a variety of veins.

Daniel M. Ravid is a doctoral candidate in industrial-organizational psychology at George Washington University. His research program broadly explores the changing nature of work, including individual and organizational adoption of emerging technologies, skill development and workforce readiness, and workforce aging and ageism/generationalism.

Jenn Rineer is a research psychologist and program manager at RTI International's Center for Policing Research and Investigative Science. In this role, Dr. Rineer conducts workplace and workforce surveys, qualitative studies, employee trainings, evaluations, and experimental research in criminal legal contexts. Her research focuses on worker health, job-related stress, diversity and inclusion, aging and work, and organizational effectiveness. Dr. Rineer has authored several peer-reviewed publications, book chapters, and conference presentations on these topics. Her professional background includes conducting research on employment-related issues for the Center for Parental Leave Leadership, Catalyst, Inc., and the Liberty Mutual Research Institute for Safety.

Kathrin Rosing is an assistant professor of psychology of entrepreneurial behavior at the Institute of Psychology at the University of Kassel, Germany. She completed her PhD in organizational psychology in 2011 at the Leuphana University Lüneburg, Germany. Her research concerns creativity and innovation, leadership, aging, and error management. Her main research interest focuses on how individuals, teams, and leaders manage contradictions and paradoxes. Kathrin has published her research in outlets such as *Academy of Management Journal*, *Leadership Quarterly*, and *Psychology and Aging*.

Ritu Sadana leads the World Health Organization's work on aging and health and on life-course trajectories. Dr. Sadana coordinated the consultation and drafting of the WHO Global Strategy on Ageing and Health (2016–2030), instigated preparation that lead to the UN Decade of Healthy Ageing 2021–2030, and was the lead author of the Decade of Healthy Ageing Baseline Report. She coordinates the WHO Consortium on Metrics and Evidence for Healthy Ageing made up of policy makers, academics, and civil society representatives. Trained in epidemiology, economics, and policy research, she holds a Doctor of Science from Harvard University and serves as an editorial advisor for *The Bulletin of the World Health Organization.*

Sarah E. Salvi is a PhD candidate at George Washington University in the industrial-organizational psychology program. In her research program, she investigates generational differences (or lack thereof) in the workplace and also work-life balance and autonomy in the gig economy. She is also currently Associate Research Fellow at the Army Research Institute in the Selection and Assessment Research Unit.

Susanne Scheibe is Professor of organizational psychology at the University of Groningen (Netherlands). She obtained her PhD from Free University Berlin and subsequently worked as research scientist at the Max Planck Institute for Human Development (Germany) and Stanford University (USA). Her research lies at the intersection of lifespan development and organizational behavior. She investigates how workplace characteristics and individual differences in emotions and self-regulation interact in shaping the well-being and effectiveness of employees at different ages and career stages.

Kenneth S. Shultz is a professor of psychology and executive board member for the Center on Aging at California State University, San Bernardino. His MA and PhD degrees are in Industrial and Organizational (I-O) Psychology from Wayne State University in Detroit, Michigan. He also completed postdoctoral work in social gerontology as a National Institute on Aging Post-Doctoral Fellow at the Andrus Gerontology Center at the University of Southern California. He has published over 50 peer-reviewed articles, 4 books, and 18 book chapters on a variety of topics, most recently focusing on bridge employment, successful aging at work, and retirement issues.

Gregory R. Thrasher is currently Assistant Professor of management at Oakland University. He completed his bachelor's in psychology at the University of Windsor and his masters and PhD in industrial-organizational psychology at Wayne State University. His research primarily focuses on the application of lifespan psychology theories to questions surrounding the effect of age on various workplace processes and outcomes. He has written several peer-reviewed articles and book chapters on the effect of age on topics such as motivation, leadership, and the work–life interface. Gregory also facilitates leader development programs applying these principles to the lifelong development of diverse organizational leaders.

Donald M. Truxillo is a professor at the Kemmy Business School, University of Limerick, Ireland, and Professor Emeritus at Portland State University. He studies issues related to the aging workforce such as age discrimination and promoting work ability across the lifespan. He is an associate editor at *Work, Aging and Retirement*. He is the author of over 120 peer-reviewed journal articles and book chapters. He is a fellow of the Society for Industrial and Organizational Psychology, the American Psychological Association, the Association for Psychological Science, and the International Association for Applied Psychology.

Ulrich Walwei is Vice Director of the Institute for Employment Research (IAB) in Nuremberg, Germany. In addition, he is honorary professor at the Department of Economics at the University of Regensburg. He studied economics and completed his doctorate in legal economics at the University of Paderborn (Dr. rer. pol.) where he was the research assistant to Chair of Public Finance Professor Dr. Friedrich Buttler. He has been published broadly, and his research interests focus on the analysis of labor market institutions. Recent work deals with trends and changes in work arrangements and the employment situation of older workers.

Mo Wang is Lanzillotti-McKethan Eminent Scholar Chair at the Warrington College of Business at University of Florida. Dr. Wang specializes in research areas of retirement and older worker employment, occupational health psychology, expatriate and newcomer adjustment, leadership and team processes, and advanced quantitative methodologies. He has published over 160 peer-reviewed journal articles, 30 book chapters, and 5 edited/coauthored books. He also received numerous career and research awards from the Academy of Management (AoM), the American Psychological Association (APA), and the Society for Industrial-Organizational Psychology (SIOP). He is a fellow of AOM, APA, APS, and SIOP and an elected member of Academia Europaea.

David Weiss is a Senior Lecturer in Developmental Psychology at Martin Luther University Halle-Wittenberg. After earning his PhD from the University of Erlangen-Nuremberg in Germany, he was as a Postdoc at University of Zurich in Switzerland, later an Assistant Professor at Columbia University, and a Heisenberg fellow at Leipzig University. His research program focuses on social-cognitive and motivational mechanisms across the life span with a focus on (a) subjective aging; (b) stereotypes, mindsets, and health; as well as (c) social status and social inequality. His studies include experimental, longitudinal, and cross-cultural methods and have been funded by competitive external grants.

Mona Weiss is Assistant Professor of management and diversity at Freie Universität Berlin. After earning her PhD from ETH Zurich, she was a postdoctoral researcher at New York University. In her research program, she studies employee behavior within complex organizational systems, examining, for example, how social categories such as age, gender, and occupational status affect employee attitudes, well-being, and behavior in various organizational settings (e.g., healthcare). Her work is published in top-tier journals, and she has received numerous distinguished grants and awards for her research.

Annika Wilhelmy is a senior researcher in work and organizational psychology at the University of Zurich. Previously, she was a visiting scholar at the Department of Psychology of Portland State University sponsored by the Swiss National Science Foundation and a postdoctoral researcher at the University of Zurich, where she also completed her PhD. Her research interests lie at the interface among recruitment, personnel selection, and unemployment. She uses a broad range of research methodologies including video coding approaches, online experiments, and qualitative research methods. She has led workshops on qualitative research at conferences such as SIOP, AOM, and EAWOP.

SERIES FOREWORD

One of the most striking trends in the global workplace is the aging of the workforce. This change is the results of many factors (e.g., falling birthrates, later retirements, healthier workforce), and different factors are in play in different parts of the world, but, no matter where you go, the workforce is getting older. This brings both challenges and opportunities. For example, older workers may suffer from more health problems and sometimes have trouble adapting to changes in the workplace, but they tend to be more reliable than younger workers, and they often bring substantial experience and a broad skill set to the workplace.

Zacher and Rudolph have assembled a volume that examines demographic changes in the workplace and their implications. They present (Chapters 1, 2) the latest data on changing age profiles in the workplace. They then examine in detail (Chapters 3–7) the implications of these changes for theory (e.g., changing definitions of age, intersectionality among age, gender, race, etc.), as well as for (Chapters 8–13) research methodology (e.g., developments in longitudinal research methods, experimental methods, qualitative methods). Their book includes a detailed discussion (Chapters 14–18) of organizational interventions designed to maximize older workers' opportunities to succeeded in organizations and to provide support for an aging workforce.

The goal of the Organizational Frontiers Series is to publish books that help to define and advance the frontiers of our knowledge about behavior in organizations and stimulate future research and applications. *Age and Work: Advances in Theory, Methods and Practice* advances this set of goals admirably. Zacher and Rudolph have not only summarized the current state of the field; they have set the agenda for research on aging and work for the foreseeable future.

Angelo S. DeNisi and Kevin R. Murphy

PROLOGUE

The World Health Organization (WHO) defines healthy aging as the process of developing and maintaining the functional ability that enables well-being in older age (WHO, 2017). Abilities reflect a combination of a person's intrinsic capacities—cognitive, psychological, vitality, physical, and sensory capacities—and interaction with a person's environment. Functional ability includes the ability to meet basic needs for food, clothing, suitable housing, and health and long-term care services; to learn, grow, and make decisions reflecting personal development and sense of control; to be mobile in order to complete daily tasks and participate in activities; to build and maintain relationships including with children and other family members; intimate relationships, and those with friends, neighbors, and colleagues; and to contribute to society including assisting friends, mentoring younger people, caring for family members, volunteering, pursuing social and cultural activities, and working (WHO, 2020). As defined in the WHO International Classification of Functioning, Disability and Health (WHO, 2001), *work* is used in the broadest sense and includes unpaid work in the home or in a family enterprise, paid work for another person or organization in the formal or informal economy, and self-employment. *Volunteering* is unremunerated work that older people choose to do for people outside of their household and for the wider community.

Environments are where people live and conduct their lives and shape what older people with a given level of capacity can "be" and "do" (Sen, 1985), and enable well-being. Environments, including policies, social attitudes, and physical spaces, can determine whether people, including older persons, are able to engage or participate in activities. This is also relevant to work environments, which are shaped by public and industrial policies, organizational contexts, and how people think (stereotyping), feel (prejudice), and act (discrimination) toward people based on their age (WHO, 2021). Public policies can institutionalize discrimination when laws and regulations codify discrimination based on chronological age, or they can mitigate ageism and ensure equal opportunity or equal protection irrespective of age. Another dimension is that healthy aging is a process relevant to everybody, not only to those who are disease-free. The environment will interact with each person, whether a person has no disease, some declines in physical or cognitive capacities, or several underlying conditions. An enabling environment will anticipate and mitigate declines and foster abilities across all ages.

Describing and improving functional ability, intrinsic capacity, and environments—the three components of healthy aging—represents a paradigm shift in thinking about older people and aging. Optimizing people's functional ability requires focusing on needs, rights, preferences, and goals. Healthy aging also reflects a person-centered approach that takes account of the complete range of abilities, capacities, and goals of an individual within the person's unique context, considering not only a snapshot but also how such features are dynamic over time. This process recognizes that most determinants of healthy aging and the approach to optimize people's abilities can be shaped by policy (Kralj et al., 2018). Optimizing people's abilities to contribute and work are important at every age; however, this approach also recognizes that some aspects may be more important for individuals at different stages across the life course. For example, some research suggests that, at older ages, work flexibility becomes increasingly important (Baumann & Madero-Cabib, 2021).

Approaches to extend working life are key policy responses to population aging that are growing in importance. Countries with different social protection and social security schemes—with and without flexible retirement policies—and different views on the sustainability of pension schemes, have documented an increase in the labor force participation rate of individuals beyond the age to qualify for a full pension (Madero-Cabib & Biehl, 2021). This is reflected in countries in the Organization for Economic Cooperation and Development (OECD), which focus on maintaining employment in the formal sector. In such countries, labor force participation rates of people aged 65 and older grew about 75.80% between 2000 and 2019 (from 9.10% to 16.00%; OECD, 2020), resulting in extended working lives (OECD, 2006). However, not all countries that have implemented policies to promote longer working lives have considered differences between men and women or differences in opportunities or in life expectancy across socioeconomic groups. Moreover, the reality is that the International Labour Organization (ILO) estimates that more than 60% of the world's working population is in the informal economy—ranging from less than 20% in some countries to 90% and over in other countries (ILO, 2018).

Despite advances in the research on the field of extended working lives over the last decades, several knowledge gaps exist that need to be addressed. For example, additional studies in a wider range of countries could further identify and evaluate whether policies that promote longer working years have considered employment conditions in which individuals have to continue working or whether these policies can mitigate gender-based discrimination and other forms of inequalities in opportunities, including age-based discrimination. Moreover, documenting environments where longer working years are coupled with, for example, lifelong learning opportunities and universal health coverage—and whether such environments increase people's satisfaction and motivation—will be important. Such research will add insight into the interrelationships between all functional abilities, highlighted previously. Relevant to such research efforts is whether policies are reversing perverse incentives that have forced older people in poor health and with limited financial resources to work longer, whereas older people who would like to work longer are forced to stop working due to a mandatory retirement age (WHO, 2020).

The way in which labor force and work participation are measured also requires a reconsideration of who is included within the "working-age population," how "dependency-ratios" are calculated, and what is valued as an outcome of society's investments. For example, the United Nation's Agenda 2030 and Sustainable Development Goals (United Nations, 2021) provide an array of indicators that are aligned with fostering functional ability of all people including older persons, including universal health coverage, public transportation, lifelong learning opportunities, built-up areas of cities that are open for public use, and decent work including accounting for time spent on unpaid domestic and care work.

The book *Age and Work: Advances in Theory, Methods and Practice* aims to advance the frontiers of knowledge on age and work though novel and challenging questions that require answers to move industrial, work, and organizational psychology and related disciplines forward. The editors, Professors Hannes Zacher and Cort W. Rudolph, deliver on this goal across the book's 18 chapters written by some 40 leading academics. This collection conveys important advances in theory, methods, and practice, extending and fostering connections across disciplines.

Among many other contributions, this book encourages the use of a lifespan and a life course theoretical and methodological approach to explore age and work dynamics. Thus far, most studies in this field have examined older people and work through a cross-sectional approach, which only provides a snapshot without a dynamic understanding of contributing factors. A life course perspective suggests that intrinsic capacity during early development and during critical stages or periods of life can be influenced by a range of factors (biological, socioeconomic, and environmental; Ben-Shlomo & Kuh, 2002; Kuh et al., 2014). Recent longitudinal lifespan and life course studies on work and older persons have yielded two main findings regarding extended working lives (Madero-Cabib et al., 2020). First, they indicate that, despite the prevalence of early retirement pathways in multiple countries, more than half of older adults retire "on time" or choose late retirement. Second—and more importantly—these empirical studies document that older people are increasingly working in full- or part-time jobs beyond retirement age, either as employees or through self-employment, partly retiring from the labor force or moving continuously in and out of the labor market. A standardized retirement transition consisting of a one-time labor market exit from a full-time job as an employee at full pension age can no longer be considered the norm (Kuh et al., 2014). Complementing these approaches, a social determinants perspective adds further insights into the cumulative impact of social and economic disadvantage or privilege—on health and other outcomes of interest—that sort people into different life course trajectories (Halfon et al., 2018). Importantly, almost all these underlying determinants are amenable to policy change and interventions.

The timing of this book is prescient, at the start of the new United Nations Decade of Healthy Ageing 2021–2030 (United Nations, 2020). We are certain that the knowledge contained here will contribute to developing practical policies and actions to optimize older adults' abilities, particularly to contribute to the workforce. To do so, we need to accelerate action to scale up "what we know now" and further address "what we need to know" to encourage healthy aging at work.

Ritu Sadana
Ignacio Madero-Cabib

References

Baumann, I., & Madero-Cabib, I. (2021). Retirement trajectories in countries with flexible retirement policies but different welfare regimes. *Journal of Aging & Social Policy, 33*(2), 138–160. https://doi.org/10.1080/08959420.2019.1685358

Ben-Shlomo, Y., & Kuh, D. (2002). A life course approach to chronic disease epidemiology: Conceptual models, empirical challenges and interdisciplinary perspectives. *International Journal of Epidemiology, 31*(2), 285–293. https://doi.org/10.1093/ije/31.2.285

Halfon, N., Forrest, C. B., Lerner, R. M., Faustman, E. M., Tullis, E., & Son, J. (2018). Introduction to the handbook of life course health development. In N. Halfon, C. Forrest, R. Lerner, & E. Faustman (Eds.), *Handbook of life course health development*. Springer. Retrieved on 4 August 2021, from https://doi.org/10.1007/978-3-319-47143-3_1

International Labour Organization. (2018). *Women and men in the informal economy: A statistical picture* (3rd ed.). International Labour Office. Retrieved on 4 August 2021, from www.ilo.org/wcmsp5/groups/public/—dgreports/—dcomm/documents/publication/wcms_626831.pdf

Kralj, C., Daskalopoulou, C., Rodríguez-Artalejo, F., García-Esquinas, E., Cosco, T. D., & Prince, M. (2018). *Healthy ageing: A systematic review of risk factors*. King's College London. Retrieved on 4 August 2021, from http://athlosproject.eu/wp-content/uploads/2018/05/KIOPPN_HealthyAgeing-Report2018.pdf

Kuh, D., Cooper, R., Hardy, R., Richards, M., & Ben-Shlomo, Y. (2014). *A life course approach to healthy ageing*. Oxford University Press, UK.

Madero-Cabib, I., & Biehl, A. (2021). Lifetime employment—Coresidential trajectories and extended working life in Chile. *The Journal of the Economics of Ageing, 19*, 100309. https://doi.org/10.1016/j.jeoa.2021.100309

Madero-Cabib, I., Corna, L., & Baumann, I. (2020). Aging in different welfare contexts: A comparative perspective on later-life employment and health. *The Journals of Gerontology: Series B, 75*(7), 1515–1526. https://doi.org/10.1093/geronb/gbz037

OECD. (2006). *Live longer, work longer.* OECD Publishing.

OECD. (2020). *Labour force participation rate (indicator).* https://doi.org/10.1787/8a801325-en

Sen, A. (1985). *Commodities and capabilities.* Elsevier.

United Nations. (2020). United Nations decade of healthy ageing (2021–2030). In *United Nations General Assembly Seventy-Fifth Session,* Agenda item 131: Global health and foreign policy. United Nations. Retrieved on 4 August 2021, from https://undocs.org/en/A/75/L.47

United Nations. (2021). *Global indicator framework for the Sustainable Development Goals and targets of the 2030 Agenda for Sustainable Development* (A/RES/71/313 Refinements up to the 52nd Session of the Statistical Commission in March 2021). United Nations. Retrieved on 4 August 2021, from https://unstats.un.org/sdgs/indicators/indicators-list/

World Health Organization. (2001). *The international classification of functioning, disability and health.* World Health Organization. Retrieved on 8 August 2021, from www.who.int/classifications/icf/en/

World Health Organization. (2017). *Global strategy and action plan on ageing and health.* World Health Organization. Retrieved on 4 August 2021, from www.who.int/ageing/WHO-GSAP-2017.pdf?ua=1

World Health Organization. (2020). *Decade of healthy ageing: Baseline report.* World Health Organization. Retrieved on 4 August 2021, from www.who.int/publications/i/item/9789240017900

World Health Organization. (2021). *Global report on ageism.* World Health Organization. Retrieved on 4 August 2021, from www.who.int/publications/i/item/9789240016866

SECTION I
Introduction and Overview

1

RESEARCH ON AGE(ING) AT WORK HAS "COME OF AGE"

Cort W. Rudolph and Hannes Zacher

The study of the role of age(ing) at work is now a well-established subfield of industrial, work, and organizational (IWO) psychology. Indeed, we have seen a notable increase in research on age(ing) at work over the past two decades. There are several reasons for this; for example, there is a growing awareness of demographic changes, especially the aging of the population, impacting the workplace (Hertel & Zacher, 2018; Rudolph & Zacher, 2019). Moreover, the publication of key articles, for instance Kanfer and Ackerman's (2004) influential paper on aging and work motivation, has inspired increased attention to the interplay between cognition and motivation across the lifespan (e.g., Hertzog et al., 2009). Additionally, new publication outlets, especially the journal *Work, Aging and Retirement* (Wang, 2015), have contributed to the growing body of research on age(ing) at work. Finally, development of—and interest in—lifespan developmental perspectives, theories, and constructs have stimulated interest in this field of study (Rudolph, 2016, see Chapter 7).

This subfield has matured to the extent that we now have several systematic, meta-analytic, and narrative reviews on age(ing) at work (e.g., Ng & Feldman, 2012; Zacher & Froidevaux, 2021), as well as several books on age(ing) at work (e.g., B. B. Baltes et al., 2019; Finkelstein et al., 2015; Shultz & Adams, 2019). Indeed, this is the second volume published in the *Organizational Frontiers Series* to address work and age(ing) in the last ten years (Finkelstein et al., 2015). With so much accumulation of knowledge, it is fair to ask, "What is novel and useful about this book?" We focus on *recent* developments in theory, methods, and practical applications related to age(ing) at work and how they may advance new directions for future research. The chapters included here review state-of-the-art knowledge in their respective areas but also propose new directions to inspire future research. We believe that this topic is so important (i.e., not a "fad") that

DOI: 10.4324/9781003089674-2

IWO psychology needs to continuously "take stock" and summarize the state of our understanding of the role of age(ing) at work.

In this introductory chapter to our edited volume, we introduce ten principles based on well-established theorizing and accumulated empirical evidence on age(ing) at work. These principles represent "what we have learned so far," representing major insights into age(ing) at work and related phenomena. This is followed by ten topics that we think need more attention. These represent "what we still need to know," and that constitutes gaps in our methodologies, understandings of age(ing) at work, or burgeoning areas of inquiry that support existing knowledge.

What We Have Learned So Far About Age(ing) at Work

1. The Average Association Between Age and Work Performance Is Weak

Several meta-analyses have examined relationships between workers' age and various work outcomes (see Zacher & Froidevaux, 2021, for a summary). A key insight from meta-analyses on age and work performance is that these relationships are typically weak. Indeed, Ng and Feldman (2008) found associations among age and task performance, organizational citizenship behavior, creative performance, and training performance that were all below $\rho = .10$, even when considering moderators. What do these findings imply? Practically, they suggest that age should not be used as a predictor in personnel selection, which has been known for quite some time (Schmidt & Hunter, 1998) and is not legal in most professions anyway (EEOC, 2021). From a scientific perspective, these findings suggest that there are likely multiple and countervailing mediating age-related factors underlying these associations. For instance, research suggests that two key predictors of work performance—fluid cognitive ability and conscientiousness—are negatively and positively related to age, respectively (Klein et al., 2015; Roberts et al., 2006). It has also been suggested that potential age-related declines in performance may be buffered by the use of self-regulation strategies, such as selection, optimization, and compensation (SOC; P. B. Baltes & M. M. Baltes, 1990; Salthouse, 2012); however, a meta-analysis did not find higher SOC strategy use among older as compared to younger workers ($\rho = .04$; Moghimi et al., 2017). Finally, the meta-analytic findings of weak associations between age and work performance dimensions should be interpreted with caution, as they are based on cross-sectional data (i.e., representing between-person differences and not within-person age-related changes over time), and many of the primary studies did not include workers older than 60 years, which may raise concerns about selection effects (Ng & Feldman, 2008).

2. To Understand Age at Work, It Is Not Sufficient to Study Older Workers

When a study focuses on relationships between two or more constructs using only a sample of "older workers" (e.g., 40 and older), it remains unclear whether the relationships under study would be similar or different in a sample of "younger workers" (e.g., younger than 40). In other words, to understand the role of age in the work context, it is not sufficient to focus only on older (or younger) workers; age should be included as a substantive variable (i.e., as a predictor or moderator) in the study. Researchers should sample workers across the entire working lifespan without restricting the age range (e.g., 16 to 80+ years, including trainees and "silver workers") and without splitting the continuous age variable into groups using arbitrary cutoffs (n.b. this also applies to research on "generations"; Bohlmann et al., 2018; see Chapter 6). For instance, based on the lifespan development perspective on job design (Truxillo et al., 2012), studies have examined interactive effects of age and job characteristics on various worker outcomes (Mühlenbrock & Hüffmeier, 2020; Zacher & Schmitt, 2016). An exception may be studies that examine constructs that cannot be assessed in a meaningful way among younger workers, such as concerns with generativity (i.e., supporting younger workers; Garcia et al., 2018) or retirement intentions (Zacher & Rudolph, 2017). However, even studies on these constructs could sample younger workers and assess their interpretation of the constructs (maybe including a "does not apply" option).

3. Lifespan and Life Course Perspectives Are Complementary Metatheories

The lifespan and life course perspective are complementary theoretical frameworks that aim to understand individual- and group-/institutional-level influences on development, respectively (Diewald & Mayer, 2009; Zacher & Froidevaux, 2021). The lifespan development perspective (P. B. Baltes, 1987)—which was primarily developed in the field of psychology—and various mid-range theories associated with it (e.g., socioemotional selectivity theory, the model of selection, optimization, and compensation) have been frequently adopted by researchers studying age(ing) at work over the last two decades. Beyond the more specific assumptions of the midrange theories, the lifespan development perspective offers a set of seven propositions or principles that have shaped the thinking and work of many scholars in this field. These principles include: (1) development as a lifelong process, (2) development as multidimensional and multidirectional, (3) development involving the dynamic and joint occurrence of gains and losses in different domains of functioning, (4) development as context-dependent (i.e., dependent on historical and sociocultural conditions), (5) development as resulting from the interplay between age-graded influences, normative history-graded influences, and nonnormative or idiosyncratic influences, (6) the potential for plasticity (i.e., within-person modifiability) in development, and (7) development as an inter-disciplinary and multilevel phenomenon (P. B. Baltes, 1987). In contrast, the life course perspective, which was primarily developed in the field of sociology, has not been widely adopted by researchers in the field of age(ing) at work. This perspective focuses on the interplay between individual agency and structure in shaping development, with a greater emphasis placed on the latter rather than the former. "Structure" includes people's membership in various social groups (e.g., family), roles (e.g., male blue-collar workers), and institutions (e.g., organizations, societies) that may impact the development of individuals and groups over time (Tomlinson et al., 2018).

4. Workers May Identify with Their Age Group

Chronological age represents the time that has passed since birth (Schwall, 2012). Research in the lifespan development tradition suggests that individuals' experi-ence and behavior can change, due to biological and/or environmental factors, in multiple directions over time (e.g., declines in neuroticism, increases in emotion regulation skills, stabilities in generalized self-efficacy). These changes, in turn, are often assumed to manifest in age-related differences that are assessed using cross-sectional surveys. Furthermore, research in the tradition of social identity and self-categorization metatheories (Hornsey, 2008) has argued that people also use age to categorize others and themselves into distinct social groups, such as "younger workers" and "older workers" (Zacher et al., 2019). Indeed, next to sex and race, age is one of the most salient characteristics used for social comparisons and social (self-)categorization (see Chapter 4).

Research suggests that people vary in the extent to which they identify in cognitive and affective terms with their respective age group (for a review, see Zacher et al., 2019). Age-based social identification, in turn, has been shown to be associated with work-related experiences (e.g., well-being, job attitudes) and behaviors (e.g., stereotypes and discrimination against outgroup members; Armenta et al., 2017; Desmette & Gaillard, 2008). Moreover, research has shown that age-based stereotype threat is negatively associated with occupational well-being and favorable job attitudes among older but not younger workers (Von Hippel et al., 2013; Von Hippel et al., 2019). This may be because younger work-ers view stereotype threat in terms of challenge demands, whereas older workers view stereotype threat in terms of hindrance demands.

5. "Successful Aging" Is Challenging to Define and Operationalize

The term "successful aging" has long been used by developmental psycholo-gists, typically meaning the experience of high life satisfaction in later life (e.g.,

Havighurst, 1961). The term was first adopted by IWO psychologists in the 1990s (Hansson et al., 1997), and only recently have work and aging scholars accepted the challenge to define and operationalize this complex phenomenon (Zacher et al., 2018b). Zacher (2015) offered a comparative approach to successful aging at work, suggesting that those workers who evidence steeper-than-average growth or flatter-than-average decline in objective or subjective work outcomes are aging successfully. More recently, researchers have proposed a more pragmatic definition of successful aging at work as "the proactive maintenance of, or adaptive recovery (after decline) to, high levels of ability *and* motivation to continue working among older workers" (Kooij et al., 2020, p. 345). Both definitions can be and have been criticized on various grounds. For instance, Zacher (2015) conceptualizes successful aging as a (positive) deviation from the norm, which may be seen as contradicting efforts to promote successful aging for all workers. Kooij et al.'s (2020) definition may be criticized for neglecting the idea that not all workers are intrinsically motivated to continue working but may have to delay retirement for financial reasons. Given these challenges, researchers have recently introduced the more specific concepts of "active aging" (i.e., focusing on the interplay between agentic workers and a supportive organizational context; Kooij, 2015; Zacher et al., 2018a) and "healthy aging" (i.e., based on the World Health Organization's definition as "the process of developing and maintaining the functional ability that enables well-being in older age"; World Health Organization, 2015, p. 28; Zacher et al., 2021) in the work context. These concepts, which describe temporal phenomena or patterns, cannot be adequately investigated using only cross-sectional designs and self-report scales. Future empirical research thus needs to employ longer-term longitudinal designs (see Chapter 10) and combine both objective and subjective measurements (see Chapter 8) to investigate successful (or active, healthy) aging at work (see Chapter 13).

6. Age Matters, But So Do Other Temporal Variables

Studying age(ing) at work is inherently about studying time. Research that investigates relationships between chronological age and work outcomes or that considers the development of work-related variables over time is inherently interested in how time or timelike proxy variables affect such processes. As alluded to variously throughout this volume, research suggests evidence for both age- and aging-related influences at work. It is also important to note the role that other temporal variables play in addition to the influence of chronological age. Examples of such temporal variables include tenure, time perspectives, and subjective age.

For example, a daily diary study by Bohlmann et al. (2021) shows that organizational tenure matters incrementally to chronological age in the prediction of proactive work behavior. Moreover, in a meta-analytic regression model, Rudolph et al. (2018) show that occupational future time perspective predicts work outcomes (e.g., job satisfaction, task performance) incrementally to chronological age. Finally, Zacher and Rudolph (2019b) show that subjective age predicts job crafting incremental to chronological age but that this relationship is accounted for, in part, by occupational future time perspective. Indeed, the relationships between chronological age, temporal variables, and work outcomes can be more complex than simple incremental variance explanation effects.

Importantly, these temporal variables are themselves proxies for related concepts that covary with time. For example, tenure (e.g., career, job, organizational) is a proxy for work experience, time perspective reflects a theoretically supported underlying shift in motivations across the lifespan (see Chapter 7), and subjective age is a self-reflexive concept that suggests how one self-contextualizes the aging process in a common (i.e., age) metric (see Chapter 3).

7. Studying Age Is Greatly Complicated by Period and Cohort Effects

Much of what we know about chronological age at work comes from research based on cross-sectional (i.e., single time point) research designs. The limitations of cross-sectional research designs in aging research have long been understood (e.g., Hofer et al., 2002); however, a particularly challenging issue emerges in the study of chronological age in such designs—the age-period-cohort confounding problem.

Anyone's chronological age (e.g., 38 years old) is a function of their year of birth (i.e., their cohort: 1984) and the time of data collection (i.e., the period: 2022). In cross-sectional research designs, the time of data collection is typically held constant (i.e., the "period" effect does not vary as data are collected only once, at a single point in time). In such a case, chronological age is defined by subtracting "cohort" from "period" (i.e., $2022_{period} - 1984_{cohort} = 38_{age}$). The perfect linear relationship of cohort and age in this case means that any variability that is attributable to one variable cannot be differentiated from the other. In other words, age and cohort effects are perfectly confounded in cross-sectional research designs. This concern has been long understood and largely believed to be an intractable problem (see Rudolph et al., 2020).

What this means is that claims about the influence of chronological age effects in cross-sectional research could just as easily be claims about cohort effects. However, to make such a claim, one must assume that there is strong theory that cohort effects matter more than age effects, which is rarely the case. Indeed, the strength of theorizing and the vast body of empirical evidence regarding aging and human development across the lifespan (see B. B. Baltes et al., 2019) speak to the robust nature of age-related change. As a proxy for such developmental change, chronological age is a far more likely source of such variability than cohort effects.

8. Control and Action Regulation Matter for the Process of Aging

The study of age(ing) at work is often concerned with motivation, and the metatheory of action regulation and the metaconcept of control dominate our understanding of developmental dynamics in motivation across the lifespan. Fundamentally, motivated behavior is goal-oriented, and action regulation theory is a theory of how such goal-oriented behavior is regulated (Zacher & Frese, 2018). Actions are the goal-oriented behaviors in need of regulation, and action regulation can occur at different levels of abstraction (e.g., cognitively, behaviorally). Control refers to one's discretion over their actions and their ability to engage in chosen actions and/or to receive rewards or desired outcomes because of their choices and actions (Rauvola & Rudolph, 2021). Given its focus on agency, control necessarily facilitates the process of action regulation, and through successful action regulation enhanced control is possible. Through this fundamental, reciprocal process, growth and development are facilitated.

Many grand and associated midrange theories of motivation across the lifespan draw from the concepts of control and the fundamental premises of action regulation theory. For example, the metatheoretical lifespan development perspective is about how people maintain control through effortful action regulation across time (see Chapter 7). Highlighting this further, Zacher et al. (2016) proposed the action regulation across the adult lifespan (ARAL) model (discussed later), which describes the reciprocal influence of workers and their environments over time. Supplementing this, Rauvola and Rudolph's (2021) lifespan control framework provides an organized set of principles for understanding control and control-related constructs and their various roles across the lifespan.

9. Retirement Is not a One-Time Thing; It Is a Process

Retirement is often spoken of in dichotomous terms—one either is or is not retired. However, research has identified retirement as a more complex transition process rather than a one-time decision. Example themes in research on retirement include retirement planning, retirement decision making and the voluntariness of retirement, retirement adjustment, and bridge employment (Shultz & Wang, 2011).

Retirement planning research has focused on aspects of the planning process, which can include formal retirement planning (e.g., financial planning) and informal retirement planning (e.g., retirement goal setting). Research has generally found that those who are better prepared for retirement (i.e., both formally and informally) and retire voluntarily (i.e., retire "on their own terms") have more favorable retirement adjustment outcomes (e.g., higher satisfaction with retirement, better health) than others (see Topa et al., 2009).

The transition to retirement can be viewed as a process of psychological adjustment, and one closely studied aspect of retirement transition and adjustment is the idea of bridge employment. Indeed, people often return to work following an initial phase of retirement from their career job, assuming "bridge employment" roles that may be within or outside the domain of their career roles. Beyond its clear economic benefits to society (Cahill et al., 2013), bridge employment provides important tangible (e.g., health insurance; Beehr & Bennett, 2015) as well as intangible resources (e.g., sense of purpose, social support; Rudolph et al., 2015) to retirees (see Zhan et al., 2009).

10. Aging at Work Takes Place Within a Social-Institutional Context

To understand truly the complexities of development in any context, it is important to take a multidisciplinary approach, especially when studying age(ing) at work. The sociological life course perspective describes the interaction between institutions and life roles over time and compliments the psychological perspective offered here. The contributions of sociological perspectives on work and aging are numerous. For example, work by Moen and colleagues (Kim & Moen, 2002; Moen, 1996) has been especially important for bridging the gap between psychological and sociological perspectives on retirement, highlighting the intersections between gendered roles and the process of retirement and links to individual well-being. Related sociological perspectives have also been important in understanding the complex relationship between gender and work and nonwork roles across the lifespan (Moen, 2011; Moen & Sweet, 2004; see Chapter 4).

Likewise, economic perspectives, especially on workforce participation (see Chapter 2) and retirement (e.g., Cahill et al., 2013) have shaped the way that psychologists and sociologists approach questions regarding work and age(ing). Such economic perspectives have been translated into "best practices" for managing the aging workforce, with direct implications for organizational policy and management practice (e.g., Hertel & Zacher, 2018).

To better account for multiple spheres of influence, more recent scholarship has adopted an ecological systems approach to understanding work and aging (Marcus et al., 2020). According to this perspective, a holistic understanding of work and aging requires a consideration of the systems that result when societal-, organizational-, and individual-level processes are considered in tandem with institutional, cultural, and normative organizational factors across time.

What We Still Need to Know about Age(ing) at Work

1. Matching Research Designs, Research Questions, and Inferences

There are real opportunities and challenges to extend our understanding of work and aging phenomena beyond cross-sectional research. To this end, it is important to distinguish the strict definition of a longitudinal study as one in which three or more waves of data are collected in a complete panel design (Wang et al., 2017; see Chapter 10), from a cross-sectional study, which collects data from a sample of respondents once (i.e., a single wave; a single time point). Importantly, there is nothing inherently wrong with cross-sectional research designs. However, the challenge of such designs stems from their inability to represent longitudinal changes. Indeed, research has long suggested that the results of longitudinal studies and cross-sectional studies (i.e., comparing developmental changes in an outcome over time vs. comparing correlations between age and the same outcome) do not necessarily triangulate with one-another (e.g., see P. B. Baltes, 1968). Beyond the obvious logical issues of inferring change in single time point research, this means that the inference of age-related *changes* in cross-sectional studies is unjustified.

As such, it is very important to be cognizant of the limitations of various research designs, and what bearing research designs have on the inferences one can draw from their data. Age is an empty/non-causal variable (Wohlwill, 1970). In cross-sectional designs where age is considered as an (exogenous) predictor or moderator, the effect of age must be understood as a proxy for some other process that covaries with development, over time. For example, age may be taken as a proxy for life or work experience.

2. (Re)focus on Intersectionality

Aging is one of the few truly universal human experiences; it cuts across race, sex, social class, and culture. However, the way in which aging manifests across these strata and within these contexts is far from heterogeneous, and research points to the idea that the experience of aging varies vastly across (sub)populations as a function of these factors (e.g., Sinnott & Shifren, 2001; Williams & Wilson, 2001).

Despite this, research on age(ing) at work has thus far rarely adopted an intersectional perspective that considers how age interacts with other person-level characteristics to predict work outcomes (for a notable recent counterexample, see Moen et al., 2020). The notion of intersectionality implies that age effects must be understood in concert with other person level characteristics that are relevant to the explanation of a given outcome (e.g., labor force participation rates vary as a function of age, but also sex and country; see Chapter 2).

Recent advancements in the development of the intersectional salience of ageism theory have considered how crossing these variables and others contribute to differential experiences of aging (see Marcus & Fritzsche, 2015 and Chapter 4). To account for and expand our understanding of intersectional effects of age, it is important for researchers to plan studies that are well-powered to test higher-order interactions between age and relevant person-level characteristics. This will allow research to explore the potential for joint relationships between variables that may manifest as differential age-graded experiences at work (i.e., moderated effects of age on work outcomes). Importantly too, these effects manifest not only in differences in substantive outcomes, but also in features external to the collection of such data. Indeed, understanding how demographics contribute to sample selection (e.g., representativeness; attrition) over time is of primary relevance to designing and interpreting the results of any study, and especially longitudinal research studies (e.g., Goodman & Blum, 1996).

3. Age(ing) at Work is Inherently Multidisciplinary

A core tenet of the lifespan development perspective is that aging is inherently multidisciplinary (P. B. Baltes, 1987). Reflecting this, studies of work and age(ing) draw from eclectic theoretical traditions ranging from core theories in psychology to sociological and economic perspectives. Indeed, the lifespan development perspective has become a predominant way of understanding a diverse array of age(ing)-related phenomena at work (B. B. Baltes et al., 2019; Rudolph, 2016).

Despite the increasing focus on studying work and age(ing) from a lifespan lens, there exist few multidisciplinary partnerships between researchers from different domains and traditions. Indeed, to move research in this domain forward, partnerships between psychologists (e.g., IWO psychologists, developmental psychologists, neuroscientists) and other fields (i.e., sociologists, anthropologists, economists) will be necessary.

Moreover, although there are clear trends in theorizing to support research on work and age(ing), there has been little effort to integrate (for an exception, see Chapter 5) and formalize these theories (see Chapter 7). The lack of integration means that there is often scant guidance for what theories predict, leaving multiple theories with essentially the same predictions in the literature. The lack of formalization means that there are not concrete "rules" that dictate the predictions made by such theories. What this leads to is ambiguity in our ability to evaluate studies that purport to test tenets thereof; the theories are left to be interpreted "in the eye of the beholder" rather than as an integrated or formalized model. Accordingly, we might argue that many "theories" are not really theories at all; rather they are loose collections of heuristics bound together by prior knowledge through vague descriptions of relationships that are not necessarily functional in their nature.

4. Triangulate the Results of Multiple Research Methodologies

Research on work and age(ing) relies heavily on self-report research methods (e.g., surveys) and less so on experimental (see Chapter 11), behavioral observation (see Chapter 8), or qualitative methods (see Chapter 12). As alluded to, the limitations of any given research design must be understood in comparison to others, and each individual technique brings unique strengths and weaknesses to bear on one's research question. To advance our understanding of phenomena related to age(ing) at work, research must advance more eclectic methodologies and triangulate the results of studies designed to test similar phenomena across methodologies. Indeed, more confidence in one's findings is possible by triangulating the results of studies that adopt multiple methodologies (e.g., "full cycle" research designs; see Chatman & Flynn, 2005).

One challenge in adopting this perspective is that it requires a strong a priori theory to be tested, and, not withstanding concerns raised here about the degree to which our theories approximate "strong theories," this is challenging to do, requiring both time and resources. Researchers would be well advised to map the features of a given theory onto the phenomenon purported to be affected though the development of testable hypotheses. Then, these hypotheses can be mapped onto research methodologies that are appropriate to answer the questions they pose. Importantly, it is not necessary for each study to test every hypothesis entirely or even in part. Rather, as a whole, the collection of studies should be useful in drawing conclusions about the hypotheses posed.

A good example of this type of approach can be found in the advice offered by Stone-Romero and Rosopa (2008, 2011) for how to test mediation models in experimental research designs. The challenge with doing so is how best to integrate the results of studies where exogenous/mediator variables are variously either manipulated or observed. Indeed, to achieve this, the results of multiple studies, using differing methodologies, need to be combined and understood together.

5. What to Do About Generations

Although there is scant reason to believe that generations exist as distinct groups and influence work-related processes, it is still important to recognize that people believe that they do (see Chapter 6). Likewise, it is common for people to apply a misguided logic to unpack differences between members of different purported generations that very likely do not exist or that can be attributed to other factors (e.g., aging, period effects).

What, then, are we left to "do" with generations? The easy and inelegant solution would be to "throw the baby out with the bathwater"—we should abandon the idea of generations altogether in favor of more tenable explanations for age-graded differences in behavior at work. As suggested by Rudolph and Zacher (2017), a more nuanced solution is to do away with time-based operationalizations of generations and favor those that reconceptualize cohort effects as interindividual differences (i.e., specific, theory-based, psychological individual differences, e.g., generational identity, see Chapter 3).

Theoretically, a shift away from temporal operationalizations of generations requires a reconceptualization of generations in socially constructed terms (Rudolph et al., 2020). This perspective offers that generations do not exist tangibly, and that they are a product of the way in which we construct and maintain the existence of generations through discourse. One way to study generations that does not require a temporal definition and that adopts a social constructive lens is to focus on the quality of intergenerational contact and exchange in organizations (Rudolph & Zacher, 2015). Such research has pointed toward promising impacts of such exchanges, including increasing knowledge transfer (see Chapter 15) and encouraging the expression of generativity, which has been linked to well-being (see Doerwald et al., 2021).

6. Toward a Multilevel Framework of Age(ing) at Work

Most research on age at work has been conducted at the between-person level, comparing people of different ages on various attributes (e.g., attitudes, beliefs, performance). More recent research has also examined age as a between-person moderator of within-person associations among work-related variables (e.g., Finkelstein et al., 2020; Yeung et al., 2020). At higher conceptual and analytical levels, studies have explored potential consequences of mean age and age diversity of teams (e.g., Schneid et al., 2016; Wegge et al., 2008) and of organizations (e.g., De Meulenaere et al., 2016; Kunze et al., 2011). However, despite early calls on this topic (Avolio, 1991), the field is still lacking an integrated multilevel framework of age at work. Such a framework could consider various ways of conceptualizing age at a higher level, such as the team or organization (see Chapter 9). For instance, research could focus on the average age of a team or organization, age diversity, or both (see Harrison & Klein, 2007). Importantly, however, the same average age would be obtained for teams that include both very young and very old workers and for teams that include only middle-aged workers. Moreover, the framework should outline how aggregated age at higher levels predicts outcomes at the same, lower, and/or higher levels and how aggregated age at higher levels moderates relationships between relevant variables at other levels. For instance, a relatively high (vs. low) organizational average age may buffer the negative association between supervisors' negative age stereotypes and older workers' well-being, because older workers' feel generally included in the organization (Böhm et al., 2014). In summary, more conceptual and empirical work is needed that considers the role of age at multiple levels in the work context and the interplay between age, age-related constructs, and work outcomes within and across levels.

7. The Need to Better Understand Midcareer

Similar to the lifespan development literature, which has generally neglected individuals in "middle age" (i.e., roughly the period between 40 and 60 years; Lachman et al., 2015), research on age(ing) at work has mostly focused on "younger workers" and "older workers" and neglected midcareer workers, who are approximately between 35 and 55 years old (however, these cutoffs are arbitrary—the boundaries are fuzzy; Sterns & Subich, 2002). Some research has suggested that midcareer workers have lower occupational well-being due to increased work and family demands and reduced resources during this life and career stage (Zacher et al., 2014). However, the idea of a "U-shape" in well-being across the life-span has recently been questioned (e.g., because most research uses cross-sectional data; Galambos et al., 2020). Nevertheless, methodologists have argued that non-linear associations between age and other variables should routinely be reported, without splitting the continuous age variable into subgroups (Bohlmann et al., 2018). For instance, based on both meta-analytic and primary data, Katz et al. (2019) find that the relationship between age and career commitment follows an inverted U-shape. Another issue that needs further attention is constructs that are thought to emerge only in midlife/midcareer (Kanfer & Ackerman, 2004). Two prominent examples are generativity—or the concern for establishing and guiding the next generation (McAdams & Logan, 2004)—and the motivation to retire or continue working. However, research suggests that measures designed to tap these constructs can also be answered by younger workers in a meaningful way (Doerwald et al., 2021; Pak et al., 2018). Overall, more rigorous empirical research is needed that examines changes in workers' characteristics and work outcomes in midcareer. Additionally, qualitative research could explore whether there are unique concerns associated with midcareer, similar to research that has focused on younger and older workers' changing concerns (Koen et al., 2012; Noonan, 2005).

8. Integrating Job and Age Crafting

Similar to IWO psychologists' interest in proactive work behaviors (i.e., future-oriented behaviors that aim to change the work environment or oneself in a posi-tive way; Parker & Bindl, 2017), lifespan psychologists and life course sociologists have focused on people's action regulation and agentic behaviors intended to actively shape their development (Heckhausen et al., 2019; Rauvola & Rudolph, 2020). However, so far, research on proactive job crafting (Rudolph et al., 2017; see Chapter 14) and successful aging or life management strategies (Freund & P. B. Baltes, 2002) has not been well integrated. A promising way to bridge these literatures may be an action theoretical perspective on proactive behaviors at work and across the working lifespan. To this end, Zacher et al. (2016) intro-duced a metatheoretical framework on action regulation across the adult life-span (ARAL), which explains how workers influence and are influenced by their work environment across different time spans. On the one hand, the framework outlines how the workers' action regulation may change with age (e.g., selection and pursuit of different goals, different needs regarding feedback). On the other hand, ARAL theory also suggests that workers' action regulation can meaning-fully shape their development (e.g., cognition, personality). For instance, workers who remain intellectually active across their careers may be able to slow down cognitive decline and even prevent dementia after retirement (Finkel et al., 2009). Future research could examine the various propositions of the ARAL theory using experimental and correlational methods and, thereby, contribute to a better alignment of the complementary approaches to proactive or agentic behaviors in IWO psychology (e.g., job crafting) and lifespan psychology (e.g., primary and secondary control striving; Shane & Heckhausen, 2019).

9. (Why) Do "Alternative Age Constructs" Matter?

Chronological age explains relatively little variance in many work outcomes (i.e., there is more interindividual variability within specific age groups than intraindividual variability within persons, over time). Based on this observation, work and aging scholars have argued that research should take "different meanings of age" or "alternative age concepts," such as "functional age," "psychosocial age," "organizational age," and "lifespan age" into account (Kooij et al., 2008). On the one hand, it can be debated whether these new age labels are needed for well-established constructs such as physical health and cognitive abilities ("functional age"), organizational tenure ("organizational age"), or family status ("lifespan age"). On the other hand, it seems important to account for these age-related constructs in research on age(ing) at work. However, particularly physical health and cognitive abilities should not be conceptualized as alternatives to chronological age but as age-related explanatory mechanisms that may mediate associations between age and work outcomes. For instance, research suggests that employees' experience and future time perspective mediate the moderating effects of age on the links between opportunity identification and entrepreneurial action (Gielnik et al., 2018). With regard to "psychosocial age," research suggests that workers' perceptions of their age (i.e., subjective age, relative age) change with age and correlate with important work outcomes, including job engagement and strain (Rudolph et al., 2019; Weiss & Weiss, 2019; see Chapter 3). However, further empirical research on the construct validity of such perceived age constructs is necessary. For instance, research has shown that moderate and significant associations between subjective age and work outcomes (controlling for chronological age) become weaker and nonsignificant when workers' core self-evaluations (i.e., their broader appraisals of themselves) are statistically controlled (Zacher & Rudolph, 2019a). Additional research suggests that subjective age does not predict work behavior (i.e., job crafting) but vice versa (Zacher & Rudolph, 2019b).

10. Which New Work-Related Topics Should Be Investigated in Relation to Age in the Future?

Due to numerous primary empirical studies and meta-analyses, associations between age and job attitudes as well as job performance are now rather well understood. However, there are several IWO psychology topics that would benefit from integrating age and a lifespan development perspective both theoretically and empirically. These topics include leadership and entrepreneurship/self-employment (e.g., how does leadership effectiveness change across the lifespan, and what role do age differences between leaders and followers play; Halvorsen & Morrow-Howell, 2017; Rosing & Jungmann, 2019), personnel recruitment and selection (e.g., age-based adverse impact; Klein et al., 2015; Lievens et al., 2012), as well as creativity and innovation (e.g., are there age differences in various aspects of the innovation process, including idea generation, communication about ideas, and idea implementation? Rietzschel et al., 2016).

The list of important IWO psychology topics that should be examined in relation to age and lifespan development could be extended for some time, illustrating the fascinating nature of this interdisciplinary research area. In this book, we decided to cover five emerging topics in this area that are of particularly high practical relevance: job crafting (Chapter 14; e.g., Why and how do older workers proactively change their jobs?), knowledge transfer and knowledge hiding (Chapter 15; e.g., Under which conditions do younger and older workers share their knowledge, and how do they benefit from this behavior?), management of the work–nonwork interface (Chapter 16; e.g., How do younger and older workers differ with regard to boundary management strategies and work–family outcomes?), absenteeism and presenteeism (Chapter 17; e.g., Why and when do younger and older workers differ with regard to health-related work behaviors?), as well as organizational metastrategies (Chapter 18; e.g., How can organizations create an inclusive climate and address age diversity?).

Conclusion and Expression of Gratitude

We hope that this volume supports and inspires new programs of research that address challenging questions in the study of age(ing) at work. Much of our inspiration for this volume comes from collaborations and relationships that we have fostered through our participation in the Age in the Workplace Meeting, a biennial small-group conference that covers topics related to age(ing) at work that has taken place in Italy, Ireland, Germany, and the Netherlands since 2011. Finally, we would like to personally thank Lisa Finkelstein, Donald M. Truxillo, Franco Fraccaroli, and Ruth Kanfer. Our first formal collaboration (Rudolph & Zacher, 2015) was on a chapter for the earlier volume of this series on age(ing) at work edited by these scholars (Finkelstein et al., 2015). We are indebted to your support over the years and so thankful that you gave us the opportunity then to work on such a challenging topic, which has grown into dozens of publications, books, and other projects over time.

References

Armenta, B. M., Stroebe, K., Scheibe, S., Postmes, T., & Van Yperen, N. W. (2017). Feeling younger and identifying with older adults: Testing two routes to maintaining well-being in the face of age discrimination. *PLoS One, 12*(11), e0187805. https://doi.org/10.1371/journal.pone.0187805

Avolio, B. J. (1991). A levels-of-analysis perspective of aging and work research. *Annual Review of Gerontology and Geriatrics, 11,* 239–260.

Baltes, B. B., Rudolph, C. W., & Zacher, H. (Eds.). (2019). *Work across the lifespan.* Academic Press.

Baltes, P. B. (1968). Longitudinal and cross-sectional sequences in the study of age and generation effects. *Human Development, 11,* 145–171. https://doi.org/10.1159/000270604

Baltes, P. B. (1987). Theoretical propositions of life-span developmental psychology: On the dynamics between growth and decline. *Developmental Psychology, 23*(5), 611–626. https://doi.org/10.1037/0012-1649.23.5.611

Baltes, P. B., & Baltes, M. M. (1990). Psychological perspectives on successful aging: The model of selective optimization with compensation. In P. B. Baltes & M. M. Baltes (Eds.), *Successful aging: Perspectives from the behavioral sciences* (pp. 1–34). Cambridge University Press. https://doi.org/10.1017/CBO9780511665684.003

Beehr, T. A., & Bennett, M. M. (2015). Working after retirement: Features of bridge employment and research directions. *Work, Aging and Retirement, 1*(1), 112–128. https://doi.org/10.1093/workar/wau007

Bohlmann, C., Rudolph, C. W., & Zacher, H. (2018). Methodological recommendations to move research on work and aging forward. *Work, Aging and Retirement, 4*(3), 225–237. https://doi.org/10.1093/workar/wax023

Bohlmann, C., Rudolph, C. W., & Zacher, H. (2021). Effects of proactive behavior on within-day changes in occupational well-being: The role of organizational tenure and emotion regulation skills. *Occupational Health Science.* https://doi.org/10.1007/s41542-021-00089-2

Böhm, S. A., Kunze, F., & Bruch, H. (2014). Spotlight on age-diversity climate: The impact of age-inclusive HR practices on firm-level outcomes. *Personnel Psychology, 67*(3), 667–704. https://doi.org/10.1111/peps.12047

Cahill, K. E., Giandrea, M. D., & Quinn, J. F. (2013). Bridge employment. In M. Wang (Ed.), *The Oxford handbook of retirement* (pp. 293–310). Oxford University Press.

Chatman, J. A., & Flynn, F. J. (2005). Full-cycle micro-organizational behavior research. *Organization Science, 16*(4), 434–447. https://doi.org/10.1287/orsc.1050.0136

De Meulenaere, K., Boone, C., & Buyl, T. (2016). Unraveling the impact of workforce age diversity on labor productivity: The moderating role of firm size and job security. *Journal of Organizational Behavior, 37*(2), 193–212. https://doi.org/10.1002/job.2036

Desmette, D., & Gaillard, M. (2008). When a "worker" becomes an "older worker": The effects of age-related social identity on attitudes towards retirement and work. *Career Development International, 13*(2), 168–185. https://doi.org/10.1108/13620430810860567

Diewald, M., & Mayer, K. U. (2009). The sociology of the life course and life span psychology: Integrated paradigm or complementing pathways? *Advances in Life Course Research, 14,* 5–14. https://doi.org/10.1016/j.alcr.2009.03.001

Doerwald, F., Zacher, H., Scheibe, S., & van Yperen, N. W. (2021). Generativity at work: A meta-analysis. *Journal of Vocational Behavior, 125,* 103521. https://doi.org/10.1016/j.jvb.2020.103521

Finkel, D., Andel, R., Gatz, M., & Pedersen, N. L. (2009). The role of occupational complexity in trajectories of cognitive aging before and after retirement. *Psychology and Aging*, 24(3), 563–573. https://doi.org/10.1037/a0015511

Finkelstein, L. M., Truxillo, D., Fraccaroli, F., & Kanfer, R. (Eds.). (2015). *Facing the challenges of a multi-age workforce: A use-inspired approach*. Routledge.

Finkelstein, L. M., Voyles, E. C., Thomas, C. L., & Zacher, H. (2020). A daily diary study of responses to age meta-stereotypes. *Work, Aging and Retirement*, 6(1), 28–45. https://doi.org/10.1093/workar/waz005

Freund, A. M., & Baltes, P. B. (2002). Life-management strategies of selection, optimization, and compensation: Measurement by self-report and construct validity. *Journal of Personality and Social Psychology*, 82(4), 642–662. https://doi.org/10.1037/0022-3514.82.4.642

Galambos, N. L., Krahn, H. J., Johnson, M. D., & Lachman, M. E. (2020). The U shape of happiness across the life course: Expanding the discussion. *Perspectives on Psychological Science*, 15(4), 898–912. https://doi.org/10.1177/1745691620902428

Garcia, P. R. J. M., Bordia, P., Restubog, S. L. D., & Caines, V. (2018). Sleeping with a broken promise: The moderating role of generativity concerns in the relationship between psychological contract breach and insomnia among older workers. *Journal of Organizational Behavior*, 39(3), 326–338. https://doi.org/10.1002/job.2222

Gielnik, M. M., Zacher, H., & Wang, M. (2018). Age in the entrepreneurial process: The role of future time perspective and prior entrepreneurial experience. *Journal of Applied Psychology*, 103(10), 1067–1085. https://doi.org/10.1037/apl0000322

Goodman, J. S., & Blum, T. C. (1996). Assessing the non-random sampling effects of subject attrition in longitudinal research. *Journal of Management*, 22(4), 627–652. https://doi.org/10.1177/014920639602200405

Halvorsen, C. J., & Morrow-Howell, N. (2017). A conceptual framework on self-employment in later life: Toward a research agenda. *Work, Aging and Retirement*, 3(4), 313–324. https://doi.org/10.1093/workar/waw031

Hansson, R. O., DeKoekkoek, P. D., Neece, W. M., & Patterson, D. W. (1997). Successful aging at work: Annual review, 1992–1996: The older workers and transitions to retirement. *Journal of Vocational Behavior*, 51, 202–233. https://doi.org/10.1006/jvbe.1997.1605

Harrison, D. A., & Klein, K. J. (2007). What's the difference? Diversity constructs as separation, variety, or disparity in organizations. *Academy of Management Review*, 32(4), 1199–1228. https://doi.org/10.5465/amr.2007.26586096

Havighurst, R. J. (1961). Successful aging. *The Gerontologist*, 1, 8–13. https://doi.org/10.1093/geront/1.1.8

Heckhausen, J., Wrosch, C., & Schulz, R. (2019). Agency and motivation in adulthood and old age. *Annual Review of Psychology*, 70, 191–217. https://doi.org/10.1146/annurev-psych-010418-103043

Hertel, G., & Zacher, H. (2018). Managing the aging workforce. In D. S. Ones, N. Anderson, C. Viswesvaran, & H. K. Sinangil (Eds.), *The Sage handbook of industrial, work and organizational psychology* (2nd ed., Vol. 3, pp. 396–428). Sage.

Hertzog, C., Kramer, A. F., Wilson, R. S., & Lindenberger, U. (2009). Enrichment effects on adult cognitive development: Can the functional capacity of older adults be preserved and enhanced? *Psychological Science in the Public Interest*, 9(1), 1–65. https://doi.org/10.1111/j.1539-6053.2009.01034.x

Hofer, S. M., Sliwinski, M. J., & Flaherty, B. P. (2002). Understanding ageing: Further commentary on the limitations of cross-sectional designs for ageing research. *Gerontology*, *48*(1), 22–29. https://doi.org/10.1159/000048920

Hornsey, M. J. (2008). Social identity theory and self-categorization theory: A historical review. *Social and Personality Psychology Compass*, *2*(1), 204–222. https://doi.org/10.11 11/j.1751-9004.2007.00066

Kanfer, R., & Ackerman, P. L. (2004). Aging, adult development, and work motivation. *Academy of Management Review*, *29*(3), 440–458. https://doi.org/10.5465/AMR.2004.13670969

Katz, I. M., Rudolph, C. W., & Zacher, H. (2019). Age and career commitment: Meta-analytic tests of competing linear versus curvilinear relationships. *Journal of Vocational Behavior*, *112*, 396–416. https://doi.org/10.1016/j.jvb.2019.03.001

Kim, J. E., & Moen, P. (2002). Retirement transitions, gender, and psychological well-being: A life-course, ecological model. *The Journals of Gerontology Series B: Psychological Sciences and Social Sciences*, *57*(3), P212-P222. https://doi.org/10.1093/geronb/57.3.P212

Klein, R. M., Dilchert, S., Ones, D. S., & Dages, K. D. (2015). Cognitive predictors and age-based adverse impact among business executives. *Journal of Applied Psychology*. https://doi.org/10.1037/a0038991

Koen, J., Klehe, U. C., & Van Vianen, A. E. M. (2012). Training career adaptability to facilitate a successful school-to-work transition. *Journal of Vocational Behavior*, *81*(3), 395–408. https://doi.org/10.1016/j.jvb.2012.10.003

Kooij, D. T. A. M. (2015). Successful aging at work: The active role of employees. *Work, Aging and Retirement*, *1*(3), 309–319. https://doi.org/10.1093/workar/wav018

Kooij, D. T. A. M., de Lange, A., Jansen, P., & Dikkers, J. (2008). Older workers' motivation to continue to work: Five meanings of age. *Journal of Managerial Psychology*, *23*, 364–394. https://doi.org/10.1108/02683940810869015

Kooij, D. T. A. M., Zacher, H., Wang, M., & Heckhausen, J. (2020). Successful aging at work: A process model to guide future research and practice. *Industrial and Organizational Psychology*, *13*, 345–365. https://doi.org/10.1017/iop.2020.1

Kunze, F., Böhm, S. A., & Bruch, H. (2011). Age diversity, age discrimination climate and performance consequences: A cross organizational study. *Journal of Organizational Behavior*, *32*(2), 264–290. https://doi.org/10.1002/job.698

Lachman, M. E., Teshale, S., & Agrigoroaei, S. (2015). Midlife as a pivotal period in the life course: Balancing growth and decline at the crossroads of youth and old age. *International Journal of Behavioral Development*, *39*(1), 20–31. https://doi.org/10.1177/0165025414533223

Lievens, F., Van Hoye, G., & Zacher, H. (2012). Recruiting/hiring of older workers. In J. W. Hedge & W. C. Borman (Eds.), *The Oxford handbook of work and aging* (pp. 380–391). Oxford University Press. https://doi.org/10.1093/oxfordhb/9780195385052.013.0121

Marcus, J., & Fritzsche, B. A. (2015). One size doesn't fit all: Toward a theory on the intersectional salience of ageism at work. *Organizational Psychology Review*, *5*(2), 168–188. https://doi.org/10.1177/2041386614556015

Marcus, J., Rudolph, C. W., & Zacher, H. (2020). An ecological systems framework on work and aging. In D. L. Stone, J. H. Dulebohn, & K. M. Lukaszewski (Eds.), *Diversity and inclusion in organizations*. Information Age Publishing.

McAdams, D. P., & Logan, R. L. (2004). What is generativity? In E. de St. Aubin, D. P. McAdams, & T.-C. Kim (Eds.), *The generative society: Caring for future generations* (pp. 15–31). American Psychological Association.

Moen, P. (1996). A life course perspective on retirement, gender, and well-being. *Journal of Occupational Health Psychology*, *1*(2), 131–144. https://doi.org/10.1037/1076-8998.1.2.131

Moen, P. (2011). From 'work-family' to the 'gendered life course' and 'fit': Five challenges to the field. *Community, Work & Family*, *14*(1), 81–96. https://doi.org/10.1080/1366 8803.2010.532661

Moen, P., Pedtke, J. H., & Flood, S. (2020). Disparate disruptions: Intersectional COVID-19 employment effects by age, gender, education, and race/ethnicity. *Work, Aging and Retirement*, *6*(4), 207–228. https://doi.org/10.1093/workar/waaa013

Moen, P., & Sweet, S. (2004). From 'work-family' to 'flexible careers': A life course reframing. *Community, Work & Family*, *7*(2), 209–226. https://doi.org/10.1080/1366 880042000245489

Moghimi, D., Zacher, H., Scheibe, S., & Von Yperen, N. W. (2017). The selection, optimization, and compensation model in the work context: A systematic review and meta-analysis of two decades of research. *Journal of Organizational Behavior*, *38*(2), 247–275. https://doi.org/10.1002/job.2108

Mühlenbrock, I., & Hüffmeier, J. (2020). Differential work design for different age groups? A systematic literature review of the moderating role of age in the relation between psychosocial work characteristics and health. *Zeitschrift für Arbeits- und Organisationspsychologie*, *64*, 171–195. https://doi.org/10.1026/0932-4089/a000330

Ng, T. W. H., & Feldman, D. C. (2008). The relationship of age to ten dimensions of job performance. *Journal of Applied Psychology*, *93*(2), 392–423. https://doi.org/10.1037/0021-9010.93.2.392

Ng, T. W. H., & Feldman, D. C. (2012). Evaluating six common stereotypes about older workers with meta-analytical data. *Personnel Psychology*, *65*(4), 821–858. https://doi.org/10.1111/peps.12003

Noonan, A. E. (2005). "At this point now": Older workers' reflections on their current employment experiences. *International Journal of Aging and Human Development*, *61*(3), 211–241. <Go to ISI>://000232355700004

Pak, K., Kooij, D. T., De Lange, A. H., & Van Veldhoven, M. J. (2018). Human resource management and the ability, motivation and opportunity to continue working: A review of quantitative studies. *Human Resource Management Review*. https://doi.org/10.1016/j.hrmr.2018.07.002

Parker, S. K., & Bindl, U. K. (2017). *Proactivity at work: Making things happen in organizations*. Routledge.

Rauvola, R. S., & Rudolph, C. W. (2020). On the limits of agency for successful aging at work. *Industrial and Organizational Psychology: Perspectives on Science and Practice*, *13*(3), 383–387. https://doi.org/10.1017/iop.2020.61

Rauvola, R. S., & Rudolph, C. W. (2021). Control at work: An integrative, lifespan-informed review. *Work, Aging and Retirement*. https://doi.org/10.1093/workar/waab015

Rietzschel, E. F., Zacher, H., & Stroebe, W. (2016). A lifespan perspective on creativity and innovation at work. *Work, Aging and Retirement*, *2*(2), 105–129. https://doi.org/10.1093/workar/waw005

Roberts, B. W., Walton, K. E., & Viechtbauer, W. (2006). Patterns of mean-level change in personality traits across the life course: A meta-analysis of longitudinal studies. *Psychological Bulletin*, *132*(1), 1–25. https://doi.org/10.1037/0033-2909.132.1.1

Rosing, K., & Jungmann, F. (2019). *Lifespan perspectives on leadership*. Academic Press.

Rudolph, C. W. (2016). Lifespan developmental perspectives on working: A literature review of motivational theories. *Work, Aging and Retirement*, *2*, 130–158. https://doi.org/10.1093/workar/waw012

Rudolph, C. W., De Lange, A. H., & Van der Heijden, B. (2015). Adjustment processes in bridge employment: Where we are and where we need to go. In P. M. Bal, D. T. A. M. Kooij, & D. Rousseau (Eds.), *Aging workers and the employee-employer relationship* (pp. 221–242). Springer.

Rudolph, C. W., Katz, I. M., Lavigne, K. N., & Zacher, H. (2017). Job crafting: A meta-analysis of relationships with individual differences, job characteristics, and work outcomes. *Journal of Vocational Behavior, 102*, 112–138. https://doi.org/10.1016/j.jvb.2017.05.008

Rudolph, C. W., Kooij, D. T. A. M., Rauvola, R. S., & Zacher, H. (2018). Occupational future time perspective: A meta-analysis of antecedents and outcomes. *Journal of Organizational Behavior, 39*(2), 229–248. https://doi.org/10.1002/job.2264

Rudolph, C. W., Kunze, F., & Zacher, H. (2019). Getting objective about subjective age: Introduction to a special issue. *Work, Aging and Retirement, 5*(4), 265–272. https://doi.org/10.1093/workar/waz019

Rudolph, C. W., Rauvola, R. S., Costanza, D. P., & Zacher, H. (2020). Generations and generational differences: Debunking myths in organizational science and practice and paving new paths forward. *Journal of Business and Psychology.* https://doi.org/10.1007/s10869-020-09715-2

Rudolph, C.W. & Zacher, H. (2015). Intergenerational perceptions and conflicts in multi-age and multigenerational work environments. In L. M. Finkelstein, D. M. Truxillo, F. Fraccaroli, F., & R. Kanfer (Eds.), *SIOP Organizational Frontier Series—Facing the Challenges of a Multi-Age Workforce: A Use Inspired Approach* (pp. 253–282). New York, NY: Psychology Press.

Rudolph, C. W., & Zacher, H. (2017). Considering generations from a lifespan developmental perspective. *Work, Aging and Retirement, 3*(2), 113–129. https://doi.org/10.1093/workar/waw019

Rudolph, C. W., & Zacher, H. (2019). Managing employees across the lifespan. In B. Hoffman, M. Shoss, & L. Wegman (Eds.), *The Cambridge handbook of the changing nature of work* (pp. 425–445). Cambridge University Press.

Salthouse, T. A. (2012). Consequences of age-related cognitive declines. *Annual Review of Psychology, 63*, 201–226. https://doi.org/10.1146/annurev-psych-120710-100328

Schmidt, F. L., & Hunter, J. E. (1998). The validity and utility of selection methods in personnel psychology: Practical and theoretical implications of 85 years of research findings. *Psychological Bulletin, 124*(2), 262–274. https://doi.org/10.1037/0033-2909.124.2.262

Schneid, M., Isidor, R., Steinmetz, H., & Kabst, R. (2016). Age diversity and team outcomes: A quantitative review. *Journal of Managerial Psychology, 31*(1), 2–17. https://doi.org/10.1108/JMP-07-2012-0228

Schwall, A. R. (2012). Defining age and using age-relevant constructs. In J. W. Hedge & W. C. Borman (Eds.), *The Oxford handbook of work and aging* (pp. 169–186). Oxford University Press. https://doi.org/10.1093/oxfordhb/9780195385052.013.0080

Shane, J., & Heckhausen, H. (2019). Motivational theory of lifespan development. In B. B. Baltes, C. W. Rudolph, & H. Zacher (Eds.), *Work across the lifespan* (pp. 111–134). Academic Press.

Shultz, K. S., & Adams, G. A. (2019). *Aging and work in the 21st century* (2nd ed.). Routledge.

Shultz, K. S., & Wang, M. (2011). Psychological perspectives on the changing nature of retirement. *American Psychologist, 66*(3), 170–179. https://doi.org/10.1037/a0022411

Sinnott, J. D., & Shifren, K. (2001). Gender and aging: Gender differences and gender roles. In J. E. Birren & K. W. Schaie (Eds.), *Handbook of the psychology of aging* (pp. 454–476). Academic Press.

Sterns, H. L., & Subich, L. M. (2002). Career development in midcareer. In D. C. Feldman (Ed.), *Work careers: A developmental perspective* (pp. 186–213). Jossey-Bass.

Stone-Romero, E. F., & Rosopa, P. J. (2008). The relative validity of inferences about mediation as a function of research design characteristics. *Organizational Research Methods, 11*, 326–352. https://doi.org/10.1177/1094428107300342

Stone-Romero, E. F., & Rosopa, P. J. (2011). Experimental tests of mediation models: Prospects, problems, and some solutions. *Organizational Research Methods, 14*(4), 631–646. https://doi.org/10.1177/1094428110372673

Tomlinson, J., Baird, M., Berg, P., & Cooper, R. (2018). Flexible careers across the life course: Advancing theory, research and practice. *Human Relations, 71*(1), 4–22. https://doi.org/10.1177/0018726717733313

Topa, G., Moriano, J. A., Depolo, M., Alcover, C. M., & Morales, J. F. (2009). Antecedents and consequences of retirement planning and decision-making: A meta-analysis and model. *Journal of Vocational Behavior, 75*(1), 38–55. https://doi.org/10.1016/j.jvb.2009.03.002

Truxillo, D. M., Cadiz, D. M., Rineer, J. R., Zaniboni, S., & Fraccaroli, F. (2012). A lifespan perspective on job design: Fitting the job and the worker to promote job satisfaction, engagement, and performance. *Organizational Psychology Review, 2*(4), 340–360. https://doi.org/10.1177/2041386612454043

United States Equal Employment Opportunity Commission. (2021). *The age discrimination in employment act of 1967.* Retrieved on 29 June 2021, from www.eeoc.gov/laws/statutes/adea.cfm

Von Hippel, C., Kalokerinos, E. K., Haanterä, K., & Zacher, H. (2019). Age-based stereotype threat and work outcomes: Stress appraisals and rumination as mediators. *Psychology and Aging, 34*(1), 68–84. https://doi.org/10.1037/pag0000308

Von Hippel, C., Kalokerinos, E. K., & Henry, J. D. (2013). Stereotype threat among older employees: Relationships with job attitudes and turnover intentions. *Psychology and Aging, 28*(1), 17–27. https://doi.org/10.1037/a0029825

Wang, M. (2015). Inaugural editorial. *Work, Aging and Retirement, 1*(1), 1–3. https://doi.org/10.1093/workar/wau010

Wang, M., Beal, D. J., Chan, D., Newman, D. A., Vancouver, J. B., & Vandenberg, R. J. (2017). Longitudinal research: A panel discussion on conceptual issues, research design, and statistical techniques. *Work, Aging and Retirement, 3*(1), 1–24. https://doi.org/10.1093/workar/waw033

Wegge, J., Roth, C., Neubach, B., Schmidt, K. H., & Kanfer, R. (2008). Age and gender diversity as determinants of performance and health in a public organization: The role of task complexity and group size. *Journal of Applied Psychology, 93*(6), 1301–1313. https://doi.org/10.1037/a0012680

Weiss, D., & Weiss, M. (2019). Why people feel younger: Motivational and social-cognitive mechanisms of the subjective age bias and its implications for work and organizations *Work, Aging and Retirement, 5*(4), 273–280. https://doi.org/10.1093/workar/waz016

Williams, D. R., & Wilson, C. M. (2001). Race, ethnicity, and aging. In R. H. Binstock & L. K. George (Eds.), *Handbook of aging and the social sciences* (4th ed., pp. 160–178). Academic Press.

Wohlwill, J. F. (1970). The age variable in psychological research. *Psychological Review, 77*(1), 49–64. https://doi.org/10.1037/h0028600

World Health Organization. (2015). *World report on ageing and health.* World Health Organization.

Yeung, D. Y., Fung, H. H., & Chan, D. K.-S. (2020). Roles of age and future time perspective of the work relationship in conflict management: A daily diary study. *International Journal of Stress Management, 27*(4), 358–369. https://doi.org/10.1037/str0000155

Zacher, H. (2015). Successful aging at work. *Work, Aging and Retirement, 1*(1), 4–25. https://doi.org/10.1093/workar/wau006

Zacher, H., Esser, L., Bohlmann, C., & Rudolph, C. W. (2019). Age, social identity and identification, and work outcomes: A conceptual model, literature review, and future research directions. *Work, Aging and Retirement, 5*(1), 24–43. https://doi.org/10.1093/workar/way005

Zacher, H., & Frese, M. (2018). Action regulation theory: Foundations, current knowledge, and future directions. In D. S. Ones, N. R. Anderson, C. Viswesvaran, & H. K. Sinangil (Eds.), *The SAGE handbook of industrial, work and organizational psychology, Vol. 2. Organizational psychology* (2nd ed., pp. 80–102). Sage.

Zacher, H., & Froidevaux, A. (2021). Life stage, lifespan, and life course perspectives on vocational behavior and development: A theoretical framework, review, and research agenda. *Journal of Vocational Behavior.* https://doi.org/10.1016/j.jvb.2020.103476

Zacher, H., Hacker, W., & Frese, M. (2016). Action regulation across the adult lifespan (ARAL): A meta-theory of work and aging. *Work, Aging and Retirement, 2*(3), 286–306. https://doi.org/10.1093/workar/waw015

Zacher, H., Jimmieson, N. L., & Bordia, P. (2014). Time pressure and coworker support mediate the curvilinear relationship between age and occupational well-being. *Journal of Occupational Health Psychology, 19*(4), 462–475. https://doi.org/10.1037/a0036995

Zacher, H., Kooij, D. T. A. M., & Beier, M. E. (2018a). Active aging at work: Contributing factors and implications for organizations. *Organizational Dynamics, 47*(1), 37–45. https://doi.org/10.1016/j.orgdyn.2017.08.001

Zacher, H., Kooij, D. T. A. M., & Beier, M. E. (2018b). Successful aging at work: Empirical and methodological advancements. *Work, Aging and Retirement, 4*(2), 123–128. https://doi.org/10.1093/workar/way002

Zacher, H., & Rudolph, C. W. (2017). Change in job satisfaction negatively predicts change in retirement intentions. *Work, Aging and Retirement, 3*(3), 284–297. https://doi.org/10.1093/workar/wax009

Zacher, H., & Rudolph, C. W. (2019a). Just a mirage: On the incremental predictive validity of subjective age. *Work, Aging and Retirement, 5*(2), 141–162. https://doi.org/10.1093/workar/wax031

Zacher, H., & Rudolph, C. W. (2019b). Why do we act as old as we feel? The role of occupational future time perspective and core self-evaluations in the relationship between subjective age and job crafting behavior. *European Journal of Work and Organizational Psychology, 28*(6), 831–844. https://doi.org/10.1080/1359432X.2019.1677609

Zacher, H., Sagha Zadeh, R., Heckhausen, J., & Oettingen, G. (2021). Motivation and healthy aging at work. *Journal of Gerontology: Psychological Sciences.* https://doi.org/10.1093/geronb/gbab042

Zacher, H., & Schmitt, A. (2016). Work characteristics and occupational well-being: The role of age. *Frontiers in Psychology, 7*, 1411. https://doi.org/10.3389/fpsyg.2016.01411

Zhan, Y., Wang, M., Liu, S., & Shultz, K. S. (2009). Bridge employment and retirees' health: A longitudinal investigation. *Journal of Occupational Health Psychology, 14*(4), 374–389. https://doi.org/10.1037/a0015285

2

WORKFORCE AGE TRENDS AND PROJECTIONS[1]

Jürgen Deller and Ulrich Walwei

Aging is a phenomenon shared by many societies. However, it affects industrialized countries much more strongly than less-developed countries. On average, both the population and working population are living longer, which is good news per se. However, the process of aging raises numerous questions for economic systems. What does it mean for economic development or trends in labor productivity in the long term? How long can implicit knowledge be maintained and skill shortages be avoided? Are social security systems based on workers' contributions sustainable? A key factor in this context is the employment-to-population rate for workers, particularly older workers, i.e., people aged 55 years and older. The longer older workers are employed, the more they contribute to economic activities, facilitate knowledge transfer, offer valuable skills, ease the burden on social security systems, and generate their own income.

Taking a comparative perspective, this chapter deals with driving forces of employment-to-population rates for older workers. In order to do so, it particularly focuses on comparing the process of aging in both the population and the workforce. The following section starts by adopting a global perspective and examining worldwide population developments. In the next step, it compares trends in ten industrial countries representing three continents, diverse cultural backgrounds, and notable differences in their economic and social development. The third section touches upon four brief cases in four different countries that seem to be particularly prototypical for different contexts. Given the high variance in cultures of work and welfare state systems in and around Europe, we have selected Germany, Israel, Italy, and Sweden. Each country stands for a specific configuration, for instance, because it may represent a trend reversal, a continuously outstanding performance, or lasting problems. The conclusion summarizes the main findings and provides guidelines for further research in this context.

DOI: 10.4324/9781003089674-3

Population and Employment: Trends in Aging

Population development is characterized by various changes. These changes entail either variations in level—such as growth or shrinkage—or shifts in its composition, such as aging. Such changes are highly relevant for the labor market because they influence the size and the structure of the working population. Population development differs greatly among continents and among countries. This section first draws a broader picture and looks at variations in population development among continents. Given the focus of the chapter on labor market issues and particularly on employment-to-population rates of older workers, it then compares developments in ten industrial countries representing three continents, different cultural backgrounds, and diverse welfare state models: Canada, Denmark, France, Germany, Italy, Israel, Japan, Sweden, the UK, and the USA. In particular, it looks at the process of population aging and at different labor market indicators in these countries.

Population Aging

Over the past three decades, the world population has increased from 5.3 billion to 7.8 billion inhabitants, which corresponds to a growth rate of more than 46% (for the following, see United Nations, 2019). The fastest growth has been registered in Africa with a rate of almost 130%, whereas the lowest rate has been observed in Europe with less than 4%. Closer to the world average were growth rates in Oceania (56%), South America (46%), Asia (44%), and North America (32%). The United Nations' projections for up to 2050 suggest that population growth will most probably slow down: In the next three decades, the world population may grow by around 25%. The reduction in growth rate will affect all continents to a varying extent. However, Europe will be the only continent in which the population may even shrink by the year 2050 (by around 5%).

To a certain degree, population growth corresponds with aging. That is because high (low) fertility rates go along with a lower (higher) life expectancy. Wang et al. (2020) argue that, with few exceptions, fertility rates have been dropping steadily and life expectancy has been increasing over the past 20 years. Since 1990, the median age of the world population has climbed from 24.1 years to 30.9 years. The currently highest median age can be identified in Europe with 42.5 years, followed by North America with 38.6 years. By far the lowest median age can be found in Africa with 19.7 years. According to UN projections, the order of median ages between the continents will not change up to 2050. Nevertheless, the median age will rise even further due to increased life expectancy. In 2050, Africa will remain the youngest continent (median age: 24.8 years), whereas North America (median age: 43.0 years) and Europe (47.1 years) will most probably be home to the oldest populations.

Evidently, aging is a global phenomenon. However, it affects industrialized countries much more strongly than less-developed countries. In order to understand the process of aging, we concentrate in the following on more-developed countries, as they are the first to experience the challenges of aging populations. Data from labor force surveys gathered by the organization for economic cooperation and development (OECD) offer differentiated information. To illustrate past and future developments in population, total numbers are divided here into four age groups: 0–14; 15–54; 55–64; 65 and older. The focus will be on long-term trends: We look back at previous decades and look ahead to future decades. Therefore, the following charts present data for the past three decades, between 1988 and 2018, as well as projections for the three forthcoming decades up to 2050. For the year 1988, Figure 2.1 illustrates that Israel was by far the youngest of the selected countries. Its share of the youngest age group between 0 and 14 years was the highest of all 10 countries. By contrast, the European countries (Denmark, France, Germany, Italy, and Sweden) had the highest share of persons 65 and older. In 1988, the share of the working population aged between 15 and 64 years was highest in Germany (69.4 percent of total population) and lowest in Israel (59.1 percent of total population).

The development between 1988 and 2018 indicates a process of continuous aging in all selected countries. Nevertheless, one can observe different speeds of this process (Figure 2.2). On one end, Israel is still the country with the largest group of children and youngsters aged up to 14 years. On the other end, the highest share of citizens aged 65 years and older can now be found in Japan. The corresponding shares of the selected European countries are only slightly lower than in Japan. In most countries, the share of the working population has decreased

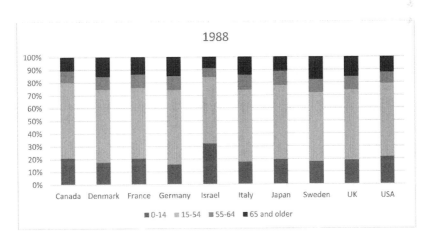

FIGURE 2.1 Population in selected countries by different age groups, 1988

Source: data.oecd.org; authors' own analysis

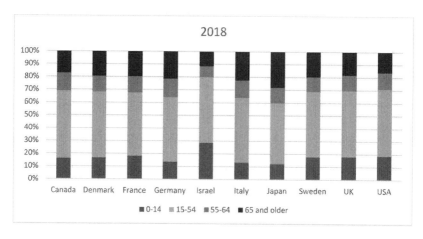

FIGURE 2.2 Population in selected countries by different age groups, 2018

Source: data.oecd.org; authors' own analysis

over time, whereas—due to aging—the share of older (55- to 64-year-old) workers has grown. In 2018, the working population between 15 and 64 years of age was highest in Canada (66.7% percent of total population) and lowest in Japan (59.7% of total population).

The projection of population growth by age for the year 2050, based on data from the United Nations, indicates in its medium variant that future developments will move in the same direction as in the past (see Figure 2.3). Even then, Israel will be the youngest country. The highest shares of older persons can be expected in Italy and Japan, closely followed by Germany and Sweden, countries with a comparatively high and increasing share of older people. At the same time, the share of the population in the age group 15–64 will drop in almost all of the selected countries.

Past and future population developments suggest an increasing share of older persons in industrial countries. Older persons usually belong to the so-called potential workforce. Its size largely depends on institutional issues such as retirement regulations or on sociodemographic characteristics such as health status. To what extent this potential share of the workforce can be utilized is a particularly relevant question for the future size of labor supply in a given country. That is because demographic change is severely affecting both the economy and the labor market. As has already been shown, the population of industrialized countries will most likely grow more slowly or even shrink in due course, as will the labor force. At the same time, the labor force is growing older. A more slowly increasing or shrinking labor force has the potential to reduce economic growth and income opportunities for older workers and also to make it more difficult to maintain and transfer knowledge (Ottaviano & Peri, 2006).

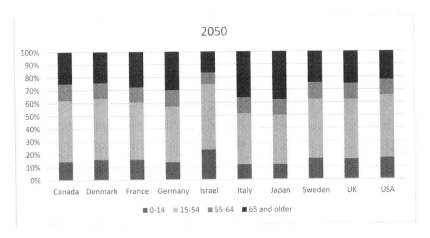

FIGURE 2.3   Population projection in selected countries by different age groups, 2050

Source: UN, Department of Economic and Social Affairs, Population Division. World Population Prospects 2019; authors' own analysis

Workforce Aging

The process of aging within the workforce can be illustrated best by making use of employment-to-population rates. These ratios are defined as the proportion of employed persons within the corresponding population. They can be disaggregated by various characteristics, such as by age. The following comparison again includes the ten countries mentioned earlier. It looks at two different age groups (25–54 years and 55–64 years) at two points in time (1988 and 2018). The youngest members of the workforce (15–24 years) have been excluded here because, unlike most people 25 years of age or older, many have not yet completed school, training, and studies. For 1988, the general picture shows that employment-to-population rates for the age group 55–64 were consistently lower than for the age group 25–54 across countries. The highest employment rate of older workers could be observed in Sweden and Japan, the lowest in Italy, France, and Germany (Figure 2.4). In the last three decades, the employment rate of older workers increased in all selected countries, particularly in Germany, where it almost doubled (Figure 2.5). In 2018, the employment-to-population rate for older workers was highest in Japan and Sweden and lowest in Italy and France. Large differences between the older and the younger age group can still be found in France and Italy.

Of further interest is that employment-to-population rates for older workers differ to a certain extent by sex. Figures 2.6 and 2.7 show employment-to-population rates for the age group 55–64 for each sex in 1988 and 2018. One can observe comparatively large differences between men and women in Italy

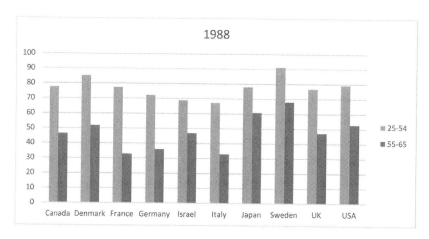

FIGURE 2.4 Employment rates in selected countries by age groups, 1988

Source: data.oecd.org; authors' own analysis

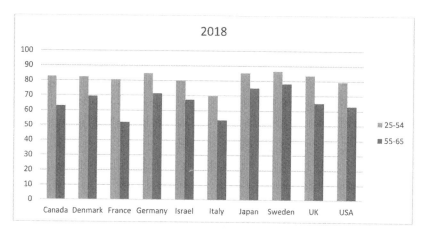

FIGURE 2.5 Employment rates in selected countries by age groups, 2018

Source: data.oecd.org; authors' own analysis

and the lowest difference in Sweden at both points in time. In all countries, the differences were much lower in 2018 than they were in 1988. This development reflects an overall increase in female participation in labor markets.

Besides age groups who are part of the "regular" working population (usually 15 to 64 years), employment-to-population rates of those aged 65 and above are also of relevance here. This group can also be seen as part of the potential work-force. Particularly in European countries, there are clear indications that the 65+ age group is now much more involved in employment than before (Eurofound,

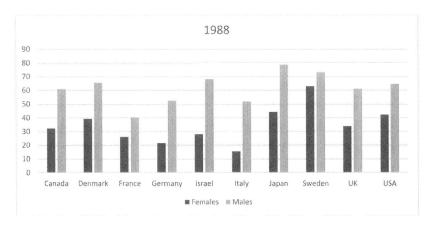

FIGURE 2.6   Employment rates of workers by sex aged 55–64 years in selected countries, 1988

Source: data.oecd.org; authors' own analysis

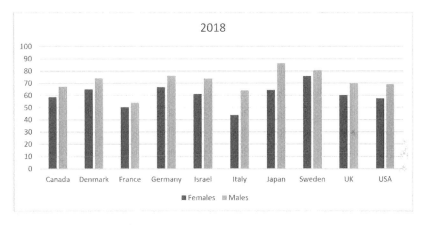

FIGURE 2.7   Employment rates of workers by sex aged 55–64 years in selected countries, 2018

Source: data.oecd.org; authors' own analysis

2012, 2014). Nevertheless figures for 2018 show that these rates are highest in non-European countries such as Japan, Israel, and the US (see Figure 2.8). Such figures can, on the one hand, indicate a need for older people to stay employed in order to secure their cost of living, e.g. due to low pensions. On the other hand, comparatively high employment-to-population rates of 65-year-olds and older can also be seen as an interest in spending their time in a meaningful way as characterized by work.

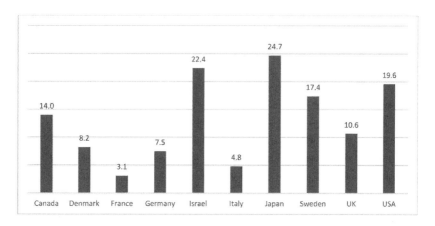

FIGURE 2.8 Employment rates of 65-year-olds and older in selected countries, % in same age group, 2018

Source: data.oecd.org; authors' own analysis

For a more complete picture of older workers' employment situation, it also helps to know to what extent they face difficulties in (re-)entering the labor market. This can be estimated by a comparison of unemployment rates for different age groups (25–54 and 55–64) and by distinguishing between different durations of unemployment. Figures 2.9 and 2.10 illustrate the incidence of short-term and long-term unemployment for the two age groups in the selected countries. In 1988, some countries, such as Germany, the UK, and Japan, showed higher unemployment rates for older workers than for younger workers. The highest share of long-term unemployed among total unemployed could be found in Italy, France, Germany, and the UK (Figure 2.9). Comparing 1988 and 2018, we recognize a sharp reduction in unemployment among older workers in Germany and the UK for both age groups and a significant increase in old-age unemployment in Italy and Sweden (Figure 2.10). The more recent figures also show that the unemployment rate of older workers is, in most countries, now lower than for the younger age group. Exemptions are Anglo-American countries such as Canada, the UK, and the USA. The incidence of long-term unemployment among older unemployed is highest in France, Germany, and Italy and relatively low in Canada, the US, and Israel, indicating differences in labor market institutions and dynamics.

Finally, comparative information about the time of retirement is available at least for European countries (Axelrad, 2018). It allows for distinguishing between workers who retired early, at the regular time, or late. Concerning the countries of interest here, the rate of early retirees was highest in Italy and Israel and lowest in the two Scandinavian countries Denmark and Sweden. The highest proportion of late retirees can be found in Denmark and again in Israel, showing a

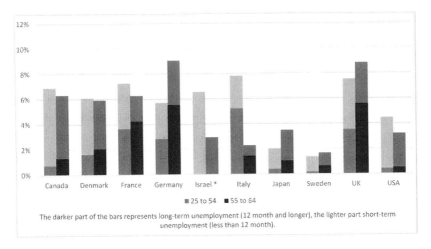

FIGURE 2.9   Unemployment rate and incidence of short-term and long-term unemployment by age groups in selected countries, 1988

Source: data.oecd.org; authors' own analysis

Note: * no data available for long-term unemployment

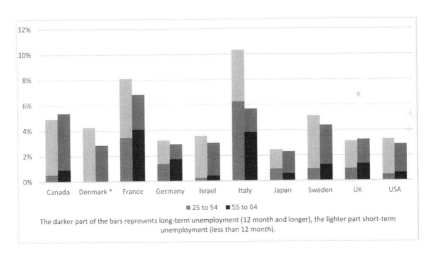

FIGURE 2.10   Unemployment rate and incidence of short-term and long-term unemployment by age groups in selected countries, 2018

Source: data.oecd.org; authors' own analysis

Note: * no data available for long-term unemployment

polarized distribution, whereas relatively low rates are reported for France, Germany and Italy. All in all, the differences in retirement decision among countries seem largely associated with the generosity of pension systems. Furthermore, early retirement was found to be more likely when GDP was lower and/or health conditions of people were poorer.

Due to the differences over time and between countries in employment-to-population ratios for older workers and their great significance for future developments, a major question is what drives changes to these ratios. Employment rates of older workers can be influenced by three main factors (Walwei, 2018a). First, differences in the particular labor market situation and development of a country are relevant here in two respects. A favorable labor market development improves the chances of all groups of workers, including older workers. This argument is perfectly illustrated by the aphorism popularized by John F. Kennedy that "a rising tide lifts all boats" (Kennedy, 1963). In addition, specific labor market features, such as the industrial composition of employment, can be associated with different opportunities for the various kinds of workers. Compositional differences may offer more or fewer options for older workers to stay in or (re-)enter the labor market.

Second, changes in characteristics of jobs and workers may also play a role. There are indications that—independent of age—educational attainment is positively associated with labor market participation. An increase in younger women's labor market participation most likely influences their lifelong presence in employment. Of importance here are also changes in the health situation of the population and variations in specific job requirements. In addition, life partners' preferences in retirement decisions need to be put under scrutiny. Third, changes in relevant institutions and reforms may create incentives or disincentives for older workers to participate in the labor market. Of main importance are regulations dealing with retirement and unemployment benefits that affect older persons.

Finally, in the current situation, the potential impacts of the ongoing COVID-19 pandemic need to be addressed. The pandemic may have several effects on older workers' employment situation. Like other workers, they may also suffer from at least temporary job losses and fewer opportunities in certain areas of the labor market. In this respect, it is of relevance that older workers are more likely to be self-employed, a group that has particularly suffered from pandemic-related containment measures in almost all countries (de Bruin & Firkin, 2001; Baer, 2015). In addition, physical distancing has become decisive due to higher health risks in connection with the virus, for instance, working from home is a potential alternative, particularly for groups who are specifically threatened by the pandemic, including older workers. Of additional importance for the long-term employability of older workers is the fact that the diffusion of digital technologies has been clearly and strongly pushed, implying an increased need for new capabilities of workers. For a more detailed look at forces that may have driven the employment-to-population rates for older workers, the following section outlines four country cases.

Labor Market Participation of Older Workers: Short Country Cases

Four countries were selected as specific short cases (more detailed information on these can be found in Walwei and Deller (2021a, 2021b)). These countries represent different cultural backgrounds and varying welfare state models. In addition, they appear to be prototypical for developments in industrialized countries. The short country cases cover Germany, Sweden, Italy, and Israel, whose welfare state models differ. Each of these countries is of interest for different reasons. Germany has been chosen for its trend reversal regarding the labor market integration of older workers, Sweden for its consistently high participation rate of older workers, Italy for its difficulties in achieving a high labor market participation among older workers, and Israel for its young population as a highly interesting countermodel.

The following case studies will address the specificities of these four countries in more detail. They do not aim at providing any causal explanation for developments of employment-to-population ratios in the countries. Instead, they offer circumstantial evidence to illustrate which factors may have been of consequence for developments of employment-to-population ratios in the four countries.

First, however, further systematic information of relevance for the four countries needs to be given: The median age in years as an indicator for the age composition of the total population and employment-to-population ratios for older workers over time by different age groups and by sex.

Table 2.1 indicates that in 2018 the employment rate of older workers (55–64 years) was highest in Sweden for both men and women. The largest increase in the employment-to-population ratio for older workers between 1988 and 2018 could be observed in Germany, whereas Italy showed the lowest increase. Israel had by far the youngest population—as measured by the median age—but also the highest share of workers older than 65 years.

In Germany, one can observe a longer-lasting trend of an increasing employment-to-population ratio for older workers that gained momentum in the last decades, particularly during the more recent years of strong economic growth. Until the early 1990s, the labor market situation was poor for older workers compared with younger groups of workers as well as with older workers in several other countries. This applies even more for women than for men. In recent years, however, older workers' participation in the labor market has improved considerably. The positive development of the employment-to-population rate for older workers is associated with a higher stability of existing employment relationships, for instance, one can observe a lower exit rate of older workers (Dietz & Walwei, 2011). The positive trend applies not only to older workers aged 55–64 years who

TABLE 2.1 Aging of Population and Workforce

		Germany	Israel	Italy	Sweden	OECD total
Median age of total population in years, 2018		46.0	29.8	46.3	40.6	39.8
Total employment rates by age groups						
1993	25–54	76.8	68.9	66.7	83.2	74.4
	55–64	35.9	45.2	30.4	63.4	46.1
2018	25–54	84.9	80.1	69.8	86.6	78.4
	55–64	71.5	67.3	53.7	78.2	61.4
Employment rates by gender, age 55–64						
1993	male	47.8	62.2	48.2	65.9	59.7
	female	24.2	29.6	14.1	60.9	33.4
2018	male	76.1	73.7	64.2	80.5	70.2
	female	66.9	61.2	43.9	75.8	53.1
Employment rates 65+						
	2018	7.4	21.9	4.7	16.9	15.1

Sources: United Nations (2019), Department of Economic and Social Affairs, Population Division World Population Prospects 2019, custom data acquired via website. OECD (2021), Employment/population ratio (Accessed on April 9, 2021).

are still part of the workforce but also to older workers who are already pensioners (Anger et al., 2018; Walwei, 2018b). Due to increasing skill shortages, firms have made great efforts to retain workers otherwise eligible for pensions (Czepek et al., 2017). Further evidence shows that a stable employment biography before entering retirement age favors the likelihood of pensioners' participating in the labor market. The economic upswing vitalized the labor market in general, with a positive effect on older workers' employment situation. However, it is important to note that the situation was already improving in times of weak economic and employment growth prior to the upswing—meaning that the improved labor market participation of older workers is not solely growth-induced. Pension and labor market reforms have initiated an institutional turnaround and can claim a considerable share of success in improving the situation of older workers on the labor market. Nevertheless, it seems unlikely that labor market and pension policies alone can explain the strong increase (Steiner, 2017). With respect to future developments, the topic of employability clearly requires more attention. Continuous skill improvement and a healthy work environment need to be addressed more intensively in order to keep older workers in Germany employed.

Israel, by contrast, is a young country. The Israeli labor market is faring remarkably well overall. A series of successful policy measures have laid the foundation for the rise in employment: incentives to work, lowered welfare payments and an increase in the mandatory retirement age. Following a period of exceptionally rapid growth, Israel's employment rate increased by 10 percentage points in the last 15 years, barely affected by the global financial crisis. Axelrad (2020) reports an overall labor force participation rate of 19.5% for individuals aged 65 and older compared with 10.4% in 2004. With this higher rate, Israel now comes second to Denmark in a comparison with 20 European countries (Axelrad, 2018). Israel's success may result from the increased retirement age or from immigrants without pension plans who are entitled only to low social security retirement benefits (Axelrad, 2020). However, serious challenges face two large minority groups: Arabs and Haredi Jews (on ethnicity at work, see Chapter 4). They lag behind in both employment and earnings. Employment could be promoted with a special focus on these two groups, as well as by encouraging investments in their human capital through higher education and training in order to address the high, upward-trending level of net income inequality. According to Larom and Lifshitz (2018), almost a third (30%) of the increase in employment can be attributed to educational attainment.

Retirement age in Israel is characterized by a gender gap. This gap is not expected to close. In 2004, the mandatory retirement age was raised from 65 to 67 for men and from 60 to 62 for women. For over a decade, the Israeli government has unsuccessfully attempted to raise women's retirement age by another two years, to 64 (Fuchs & Weiss, 2018). The higher retirement ages have had a direct effect on employment for all ages. Compared with other age groups, the 55–64 age group has the lowest employment rate but the fastest increase in employment. While men and women face different legal regulations on retirement age, the reasons for the relatively high percentage of individuals of either sex retiring late have not been identified so far. Highly interesting is the finding that Israel is a country of extremes in terms of early versus later retirement. It has both a large group of individuals leaving the workplace early and a large group leaving late. Better understanding the drivers behind this variance is definitely a worthwhile endeavor.

Italy is one of the largest economies in Europe. Its labor market is characterized by a growing labor force participation among the oldest age group, while the youngest age group encounters major problems in entering the work force. Young individuals (age 15–24) face high unemployment, and their participation rates, already low, in fact decreased between 2000 and 2016 by 15 percentage points. Only around one quarter of this group is currently working. This is also due to the emergence of the NEET youth (those not in education, employment or training), which totals about a fifth of the age group. Additionally, undeclared employment is high. Since 2009, Italy has experienced a moderate economic recovery, and job vacancies have increased. Another main challenge is a north–south disparity, with the north continuing to be more dynamic (Marino & Nunziata, 2017). Nevertheless, promising signs can be identified in several regions. These developments need to be continued and strengthened.

Italy is also a good example that demographically driven pension reforms can be impactful and lead to behavior change. In 2012, the retirement age for men was set between 66 and 70 years of age, and the respective age for women was set at 62, to be raised to 66. Since 2000, older workers' (aged 55–64) labor market participation has accelerated and increased substantially, particularly after the 2011 "Fornero" pension reforms (which increased minimum retirement age), by 25 percentage points between 2000 and 2016 to reach 53.4% (Marino & Nunziata, 2017). At the same time, older workers may also contribute to unbalanced groups in the labor market. Although female labor force participation is still low, it has increased by five percentage points from 2000 to 2016. The importance of education and a smooth entrance into the labor market is illustrated by the situation of Italy's youth. Changing this development successfully may set an example for other countries as well. In Italy, as Socci et al. (2017) summarize, the sensibility, willingness, and ability to manage a mature and aging workforce is not particularly developed compared with other European countries. At the same time, the authors identify main labor market indicators relative to older workers as showing a trend toward gradual improvement in the last decade, although several critical aspects still persist.

For quite some time, Sweden has had one of the highest labor force participation rates among older workers, to a large extent driven by high female labor market participation. The latter is one of the major explanations for steadily high employment-to-population rates for all groups of workers, particularly for older workers. Women's participation in the labor market increased particularly in the 1990s, when a "feminization of the labor force" took place (Albin et al., 2015). "Housewifes" have since then more or less disappeared from Swedish society. Overall, statistics indicate that the population in Sweden has experienced improved health over time. Particularly between the 1960s and 1980s, mortality decreased, and surveys report a steady improvement in self-assessed health, especially in older men (Laun & Palme, 2018). Research also identifies other important determinants for an increasing retirement age. First, it shows that a good mental and physical work environment potentially avoids high-risk jobs, risky physical exposure, and disability. Second, education in Sweden is an important gradient for retirement age. Current cohorts of older workers are more educated than previous ones and tend to retire later (Venti & Wise, 2015). Third, the retirement age is also associated with retirement decisions by life partners or close friends (Laun & Palme, 2018). Joint decision-making of couples leads to an earlier exit for women and later exits for men. Fourth, with respect to work requirements there are hints that jobs are becoming less demanding in Sweden. Self-reported assessments indicate lower physical demands (Laun & Palme, 2018).

There is evidence that retirement policies may have led to delayed exit from the labor market, mainly through stricter rules for disability eligibility. Exit patterns from employment to retirement have become increasingly heterogeneous. They augment inequalities between older people in retirement, particularly regarding educational attainment. Findings for Sweden suggest that good health and high education are the most important factors for a long career and late retirement. It is argued that policies should focus more on providing education and training (e.g., language and job-specific skills) to vulnerable groups (Albin et al., 2015).

Conclusion and Discussion

This chapter reflects workforce age trends and projections. It analyses available data on different workforce age aspects, including population age groups, employment rates, and unemployment to give an overview of selected yet typical countries. Four brief country case studies depict the country-specific situations and present special attributes, including the age profiles, developments of age groups over several decades, differences between male and female labor market participation, and changes in characteristics of jobs and workers. As the cases reveal, situations and processes in different countries vary. Some aspects are similar; others very different. What do we learn from the cases, and what is unique to each? Given the different country situations, we do not look for best practices but rather for design options. The case studies show that it is important to understand the mechanisms behind different developments. They make it clear that one size does not fit all; instead, changes must be tailor-made to fit to specific country situations. As this chapter shows, we have gathered some specialist knowledge about workforce age trends and projections. However, our knowledge is far from being sufficient to understand the interaction of individual, organizational, and institutional aspects. This necessitates more multidisciplinary research. Several topics need to be addressed in the future, to name just a few:

First, plenty of data is available on the institutional level. Available data provides differentiated data on supranational, national, and in part also organizational levels. This holds true for the age groups relevant for traditional labor force participation up to and including 64 years. And, across our country examples, they show the growing number of older persons participating in the labor markets. Nevertheless, we do not know enough about the motives of older workers and of the older nonemployed across countries and over time. Are they still able to work? Do they want to work, and, if so, which motives play a role and how do these develop? Might they even have to work to make a living? Are certain people less open to new experience than others? Are there sex differences? Given their substantial numbers of working retirees, the countries analyzed in the case studies, among others, offer interesting samples for research to better understand the interplay of intention in the field of motivation, capability, the should and may of social norms, and the enabling situation. Extrinsic motivation and financial need can be aspects of situational parameters; education and a job that fits with a person's intrinsic motivation may be important individual aspects that support the intention to work. Furthermore, simple physical or service work without noticeable mental challenges may interest one group while appearing unattractive for others.

Second, robust representative data on workers above the retirement age is not easily available, if it even exists. Therefore, data on work in retirement is usually nonrepresentative, incomplete, or sparse. This lack of evidence must be addressed in order to provide research and policymakers alike with the data they need for evidence-based decision-making. One way to look for new evidence is the analysis of existing data, e.g., social security data or data from social-economic population household panel surveys, integrated into the Cross National Equivalent File (CNEF), Health and Retirement Study (HRS), English Longitudinal Study of Ageing (ELSA), and others. Additionally, a proper linkage of datasets may yield new results. This may include organizational and individual data such as company data and employee surveys. The role artificial intelligence can play in this field is underexplored to date as well.

Third, longitudinal research on relevant variables has rarely been conducted (see Chapter 10). Therefore, cause-and-effect relationships have yet to be substantiated empirically. To fill this gap, future research needs to apply longitudinal research designs. This can even start by observing individuals from early on in life. Only with a longitudinal research design will we be able to investigate whether and how situational changes such as pension reforms unfold over time and affect the behavioral component, namely individuals' behavior in relation to the labor market. At the same time, it is important to look for potential specificities of cohort effects, as behavior may also be a function of specific situational characteristics that change over time and have effects on individual behavior. Also, there are indications that path dependencies and education over time may play a role; further validation, however, is needed. Different academic disciplines can cooperate in this field, combining their forces and multiple perspectives.

Fourth, to further develop the field, additional population-representative data collection projects are needed that focus on retirement transitions and the potential of older adults on the labor market, in civil society and in the family. Alongside the Survey of Health, Ageing and Retirement in Europe (50+ in Europe; SHARE) and its sister studies around the world (see chapter 13), "TOP: Transitions and old age potential" is a good example of such a project (Mergenthaler et al., 2020). This longitudinal research project of the German Federal Institute for Population Research uses several waves of population representative data to find out more about older adults' potential for different areas of activity. The importance and interplay of individual and situational variables need to be analyzed. Such a representative survey should be conducted across countries in order to better understand similarities and differences.

Fifth, activities can also take place outside the traditional labor market, as motivation is not purely labor market oriented. Options are manifold: For instance, the Senior Expert Service (SES) works around the world with retired individuals as volunteers only (Deller & Pundt, 2014). Most of its assignments are completed in developing and emerging countries. SES follows the principle of helping people help themselves. To recruit retired volunteers, organizations need to offer attractive work conditions.

There are additional scientific challenges, such as how to develop robust methods that do not label individuals and neglect their potential developments, how to predict unemployment on the basis of data, and questions of "scarring" about the consequences of when individuals face difficulties in entering the labor market and its long-term impact.

Practical questions include the impact of COVID-19 on the labor market for older employees, the effects of digitization on aging workforces, and how transitions into, within, and out of the workforce can be organized. Different models of the transition to retirement, experiences, and obstacles need to be tested and applied.

Finally, another challenge is how to connect the societal and demographic levels to age-inclusive practices at the organizational level (see Chapters 9, 14, 15, 17, and 18). The latter are important in order to create relevant framework conditions for fostering work across all ages. These practices appear to be a prerequisite for securing labor market participation of all age groups, especially the oldest age group. Many organizations are not yet prepared to support the participation of all age groups. Evidence-based and validated instruments, such as the Later Life Workplace Index (LLWI; Wilckens et al., 2020), have been developed to support organizations in shaping workplaces for an aging workforce. To reach this objective, the LLWI measures nine distinct and multifaceted domains of organizational practices relevant to an aging workforce. Influenced by the LLWI, the International Standards Organization is in the process of publishing a guideline for an age-inclusive workforce (ISO 25550) that contains several dimensions of appropriate work conditions for older workers in small, medium, and large organizations. It addresses, among others, aspects such as leadership and age-inclusive organizational culture, health and well-being, work design, knowledge management, and transition to retirement. These tools will give organizations orientation for appropriately managing their aging workforce. Eventually, these practices at the organizational level can contribute to a better and more sustainable foundation for a higher labor market participation of older workers globally.

Note

1 Both authors contributed equally to this manuscript. The authors thank Marie Lena Muschik for technical assistance in preparing figures and tables.

References

Albin, M., Bodin, T., & Wadensjö, E. (2015). National report: Sweden. In H. M. Hasselhorn & W. Apt (Eds.), *Understanding employment participation of older workers: Creating a knowledge base for future labor market challenges*. Research Report, Federal Ministry of

Labor and Social Affairs (BMAS) and Federal Institute for Occupational Safety and Health (BAuA).

Anger, S., Trahms, A., & Westermeier, C. (2018). Erwerbsarbeit nach Renteneintritt. *Wirtschaftsdienst, 98*(12), 904–906.

Axelrad, H. (2018). Early retirement and late retirement: Comparative analysis of 20 European countries. *International Journal of Sociology, 48*(3), 231–250. https://doi:10.1080/00207659.2018.1483004

Axelrad, H. (2020). Perception versus official data: Employers' knowledge about the aging workforce. *Journal of Aging and Social Policy*. Advance online publication. https://doi.org/10.1080/08959420.2020.1769535

Baer, D. (2015, February). *Older workers are more likely to be self-employed.* Fact Sheet. AARP Public Policy Institute.

Czepek, J., Gürtzgen, N., Moczall, A., & Weber, E. (2017). Halten rentenberechtigter Mitarbeiter in den Betrieben: Vor allem kürzere und flexiblere Arbeitszeiten kommen zum Einsatz. *IAB-Kurzbericht, 16/2017.*

de Bruin, A., & Firkin, P. (2001). *Self-employment of the older worker.* Working Paper No. 4, Labour Market Dynamics Research Programme, Albany and Palmerston North Labour Market Dynamics Research Programme.

Deller, J., & Pundt, L. (2014). Flexible transitions from work to retirement in Germany. In C. M. Alcover, G. Topa, E. Parry, F. Fraccaroli, & M. Depolo (Eds.), *Bridge employment: A research handbook* (pp. 167–192). Routledge.

Dietz, M., & Walwei, U. (2011). Germany—no country for old workers? *Zeitschrift für ArbeitsmarktForschung, 44*(4), 363–376.

Eurofound. (2012). *Sustainable work and the ageing workforce.* https://www.eurofound.europa.eu/publications/report/2012/working-conditions-social-policies/sustainable-work-and-the-ageing-workforce

Eurofound. (2014). *Living and Working in Europe 2014: Adapting to the realities of an ageing labour market.* https://www.eurofound.europa.eu/news/news-articles/living-and-working-in-europe-2014-adapting-to-the-realities-of-an-ageing-labour-market

Fuchs, H., & Weiss, A. (2018). *Israel's labor market: An overview.* Taub Center for Social Policy Studies in Israel.

Kennedy, J. F. (1963, October 3). *Remarks in Heber Springs, Arkansas, at the dedication of Grers Ferry dam.* The American Presidency Project. Retrieved on 16 May 2021, from www.presidency.ucsb.edu/ws/index.php?pid=9455

Larom, T., & Lifshitz, O. (2018). The labor market in Israel, 2000–2016. *IZA World of Labor, 415.* https://doi.org/10.15185/izawol.415

Laun, L., & Palme, M. (2018). *The recent rise of labor force participation of older workers in Sweden.* Working Paper 24593, National Bureau of Economic Research.

Marino, F., & Nunziata, L. (2017). The labor market in Italy, 2000–2016. *IZA World of Labor, 407.* https://doi.org/10.15185/izawol.407

Mergenthaler, A., Konzelmann, L., Cihlar, V., Micheel, F., & Schneider, N. F. (2020). *Vom Ruhestand zu (Un-)Ruheständen. Ergebnisse der Studie "Transitions and Old Age Potential" (TOP) von 2013 bis 2019.* Bundesinstitut für Bevölkerungsforschung.

OECD. (2021). *OECD data.* Data.oecd.org.

Ottaviano, G., & Peri, G. (2006). *Rethinking the effects of immigration on wages.* NBER Working Paper No. 12497. https://www.nber.org/system/files/working_papers/w12497/w12497.pdf

Socci, M., Principi, A., with the cooperation of Bauknecht, J., Naegele, G., & Gerling, V. (2017). *Final country report: Italy*. In MoPAct—Mobilising the potential of active ageing in Europe: Work package 3: Extending working lives. European Centre for Social Welfare Policy and Research.

Steiner, V. (2017). The labor market for older workers in Germany. *Journal for Labor Market Research, 50*(1), 1–14.

United Nations Department of Economic and Social Affairs. (2019). *Revision of world population prospects*. United Nations Population Division.

Venti, S., & Wise, D. A. (2015). The long reach of education: Early retirement. *The Journal of the Economics of Ageing, 6*, 133–148. https://doi.org/10.1016/j.jeoa.2015.08.001

Walwei, U. (2018a). Silver Ager im Arbeitsmarktaufschwung: Wie steht es um die Qualität der Beschäftigung. *Deutsche Rentenversicherung, 73*(2), 144–158.

Walwei, U. (2018b). Trends in der Beschäftigung Älterer: Rahmenbedingungen für betriebliche Personalpolitik. *WSI-Mitteilungen, 71*(1), 3–11.

Walwei, U., & Deller, J. (2021a). *Labor market participation of older workers in international comparison*. IAB-Discussion Paper, 16/2021. Nuremberg.

Walwei, U., & Deller, J. (2021b). Older workers: Drivers and obstacles of labour market participation. *Intereconomics: Review of European Economic Policy, 56*(6). https://doi.org/10.1007/s10272-021-1010-9

Wang, H. D., et al. (2020). Global age-sex-specific fertility, mortality, healthy life expectancy (HALE), and population estimates in 204 countries and territories, 1950–2019: A comprehensive demographic analysis for the Global Burden of Disease Study 2019. *Lancet, 396*(10258), 1160–1203.

Wilckens, M. R., Wöhrmann, A. M., Deller, J., & Wang, M. (2021). Organizational practices for the aging workforce: Development and validation of the Later Life Workplace Index (LLWI). *Work, Aging and Retirement, 7*(4), 352–386. https://doi.org/10.1093/workar/waaa012

SECTION II

Advances in Theory on Age and Work

3

BEYOND CHRONOLOGICAL AGE

Alternative Age Constructs and Their Implications at Work

David Weiss and Mona Weiss

Across the last decades, work and organizational researchers have increasingly focused on examining chronological age to predict work and organizational outcomes, such as productivity, trainability, job attitudes, work motives, retirement decisions (e.g., for overviews see Kooij et al., 2011; Truxillo et al., 2015; Wang & Shi, 2014; please see also Chapter 1). However, in most of this research chronological age tends to be only weakly correlated with these work outcomes, suggesting that it is not chronological age per se that can explain age-related changes and interindividual differences in key work outcomes. In addition, there is strong consensus that chronological age is often only a superficial indicator of aging as it does not capture the complex and multifaceted nature of the aging process (P. B. Baltes, 1987). Relying on chronological age alone thus fails "to explain how and why, or through what mechanism the aging of an individual affects a given outcome" (Schwall, 2012, p. 2). Therefore, scholars across different disciplines have argued that chronological age should be merely understood as a placeholder for changes that occur across the lifespan, and a growing body of research has focused on understanding the processes that aging entails (e.g., Wohlwill, 1970; Zacher et al., 2010). Even though this research has yielded fruitful insight into the psychology of aging by investigating the predictive validity of alternative age constructs, such as subjective age and age-related beliefs, many open questions remain. First, what types of alternative age constructs are meaningful in the work context? For example, what are individuals' perceptions of age and aging, and what are the consequences for attitudes, motivation, and behavior at work? Second, which alternative age constructs capture the multidimensional nature of aging? For example, how do individuals perceive their own age, the process of aging, or different age groups and generations at work? Third, which alternative age constructs allow for precise measurement as well as manipulability such that

DOI: 10.4324/9781003089674-5

organizations can implement interventions to leverage the unique skills and abilities of older employees?

In the present chapter, we provide answers to these questions by introducing three alternative age constructs that have important implications at work: (1) subjective age, (2) essentialist beliefs about aging, and (3) age group vs. generation identity. First, we review research providing insights into the implications of subjective age (i.e., how old people feel) for important cognitive, health, and work outcomes. Second, we introduce essentialist beliefs about aging as a relatively new yet highly relevant alternative age construct indicating how fixed vs. malleable people perceive the aging process and discuss how this may affect important work outcomes, such as individuals' motivation to continue working after retirement. Third, we summarize research addressing alternative age identities such as generational membership, which highlights that the identification with one's generation can serve as a resource for dealing with aging-related challenges at work. In each section, we discuss how employees and organizations can leverage the benefits of these alternative age constructs by pointing out possibilities for interventions, and we conclude with recommendations for future research.

Subjective Age

The first alternative age construct that goes beyond chronological age is *subjective age*, that is, the age individuals think of themselves as being. Although everyone grows older, this does not necessarily imply that one also *feels* older. Studies across a variety of countries and cohorts repeatedly show and have established that the older individuals get, the younger they feel. The discrepancy between the age individuals feel and their chronological age has been examined as early as the 1950s. In a classic study, Blau (1956) asked older adults "How do you think of yourself as far as age goes—middle-aged, elderly, old; or what?" Zola (1962) asked participants "How old do you feel?" and Kastenbaum and colleagues (1972) assessed subjective age as a multidimensional construct asking participants about the age they feel, look, and act and the age of people whose interests are like theirs.

A large body of research has confirmed that from childhood to old age the majority of people feel significantly younger or older than their chronological age (Montepare, 2009; D. Weiss & M. Weiss, 2019). These studies suggest that, while younger adults (up to the age of 25) may often feel older, the majority of middle-aged and older adults (> 70%) feels significantly younger than their chronological age (Chopik et al., 2018; Rubin & Berntsen, 2006). Older adults generally consider themselves as middle-aged and show an implicit bias for younger ages (Blau, 1956; Chopik et al., 2018). By contrast, adolescents and young adults often report a relatively older subjective age, and in their mid-20s individuals shift from feeling relatively older to feeling younger than their chronological age (Galambos et al., 2005). A recent meta-analysis (Pinquart & Wahl, 2021) including subjective age data of 148 different countries confirmed that adults older than 40 years of age felt relatively younger, whereas children and adolescents felt relatively older than their chronological age. In line with previous studies that point to a large cross-cultural variability in the magnitude of the subjective age bias between modern and more traditional cultures (Ackerman & Chopik, 2021; Barak, 2009; D. Weiss & Halawa, 2016), this meta-analysis suggests that the subjective age bias is larger in Western countries.

Research also suggests that, for older adults, feeling younger than one's chronological age appears to be beneficial and has been associated with better health, well-being, cognitive functioning, and even a longer life (for a reviews see Kotter-Grühn et al., 2016). With regard to the workplace, studies suggest that employees' subjective age can affect work motivation, attribution processes, job-related behavior, job performance, and stress at and off work (Akkermans et al., 2016; Barnes-Farrell et al., 2002; Kunze et al., 2015; Nagy et al., 2019). For example, Cleveland and colleagues (1997) showed that a relatively younger subjective age was linked to a higher self-rated promotability, lower retirement intentions, and higher transferability, as well as to higher manager-rated promotability and health, above and beyond the effect of chronological age. In addition, longitudinal research showed that feeling progressively younger than one's chronological age predicted increased levels of perceived control over and motivational investment in one's work situation (Shane et al., 2019). Together these findings have contributed to the "young(er)-is-better perspective," arguing that a relatively younger subjective age is a biopsychosocial marker of healthy aging and better work outcomes (Stephan et al., 2013; Kunze et al., 2015).

Yet, recent research suggests that there seem to be important boundary conditions affecting the link between subjective age and beneficial outcomes. For example, a 10-year longitudinal study (Zee & D. Weiss, 2019) demonstrated a positive association between a younger subjective age and better memory performance as well as better cardiovascular health over time. However, the link between subjective age and these two outcomes was stronger for adults who reported to be in high- rather than in low-quality relationships. These results suggest that psychological resources (i.e., a subjective age that is younger than one's chronological age) interact with interpersonal resources (i.e., relationship quality) to benefit cognitive and physical functioning over time. The authors argue that social relationships offer resources that help individuals adapt to aging-related changes and that partner affirmation for one's younger subjective age could be a critical prerequisite for its positive effects.

Although findings suggest that a younger subjective age tends to be beneficial in the second half of life, recent research suggests that feeling younger is not always better and that distancing oneself from one's own age might become psychologically harmful at some point (D. Weiss & Kornadt, 2018). For example, studies show that idealizing youthfulness and attempts to appear younger among older adults can trigger negative social feedback and can have negative health-related consequences (Chasteen et al., 2011; Levy et al., 2019). A recent study

(Blöchl et al., 2020) applying polynomial regression and response surface methodology including $N = 7,356$ participants between 36–89 years of age showed that a relatively younger subjective age is linked to higher life satisfaction to a certain point, at which it then ceases, and this optimal margin of feeling younger increases across adulthood. This suggests that feeling younger than one's chronological age is only beneficial up to a certain point and that feeling younger to an extreme degree is less beneficial and can even be detrimental. Aspiring to an extremely young subjective age might be unrealistic and, thus, lead to dissatisfaction in the long run.

The *younger-is-better perspective* also assumes that subjective age is stable, thus neglecting the dynamic, changing, and interactive nature of aging perceptions that contribute to individuals' subjective age. The age stereotype internalization and dissociation model (SIDI; D. Weiss & Kornadt, 2018) argues that a younger subjective age serves as a means to distance oneself from negative age stereotypes. In support of this perspective, studies have shown that, when negative aging-related information was made salient, older adults distanced themselves from older adults on a cognitive (disidentification from older adults; D. Weiss & Lang, 2012a) and behavioral level (looking away from older targets, D. Weiss & Freund, 2012). Moreover, the self-protective role of age group dissociation has also been confirmed, showing that when negative age stereotypes were activated older adults who distanced themselves from older people benefited in terms of higher implicit und explicit self-esteem (D. Weiss et al., 2013). In a recent study, Armenta and colleagues (2018) investigated daily variations in employees' subjective age. The results of this daily-diary study showed that variations in employees' subjective age positively predicted their responses to negative events at work. Specifically, older employees with a younger subjective age were less likely to attribute negative daily work events to their chronological age (i.e., this happened to me because of my age), and this positively affected their cognitive engagement and well-being.

A dynamic lifespan perspective on subjective age (D. Weiss & M. Weiss, 2019) predicts that, individuals adopt ages that are associated with being favorable and distance themselves from ages that are associated with unfavorable characteristics. However, a systematic test of this hypothesis across the adult life span has been lacking so far (see Zacher & Rudolph, 2018). Hence, we tested exactly this idea in a recent set of experimental and field studies including younger and older adults in the work context (M. Weiss & D. Weiss, 2020). The starting point of this research was the well-established finding that age stereotypes in the workplace often center around competence and social prestige (Posthuma & Campion, 2009; Robertson & D. Weiss, 2017). We hypothesized that younger adults would adopt older ages and older adults would adopt younger ages due to negative stereotypes about younger (less mature, less persistent, more naïve and emotionally unstable) and older workers (less trainable, less adaptable, less effective, slower) (Posthuma & Campion, 2009; D. Weiss & Zhang, 2020). Across three studies (Ns > 600, 16–85 years), we found that feeling older (among younger adults) and younger (among older adults) was triggered by undesirable age stereotypes in the workplace concerning competence and status of young and later adulthood and desirable age stereotypes of midlife. This research also showed that subjective age can be manipulated through an intervention, which significantly increased individuals' self-perceived competence at work and predicted voice behavior.

Summary and Recommendations for Research and Practice Regarding Subjective Age

Taken together, we have summarized empirical evidence suggesting that subjective age has meaningful implications for work and organizational outcomes such as promotability, health, competence, and proactive behavior. Even though a younger subjective age among older employees can be highly beneficial, there seems to be an optimal margin of the discrepancy between one's chronological and subjective age. Moreover, there are also some contextual boundary conditions (e.g., social support) that need to be taken into account in addition to merely feeling younger.

Due to its significance, work and organizational psychology researchers should assess subjective age in addition to chronological age (please see also Chapter 9). Although the assessment of subjective age has been criticized as a reductionist approach at the expense of a multifaceted understanding of aging, we believe this is an important piece of the puzzle capturing the subjective age bias phenomenon. Thus, we recommend using the established one-item measure assessing how young or old people feel as it represents a highly effective and parsimonious measure (Kotter-Grühn et al., 2016). Moreover, we recommend assessing subjective age not only in the context of investigations on the "older workforce" but across the lifespan, as recent research shows that feeling older among younger employees can also have meaningful implications. Future research should also test a potential bidirectional relationship between subjective age and key work outcomes. It might be likely that adults who excel at work and are satisfied with their jobs are more likely to feel younger, as positive feedback from one's job can boost core self-evaluations (i.e., self-esteem, generalized self-efficacy, emotional stability, and locus of control). Previous studies have shown that core self-evaluations account for some of the effects of subjective age, suggesting that a younger subjective age reflects more positive core self-evaluations (Zacher & Rudolph, 2018, 2019). Finally, we believe one important advantage of subjective age is that various approaches exist for its experimental manipulation (please see also Chapter 11). Table 3.1 provides an overview about the measurement and manipulability of different alternative age constructs.

We advise organizational decision-makers to consider subjective age as an important factor affecting employee well-being, attitudes, and behavior.

TABLE 3.1 Measurement and Manipulation of (Alternative) Age Constructs

Construct	Measurement	Manipulation
Chronological Age	*"How old are you?"*	Not possible
Cohort	*"What is your year of birth?"*	Not possible
Generation	*"To which generation do you belong?"* (D. Weiss & Perry, 2020)	Not possible
Subjective Age	*"How young or old do you feel?"*	Activating (1) individual aging experiences, (2) upward or downward social comparison, and (3) negative age stereotypes (Stephan et al., 2013; Eibach et al., 2010; D. Weiss & Freund, 2012)
Essentialist Beliefs About Aging	*"Aging is set in stone and cannot be changed"* (brief 4-item and extended 10-item scale, D. Weiss & Diehl, 2021)	Mock newspaper article highlighting the (1) immutability or (2) malleability of aging (D. Weiss et al., 2016)
Age and Generation Identity	*"I identify with people my age/my generation"* (4-item scale; D. Weiss & Lang, 2009)	Activating age and generational identity or metastereotypes (D. Weiss & Lang, 2012b; D. Weiss & Perry, 2020)

Practitioners should also take into account that subjective age is malleable and can be altered, for example, through activating meaningful and positive images of aging at work.

Essentialist Beliefs About Aging

Chronological age is just one aspect associated with our perceptions of age and aging. A second alternative age construct that goes beyond chronological age is essentialist beliefs about aging. Change is an inextricable aspect of aging, and an alternative way to think about age and aging is to think about the inevitability or malleability of aging-related changes. Thus, aging can be conceived of as a result of biological determinism emphasizing the role of genes or of human plasticity highlighting the potential for systematic change across the whole life span (Lerner, 1984). Research suggests that people differ in how they conceive of the aging process and that some people are more likely than others to believe that the process of aging is malleable ("age is just a number") while others believe that aging is inevitable ("aging is set in stone") (D. Weiss et al., 2016). In the following, we will explain why these beliefs have the potential to influence important work and organizational outcomes and behavior.

Beliefs are defined as learned cause-effect associations that inform individuals' expectations and provide individuals with a framework or schema for experience and action (e.g., Dweck, 1975; Snyder, 1984). In the work context, they play a crucial role for how individuals deal with occupational transitions across the lifespan (D. Weiss et al., 2012). Essentialist beliefs about aging construe aging as a "fixed rather than malleable process including a set of inevitable and uncontrollable changes that occur over time" (D. Weiss et al., 2016, pp. 997–998) and have been shown to predict how older adults deal with aging-related changes (D. Weiss et al., 2019; D. Weiss & M. Weiss, 2016; D. Weiss, 2018). One set of studies showed that individuals who believe that aging is a fixed, biologically determined, and inevitable process (i.e., essentialist view) feel more threatened by aging-related changes and perceive their future time in life as more limited than individuals who believe that aging is modifiable and flexible (i.e., nonessentialist view; D. Weiss et al., 2016). Studies also show that essentialist beliefs moderate the impact of negative age stereotypes on cognitive performance and physiological reactivity. Specifically, a more malleable view of aging can buffer the detrimental consequences of negative age stereotypes and low social status such that older adults exhibit less physiological stress and perform better when faced with cognitively challenging tasks (D. Weiss, 2018; D. Weiss & M. Weiss, 2016). Longitudinal research also suggests that people who are less likely to endorse essentialist beliefs about aging perceive a greater discrepancy between their chronological and subjective age as they grow older (D. Weiss et al., 2019). Thus, a more malleable view of aging defining age and aging as modifiable (e.g., "you're as young as you feel") seems to represent a necessary precondition to feeling younger than one's chronological age.

In terms of antecedents and correlates of essentialist beliefs about aging, research suggests that adults who construe aging as a malleable rather than fixed process are higher in openness to experience, hold more incremental implicit theories of personality, have higher levels of perceived control, have more positive self-perceptions of aging, have a higher subjective social status, and have better self-reported health (D. Weiss & Diehl, 2021). Studies further show that essentialist beliefs about aging are related with these constructs but are also empirically distinct and conceptually different. For example, essentialist beliefs are different from perceived control and agency beliefs referring to the perception that a person believes that she or he possesses the means to affect an outcome and not whether growing old is a process that can *generally* be influenced or not. Thus, people can endorse the belief that aging is malleable but can feel that they personally do not have the means to do so.

Emerging research reveals that essentialist beliefs about aging play a role in predicting work-related outcomes. A recent study (M. Weiss et al., 2021) examined how essentialist beliefs about aging affect the retirement decision-making process. Because workforce participation of older adults is rather low (e.g., in Europe only 55% of adults between 55 and 65 years are working; Eurostat, 2017; please see also Chapter 2), this study focused on whether essentialist beliefs about aging affect older workers' motivation to continue working until retirement and beyond. The recent set of studies, including longitudinal and experimental designs, demonstrated that older workers (40–65 years) who strongly endorsed essentialist beliefs about aging were less motivated to continue working beyond traditional retirement age because they had a more constrained occupational future time perspective, (after controlling for important covariates such as chronological age and subjective health). One possible explanation is that believing aging inevitably leads to cognitive and physical decline leads individuals to protect their resources and opt for earlier retirement (Wang & Shi, 2014). These findings underscore the fact that it is not chronological age per se that explains why some older workers continue to work while others may opt for early retirement but rather their beliefs about the immutability or malleability of aging.

Summary and Recommendations for Research and Practice Regarding Essentialist Beliefs About Aging

We have reviewed studies suggesting that the extent to which people believe that the aging process is "just a number" vs. "set in stone" can affect not only how threatening people perceive age-related changes but also a variety of work outcomes, including perceptions of one's future occupational possibilities at work and one's motivation to continue working. Essentialist aging beliefs thus seem to have a substantial impact on the perception that one can still set and achieve occupational goals and may explain why some older workers may quit their jobs earlier than others. Given these important effects, future research may also investigate how essentialist beliefs about aging affect employee performance, trainability, as well as key job attitudes (e.g., job satisfaction, work engagement, perceived organizational support).

Essentialist beliefs have been commonly assessed with a brief 4-item and an extended 10-item scale with 2 (5) items assessing a more malleable view of aging and 2 (5) items assessing a more flexible view of aging. The scales have been successfully used and validated across many different working and nonworking populations in different social contexts (D. Weiss & Diehl, 2021). It thus represents a ready-to-use measure for organizational researchers and practitioners that seek to investigate how age-related beliefs influence important employee outcomes. In this context, it is also noteworthy that prior studies have also manipulated essentialist beliefs about aging through a simple yet powerful intervention (see Table 3.1). For example, in one study (D. Weiss et al., 2016), participants read an ostensible newspaper article portraying age either as a flexible process that individuals can influence through mental training and physical exercise (i.e., nonessentialist condition) or as a biologically determined and inherited process that is written into our genes (i.e., essentialist condition). The manipulation led to a higher endorsement of the respective statements about the process of aging and influenced important outcomes (e.g., perception of aging-related threat).

Taken together, employees can benefit from a more malleable view of aging, and, thus, organizations should support the view that aging is a flexible process allowing for modification and influence. This seems to be of particular importance when offering training and development programs for older employees or in the context of postretirement career options (Wang & Shi, 2014).

Dual Age Identity

Chronological age links people to a specific age cohort and generation. Therefore, a third alternative age concept is individuals' membership in different age groups and generations that originate in the same birth cohort. Age builds the basis for multiple age identities as formulated in the model of the dual age identity (D. Weiss & Lang, 2009). On the basis of chronological age, individuals can be assigned to age groups such as adolescents, young adults, middle-aged adults, young-old adults, and old-old adults. At the same time, however, belonging to a certain cohort assigns individuals to different generations (e.g., "Baby Boomers" or "Millennials"). While these labels may differ from one cultural context to another or across time, they derive meaning from the specific collective, historical experiences that transform a birth cohort into a generation. Research suggests that generational distinctions are often arbitrary (Rudolph et al., 2020) and only become "real" for individuals who actually adopt a specific generation identity (D. Weiss & Lang, 2009).

Although research has documented that people categorize themselves and others based on age, emerging evidence suggests that people may perceive themselves and others in terms of their generational membership (Joshi et al., 2010; Mannheim, 1928/1952; Perry et al., 2017; Rudolph & Zacher, 2017; D. Weiss & Lang, 2012b; D. Weiss & Perry, 2020; please see also Chapter 6). One consequence is that membership in specific age groups and generations represents important social age identities and provides a sense of self-definition (Tajfel & Turner, 1979). In contrast to age group identities that are transient in nature, generation represents a permanent social identity that is embedded in a specific social, cultural, and historical context. Thus, individuals remain members of the same generation throughout their whole life, while they become members of different age groups as they grow older. Generation is a purely social phenomenon and thus differs from the implications of biological aging including biological decline and a limited lifespan (Mannheim, 1928/1952). Moreover, generational membership comprises collective experiences of growing older in a unique historical context (Lyons & Schweitzer, 2016). Specifically, Mannheim (1928/1952) argued that, throughout their life, members of a given birth cohort are collectively exposed to historical events and changes, which gives rise to a consciousness of belonging to a distinct generation. Thus, identification with one's generation may reflect an awareness of the changing social, political, and economic conditions during one's life time (Mannheim, 1928/1952).

Although studies show that generations hardly differ in their life goals, values, work behavior, concerns, or social and political engagement (Costanza & Finkelstein, 2015; Rudolph et al., 2020; Rudolph & Zacher, 2017), generation appears as a distinct and powerful social category. Studies show that stereotypes about generations are often different from stereotypes about age groups. Perceptions of aging often reflect generalized expectations concerning biologically based differences in functioning, and these stereotypes are often very similar across cultures (Löckenhoff et al., 2009). While negative old-age stereotypes discourage older workers from participating in the workforce altogether (von Hippel et al., 2019), there is evidence that older generations are perceived as significantly more positive. For example, research by Perry and colleagues (2013) demonstrated that generational stereotypes linked to older workers (Baby Boomers) were associated with positive characteristics such as strong work identity and being career driven, achievement oriented, hardworking, and competitive. In contrast, age stereotypes about older workers (representing the same birth cohort) were more likely to be associated with perceptions of lower ability to perform tasks as well as being less productive and motivated. In another study, Perry et al. (2017) showed that, when a job candidate was introduced as a "60-year-old" applicant, this person was perceived as significantly less adaptable and motivated than the same job candidate introduced as a "Baby Boomer" and was less likely to be hired. A recent cross-cultural study compared attitudes and stereotypes toward age and generational groups across the life span in China, Germany, and the United States including more than 1,000 participants between 18 and 86 years of age (D. Weiss & Zhang, 2020). In this study, the perception of six age groups (e.g., adolescents, young adults, middle-aged adults, young-old, older, and old-old adults) and six matching generational groups (e.g., Generation Z, Millennials, Generation X, Baby Boomer, Silent Generation, and Greatest Generation) on various characteristics (e.g., happy, competent, selfish) was compared. Results demonstrated that across all three countries older generations were perceived as consistently more positive, whereas older age groups were perceived as less positive, suggesting that generations represent a source of positive regard and high social status in later life across different countries with different historical backgrounds and cultures.

According to the dual age identity model (D. Weiss & Lang, 2009), as individuals grow older, they develop two closely related but different age-related identities that can affect their self-definition. Studies show that older adults strongly identify with people of their generation and distance themselves from people their age (D. Weiss & Lang, 2009, 2012b; D. Weiss, 2014). By contrast, these studies also show that young and middle-aged adults do not seem to differentiate between people their age or their generation. This seemingly paradoxical effect can be explained by a different social cognitive representation of older generations as compared to older age groups that build the basis for two distinct social age identities in later adulthood (age group identity vs. generation identity). Research demonstrates that, in contrast to age identity, which is often perceived as threatening in later adulthood due to the salience of negative age stereotypes, generation identity is perceived as more positive and meaningful, representing a resource in later adulthood that provides a sense of agency, positive self-regard, and continuity (D. Weiss, 2014; D. Weiss & Lang, 2012b).

As previous research has shown that people over the age of 50 years receive fewer job offers, stay unemployed longer, and are less likely to find reemployment (Wanberg et al., 2016), it is important to find ways in supporting older workers' employability. A recent study (D. Weiss & Perry, 2020) examined whether generational (meta)stereotypes may have the capacity to empower older adults and mitigate perceptions of stereotype threat at work. Although old-age stereotypes can have detrimental effects on older workers, this experimental study showed that activating generational compared to age metastereotypes (i.e., what people think other people believe about their generation/age group) positively influences older adults' job search self-efficacy. Older employees who focused on their generational identity felt greater agency and diminished stereotype threat. This, in turn, improved older workers' confidence in finding a new job and encouraged them to remain in the workforce. Therefore, activating generational identities and metastereotypes can entail benefits for employees as well as for organizations that employ older workers whose greater perceived agency likely results in greater engagement and prolonged occupational goals.

Summary and Recommendations for Research and Practice Regarding Dual Age Identity

Generation identity provides older adults with positive roles and meaningful identities in light of negative age stereotypes. Identification with one's age group and generation can be assessed with a two- or four-item scale and manipulated through a cognitive activation of age or generational membership (see Table 3.1). Organizational empowerment strategies could focus on highlighting older workers' generation identity as opposed to their age identity as one means to increase older employees' perceptions of agency and reduce their perceptions of age-based stereotype threat. Yet, we caution against an excessive use of generational labels within intergenerational work relationships as this may increase the potential of intergenerational tension and conflict. Thus, highlighting different generations at work should not be used to create "us" vs. "them" mindsets (e.g., by denoting older generations as more industrious than younger ones or vice versa).

Conclusion

Given that chronological age only shows weak relationships with key work outcomes and does not capture the dynamic, multidimensional, and idiosyncratic nature of the aging process, we have reviewed three alternative age constructs (i.e., subjective age, essentialist beliefs about aging, age vs. generation identity) that have recently gained attention in the aging literature. Studies suggest that each of these alternative age concepts has significant implications at work affecting, for example, employees' cognitive performance, occupational future time perspective, retirement decision-making, and possibilities for reemployment. We have shown that, in contrast to chronological age, these constructs can be reliably measured and even manipulated, opening up a new field for organizational interventions. We have further pointed out how each of these concepts can be utilized by organizational researchers and practitioners to support an alternative, more flexible, and subjective approach to aging at work to most effectively reap the benefits of an aging workforce.

References

Ackerman, L. S., & Chopik, W. J. (2021). Cross-cultural comparisons in implicit and explicit age bias. *Personality and Social Psychology Bulletin, 47*, 953–968. https://doi.org/10.1177/0146167220950070

Akkermans, J., de Lange, A. H., van der Heijden, B. I., Kooij, D. T., & Jansen, P. G. (2016). What about time? Examining chronological and subjective age and their relation to work motivation. *Career Development International, 21*, 419–439. https://doi.org/10.1108/CDI-04-2016-0063

Armenta, B. M., Scheibe, S., Stroebe, K., Postmes, T., & Van Yperen, N. W. (2018). Dynamic, not stable: Daily variations in subjective age bias and age group identification predict daily well-being in older workers. *Psychology and Aging, 33*, 559–571. https://doi.org/10.1037/pag0000263

Baltes, P. B. (1987). Theoretical propositions of life-span developmental psychology: On the dynamics between growth and decline. *Developmental Psychology, 23*, 611–626. https://doi.org/10.1037/0012-1649.23.5.611

Barak, B. (2009). Age identity: A cross-cultural global approach. *International Journal of Behavioral Development, 33*, 2–11. https://doi.org/10.1177/0165025408099485

Barnes-Farrell, J. L., Rumery, S. M., & Swody, C. A. (2002). How do concepts of age relate to work and off-the-job stresses and strains? A field study of health care workers in five nations. *Experimental Aging Research, 28*, 87–98. https://doi.org/10.1080/036107302753365577

Blau, Z. S. (1956). Changes in status and age identification. *American Sociological Review, 21*, 198–203. https://doi.org/10.2307/2088522

Blöchl, M., Nestler, S., & Weiss, D. (2020). A limit of the subjective age bias: Feeling younger to a certain degree, but no more, is beneficial for life satisfaction. *Psychology and Aging.* Advance online publication. http://dx.doi.org/10.1037/pag0000578

Chasteen, A. L., Bashir, N. Y., Gallucci, C., & Visekruna, A. (2011). Age and antiaging technique influence reactions to age concealment. *The Journals of Gerontology, Series B:*

Psychological Sciences and Social Sciences, *66*, 719–724. https://doi.org/10.1093/geronb/gbr063

Chopik, W. J., Bremner, R. H., Johnson, D. J., & Giasson, H. L. (2018). Age differences in age perceptions and developmental transitions. *Frontiers in Psychology*, *9*. https://doi.org/10.3389/fpsyg.2018.00067

Cleveland, J. N., Shore, L. M., & Murphy, K. R. (1997). Person- and context-oriented perceptual age measures: Additional evidence of distinctiveness and usefulness. *Journal of Organizational Behavior*, *18*, 239–251. https://doi.org/10.1002/(sici)1099-1379(199705)18:3<239::aid-job794>3.0.co;2-a

Costanza, D. P., & Finkelstein, L. M. (2015). Generationally based differences in the workplace: Is there a there there? *Industrial and Organizational Psychology*, *8*, 308–323. http://dx.doi.org/10.1017/iop.2015.15

Dweck, C. S. (1975). The role of expectations and attributions in the alleviation of learned helplessness. *Journal of Personality and Social Psychology*, *31*, 674. https://doi.org/10.1037/h0077149

Eibach, R. P., Mock, S. E., & Courtney, E. A. (2010). Having a "senior moment": Induced aging phenomenology, subjective age, and susceptibility to ageist stereotypes. *Journal of Experimental Social Psychology*, *46*, 643–649. https://doi.org/10.1016/j.jesp.2010.03.002

Eurostat. (2017). https://ec.europa.eu/eurostat/

Galambos, N. L., Turner, P. K., & Tilton-Weaver, L. C. (2005). Chronological and subjective age in emerging adulthood: The crossover effect. *Journal of Adolescent Research*, *20*, 538–556. https://doi.org/10.1177/0743558405274876

Joshi, A., Dencker, J. C., Franz, G., & Martocchio, J. J. (2010). Unpacking generational identities in organizations. *Academy of Management Review*, *35*, 392–414. https://dx.doi.org/10.5465/amr.35.3.zok392

Kastenbaum, R., Derbin, V., Sabatini, P., & Artt, S. (1972). "The ages of me": Toward personal and interpersonal definitions of functional aging. *Aging and Human Development*, *3*, 197–211. https://doi.org/10.2190/TUJR-WTXK-866Q-8QU7

Kooij, D. T., De Lange, A. H., Jansen, P. G., Kanfer, R., & Dikkers, J. S. (2011). Age and work-related motives: Results of a meta-analysis. *Journal of Organizational Behavior*, *32*, 197–225. https://doi.org/10.1002/job.665

Kotter-Grühn, D., Kornadt, A. E., & Stephan, Y. (2016). Looking beyond chronological age: Current knowledge and future directions in the study of subjective age. *Gerontology*, *62*, 86–93. https://doi.org/10.1159/000438671

Kunze, F., Raes, A. M., & Bruch, H. (2015). It matters how old you feel: Antecedents and performance consequences of average relative subjective age in organizations. *Journal of Applied Psychology*, *100*, 1511–1526. https://doi.org/10.1037/a0038909

Lerner, R. M. (1984). *On the nature of human plasticity*. Cambridge University Press.

Levy, B. R., Slade, M. D., & Lampert, R. (2019). Idealization of youthfulness predicts worse recovery among older individuals. *Psychology and Aging*, *34*, 202–207. http://dx.doi.org/10.1037/pag0000330

Löckenhoff, C. E., De Fruyt, F., Terracciano, A., McCrae, R. R., De Bolle, M., Costa, P. T., . . . Yik, M. (2009). Perceptions of aging across 26 cultures and their culture-level associates. *Psychology and Aging*, *24*, 941–954. http://dx.doi.org/10.1037/a0016901

Lyons, S. T., & Schweitzer, L. (2016). A qualitative exploration of generational identity: Making sense of young and old in the context of today's workplace. *Work, Aging and Retirement*, *3*, 209–224. https://doi.org/10.1093/workar/waw024

Mannheim, K. (1952). The problem of generations. In K. Mannheim (Ed.), *Essays on the sociology of knowledge* (pp. 276–321). Routledge & Keegan Paul. [Original work published 1928]

Montepare, J. M. (2009). Subjective age: Toward a guiding lifespan framework. *International Journal of Behavioral Development, 33*(1), 42–46. https://doi.org/10.1177/0165025408095551

Nagy, N., Johnston, C. S., & Hirschi, A. (2019). Do we act as old as we feel? An examination of subjective age and job crafting behaviour of late career employees. *European Journal of Work and Organizational Psychology, 28*, 373–383. https://doi.org/10.1080/1359432X.2019.1584183

Perry, E. L., Golom, F. D., Catenacci, L., Ingraham, M. E., Covais, E. M., & Molina, J. J. (2017). Talkin' bout your generation: The impact of applicant age and generation on hiring-related perceptions and outcomes. *Work, Aging and Retirement, 3*, 186–199. https://doi.org/10.1093/workar/waw029

Perry, E. L., Hanvongse, A., & Casoinic, D. (2013). Making a case for the existence of generational stereotypes: A literature review and exploratory study. In R. Burke, C. Cooper, & J. Field (Eds.), *Handbook on aging, work and society* (pp. 416–442). Sage.

Pinquart, M., & Wahl, H.-W. (2021). Subjective age from childhood to advanced old age: A meta-analysis. *Psychology and Aging*. Advance online publication. https://doi.org/10.1037/pag0000600

Posthuma, R. A., & Campion, M. A. (2009). Age stereotypes in the workplace: Common stereotypes, moderators, and future research directions. *Journal of Management, 35*, 158–188. https://doi.org/10.1177/0149206308318617

Robertson, D. A., & Weiss, D. (2017). In the eye of the beholder: Can counter-stereotypes change perceptions of older adults' social status? *Psychology and Aging, 32*, 531–542. https://doi.org/10.1037/pag0000186

Rubin, D. C., & Berntsen, D. (2006). People over forty feel 20% younger than their age: Subjective age across the lifespan. *Psychonomic Bulletin & Review, 13*, 776–780. https://doi.org/10.3758/BF03193996

Rudolph, C. W., Rauvola, R. S., Costanza, D. P., & Zacher, H. (2020). Generations and generational differences: Debunking myths in organizational science and practice and paving new paths forward. *Journal of Business and Psychology*, 1–23. https://doi.org/10.1007/s10869-020-09715-2

Rudolph, C. W., & Zacher, H. (2017). Considering generations from a lifespan developmental perspective. *Work, Aging and Retirement, 3*, 113–129. https://doi.org/10.1093/workar/waw019

Schwall, A. R. (2012). Defining age and using age-relevant constructs. In J. Hedge & W. Borman (Eds.), *The Oxford handbook of work and aging* (pp. 169–186). Oxford University Press.

Shane, J., Hamm, J., & Heckhausen, J. (2019). Subjective age at work: Feeling younger or older than one's actual age predicts perceived control and motivation at work. *Work, Aging and Retirement, 5*, 323–332. https://doi.org/10.1093/workar/waz013

Snyder, M. (1984). When belief creates reality. In *Advances in experimental social psychology* (Vol. 18, pp. 247–305). Academic Press.

Stephan, Y., Chalabaev, A., Kotter-Grühn, D., & Jaconelli, A. (2013). "Feeling younger, being stronger": An experimental study of subjective age and physical functioning among older adults. *The Journals of Gerontology, Series B: Psychological Sciences and Social Sciences, 68*, 1–7. https://doi.org/10.1093/geronb/gbs037

Tajfel, H., & Turner, J. C. (1979). An integrative theory of intergroup conflict. In W. G. Austin & S. Worchel (Eds.), *The social psychology of intergroup relations* (pp. 33–47). Brooks/Cole.

Truxillo, D. M., Cadiz, D. M., & Hammer, L. B. (2015). Supporting the aging workforce: A review and recommendations for workplace intervention research. *Annual Review of Organizational Psychology and Organizational Behavior, 2*, 351–381. https://doi.org/10.1146/annurev-orgpsych-032414-111435

Von Hippel, C., Kalokerinos, E. K., Haanterä, K., & Zacher, H. (2019). Age-based stereotype threat and work outcomes: Stress appraisals and rumination as mediators. *Psychology and Aging, 34*, 68–84. http://dx.doi.org/10.1037/pag0000308

Wanberg, C. R., Kanfer, R., Hamann, D. J., & Zhang, Z. (2016). Age and reemployment success after job loss: An integrative model and meta-analysis. *Psychological Bulletin, 142*, 400–426. https://doi.org/10.1037/bul0000019

Wang, M., & Shi, J. (2014). Psychological research on retirement. *Annual Review of Psychology, 65*, 209–233. https://doi.org/10.1146/annurev-psych-010213-115131

Weiss, D. (2014). What will remain when we are gone? Finitude and generation identity in the second half of life. *Psychology and Aging, 29*, 554–562. https://doi.org/10.1037/a0036728

Weiss, D. (2018). On the inevitability of aging: Essentialist beliefs moderate the impact of negative age stereotypes on older adults' memory performance and physiological reactivity. *The Journals of Gerontology, Series B: Psychological Sciences and Social Sciences, 73*, 925–933. https://doi.org/10.1093/geronb/gbw087

Weiss, D. & Diehl, M. (2021). Measuring (non)essentialist beliefs about the process of aging. *The Journals of Gerontology, Series B: Psychological Sciences, 76*(7), 1340–1348. https://doi.org/10.1093/geronb/gbaa113

Weiss, D., & Freund, A. M. (2012). Still young at heart: Negative age-related information motivates distancing from same-aged people. *Psychology and Aging, 27*, 173–180. https://doi.org/10.1037/a0024819

Weiss, D., Freund, A. M., & Wiese, B. S. (2012). Mastering developmental transitions in young and middle adulthood: The interplay of openness to experience and traditional gender ideology on women's self-efficacy and subjective well-being. *Developmental Psychology, 48*(6), 1774.

Weiss, D., & Halawa, O. (2016). Subjective age around the world: The role of power distance and hierarchy beliefs. *Gerontologist, 56*, 313–313. https://doi.org/10.1093/geront/gnw162.1280

Weiss, D., Job, V., Mathias, M., Grah, S., & Freund, A. M. (2016). The end is (not) near: Aging, essentialism, and future time perspective. *Developmental Psychology, 6*, 996–1009. https://doi.org/10.1037/dev0000115

Weiss, D., & Kornadt, A. E. (2018). Age-stereotype internalization and dissociation: Contradictory processes or two sides of the same coin? *Current Directions in Psychological Science, 27*, 477–483. https://doi.org/10.1177/0963721418777743

Weiss, D., & Lang, F. R. (2009). Thinking about my generation: Adaptive effects of a dual age identity in later adulthood. *Psychology and Aging, 24*, 729–734. https://doi.org/10.1037/a0016339

Weiss, D., & Lang, F. R. (2012a). "They" are old but "I" feel younger: Age-group dissociation as a self-protective strategy in old age. *Psychology and Aging, 27*, 153–163. https://doi.org/10.1037/a0024887

Weiss, D., & Lang, F. R. (2012b). Two faces of age identity. *The Journal of Gerontopsychology and Geriatric Psychiatry, 25*, 5–14. https://doi.org/10.1024/1662-9647/a000050

Weiss, D., & Perry, E. (2020). Implications of generational and age metastereotypes for older adults at work: The role of agency, stereotype threat, and job search self-efficacy. *Work, Aging & Retirement, 1*, 15–27. https://doi.org/10.1093/workar/waz010

Weiss, D., Reitz, A. K., & Stephan, Y. (2019). Is age more than a number? The role of openness and (non)essentialist beliefs about aging for how young or old people feel. *Psychology and Aging, 34*, 729–737. https://doi.org/10.1037/pag0000370

Weiss, D., Sassenberg, K., & Freund, A. M. (2013). When feeling different pays off: How older adults can counteract negative age-related information. *Psychology and Aging, 28*, 1140–1146. https://doi.org/10.1037/a0033811

Weiss, D., & Weiss, M. (2016). The interplay of subjective social status and essentialist beliefs about cognitive aging on cortisol reactivity to challenge in older adults. *Psychophysiology, 53*, 1256–1262. https://doi.org/10.1111/psyp.12667

Weiss, D., & Weiss, M. (2019). Why people feel younger: Motivational and social-cognitive mechanisms of the subjective age bias and its implications for work and organizations. *Work, Aging & Retirement, 5*, 273–280. https://doi.org/10.1093/workar/waz016

Weiss, D., & Zhang, X. (2020). Multiple sources of aging attitudes: Perceptions of age groups and generations from adolescence to old age across China, Germany, and the US. *Journal of Cross-Cultural Psychology, 6*, 407–423. https://doi.org/10.1177/0022022120925904

Weiss, M., & Weiss, D. (2020). When and why does subjective age boost competence and proactive work behavior? *Innovation in Aging, 4*(Suppl. 1), 620. https://doi.org/10.1093/geroni/igaa057.2110

Weiss, M., Weiss, D., & Zacher, H. (2021). *All set in stone? How and why essentialist beliefs about aging affect older workers' motivation to continue working* (Unpublished Manuscript). Freie Universität Berlin.

Wohlwill, J. F. (1970). The age variable in psychological research. *Psychological Review, 77*, 49–64. http://dx.doi.org/10.1037/h0028600

Zacher, H., Heusner, S., Schmitz, M., Zwierzanska, M. M., & Frese, M. (2010). Focus on opportunities as a mediator of the relationships between age, job complexity, and work performance. *Journal of Vocational Behavior, 76*, 374–386. https://doi.org/10.1016/j.jvb.2009.09.001

Zacher, H., & Rudolph, C. W. (2018). Just a mirage: On the incremental predictive validity of subjective age. *Work, Aging and Retirement.* https://doi.org/10.1093/workar/wax031

Zacher, H., & Rudolph, C. W. (2019). Why do we act as old as we feel? The role of occupational future time perspective and core self-evaluations in the relationship between subjective age and job crafting behaviour. *European Journal of Work and Organizational Psychology, 28*, 831–844. https://doi.org/10.1080/1359432X.2019.1677609

Zee, K. S., & Weiss, D. (2019). High-quality relationships strengthen the benefits of a younger subjective age across adulthood. *Psychology and Aging, 34*, 374–388. https://doi.org/10.1037/pag0000349

Zola, I. K. (1962). Feelings about age among older people. *Journal of Gerontology, 17*, 65–68. https://doi.org/10.1093/geronj/17.1.65

4

INTERSECTIONAL EFFECTS OF AGE, GENDER, AND SOCIAL CLASS ON SUCCESSFUL AGING AT WORK

Justin Marcus

Intersectionality in diversity research refers to the interactive effects of multiple demographic variables such as gender, race, and age. These demographic variables reflect societal power dynamics associated with an individual's social location, whereby an individual's position on the societal hierarchy is determined based on the intersection of multiple, and often competing, aspects of his or her demography (e.g., "poor white man"; "rich Black woman"; Ozbilgin et al., 2011). Such intersectional effects of demographic variables are multiplicative, leading to different patterns of effects for individuals given the particular social positions that they occupy as a function of the constellations of their demographic category memberships (Ozbilgin et al., 2011). Work and organizational psychology scholars have used the intersectional lens to examine the confluence of sex (being biologically male or female) with race or ethnicity (e.g., Black women, Arab men; Berdahl & Moore, 2006; Derous et al., 2012). Yet, despite burgeoning interest in intersectional research over the last decade or so, studies adopting an intersectional perspective remain few. A meta-analysis on the effects of age, sex, and race on unfair work discrimination by Jones et al. (2017) found that only 3 out of 83 primary studies examined the interactive effects of demographic categories; notably and of the present interest, no included studies examined the interactive effects of age with other demographic variables.

A first theory for understanding the intersectional effects of age with other demographic variables was the Intersectional Salience of Ageism framework (ISA; Marcus & Fritzsche, 2015). The ISA suggested that gender and "tribe" (including race, ethnicity, religion, and nationality) would interact with age and the age-salience of the work context to predict qualitatively different patterns of cognitive, affective, and behavioral outcomes for older and younger workers of different demographic types. Since then, three empirical studies have used the ISA as a basis to study the confluence of worker age and work outcomes: Marcus

DOI: 10.4324/9781003089674-6

et al. (2019) studied the interactive effects of sex and objective/subjective age on age and sex discrimination, self-esteem, and burnout; Bohlmann and Zacher (2020) studied the interactive effects of sex, age, and work motivation on proactive behavior; and Reeves et al. (2021) studied the interactive effects of sex, age, and job age norms on age and sex discrimination. All three studies found different patterns of work outcomes for older and younger men and women.

Accordingly, given a nascent yet emerging body of research on the intersectional effects of age and given repeated calls by scholars to more deeply examine the effects of age from an intersectional perspective (Finkelstein et al., 2019; Hertel & Zacher, 2018; Jones et al., 2017; Rudolph et al., 2019; van Dijk et al., 2020), the goal of this chapter is to expand upon the ISA framework by better specifying the scope of intersectional demographic memberships, contextual boundary conditions, and work outcomes, as depicted in Figure 4.1. Because age dominates category representation over sex and race for older adults (Schneider, 2004), it is situated as the central demographic factor with respect to successful aging at work; gender and social class are theorized as intersecting demographic variables. Institutional, cultural, occupational, and organizational factors are shown in Figure 4.1 to represent contextual boundary conditions impacting upon these intersectional relations.

An important omission in Figure 4.1 pertains to the underlying psychological mechanisms driving associations between intersectional demographic factors

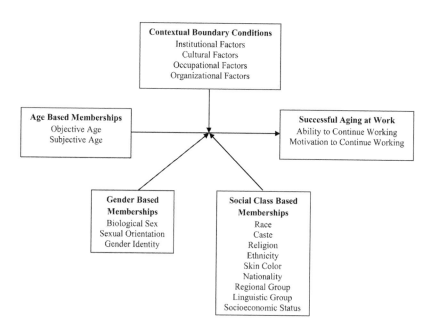

FIGURE 4.1 The Intersectional Salience of Ageism (ISA) framework: An update

and work outcomes. Many interesting questions arise when one considers such mediating factors. For instance, although it is well documented that stereotypes mediate the relations between categorical group membership and unfair discrimination (Gaertner & Dovidio, 2000), would the *strength* of that mediating association be different for different types of older and younger workers? Would that mediating association play out through different cognitive or neural pathways for different types of aging workers? How are the content of age stereotypes and metastereotypes (see Finkelstein et al., 2015, for more on age metastereotypes) regarding younger and older majority- and minority-group men and women similar or different? Given the complexity of the issue, it is beyond the scope of this chapter to delve into the nuances of such underlying psychological mechanisms. Rather, this chapter adopts an ecological systems perspective on work and aging (Marcus et al., 2020), situating the demographic group member as an actor who interacts with the social context across multiple levels of analysis (e.g., institutional, organizational) to determine outcomes. Viewed in this light, demography is treated as psychological process giving rise to sociobehavioral outcomes (see Chao & Moon, 2005, for theory on demography as psychological process).

Following Marcus and Fritzsche (2015), Figure 4.1 retains the scope of age to include both objective (chronological) and subjective age (biological, social, life-span, psychological, and organizational; Kooij et al., 2008; Zacher & Rudolph, 2019; see also Chapter 3). Similarly, gender is defined to include both objective biological sex and subjective sexual orientations and gender identities (Sawyer et al., 2016). An important difference, however, is the inclusion of social class as an overarching demographic variable subsuming all intrasocietal intergroup memberships. That is, the meanings of concepts such as race (e.g., Black or Latinx in North America), ethnicity (e.g., Arab or North African in Western Europe), religion (e.g., devout Muslims in Central Asia), nationality (e.g., South or Southeast Asian in the Middle East), linguistic group (e.g., Anglophones in the Ivory Coast or Oromo in Ethiopia), caste (e.g., Dalit or non-Hindu in India), and skin color (e.g., Mestizo or indigenous in Central America) are inherently bounded by the societies they are idiosyncratic to and are not meaningful markers of intersocietal comparisons for a globally aging workforce.

Rather, the common strand underlying all such intergroup demographic variables is the notion of *social class*, whereby minority group members, such as all of the just-noted exemplars, are usually situated outside the axes of power, typically experience social and economic marginalization, and are always "othered" (Ozbilgin et al., 2011). Majority–minority societal group distinctions may thus be understood as social class distinctions, with majority group members usually occupying the higher social class and minorities usually the lower. Exceptions may occur. Illustratively, Asians in contemporary North America and Jews in pre-World War II Europe constitute high social class minority groups, whereas Blacks in apartheid-era South Africa constituted a low social class majority group. Hence, the umbrella term "social class" is here used to represent both the socioeconomically rich or poor[1] (the traditional sense of the word) and *all demographically defined intergroup memberships involving socially marginalized groups that may be particular to a given society*. This definition involving higher vs. lower social class places socially marginalized minorities (e.g., Blacks and Latinxs in the US) in the lower social class groups. (Most) majority groups and high social class minority groups (e.g., whites and Asians in the US) represent the countervailing higher social class groups.

Additionally, while the initial ISA framework (Marcus & Fritzsche, 2015) included only job contexts[2] as boundary conditions impacting relations between intersectional demographic membership and work outcomes, the current framework expands the scope of contextual factors to include institutional, cultural, occupational, and organizational factors. The expected moderating effects of said contextual factors on the intersectional associations between demography and work outcomes are discussed. In turn, better reflecting the scope of work and aging, "work outcomes" are here defined as "successful aging at work," namely, an individual's *ability and motivation to continue working* (Kooij et al., 2020). "Ability" refers to any variable that represents *being physically or psychologically able to work* such as physical health, mental well-being, stress and strain, and physical or cognitive capacity. "Motivation" refers to any variable that represents *wanting to work* such as work engagement, burnout, job satisfaction, and turnover intentions (Kooij et al., 2020; italics mine). Hence, "ability and motivation to continue working" may be conceptualized as constituting a large family of interrelated variables that are ultimately aimed at understanding the myriad ways by which the successful aging of workers from across the many walks of life may best be understood.

Intersectional Effects of Age and Gender

Intersectionality of Age and Biological Sex

Prescriptive stereotypes of the sexes relegate women to more subordinate organizational positions vis-à-vis men—women are stereotyped as communal caregivers, whereas men are stereotyped as possessing agency and work dynamism (Heilman, 2001; Powell et al., 2002). Intersectional stereotypes of older men and women follow suit—whereas older women are perceived as being vulnerable, weak, and frail, older men are perceived as being wise and experienced leaders (Hummert, 1990; Marcus & Sabuncu, 2016). Consequent of such social cognitions, women are promoted into leadership positions at significantly lower rates than men (Lyness & Heilman, 2006) and occupy significantly fewer managerial positions throughout the course of their careers (Kirchmeyer, 2002). Likewise, older women have been found to report more sex discrimination and less self-esteem at work relative to other age and sex groups, whereas older men have been found to report less sex discrimination and more self-esteem at work relative to said groups (Marcus et al., 2019). Whereas older women's proactive behaviors are rated as less effective than their younger counterparts, the reverse holds true for older men (Bohlmann & Zacher, 2020).

These findings regarding the intersectionality of age and sex at work may be interpreted in light of theory on the social identity of age (Zacher et al., 2019). Advanced age may be understood as being associated with negative social identification for women given negative prescriptive stereotypes about women at work but positive social identification for men given positive prescriptive stereotypes about men at work (Heilman, 2001; Powell et al., 2002). As such, negative social identification for older women may be expected to result in more negative work outcomes, whereas positive social identification for older men may be expected to result in more positive work outcomes (Zacher et al., 2019). From the perspective of power and demography (Ozbilgin et al., 2011), older women may thus be conceptualized as a marginalized social group located outside of the axes of power; the opposite may hold true for older men, given their benefit of being stereotyped as leaders and promoted into positions of leadership. Hence, given more negative social identification and the presence of social marginalization, the ability and motivation to work of older women may expectedly be lower relative to similar others; given more positive social identification and the relative absence of social marginalization, the opposite pattern of effects may be expected for older men (Zacher et al., 2019).

Proposition 1a: Older women's ability and motivation to continue working will be lower relative to men and younger women.

Proposition 1b: Older men's ability and motivation to continue working will be higher relative to women and younger men.

Intersectionality of Age and Gender Identity

Sexual orientation and gender identity prejudice (SOGIP) refers to negative perceptions about individuals and groups based on their perceived sexual orientation, perceived sexual identity, gender role, or gender expression (Cramwinckel et al., 2018). Prejudice based on gender identity refers to perceptions of whether a given individual is typically "male" or "female" in terms of behavior and appearance; it is distinct from prejudice based on sexual orientation, which focuses on nonheteronormative lifestyle choices such as homosexuality or sadomasochism (Mor-Barak, 2017). Given the present focus on older vs. younger *men vs. women*, the scope of the discussion will concern gender identity. Although other conceptualizations exist, "gender identity" as discussed presently is defined as either the advent of a biological male expressing a feminine gender identity or as the advent of a biological female expressing a masculine gender identity (i.e., gender nonconformity; Cramwinckel et al., 2018).

Although no published research has investigated the intersection of age and gender nonconformity, the previously noted literature on social identity and the confluence of power and demography may be instructive. Gender nonconforming identities lie outside of the heteronormative and cisgender mainstream (Cramwinckel et al., 2018). As such, gender nonconforming individuals would be socially located outside of the axes of societal power and thereby marginalized (Ozbilgin et al., 2011). Gender nonconforming older men would thus likely not benefit from stereotypes of experience, leadership, and wisdom typically attributed to (cisgender) older men; to the extent that their visible mannerisms and dress are expressive of a feminine gender identity, such positive old age stereotypes typically attributed to older men would likely not be attributed to them. Bereft of the privileged social position typically accorded to older working men (Kirchmeyer, 2002; Lyness & Heilman, 2006) and of the positive stereotypes typically accorded to older men in general (Hummert, 1990; Marcus & Sabuncu, 2016), gender nonconforming older men would thus occupy a similarly (lower) social position as older women. Given the lack of positive stereotypes that would otherwise be attributed to them on account of their biological sex, gender nonconforming older men may thus be expected to experience negative social identification and work outcomes (Zacher et al., 2019).

Similarly, gender nonconforming older *women* would nevertheless be located outside of the heteronormative and cisgender patriarchal social power structure even if they were to behave as if they were men or otherwise possess a nonfeminine gender identity because the advent of being biologically female would preclude them from the said patriarchy. As such, gender nonconforming older women may also not expect to experience the positive benefits of a male gender identity. Lacking the benefit of positive (male-oriented) old age stereotypes, gender nonconforming older women would thus be expected to experience negative social identification and work outcomes (Zacher et al., 2019). Buttressing this line of reasoning regarding the overall negative effects of gender nonconformity, a meta-analysis of the literature on stigmatized identities found associations between transgender identity expression and positively valanced work (e.g., job satisfaction, organizational commitment) and life outcomes (e.g., life satisfaction, positive affect) to be negative (Sabat et al., 2020).

Proposition 2: Gender nonconforming older men and women's ability and motivation to continue working will be lower relative to their cisgender counterparts.

Intersectional Effects of Age, Gender, and Social Class

Social class-based categorization is inherently gendered. Whereas younger minority men are viewed as aggressive and criminal, younger minority women are viewed as passive and invisible; whereas older minority men are viewed as passive and wise, older minority women are viewed as dominant and aggressive

(Marcus & Fritzsche, 2015). As such, it is necessary to discuss the intersection of age and social class separately for each sex.

In turn, such age-by-social-class intersections may be viewed from the prism of the stereotype content model (SCM; Cuddy et al., 2009; Fiske et al., 2002), whereby social groups are classified into quadrants based upon the confluence of perceived competence and warmth. Lower social class minority groups, perceived to be low on both competence and warmth (e.g., poor Blacks and the homeless), are subject to hostile, hate-based prejudice, whereas higher social class minority groups (e.g., Black professionals and the rich), perceived to be high on competence but low on warmth, are subject to envy-based prejudice (Fiske et al., 2002). Older adults, perceived to be low on competence but high on warmth, are subject to paternalistic, pity-based prejudice (Fiske et al., 2002). Fiske et al.'s (2002) findings from the US have been replicated in other European and Asian societies. Illustratively, Pakistanis and Filipinos in Hong Kong replace poor US Blacks in the low competence–low warmth quadrant; Asians and Jews occupy the same high competence–low warmth quadrant in both the US and Belgium; older adults occupy the same low competence–high warmth quadrant in both the US and South Korea (Cuddy et al., 2009).

Although the previously noted research did not specifically examine the confluence of age and gender or social class, triangulating evidence from the intersectionality literature is instructive. Perceived anger has been attributed more readily to younger vs. older Black male faces, whereas perceived happiness has been attributed more readily to older vs. younger Black male faces (Kang & Chasteen, 2009). Younger minority men in the US are stereotyped as lazy, unmotivated, and delinquent, whereas older Black men are stereotyped as wise, paternal, and patient (Kang & Chasteen, 2009; Shih, 2002). Older Black men are perceived to be warmer than younger Black and even older white men (Kang et al., 2014). Although older Black men are perceived to be less powerful than younger Black men, Black men, in general, are perceived to be more powerful than their white counterparts (Kang et al., 2014). Overall, stereotypes of younger Black men are associated with threat and incompetence, whereas stereotypes of older Black men place them as warm and arguably also competent, by virtue of being viewed both as strong "Black men" and as wise "older men."

Extrapolating from the previous findings regarding race-based differences for men, it may be construed that stereotypes of younger lower social class men (e.g., angry, delinquent, lazy, and threatening) are net negative for the work context. On the other hand, stereotypes of their older counterparts (e.g., genial, patient, warm, and wise) may be construed as net positive for the work context. It may thus be expected that younger lower social class men would experience negative work outcomes given negative social categorization; vice versa for older lower social class men (Zacher et al., 2019).

Proposition 3a: Younger lower social class men will have less ability and motivation to continue working relative to other comparable demographic subgroups.

Proposition 3b: Older lower social class men will have more ability and motivation to continue working relative to other comparable demographic subgroups.

Findings regarding the intersection of age and social class are ambiguous for women. In comparison to whites and Black men, faces of Black women are least likely to be recognized, and statements made by Black women in group discussion are least likely to be correctly attributed (Sesko & Biernat, 2010). Black women are less represented than white women and men in the upper management of Fortune 500 companies (Davidson, 1997). Yet, Black women receive higher suitability for hire ratings than their male counterparts (Hosoda et al., 2003), and Black women faculty members have been found to earn 24% more in gross wages than comparable faculty of other demographic subgroups (Toutkoushian et al., 2007). Younger minority women are, in particular, "intersectionally invisible"—they are viewed as nominal token minorities that are not readily represented in contemporary social discourse (Purdie-Vaughns & Eibach, 2008). Either their social class or their gender may take prominence—younger Asian women targets are perceived to be competent when their race is made salient but less so when their sex is made salient (Rattan et al., 2019); Asian women also have been found to make stronger internal attributions to explain racism than sexism (Remedios et al., 2012).

As with prejudice and unfair discrimination against them, stereotypes of minority women are similarly ambiguous. While younger minority women are nominal and "invisible" token minorities, older minority women are stereotyped as strong and dominant "matriarchs" (Marcus & Fritzsche, 2015). Smaller magnitudes of racial and gender bias have been found against Black women targets as compared to Black men and white women (Thiem et al., 2019). Black women are stereotyped as less dangerous than Black men but more dangerous than white women, and seen as neither prototypical of women nor of Blacks (Thiem et al., 2019; Thomas et al., 2014). Hence, given ambiguous and inconsistent patterns of stereotyping and bias against minority women:

Proposition 4a: The intersectional effects of age and social class on successful aging at work will be weaker for women than for men.

Although there is much less research on the intersectionality of race and gender identity, given the social marginalization of gender nonconforming individuals (Cramwinckel et al., 2018), it is possible that gender nonconforming men of lower social classes, both younger and older, will have similarly obfuscated effects as their biologically female counterparts. Triangulating toward this view, Preddie and Biernat (2020) found that the category "gay Black man" was rated as least similar to the category "men" vis-à-vis other comparison categories such as "straight Black man" and "gay white man"; stereotypes of gay Black men were unique by comparison, with stereotype content involving both femininity (e.g., fashionable, flamboyant) and threat (e.g., criminal, drug user). Hence, given ambiguous patterns of stereotyping against homosexual men:

> *Proposition 4b: The intersectional effects of age and social class on successful aging at work will be weaker for gender nonconforming men than for cisgender men.*

Contextual Boundary Conditions

Contextual boundary conditions are discussed based on the ecological systems framework of work and aging (Marcus et al., 2020). Macrolevel institutional and cultural factors are discussed first, followed by mesolevel occupational and organizational factors.

Institutional Factors

Institutional factors include governmental policies such as the setting of the retirement age, the legal environment such as laws surrounding the minimum or maximum age of work in particular occupations, industry standards and practices, and the market environment (e.g., economic boom-bust periods; Marcus et al., 2020). Research on associations between institutional practices and age-related work outcomes is scarce (Marcus, 2017). As such, rather than speculating on the effects of any particular institutional factor, the extent to which the institutional environment may be net age-positive or net age-negative (i.e., more or less favorable toward older workers) will hereby be considered.

Insofar as the previously noted institutional factors are subject to change, work conditions may become either net age-positive or negative. Because historically disadvantaged groups such as women and racial minorities are more likely to suffer negative work outcomes from poor labor market conditions (Feldman, 1994), it is reasonable to expect that net age-negative institutional environments would more greatly impact older women and older lower social class members. Illustratively, job losses consequent of the COVID-19 pandemic have been found to be especially pronounced for women, Black, and Latinx workers (Couch et al., 2020; UN Women, 2020). Older workers have been found to be disproportionately impacted by the economic fallout that followed the onset of said pandemic (Terrell, 2020).

> *Proposition 5: Negative institutional conditions will have a greater impact on the successful aging of older women and older members of the lower social classes as compared to their male and higher social class counterparts.*

Cultural Factors

The Cultural Anchors of Ageism framework (CAA; Marcus & Fritzsche, 2016) posits that psychological dimensions of culture relating to the formation and permeability of in- and out-groups are most relevant to age-based outcomes, including collectivism and tightness. Collectivism focuses on the role of individuals and groups in social relationships and deals with the relative permeability of group boundaries, whereby cultures with relatively impermeable in-groups are more likely to exhibit tendencies toward prejudice and unfair discrimination (Fiske, 2000). Tightness focuses on the relative importance of rules vs. relationships in behavioral control and deals with the degree to which deviances from group norms are permissible, whereby cultures with relatively greater norm impermissibility are more likely to exhibit tendencies toward prejudice and unfair discrimination (Gelfand et al., 2006). Accordingly, cultures that are *both* collectivistic (strict in- and out-group distinctions) and tight (deviances from group norms are sanctioned) are theorized to be typified by the most age bias; vice versa for individualistic-loose cultures (Marcus & Fritzsche, 2016).

Proposition 6: The intersectional effects of age, gender, and social class on successful aging at work will be larger in cultures that are both collectivistic and tight than in cultures that are both individualistic and loose.

Occupational Factors

Marcus and Fritzsche (2015) posited that the intersectional effects of age, gender, and tribe would be most pronounced in job contexts that make age salient. Such contexts include occupations that are deemed to be particularly suitable for workers of a given age (job age-type; Reeves et al., 2021), jobs that are mismatched to career-graded age norms within specific occupations (job level; Lawrence, 1988), and jobs that do not match a workers' occupational history (job-experience match; Fritzsche & Marcus, 2013). Ageism against older and younger workers is expected to be most pronounced when the job context is mismatched to the worker's age, making raters more likely to rely upon age-stereotypical cognitions while conducting attitudinal and behavioral evaluations (Perry & Finkelstein, 1999). Triangulating toward these notions, Reeves et al. (2021) investigated the confluence of age, sex, and job age norms on age and sex discrimination. Older and younger women reported experiencing more age and sex discrimination when they were age-mismatched to their jobs, but older and younger men reported experiencing less age discrimination in age-mismatched jobs. Hence, given evidence of crossover interactive effects when considering intersectionality in job age-salient contexts, it may thus be construed that the interactive effects of age and gender or social class on successful aging at work will be particularly pronounced in such occupational contexts.

Proposition 7: The intersectional effects of age, gender, and social class on successful aging at work will be most pronounced in occupational contexts that make age salient.

Organizational Factors

Reviewing the literature on organizational boundary conditions related to work and aging, Marcus et al. (2020) highlighted two factors of particular relevance, including norm strength and rank hierarchies. Organizations with stronger norms have stronger socialization and training processes, with higher socially shared cognition and greater behavioral similarity among members (Gelfand et al., 2006). Theory and evidence indicate prejudice and unfair discrimination to be most pronounced in norm-salient contexts because such contexts sanction individuals whose behaviors and personal characteristics are deviant from the norm (Gelfand et al., 2006; Harrington & Gelfand, 2014; see also Chapter 9 for more on age at the organizational levels). It is thus reasonable to expect the intersectional effects of age, gender, and social class to be stronger in organizations with strong norms. Similarly, institutions with rigid rank hierarchies, such as the military and academia, may also be construed to represent norm-salient situations for older workers (Marcus et al., 2020), whereby individuals are more likely to experience positive or negative unfair discrimination when their ages are mismatched to age norms relevant to their organizational ranks (Lawrence, 1988).

Proposition 8: The intersectional effects of age, gender, and social class on successful aging at work will be most pronounced in organizations with stronger norms and/or more rigid rank hierarchies.

Other Understudied Factors[3]

Subjective Age

Chronological age refers to the number of years elapsed since one was born, whereas subjective age is based on how old one feels, looks, or acts; how old one desires to be; or the age cohort that one identifies with (Kooij et al., 2008; see also Chapter 3). The main effects of subjective age on work outcomes have been found to be trivial. After controlling for core self-evaluations and chronological age, Zacher and Rudolph (2019) found that subjective age is not related to life and job satisfaction, task performance, emotional exhaustion, or job engagement; however, the joint effect of subjective and chronological age on emotional exhaustion was significant. Although subjective age has been found to interact with chronological age and sex to predict emotional exhaustion, depersonalization, self-esteem, and sex discrimination, its main effects on these variables have been found to be mostly nonsignificant (Marcus et al., 2019). Overall, it appears that subjective age may be an individual difference variable that jointly moderates the interactive effects of chronological age and/or gender and social class, as opposed to being simply a substitute for chronological age itself. Much research is needed to examine this possibility.

Time

Reviewing the literature on temporal factors related to work and aging, Marcus et al. (2020) theorized that individuals' perceived remaining time and life stage would act as boundary conditions regarding associations between age and work outcomes. Although temporal factors have been theorized to moderate relations between age and successful aging at work (Marcus, 2020), research examining associations between worker age and such temporal factors is still nascent, and no research has empirically examined the intersectional effects of age, time, and other demographic variables on work outcomes. There is thus much need to investigate deeper the role of time in demographic intersectionality (see also Chapters 7 and 10 for more on work and aging across time).

Underlying Psychological Variables

The intersectionality of age, gender/social class, and underlying psychological variables such as work motives, personality, and cultural values have also not been investigated much (see Chapter 8 for the measurement of such variables). Here, a study by Bohlmann and Zacher (2020) investigating the joint effects of chronological age, biological sex, and achievement/benevolence motivation on the perceived effectiveness of proactive behavior is instructive. Theorizing different patterns of effects for older and younger women relative to older and younger men, given different types of stereotypes associated with older and younger women, these authors found significant three-way interactive associations between age, sex, and achievement motivation on the perceived effectiveness of proactive behavior. In line with study hypotheses, the perceived effectiveness of proactive behavior motivated by achievement was higher for younger women compared to younger men but lower for older women compared to older men. Much research examining the confluence of such surface-level demographic and deep-level psychological variables is needed.

Nontraditional Demographic Variables

No research has examined the intersectional effects of age and nontraditional demographic variables such as disability status or body weight on work outcomes. Intersectionality theory regarding the confluence of demography and power dynamics (Ozbilgin et al., 2011) and tokenism (Purdie-Vaughns & Eibach, 2008; Sesko & Biernat, 2010) are relevant in this regard. Given societal power structures relegating socially marginalized persons such as those with disabilities to the peripheries of careers and organizations (Ozbilgin et al., 2011), it is reasonable to expect a "double jeopardy" effect (see Berdahl & Moore, 2006) for individuals that are both older and disabled, particularly so if they are women. Conversely, given the obfuscation of attitudinal and behavioral work outcomes with regard to token minorities such as Black women (Davidson, 1997; Hosoda et al., 2003; Sesko & Biernat, 2010; Toutkoushian et al., 2007), it is likewise reasonable to expect obfuscated and overall weak effects at the intersection of age and nontraditional demographic variables. There is much need to investigate these and other notions regarding the intersectionality of age and nontraditional demographic variables.

Notes

1 Because socioeconomic distinctions are typically visible (e.g., through dress or mannerism) and give rise to intergroup differences whereby the poor are located outside the axes of power, socially marginalized, and "othered," they are here treated like majority–minority group distinctions, under the umbrella term "social class."
2 Although the scope of the current chapter refers only to the work context and associated work outcomes, the theorized propositions may equally be applied to the broader social and life contexts also.
3 No theoretical propositions are advanced in this subsection because the discussed topics each currently lack a well-developed body of research.

References

Berdahl, J. L., & Moore, C. (2006). Workplace harassment: Double jeopardy for minority women. *Journal of Applied Psychology*, *91*(2), 426–436. https://doi.org/10.1037/0021-9010.91.2.426

Bohlmann, C., & Zacher, H. (2020). Making things happen (un)expectedly: Interactive effects of age, gender, and motives on evaluations of proactive behavior. *Journal of Business and Psychology*, *36*, 609–631. https://doi.org/10.1007/s10869-020-09691-7

Chao, G. T., & Moon, H. (2005). The cultural mosaic: A metatheory for understanding the complexity of culture. *Journal of Applied Psychology*, *90*(6), 1128–1140. https://doi.org/10.1037/0021-9010.90.6.1128

Couch, K. A., Fairlie, R. W., & Xu, H. (2020). Early evidence of the impacts of COVID-19 on minority unemployment. *Journal of Public Economics*, *192*, 104287. https://doi.org/10.1016/j.jpubeco.2020.104287

Cramwinckel, F., Scheepers, D. T., & van der Toorn, J. (2018). Interventions to reduce blatant and subtle sexual-orientation and gender identity prejudice (SOGIP): Current knowledge and future directions. *Social Issues and Review Policy*, *12*(1), 183–217. https://doi.org/10.1111/sipr.12044

Cuddy, A. J., Fiske, S. T., Kwan, V. S., Glick, P., Demoulin, S., Leyens, J.-P., Bond, M. H., Croizet, J.-C., Ellemers, N., Sleebos, E., Htun, T. T., Kim, H.-J., Maio, G., Perry, J., Petkova, K., Todorov, V., Rodriguez-Bailon, R., Morales, E., Moya, M., . . . & Ziegler, R. (2009). Stereotype content model across cultures: Towards universal similarities and some differences. *British Journal of Social Psychology*, *48*(1), 1–33. https://doi.org/10.1348/014466608X314935

Davidson, M. J. (1997). *The Black and ethnic minority woman manager: Cracking the concrete ceiling*. Paul Chapman.

Derous, E., Ryan, A. M., & Nguyen, H.-H. D. (2012). Multiple categorization in resume screening: Examining effects on hiring discrimination against Arab applicants in field and lab settings. *Journal of Organizational Behavior, 33*(4), 544–570. https://doi.org/10.1002/job.769

Feldman, D. C. (1994). The decision to retire early: A review and conceptualization. *Academy of Management Review, 19*(2), 285–311. https://doi.org/10.2307/258706

Finkelstein, L. M., Hanrahan, E. A., & Thomas, C. L. (2019). An expanded view of age bias in the workplace. In K. S. Shultz & G. A. Adams (Eds.), *Aging and work in the 21st century* (2nd ed., pp. 59–101). Routledge.

Finkelstein, L. M., King, E. B., & Voyles, E. C. (2015). Age metastereotyping and cross-age workplace interactions: A meta view of age stereotypes at work. *Work, Aging and Retirement, 1*(1), 26–40. https://doi.org/10.1093/workar/wau002

Fiske, S. T. (2000). Stereotyping, discrimination, and prejudice at the seam between the centuries: Evolution, culture, mind, and brain. *European Journal of Social Psychology, 30*(3), 299–322. https://doi.org/10.1002/(SICI)1099-0992(200005/06) 30:3<299::AID-EJSP2>3.0.CO;2-F

Fiske, S. T., Cuddy, A. J., Glick, P., & Xu, J. (2002). A model of (often mixed) stereotype content: Competence and warmth respectively follow from perceived status and competition. *Journal of Personality and Social Psychology, 82*(6), 878–902. https://doi.org/10.1037/0022-3514.82.6.878

Fritzsche, B. A., & Marcus, J. (2013). The senior discount: Biases against older career changers. *Journal of Applied Social Psychology, 43*(2), 350–362. https://doi.org/10.1111/j.1559-1816.2012.01004.x

Gaertner, S. L., & Dovidio, J. F. (2000). *Reducing intergroup bias: The common ingroup identity model.* Psychology Press.

Gelfand, M. J., Nishii, L. H., & Raver, J. L. (2006). On the nature and importance of cultural tightness-looseness. *Journal of Applied Psychology, 91*(6), 1225–1244. https://doi.org/10.1037/0021-9010.91.6.1225

Harrington, J. R., & Gelfand, M. J. (2014). Tightness-looseness across the 50 United States. *PNAS Proceedings of the National Academy of Sciences of the United States of America, 111*(22), 7990–7995. https://doi.org/10.1073/pnas.1317937111

Heilman, M. E. (2001). Description and prescription: How gender stereotypes prevent women's ascent up the organizational ladder. *Journal of Social Issues, 57*(4), 657–674. https://doi.org/10.1111/0022-4537.00234

Hertel, G., & Zacher, H. (2018). Managing the aging workforce. In N. Anderson, D. S. Ones, C. Viswesvaran, & H. K. Sinangil (Eds.), *Handbook of industrial, work, and organizational psychology, Vol. 3. Managerial psychology and organizational approaches* (2nd ed., pp. 396–428). Sage.

Hosoda, M., Stone, D. L., & Stone-Romero, E. F. (2003). The interactive effects of race, gender, and job type on the suitability ratings and selection decisions. *Journal of Applied Social Psychology, 33*(1), 145–178. https://doi.org/10.1111/j.1559-1816.2003.tb02077.x

Hummert, M. L. (1990). Multiple stereotypes of elderly and young adults: A comparison of structure and evaluations. *Psychology and Aging, 5*(2), 182–193. https://doi.org/10.1037/0882-7974.5.2.182

Jones, K. P., Sabat, I. E., King, E. B., Ahmad, A., McCausland, T. C., & Chen, T. (2017). Isms and schisms: A meta-analysis of the prejudice-discrimination relationship across racism, sexism, and ageism. *Journal of Organizational Behavior, 38*(7), 1076–1110. https://doi.org/10.1002/job.2187

Kang, S. K., & Chasteen, A. L. (2009). Beyond the double-jeopardy hypothesis: Assessing emotion on the faces of multiply-categorizable targets of prejudice. *Journal of Experimental Social Psychology*, *45*(6), 1281–1285. https://doi.org/10.1016/j.jesp.2009.07.002

Kang, S. K., Chasteen, A. L., Cadieux, J., Cary, L. A., & Syeda, M. (2014). Comparing young and older adults' perceptions of conflicting stereotypes and multiply-categorizable individuals. *Psychology and Aging*, *29*(3), 469–481. https://doi.org/10.1037/a0037551

Kirchmeyer, C. (2002). Gender differences in managerial careers: Yesterday, today, and tomorrow. *Journal of Business Ethics*, *37*, 5–24. https://doi.org/10.1023/a:1014721900246

Kooij, D. T. A. M., De Lange, A., Jansen, P., & Dikkers, J. (2008). Older workers' motivation to continue to work: Five meanings of age: A conceptual review. *Journal of Managerial Psychology*, *23*(4), 364–394. https://doi.org/10.1108/02683940810869015

Kooij, D. T. A. M., Zacher, H., Wang, M., & Heckhausen, J. (2020). Successful aging at work: A process model to guide future research and practice. *Industrial and Organizational Psychology: Perspectives on Science and Practice*, *13*(3), 345–365. https://doi.org/10.1017/iop.2020.1

Lawrence, B. S. (1988). New wrinkles in the theory of age: Demography, norms, and performance ratings. *Academy of Management Journal*, *31*(2), 309–337. https://doi.org/10.2307/256550

Lyness, K. S., & Heilman, M. E. (2006). When fit is fundamental: Performance evaluations and promotions of upper-level female and male managers. *Journal of Applied Psychology*, *91*(4), 777–785. https://doi.org/10.1037/0021-9010.91.4.777

Marcus, J. (2017). Age discrimination. In N. A. Pachana (Ed.), *Encyclopedia of geropsychology* (pp. 75–81). Springer Reference.

Marcus, J. (2020). Clarifying multilevel and temporal influences on successful aging at work: An ecological systems perspective. *Industrial and Organizational Psychology*, *13*(3), 408–412. https://doi.org/10.1017/iop.2020.67

Marcus, J., & Fritzsche, B. A. (2015). One size doesn't fit all: Toward a theory on the intersectional salience of ageism at work. *Organizational Psychology Review*, *5*(2), 168–188. https://doi.org/10.1177/2F2041386614556015

Marcus, J., & Fritzsche, B. A. (2016). The cultural anchors of age discrimination in the workplace: A multilevel framework. *Work, Aging and Retirement*, *2*(2), 217–229. https://doi.org/10.1093/workar/waw007

Marcus, J., Fritzsche, B. A., & Ng, Y. L. (2019). On the interactive effects of objective and subjective age on work outcomes for men and women. *Work, Aging and Retirement*, *5*(4), 287–306. https://doi.org/10.1093/workar/waz018

Marcus, J., Rudolph, C. W., & Zacher, H. (2020). An ecological systems framework for work and aging. In D. L. Stone, J. H. Dulebohn, & K. M. Lukaszewski (Eds.), *Advancing theory and research on diversity in organizations (Research in human resources management)*. Information Age Publishing.

Marcus, J., & Sabuncu, N. (2016). "Old oxen cannot plow": Stereotype themes of older adults in Turkish folklore. *The Gerontologist*, *56*(6), 1007–1022. https://doi.org/10.1093/geront/gnv108

Mor-Barak, M. E. (2017). *Managing diversity: Toward a globally inclusive workplace* (4th ed.). Sage.

Ozbilgin, M. F., Beauregard, T. A., Tatli, A., & Bell, M. P. (2011). Work-life diversity and intersectionality: A critical review and research agenda. *International Journal of Management Reviews*, *13*(2), 177–198. https://doi.org/10.1111/j.1468-2370.2010.00291.x

Perry, E. L., & Finkelstein, L. M. (1999). Toward a broader view of age-discrimination in employment-related decisions: A joint consideration of organizational factors and cognitive processes. *Human Resource Management Review, 9*(1), 21–49. https://doi.org/10.1016/S1053-4822(99)00010-8

Powell, G. N., Butterfield, D. A., & Parent, J. D. (2002). Gender and managerial stereotypes: Have the times changed? *Journal of Management, 28*(2), 177–193. https://doi.org/10.1177/014920630202800203

Preddie, J. P., & Biernat, M. (2020). More than the sum of its parts: Intersections of sexual orientation and race as they influence perceptions of group similarity and stereotype content. *Sex Roles, 84*(9–10), 554–573. https://doi.org/10.1007/s11199-020-01185-3

Purdie-Vaughns, V., & Eibach, R. P. (2008). Intersectional invisibility: The distinctive advantages and disadvantages of multiple subordinate-group identities. *Sex Roles, 59*(5–6), 377–391. https://doi.org/10.1007/s11199-008-9424-4

Rattan, A., Steele, J., & Ambady, N. (2019). Identical applicant but different outcomes: The impact of gender versus race salience in hiring. *Group Processes and Intergroup Relations, 22*(1), 80–97. https://doi.org/10.1177/1368430217722035

Reeves, M. D., Fritzsche, B. A., Marcus, J., Smith, N. A., & Ng, Y. L. (2021). "Beware the young doctor and the old barber": Development and validation of a job age-type spectrum. *Journal of Vocational Behavior, 129*, 103616. https://doi.org/10.1016/j.jvb.2021.103616

Remedios, J. D., Chasteen, A. L., & Paek, J. D. (2012). Not all prejudices are experienced equally: Comparing experiences of racism and sexism in female minorities. *Group Processes and Intergroup Relations, 15*(2), 273–287. https://doi.org/10.1177/1368430211411594

Rudolph, C. W., Marcus, J., & Zacher, H. (2019). Global issues in work, aging and retirement. In K. S. Shultz & G. A. Adams (Eds.), *Aging and work in the 21st century* (2nd ed., pp. 292–324). Taylor & Francis.

Sabat, I. E., Lindsey, A. P., King, E. B., Winslow, C., Jones, K. P., Membere, A., & Smith, N. A. (2020). Stigma expression outcomes and boundary conditions: A meta-analysis. *Journal of Business and Psychology, 35*(2), 171–186. https://doi.org/10.1007/s10869-018-9608-z

Sawyer, K., Thoroughgood, C., & Webster, J. (2016). Queering the gender binary: Understanding transgender workplace experiences. In T. Köllen (Ed.), *Sexual orientation and transgender issues in organizations* (pp. 21–42). Springer International.

Schneider, D. J. (2004). *The psychology of stereotyping*. Guilford Press.

Sesko, A. K., & Biernat, M. (2010). Prototypes of race and gender: The invisibility of Black women. *Journal of Experimental Social Psychology, 4*(2), 356–360. https://doi.org/10.1016/j.jesp.2009.10.016

Shih, J. (2002). ' . . . Yeah, I could hire this one, but I know it's gonna be a problem': How race, nativity, and gender affect employers' perceptions of the manageability of job seekers. *Ethnic and Racial Studies, 25*(1), 99–119. https://doi.org/10.1080/01419870120112076

Terrell, K. (2020, October 21). Unemployment's toll on older workers is worst in over half a century. *AARP*. www.aarp.org/work/working-at-50-plus/info-2020/pandemic-unemployment-older-workers/

Thiem, K. C., Neel, R., Simpson, A. J., & Todd, A. R. (2019). Are Black women and girls associated with danger? Implicit racial bias at the intersection of target age and gender. *Personality and Social Psychology Bulletin, 45*(10), 1427–1439. https://doi.org/10.1177/0146167219829182

Thomas, E. L., Dovidio, J. F., & West, T. V. (2014). Lost in the categorical shuffle: Evidence for the social non-prototypicality of Black women. *Cultural Diversity and Ethnic Minority Psychology*, *20*(3), 370–376. https://doi.org/10.1037/a0035096

Toutkoushian, R. K., Bellas, M. L., & Moore, J. V. (2007). The interaction effects of gender, race, and marital status on faculty salaries. *The Journal of Higher Education*, *78*(5), 572–601. https://doi.org/10.1080/00221546.2007.11772330

UN Women. (2020, September 16). *Covid-19 and its economic toll on women: The story behind the numbers*. www.unwomen.org/en/news/stories/2020/9/feature-covid-19-economic-impacts-on-women

van Dijk, H., Kooij, D., Karanika-Murray, M., de Vos, A., & Meyer, B. (2020). Meritocracy a myth? A multilevel perspective of how social inequality accumulates through work. *Organizational Psychology Review*, *10*(3–4), 240–269. https://doi.org/10.1177/2041386620930063

Zacher, H., Esser, L., Bohlmann, C., & Rudolph, C. W. (2019). Age, social identity and identification, and work outcomes: A conceptual model, literature review, and future research directions. *Work, Aging and Retirement*, *5*(1), 24–43. https://doi.org/10.1093/workar/way005

Zacher, H., & Rudolph, C. W. (2019). Just a mirage: On the incremental predictive validity of subjective age. *Work, Aging and Retirement*, *5*(2), 141–162. https://doi.org/10.1093/workar/wax031

5

INTEGRATION OF PARADOXICAL AGE-RELATED ACTIONS AT WORK

Kathrin Rosing and Hannes Zacher

Paradoxical work demands are omnipresent in organizational life (Schad et al., 2016). Individuals, teams, and organizations are confronted with a multitude of interrelated but seemingly opposing demands. Such paradoxical demands are challenging, especially for individuals, because they are conflicting by definition, and they draw on the same limited resources (Kauppila & Tempelaar, 2016). However, paradoxical work demands can potentially be addressed successfully when employees show a combination of different behaviors (i.e., integration of paradoxical actions), and thus result in enhanced performance and well-being (Cañibano, 2019; Waldman et al., 2019). For example, employees are often expected to make use of their existing knowledge and skills, focus on present tasks, and take care of themselves at work, but, at the same time, they may be also expected to continuously acquire new knowledge and skills, consider future career options, and take responsibility for others, respectively (García-Sánchez et al., 2017; Zhang et al., 2015). We suggest that a subset of paradoxical work demands requires behaviors that represent typical (or average) age-related strengths or preferences of younger or older employees, respectively. In other words, these work demands are paradoxical because they require behaviors that are typical age-related strengths or preferences of both younger and older employees. For example, they may require both high levels of fluid cognitive abilities, such as fast information processing capacity (i.e., a strength of younger employees) and crystallized cognitive abilities, such as experience-based judgment (i.e., a strength of older employees; Fisher et al., 2017).

Paradox theory has not yet been applied to lifespan research. However, we posit that paradoxes are an inherent part of many lifespan theories. Based on the lifespan developmental perspective (P. B. Baltes, 1987), research has identified various multidirectional age-related changes (i.e., gains, losses, maintenance)

DOI: 10.4324/9781003089674-7

in psychological functions and individual characteristics (e.g., cognitive abilities, motivational and socioemotional priorities, personality characteristics, proactive and adaptive behaviors; Ng & Feldman, 2013; see Table 5.1 for a summary). These age-related changes can be explained by a set of prominent lifespan theories (see also Chapter 7), including: the dual component theory of cognitive abilities (P. B. Baltes et al., 1999; Fisher et al., 2017); the neosocioanalytic model of personality change (Roberts & Wood, 2006) and other theories of personality development across the lifespan (McAdams & de St. Aubin, 1992); the model of selective optimization with compensation (P. B. Baltes & M. M. Baltes, 1990); socioemotional selectivity theory (Carstensen et al., 1999) and its extension, the strength and vulnerability integration model (Charles, 2010); as well as assimilation-accommodation theory (Brandtstädter & Renner, 1990; Brandtstädter & Rothermund, 2002) and the motivational theory of lifespan development (Heckhausen et al., 2010; for recent reviews of these lifespan development theores, see B. B. Baltes et al., 2019; Rudolph, 2016).

We suggest that the lifespan literature can benefit from integrating paradox theory because this theory provides a meaningful lens to understand how employees deal with demands for different age-related actions. Specifically, we argue that it is important to understand how the interplay between age-related paradoxical work demands and individual characteristics changes with age and how employees at different points of the working lifespan deal with age-related paradoxical work demands. We argue that, given that many jobs entail age-related paradoxical work demands, focusing only on certain age-related strengths of employees from different age groups (e.g., greater experience of older employees, higher information processing capacity of younger employees) may not be an optimal strategy in the context of demographic and economic changes. Instead, for individuals to maintain high levels of performance and well-being at work, we propose that employees need to integrate various paradoxical age-related actions that are instrumental in achieving corresponding work demands.

The central aim of this chapter is, accordingly, the development of a novel conceptual model on the integration of paradoxical age-related actions (IPARA) at work. To this end, we first review theoretical and empirical research on paradoxes and paradoxical work demands and, based on the lifespan developmental literature, different age-related characteristics and corresponding actions. Next, building on this literature review, we develop the IPARA theoretical model, which suggests that employees are able to maintain high levels of performance and well-being with increasing age when they are able to meet age-related paradoxical work demands by actively regulating their behavior. We offer a number of testable propositions implied by the IPARA model. For example, we argue that older and younger employees attain better outcomes at work if they focus not only on using their typical age-related strengths and preferences but, at the same time, also attempt to integrate those strengths and preferences with behaviors that correspond to typical age-related strengths and preferences of younger

TABLE 5.1 Age-Related Paradoxical Work Demands and Corresponding Employee Actions for Different Psychological Functions

Psychological Function	Theoretical Basis	Age-Related Individual Changes	Age-Related Paradoxical Work Demands	Corresponding Employee Actions at Work
Cognition	Dual component theory of cognitive abilities (P. B. Baltes et al., 1999)	• Decrease in fluid cognitive abilities • Increase in crystallized cognitive abilities	Possessing up-to-date knowledge and skills vs. possessing a broad and deep knowledge base	Learning new knowledge and skills vs. relying on existing knowledge and skills
Motivation	Model of selection, optimization, and compensation (P. B. Baltes & M. M. Baltes, 1990)	• Decrease in personal resources • Increase in goal selectivity	Managing many projects at once vs. focusing on specific projects	Pursuing multiple goals at once vs. pursuing a few selected goals (and using optimization and compensation)
Socioemotional experience	Socioemotional selectivity theory (Carstensen et al., 1999), strength and vulnerability integration model (Charles, 2010)	• Decrease in future time perspective • Increase in priority of positive socioemotional experiences	Having a broad occupational network vs. having close collaborations	Seeking new contacts vs. relying on a smaller network of familiar colleagues
Personality and motives	Neosocioanalytic model of personality development (Roberts & Wood, 2006), generativity theory (McAdams & de St. Aubin, 1992)	• Decrease in agentic motives • Increase in communal motives	Making progress in one's own career vs. mentoring others	Developing oneself and one's career vs. developing and helping others
Behavior	Motivational theory of lifespan development (Heckhausen et al., 2010), assimilation–accommodation theory (Brandtstädter & Rothermund, 2002)	• Decrease in primary control capacity • Increase in secondary control striving	Showing proactivity vs. showing adaptability	Initiating changes/tenaciously pursuing goals vs. adapting to changes/goal adjustment

or older employees, respectively (see Table 5.1). Finally, we discuss several directions for future research based on the IPARA model, including methodological recommendations.

With this chapter, we contribute to research and practice regarding work and aging in two important ways. First, by integrating the literatures on paradoxes and work and aging, we emphasize the complexity of successful aging at work. Previous theorizing and research has highlighted the role of different age-related strengths for successful aging at work (Zacher, 2015). However, our theoretical model goes one step further and suggests that focusing on behaviors that correspond to age-related strengths of older and younger employees alone is not enough, but these behaviors need to be integrated with their alleged opposites (i.e., behaviors corresponding to age-related strengths of younger and older employees, respectively) to enhance performance and well-being. Second, research on paradoxes in the organizational behavior literature, that is, research on microperspectives on organizational paradoxes, is still in its infancy (Waldman et al., 2019). With the IPARA model, we provide a specific understanding of paradoxes within the context of work and aging at the individual level and, thus, contribute to a more comprehensive perspective on individual-level approaches to paradoxes at work. Moreover, research on paradoxes is likely to profit from integrating a more dynamic, temporal, and lifespan developmental perspective as such aspects have been largely overlooked in previous research (Schad et al., 2016). Specifically, the components of different sets of paradoxical actions, as well as their integration, are likely to change across people's working lifespan. For instance, an employee's motivation may change from tenaciously pursuing their own career goals to promoting the careers of other people over time, which, depending on their age-related paradoxical work demands and capacity to integrate different behaviors, likely influences their performance and well-being at work (Brandtstädter & Rothermund, 2002).

Paradoxical Work Demands

In many jobs, employees are increasingly expected to deal with paradoxical work demands (Cañibano, 2019; Rosing et al., 2018). In the management science literature, paradoxes have been described as "contradictory yet interrelated elements that exist simultaneously and persist over time" (Smith & Lewis, 2011, p. 382), such as exploration and exploitation (e.g., Benner & Tushman, 2003), flexibility and efficiency (e.g., Adler et al., 1999), or change and stability (e.g., Leana & Barry, 2000). The opposing elements of paradoxes create tensions that are often resolved by choosing one element over the other ("either-or" logic). In contrast, paradox theory suggests that pursuing both elements simultaneously ("both-and" logic) is not only possible but results in synergies and, thus, enhanced outcomes (Lewis, 2000; Smith & Lewis, 2011). For example, when leaders are able to both maintain control and let go of control, this has beneficial implications for employees' goal clarity and performance (Kearney et al., 2019). Accordingly, paradoxical work demands that involve tasks and duties that at first seem contradictory or conflicting can potentially be integrated and lead to enhanced individual functioning (Bledow et al., 2009). For instance, employees may not only be required to make use of their existing knowledge and skills; they may also be expected to continuously acquire new knowledge and skills (García-Sánchez et al., 2017). Other paradoxical demands include the expectations that employees focus on their present tasks but also consider future career options, or that they develop themselves but also take responsibility for others at work (Zhang et al., 2015). As we will further elaborate later, many paradoxical work demands (see also Table 5.1) entail requirements that correspond to typical age-related strengths or preferences of both younger and older employees.

Paradox theory has been predominantly focused on the organizational level, but there is an emergent research stream to address the "micro-foundations" of paradox at the individual and team levels (Miron-Spektor et al., 2018). Specifically, theory and empirical research on paradoxes have examined the individual, behavioral, and contextual factors that increase the likelihood that employees successfully integrate or balance behaviors that help meet paradoxical demands, with beneficial effects on performance and well-being (e.g., Miron-Spektor et al., 2018; Waldman et al., 2019; Zhang et al., 2015). In particular, research on paradoxes in the work context highlights the role of employees' integrative capacity, an umbrella term used to describe characteristics such as a paradoxical mindset (i.e., "to value, accept, and feel comfortable with tensions"; Miron-Spektor et al., 2018, p. 27) and functional flexibility (i.e., the ability of individuals to adapt their behavior to the specific requirements of very different situations; Paulhus & Martin, 1988). Employees with higher integrative capacity should be better able to address paradoxical work demands by simultaneously engaging in "opposing" actions, and they should be more likely to embrace and successfully deal with tensions implied by paradoxical work demands. For example, Shao et al. (2019) show that high levels of integrative capacity help followers deal with paradoxical leadership, that is, leadership that includes seemingly contradictory behaviors, such as controlling adherence to rules while allowing flexibility (Zhang et al., 2015).

Age-Related Paradoxical Work Demands and Actions

The lifespan developmental literature suggests that the aging process is accompanied not only by losses but also by maintenance and gains in various individual characteristics, including knowledge, skills, abilities, and other factors (KSAOs) such as personality and motives (P. B. Baltes, 1987). On average, these age-related changes result in a variety of typical strengths and weaknesses or typical preferences of employees at different ages (importantly, we focus here on actual age-related differences and not on descriptive or prescriptive age stereotypes). For example, while younger employees tend to be relatively stronger in acquiring new knowledge and skills quickly (due to higher capacity for fast information processing), older employees tend to be stronger in applying and sharing their knowledge and skills (Beier & Ackerman, 2005). Accordingly, it might be suggested that younger and older employees are better suited for different types of jobs that entail different age-related work demands, such as air traffic controllers (i.e., high demands for fast information processing capacity) or elementary school teachers (i.e., high demands for sharing knowledge and skills), respectively (Kanfer & Ackerman, 2004). However, many modern jobs entail paradoxical work demands that require behaviors that reflect the strengths and preferences of both younger and older employees. Thus, focusing only on specific age-related strengths of younger or older employees is not an optimal strategy to maintain and enhance performance and well-being. For example, given the pace of technological advancements, older employees cannot rely only on their accumuated knowledge and skills but also need to acquire new knowledge and skills. Accordingly, we propose that employees need to demonstrate and integrate behaviors that help address age-related paradoxical demands at work, such as engaging in both the acquisition and application of knowledge at work. In the following sections, we review prominent theories and key findings in the areas of cognition, motivation, socioemotional experience, personality, and behavior. Based on propositions of these lifespan developmental theories and corresponding age-related changes identified in empirical studies, we created an illustrative taxonomy of key paradoxical age-related actions (see Table 5.1).

Cognition

According to the dual component theory of cognitive abilities (P. B. Baltes et al., 1999; Fisher et al., 2017), aging is associated with average decreases in fluid cognitive abilities, such as memory, reasoning, and fast information processing. These declines start around the age of 20 and accelerate around the age of 50 years (Verhaeghen & Salthouse, 1997). At the same time, aging is associated with increases in crystallized cognitive abilities, including experiential knowledge, verbal abilities, and wise judgment (Salthouse, 2012). Thus, a set of age-related paradoxical work demands is to possess up-to-date knowledge and skills and to possess a both broad and deep knowledge base and skill set. Corresponding actions to meet these demands represent the exploration of new knowledge and skills (i.e., a typical "younger age" action) versus the use of existing knowledge and skills (i.e., a typical "older age" action).

Motivation

The lifespan model of selection, optimization, and compensation assumes that the ratio of gains to losses becomes smaller with increasing age, and, therefore, individuals have to use action regulation strategies to achieve their goals (P. B. Baltes & M. M. Baltes, 1990). In particular, the model suggests that, to maintain high levels of performance and well-being, people should focus on their most important goals (i.e., selection), increase their resource investment toward goal achievement (optimization), and potentially compensate for losses in means (compensation). Indeed, empirical research has demonstrated age-related changes in motivational priorities from striving for gains to maintenance and avoidance of losses (Ebner et al., 2006). A set of age-related paradoxical work demands is to "multitask" and to focus on specific projects at the same time. Corresponding actions to meet these demands are thus the pursuit of multiple work goals at once (i.e., a typical "younger age" action) versus the pursuit of few selected goals and the use of optimization and compensation strategies (i.e., a typical "older age" action).

Socioemotional Experience

Two prominent lifespan theories have focused on changes in socioemotional abilities and experiences with age. First, socioemotional selectivity theory proposes that older adults, due to a constrained future time perspective, prioritize positive emotional experiences and close social partners, whereas younger adults prioritize instrumental goals, such as broadening their social network and knowledge acquisition (Carstensen et al., 1999). The extension of socioemotional selectivity theory, the strength and vulnerability integration model, argues similarly that, due to increased emotion regulation skills and lower physiological flexibility, older adults are motivated to avoid stressful situations and seek out situations that maximize emotional well-being (Charles, 2010). Accordingly, relevant examples of age-related paradoxical work demands are to establish a broad occupational network and to have close collaborations. Corresponding actions to meet these demands involve seeking new contacts to maximize human and social capital (i.e., a typical "younger age" action) versus the reliance on a smaller network of familiar coworkers that promises to maximize emotional well-being (i.e., a typical "older age" action).

Personality and Motives

Consistent with propositions of the neosocioanalytic model of personality change (Roberts & Wood, 2006), research has shown that personality characteristics and motives change across the lifespan. In particular, there are age-related increases in emotional stability, agreeableness, conscientiousness (Roberts et al., 2006), and intrinsic motives such as generativity (i.e., helping younger people), as well as decreases in social dominance, growth, and extrinsic motives (e.g., financial compensation) with age (Kooij et al., 2011). Overall, there appears to be a decrease in agentic tendencies and an increase in communal tendencies with age (Doerwald et al., 2021; McAdams & de St. Aubin, 1992). Thus, an example set of age-related paradoxical work demands is to make progress in one's career and to mentor others. Corresponding actions to meet these demands may include focusing on one's own (career) development (i.e., a typical "younger age" action) versus helping and developing other people, such as younger coworkers, in the work context (i.e., a typical "older age" action).

Behavior

In terms of employee behavior, lifespan research suggests that younger adults are more likely to take agentic action to change their environment (i.e., goal pursuit), whereas older adults focus more on internal, self-related changes (i.e., goal adjustment; Haase et al., 2013). The distinction between these two basic strategies is described by both the assimilation-accommodation theory (Brandt-städter & Renner, 1990) and the motivational theory of lifespan development (Heckhausen et al., 2010). Assimilation-accommodation theory posits a dual process framework including an assimilative mode, in which individuals invest effort to change the situation consistent with their goals, as well as an accommodative mode, in which individuals adjust their goals based on constraints and (changes in) resources (Brandtstädter & Rothermund, 2002). The motivational theory of lifespan development proposes that individuals strive for primary control (i.e., they desire to influence their development and environment) across their entire lifespan; however, primary control capacity follows an inverted U-shaped function over the lifespan, with lowest capacity in childhood and old age and highest capacity in mid-life, whereas secondary control striving (i.e., self-regulatory skills that support goal engagement and disengagement) linearly increases over the lifespan (Shane & Heckhausen, 2019). In this regard, a set of age-related paradoxical work demands is to show high levels of proactivity and adaptability. Corresponding actions to meet these demands are to suggest changes at work (i.e., a typical "younger age" action) versus adapting oneself to work-related changes (i.e., a typical "older age" action).

Theoretical Model on the Integration of Paradoxical Age-Related Actions

In this section, we integrate theorizing on paradoxes and lifespan development to advance the IPARA theoretical model, as well as its five associated propositions on predictors and consequences of IPARA and mechanisms and boundary conditions of these effects (see Figure 5.1). IPARA refers to the active alignment or balancing of paradoxical, goal-directed behaviors to meet work demands that are more or less likely among younger and older employees due to age-related changes in strengths and preferences (as described in the previous section, see also Table 5.1). In a nutshell, we first propose that younger and older employees, due to more pronounced differences in age-related individual characteristics, have lower levels of IPARA than middle-aged employees (i.e., we hypothesize an inverted U-shaped association between age [via age-related individual differences] and

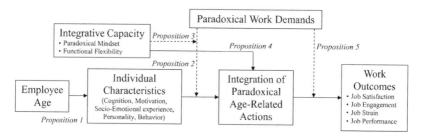

FIGURE 5.1 Integration of paradoxical age-related actions (IPARA) model

Note: Dashed lines represent moderation effects (i.e., Propositions 2, 3, and 5)

IPARA). Second, we propose that age-related paradoxical work demands moderate the strength of the curvilinear effect of age, via age-related individual characteristics, on IPARA, such that the effect is stronger when age-related paradoxical work demands are high and weaker when age-related paradoxical work demands are low. Third, there will be a three-way interaction between age (via age-related individual differences), age-related paradoxical work demands, and employees' integrative capacity. Specifically, high (vs. low) levels of integrative capacity are proposed to buffer the curvilinear effect of age on IPARA when age-related paradoxical work demands are high. Fourth, integrative capacity is positively related to IPARA. Finally, we argue that high levels of IPARA predict increased levels of positive work outcomes, including job satisfaction, engagement, low strain, and performance, when age-related paradoxical work demands are high.

Employee Age and the Integration of Paradoxical Age-Related Actions at Work

We first propose that, due to age-related changes in different domains of psychological functioning and experience (see Table 5.1), younger and older employees have lower levels of IPARA than middle-aged employees. As an illustration for our proposition, consider the following example: Based on propositions of the dual component theory of cognitive abilities (P. B. Baltes et al., 1999), younger employees should generally be better at exploring new knowledge and skills compared to older employees, whereas older employees should generally be better at utilizing existing knowledge and skills compared to younger employees (Beier & Ackerman, 2005). In contrast, middle-aged employees should be better than both younger and older employees at balancing these paradoxical age-related actions (i.e., IPARA) because they are equally likely to engage in knowledge exploration and exploitation (i.e., on average, their fluid cognitive abilities have decreased only to some extent, and they were already able to acquire knowledge and experience). Consistent with this assumption, research suggests that middle-aged adults make fewer rate-changing mistakes on home equity loans and lines of credit than younger and older adults, presumably because they rely on both fluid and crystallized cognitive abilities when making these financial decisions (Agarwal et al., 2009). Extending this example to other domains of functioning and experience, we expect that for each psychological domain listed in Table 5.1, an inverted U-shaped association between age and IPARA will emerge. Younger employees either have not yet acquired certain KSAOs or they possess KSAOs that decline with age; older employees either have obtained certain KSAOs over time or they have lost them due to aging. Middle-aged employees, in contrast, should be better at balancing age-related actions at work. Thus, it is likely that younger and older employees, compared to middle-aged employees, experience more problems with IPARA at work. For example, it might be more difficult for older employees to seek new contacts while at the same time relying on their established network than for middle-aged employees who already possess an established network of close contacts but are also highly motivated to further broaden their network.

Proposition 1: There is an inverted U-shaped relationship between age and IPARA.

The Role of Age-Related Paradoxical Work Demands

Not all jobs incorporate the same level of paradoxical work demands (Miron-Spektor et al., 2018). Therefore, we propose that age-related paradoxical work demands constitute a crucial boundary condition of the curvilinear effect of age, via age-related individual differences, on IPARA suggested by Proposition 1. Specifically, when a job does not entail age-related paradoxical work demands but requires only the use of the typical age-related strengths of preferences of either younger (i.e., establishing new contacts) or older employees' work-related strengths and preferences (i.e., working with close others), there should be no difference between younger, middle-aged, and older employees in terms of IPARA. In other words, when the job does not require employees to integrate paradoxical actions to meet work demands, middle-aged employees should not be more likely to combine different age-related behaviors than younger and older employees. In contrast, when age-related paradoxical work demands are high (e.g., establishing new contacts with a broad network of coworkers or customers *and* working closely with an established network of coworkers or customers), the curvilinear effect of age on IPARA should be stronger, thus magnifying the differences between middle-aged and younger and older employees regarding IPARA.

Proposition 2: Age-related paradoxical work demands moderate the curvilinear relationship between age and IPARA, such that the inverted U-shaped relationship is stronger when age-related paradoxical work demands are high and is weaker when age-related paradoxical work demands are low.

The Role of Integrative Capacity

We argue that integrative capacity influences, in combination with age-related paradoxical work demands, the strength of the curvilinear association between age and IPARA suggested by Proposition 1. Building on Proposition 2, we propose that high levels of integrative capacity are particularly relevant when age-related paradoxical work demands are high. More specifically, we expect integrative capacity to buffer the inverted U-shaped relationship when age-related paradoxical work demands are high. In other words, when paradoxical work demands are high, high levels of integrative capacity are particularly important for younger and older employees to achieve IPARA, whereas middle-aged employees generally engage more in IPARA because they are more likely to possess equal levels of contradictory age-related characteristics (Agarwal et al., 2009). In contrast, the proposed inverted U-shaped association between age and IPARA (Proposition 1) should be stronger for employees with both high levels of age-related paradoxical work demands and low levels of integrative capacity, as middle-aged employees will more naturally use IPARA than their younger and older counterparts, even when they do not strive for integrating paradoxes and tensions in general.

> *Proposition 3:* There is a three-way interaction between age, age-related paradoxical work demands, and integrative capacity, such that the inverted U-shaped relationship is weaker when both age-related paradoxical work demands and integrative capacity are high than when age-related paradoxical work demands are high and integrative capacity is low.

We further propose that employees' integrative capacity is generally positively related to IPARA. Based on the assumption that individual differences translate into relevant work behavior unless the work context imposes strong constraints (Meyer et al., 2010), employees with high integrative capacity should be generally more likely to show high levels of IPARA compared to employees with low integrative capacity. Specifically, employees with high levels of integrative capacity have a stronger *paradoxical mindset*, in which they "value, accept, and feel comfortable with tensions" (Miron-Spektor et al., 2018, p. 27). These individuals are comfortable with and embrace tensions implied by paradoxical actions (Miron-Spektor et al., 2018). Consequently, we suggest that a paradoxical mindset supports individuals' ability to focus on the benefits of IPARA. Moreover, employees with high integrative capacity have higher *functional flexibility*, which describes the ability of individuals to adapt their behavior to the specific requirements of very different situations (Paulhus & Martin, 1988). Functional flexibility entails a broad repertoire of behavior, and, thus, individuals with high functional flexibility are able to engage in very different actions at work (Paulhus & Martin, 1988). We therefore expect individuals with high functional flexibility to be better able to engage in "opposing" age-related actions than individuals with low functional flexibility. Taken together, we propose that integrative capacity provides individuals with both the necessary behavioral repertoire and the ability to embrace tensions between opposing actions to yield high levels of IPARA.

> *Proposition 4:* There is a positive relationship between integrative capacity and IPARA.

Integration of Paradoxical Age-Related Actions and Work Outcomes

Having discussed the antecedents of IPARA, we now turn to its consequences. Specifically, we argue that high levels of IPARA predict increased levels of positive work outcomes, including job satisfaction, engagement, low levels of strain, and performance when age-related paradoxical work demands are high. In other words, we not only expect work demands to increase the likelihood that employees show high levels of IPARA (if they are able to) but also suggest that the benefits of IPARA are dependent on the level of these demands. Specifically, employees who show high IPARA are in a better position to meet these (age-related) paradoxical demands in their work and to contribute to important organizational goals, which, in turn, should benefit their satisfaction, engagement, and performance and reduce their job-related strain. For instance, research has shown that employees who simultaneously engage in exploration and exploitation activities achieve higher levels of innovative performance (Rosing & Zacher, 2017).

> *Proposition 5:* IPARA is positively related to favorable work outcomes (i.e., job satisfaction, job engagement, low job strain, job performance) when age-related paradoxical work demands are high but not when these demands are low.

Directions for Future Research

Implications for Theory Development

The IPARA model extends current thinking on successful aging at work (e.g., Kooij et al., 2020; Zacher, 2015), which has focused on specific age-related strengths, the role of individual and contextual resources and constraints in modulating development, and the role of self-regulation. Extending this work, we posit that to maintain high levels of favorable work outcomes with increasing age and, thus, to age successfully, employees need to integrate paradoxical age-related actions. Instead of relying only on specific age-related strengths, many modern workplaces require that employees not only employ their age-related strengths at work but also engage in opposite age-related actions to achieve high performance, satisfaction, and well-being. Future theorizing could integrate the IPARA model with different approaches to successful aging at work, including Zacher's (2015) comparative approach and Kooij's self-regulation approach.

The IPARA model does not focus on a specific age-related domain of functioning or experience—such as cognition or emotions—but rather on a higher-level integration of theorizing on age-related paradoxical demands and actions and the notion of age-related changes across the working lifespan. Accordingly, our taxonomy of age-related paradoxical work demands and actions serves mostly an illustrative purpose. While wide-ranging, we do not claim that the taxonomy is complete; additional paradoxical age-related actions can be added in the future and examined through the lens provided by our model. Moreover, future theorizing could focus on a single specific domain or attempt to develop a more comprehensive set of relevant paradoxical age-related work demands and actions. For example, it may be beneficial to further advance theory on how, why, and when employees integrate specific age-related actions within one domain (e.g., cognition). This may involve a closer consideration of temporal processes, such as sequences of opposing actions contingent on current work demands (Bledow et al., 2009). At the same time, the IPARA model currently does not propose interactions between different age-related actions across domains of functioning and experience. Future theorizing could explore how simultaneously integrating paradoxical age-related actions in some domains but not in others may differentially influence work outcomes. Similarly, IPARA might be more important for some of the domains listed in the taxonomy than for others, given specific work contexts. For example, the specific work context of a mathematician might not require high levels of IPARA in terms of cognition as it places predominantly high demands on fluid cognitive abilities, but it might require high levels of IPARA in terms of personality as the mathematician needs to develop both their own career and help and support others.

The IPARA model emphasizes age-related paradoxical work demands. However, employees are embedded in multiple layers of context, including their teams, organizations, and occupations, which also may change with employee age (Edwards & Shipp, 2007) (see also Chapter 9). Thus, extensions of the model could additionally focus on specific work demands and resources linked to teams, organizations, and occupations, as well as their respective fit with the individual employee (see also Kooij et al., 2020). Further theorizing is also needed with regard to the match between age-related domains of functioning and experience and work outcomes (see de Jonge & Dormann, 2006). For instance, it may be that paradoxical demands and actions linked to socioemotional experience have stronger effects on occupational strain and well-being than on performance. In contrast, paradoxical demands and actions related to motivation may have stronger effects on work-related performance.

Implications for Empirical Studies

The ideas presented in this conceptual development chapter should be followed up not only with theoretical refinements but also with empirical examinations of the IPARA construct and the model's propositions. First, an important step seems to be the development of a reliable and valid measure of IPARA. For instance, researchers could use survey scales or a situational judgment test format (Cabrera & Nguyen, 2001). One important route toward the development of such instruments might be behavioral observations of employees of different ages in a work setting (see Chapter 8). Second, the IPARA model and propositions could be investigated using experimental and longitudinal research designs (see Chapters 10 and 11). For example, research has shown that it is possible to experimentally manipulate elements of integrative capacity, such as paradoxical mindset, in order to enhance important employee outcomes, such as creativity (Miron-Spektor et al., 2011; Miron-Spektor et al., 2018). Similarly, researchers could experimentally manipulate integrative capacity to increase IPARA among younger and older employees and investigate effects on work outcomes. Longitudinal designs could be used to test the sequential mediation process proposed by our model. It seems necessary to examine the model with at least three measurement waves, as age is an exogenous variable that could be assessed at the same time as age-related individual differences, whereas IPARA and work outcomes should be separately measured at subsequent waves. In addition, it may be possible to examine the effects of IPARA using experience sampling studies, assuming that employees' engagement in IPARA may vary from day to day and, in turn, impact on daily fluctuations in work outcomes. Third, with regard to employee age, it is important to use representative samples with appropriate numbers of participants from different age groups (e.g., even numbers of younger, middle-aged, and older employees) and to operationalize age as a continuous variable instead of splitting it into age groups to avoid loss of statistical power (Bohlmann et al., 2018). In addition, it may be important to control for job and organizational tenure to rule out alternative explanations and to routinely test curvilinear associations between age and the other variables in the model, even though only the association between age and IPARA has been proposed to be curvilinear.

Conclusion

Previous theorizing and empirical research in the literature on work and aging has focused on the unique strengths of younger and older employees, such as greater capacity to learn new knowledge quickly or greater experience. In contrast, we argue that the integration of paradoxical age-related actions (IPARA) may be a more promising approach to achieve and maintain high levels of performance and well-being with increasing age, given the increasing paradoxical nature of work demands. We integrated research on paradoxes in organizations and the lifespan

developmental perspective to develop a model and associated research propositions, which can be tested in future empirical research. We hope that future theory
development and research efforts based on this model will contribute to a better
understanding of the role of age in the context of paradoxical work demands.

References

Adler, P. S., Goldoftas, B., & Levine, D. I. (1999). Flexibility vs. efficiency? A case study of
model changeovers in the Toyota Product System. *Organization Science, 10*(1), 43–68.
https://doi.org/10.1287/orsc.10.1.43

Agarwal, S., Driscoll, J. C., Gabaix, X., & Laibson, D. (2009). The age of reason: Financial
decisions over the life cycle and implications for regulation. *Brooking Papers on Economic
Activity, 2*(51), 51–117. https://doi.org/10.1353/eca.0.0067

Baltes, B. B., Rudolph, C. W., & Zacher, H. (Eds.). (2019). *Work across the lifespan.* Academic Press.

Baltes, P. B. (1987). Theoretical propositions of life-span developmental psychology: On
the dynamics between growth and decline. *Developmental Psychology, 23*(5), 611–626.

Baltes, P. B., & Baltes, M. M. (1990). Psychological perspectives on successful aging: The
model of selective optimization with compensation. In P. B. Baltes & M. M. Baltes
(Eds.), *Successful aging: Perspectives from the behavioral sciences* (pp. 1–34). Cambridge University Press. https://doi.org/10.1017/CBO9780511665684.003

Baltes, P. B., Staudinger, U. M., & Lindenberger, U. (1999). Lifespan psychology: Theory
and application to intellectual functioning. *Annual Review of Psychology, 50,* 471–507.
https://doi.org/10.1146/annurev.psych.50.1.471

Beier, M. E., & Ackerman, P. L. (2005). Age, ability, and the role of prior knowledge on the acquisition of new domain knowledge: Promising results in a real-
world learning environment. *Psychology and Aging, 20*(2), 341–355. https://doi.
org/10.1037/0882-7974.20.2.341

Benner, M. J., & Tushman, M. L. (2003). Exploitation, exploration, and process management: The productivity dilemma revisited. *Academy of Management Review, 28*(2),
238–256. https://doi.org/10.5465/amr.2003.9416096

Bledow, R., Frese, M., Anderson, N. R., Erez, M., & Farr, J. L. (2009). A dialectic perspective on innovation: Conflicting demands, multiple pathways, and ambidexterity.
Industrial and Organizational Psychology: Perspectives on Science and Practice, 2, 305–337.

Bohlmann, C., Rudolph, C. W., & Zacher, H. (2018). Methodological recommendations to move research on work and aging forward. *Work, Aging and Retirement, 4*(3),
225–237. https://doi.org/10.1093/workar/wax023

Brandtstädter, J., & Renner, G. (1990). Tenacious goal pursuit and flexible goal adjustment: Explication and age-related analysis of assimilative and accomodative strategies of
coping. *Psychology and Aging, 5*(1), 58–67. https://doi.org/10.1037/0882-7974.5.1.58

Brandtstädter, J., & Rothermund, K. (2002). The life-course dynamics of goal pursuit and
goal adjustment: A two-process framework. *Developmental Review, 22,* 117–150.

Cabrera, M. A. M., & Nguyen, N. T. (2001). Situational judgment tests: A review of
practice and constructs assessed. *International Journal of Selection and Assessment, 9*(1-2),
103–113.

Cañibano, A. (2019). Workplace flexibility as a paradoxical phenomenon: Exploring employee experiences. *Human Relations, 72*(2), 444–470 https://doi.org/
10.1177/0018726718769716

Carstensen, L. L., Isaacowitz, D. M., & Charles, S. T. (1999). Taking time seriously: A theory of socioemotional selectivity. *American Psychologist, 54*(3), 165–181. https://doi.org/10.1037/0003-066X.54.3.165

Charles, S. T. (2010). Strength and vulnerability integration: A model of emotional well-being across adulthood. *Psychological Bulletin, 136*(6), 1068–1091. https://doi.org/10.1037/a0021232

de Jonge, J., & Dormann, C. (2006). Stressors, resources, and strain at work: A longitudinal test of the triple-match principle. *Journal of Applied Psychology, 91*(5), 1359–1374.

Doerwald, F., Zacher, H., Scheibe, S., & van Yperen, N. W. (2021). Generativity at work: A meta-analysis. *Journal of Vocational Behavior, 125*, 103521. https://doi.org/10.1016/j.jvb.2020.103521

Ebner, N. C., Freund, A. M., & Baltes, P. B. (2006). Developmental changes in personal goal orientation from young to late adulthood: From striving for gains to maintenance and prevention of losses. *Psychology and Aging, 21*(4), 664–678. https://doi.org/10.1037/0882-7974.21.4.664

Edwards, J. R., & Shipp, A. J. (2007). The relationship between person-environment fit and outcomes: An integrative theoretical framework. In C. Ostroff & T. A. Judge (Eds.), *Perspectives on organizational fit* (pp. 209–258). Jossey-Bass.

Fisher, G. G., Chaffee, D. S., Tetrick, L. E., Davalos, D. B., & Potter, G. G. (2017). Cognitive functioning, aging, and work: A review and recommendations for research and practice. *Journal of Occupational Health Psychology, 22*(3), 314–336. https://doi.org/10.1037/ocp0000086

García-Sánchez, E., García-Morales, V. J., & Bolívar-Ramos, M. T. (2017). The influence of top management support for ICTs on organisational performance through knowledge acquisition, transfer, and utilisation. *Review of Managerial Science, 11*(1), 19–51. https://doi.org/10.1007/s11846-015-0179-3

Haase, C. M., Heckhausen, J., & Wrosch, C. (2013). Developmental regulation across the life span: Toward a new synthesis. *Developmental Psychology, 49*(5), 964–972. https://doi.org/10.1037/a0029231

Heckhausen, J., Wrosch, C., & Schulz, R. (2010). A motivational theory of life-span development. *Psychological Review, 117*(1), 32–60. https://doi.org/10.1037/a0017668

Kanfer, R., & Ackerman, P. L. (2004). Aging, adult development, and work motivation. *Academy of Management Review, 29*(3), 440–458. https://doi.org/10.5465/AMR.2004.13670969

Kauppila, O.-P., & Tempelaar, M. P. (2016). The social-cognitive underpinnings of employees' ambidextrous behaviour and the supportive role of group managers' leadership. *Journal of Management Studies, 53*(6), 1019–1044. https://doi.org/10.1111/joms.12192

Kearney, E., Shemla, M., van Knippenberg, D., & Scholz, F. A. (2019). A paradox perspective on the interactive effects of visionary and empowering leadership. *Organizational Behavior and Human Decision Processes, 155*, 20–30. https://doi.org/10.1016/j.obhdp.2019.01.001

Kooij, D. T. A. M., De Lange, A. H., Jansen, P. G. W., Kanfer, R., & Dikkers, J. S. E. (2011). Age and work-related motives: Results of a meta-analysis. *Journal of Organizational Behavior, 32*(2), 197–225. https://doi.org/10.1002/job.665

Kooij, D. T. A. M., Zacher, H., Wang, M., & Heckhausen, J. (2020). Successful aging at work: A process model to guide future research and practice. *Industrial and Organizational Psychology, 13*, 345–365. https://doi.org/10.1017/iop.2020.1

Leana, C. R., & Barry, B. (2000). Stability and change as simultaneous experiences in organizational life. *Academy of Management Review, 25*(4), 753–759. https://doi.org/10.5465/amr.2000.3707707

Lewis, M. W. (2000). Exploring paradox: Toward a more comprehensive guide. *Academy of Management Review, 25*(4), 760–776. https://doi.org/10.5465/AMR.2000.3707712

McAdams, D. P., & de St. Aubin, E. (1992). A theory of generativity and its assessment through self-report, behavioral acts, and narrative themes in autobiography. *Journal of Personality and Social Psychology, 62*(6), 1003–1015. https://doi.org/10.1037/0022-3514.62.6.1003

Meyer, R., Dalal, R. S., & Hermida, R. (2010). A review and synthesis of situational strength in the organizational sciences. *Journal of Management, 36*, 121–140. https://doi.org/10.1177/0149206309349309

Miron-Spektor, E., Gino, F., & Argote, L. (2011). Paradoxical frames and creative sparks: Enhancing individual creativity through conflict and integration. *Organizational Behavior and Human Decision Processes, 116*(2), 229–240.

Miron-Spektor, E., Ingram, A., Keller, J., Smith, W. K., & Lewis, M. W. (2018). Microfoundations of organizational paradox: The problem is how we think about the problem. *Academy of Management Journal, 61*(1), 26–45. https://doi.org/10.5465/amj.2016.0594

Ng, T. W. H., & Feldman, D. C. (2013). How do within-person changes due to aging affect job performance? *Journal of Vocational Behavior, 83*(3), 500–513. https://doi.org/10.1016/j.jvb.2013.07.007

Paulhus, D. L., & Martin, C. L. (1988). Functional flexibility: A new conception of interpersonal flexibility. *Journal of Personality and Social Psychology, 55*(1), 88–101.

Roberts, B. W., Walton, K. E., & Viechtbauer, W. (2006). Patterns of mean-level change in personality traits across the life course: A meta-analysis of longitudinal studies. *Psychological Bulletin, 132*(1), 1–25. https://doi.org/10.1037/0033-2909.132.1.1

Roberts, B. W., & Wood, D. (2006). Personality development in the context of the Neo-Socioanalytic Model of Personality. In D. K. Mroczek & T. D. Little (Eds.), *Handbook of personality development* (pp. 11–39). Lawrance Erlbaum & Associates.

Rosing, K., Bledow, R., Frese, M., Baytalskaya, N., Johnson, J. E., & Farr, J. L. (2018). The temporal pattern of creativity and implementation in teams. *Journal of Occupational and Organizational Psychology, 91*(4), 798–822. https://doi.org/10.1111/joop.12226

Rosing, K., & Zacher, H. (2017). Individual ambidexterity: The duality of exploration and exploitation and its relationship with innovative performance. *European Journal of Work and Organizational Psychology, 26*(5), 694–709. https://doi.org/10.1080/1359432X.2016.1238358

Rudolph, C. W. (2016). Lifespan developmental perspectives on working: A literature review of motivational theories. *Work, Aging and Retirement, 2*, 130–158. https://doi.org/10.1093/workar/waw012

Salthouse, T. A. (2012). Consequences of age-related cognitive declines. *Annual Review of Psychology, 63*, 201–226. https://doi.org/10.1146/annurev-psych-120710-100328

Schad, J., Lewis, M. W., Raisch, S., & Smith, W. K. (2016). Paradox research in management science: Looking back to move forward. *Academy of Management Annals, 10*(1), 5–64. https://doi.org/10.1080/19416520.2016.1162422

Shane, J., & Heckhausen, H. (2019). Motivational theory of lifespan development. In B. B. Baltes, C. W. Rudolph, & H. Zacher (Eds.), *Work across the lifespan* (pp. 111–134). Academic Press.

Shao, Y., Nijstad, B. A., & Täuber, S. (2019). Creativity under workload pressure and integrative complexity: The double-edged sword of paradoxical leadership. *Organizational Behavior and Human Decision Processes*, *155*, 7–19. https://doi.org/10.1016/j.obhdp.2019.01.008

Smith, W. K., & Lewis, M. W. (2011). Toward a theory of paradox: A dynamic equilibrium model of organizing. *Academy of Management Review*, *36*(2), 381–403.

Verhaeghen, P., & Salthouse, T. A. (1997). Meta-analyses of age-cognition relations in adulthood: Estimates of linear and nonlinear age effects and structural models. *Psychological Bulletin*, *122*(3), 231–249.

Waldman, D. A., Putnam, L. L., Miron-Spektor, E., & Siegel, D. (2019). The role of paradox theory in decision making and management research. *Organizational Behavior and Human Decision Processes*, *155*, 1–6. https://doi.org/10.1016/j.obhdp.2019.04.006

Zacher, H. (2015). Successful aging at work. *Work, Aging and Retirement*, *1*(1), 4–25. https://doi.org/10.1093/workar/wau006

Zhang, Y., Waldman, D. A., Han, Y. L., & Li, X. B. (2015). Paradoxical leader behaviors in people management: Antecedents and consequences. *Academy of Management Journal*, *58*(2), 538–566. https://doi.org/10.5465/amj.2012.0995

6

GENERATIONAL DIFFERENCES AND GENERATIONAL IDENTITY AT WORK

Sarah E. Salvi, Daniel M. Ravid and David P. Costanza

Generations are commonly defined by chronological age and contemporaneous period effects that supposedly interact to create cohorts of people sharing a set of common characteristics (Costanza et al., 2012). According to the Pew Research Center (2018), for the first time in history, there are five different generations working together in the workforce. It has been suggested that the presence of these generations has profound implications for individuals, organizations, and those who study them (Knight, 2014; Clark, 2017).

Before continuing, it is critical to note that empirical evidence does not back the existence of distinct generations as they have been identified by Pew and others. There are a number of conceptual and methodological issues that raise doubts about the existence of generations as they have been conceived. These concerns have been covered at great length in other pieces (e.g., Costanza & Finkelstein, 2015; Rudolph & Zacher, 2020), and we refer interested readers to those papers for a more thorough discussion of the issues. The conclusions of this research are that generations are essentially stereotyped social constructs, popular and appealing yet unsupported by research. Using them to make individual, policy, or organizational decisions is misguided at best and seriously problematic at worst (National Academies of Sciences, 2020).

Given these concerns, readers are cautioned to view the descriptions, characteristics, and even the generational labels themselves with a healthy dose of skepticism. Although this chapter will be discussing generational identity in the workplace, we believe that the use of generational labels and common stereotypes only propagates and further legitimizes the existence of generations. Because of this, we purposefully do not use common generational labels throughout this chapter, instead focusing on how to move past labels and stereotypes.

DOI: 10.4324/9781003089674-8

Having offered this caveat, it is nonetheless clear that many people think generations exist and believe that the characteristics ascribed to the various cohorts are accurate, meaningful, and, importantly, actionable. Thus, generational labels might best be compared to horoscopes (Rauvola et al., 2019) as they similarly provide a simple way for people to make sense of their own and others' behaviors. Like horoscopes, they also provide opportunities to identify with a group and differentiate one's group from others while not actually predicting or characterizing anyone's personality or behaviors.

Despite a lack of evidence for generations as a useful construct, academics continue to research generations, practitioners and consultants sell services and advice to organizations on how to deal with generations, and managers make decisions based on generational characteristics and stereotypes. This suggests that consideration of the origin of generational stereotypes, why they persist in the absence of evidence, what else besides generational membership might be causing the characteristics of interest, and what we can learn from these other explanations is, in and of itself, important to understand. In other words, generations do not exist, but many people think they do. Why? And what should we do about it in terms of the world of work? This chapter will address these questions and consider implications and alternatives when it comes to generations and the world of work.

Objectives of the Chapter

Despite all of the problems associated with generations, generational stereotypes remain fascinating to managers, academics, and the population in general. Given the dangers of using generational stereotypes, the enduring fascination with generations, and the existence of alternate and more plausible explanations, the purpose of this chapter is to first explore how and why generational stereotypes are of interest to researchers and practitioners, discuss issues associated with these stereotypes, and then review what we actually know about age (A) and period (P) effects relative to supposed cohort (C, aka generational) effects on work and work outcomes. We briefly review theory and research regarding age effects, period effects, and age by period effects. We conclude by discussing the theoretical and practical reasons we need to refocus generations research away from cohorts created by being a certain age in a certain period (i.e., cohorts created by an Age × Period interaction; being a certain age, in a certain period) and toward more plausible explanations and provide recommendations for practice and research in the future.

How Do Generational Stereotypes Form?

The media, popular press writers, and management consultants were quick to latch on to the prevalence of multiple generations living and working together at the same time. As far back as the 1950s, numerous outlets wrote stories that engaged their readers by reviewing and seeming to confirm many of the biases associated with generational stereotypes. Common stereotypes characterize older generations as being conservative and disciplined (Strauss & Howe, 1991) and younger generations as socially conscious but narcissistic (Twenge et al., 2010), skeptical, and individualistic (Twenge et al., 2010). It is hard to determine whether the media began the fascination with generations and society followed or the reverse, with media reflecting societal trends and reinforcing the stereotypes. Either way, the cycle continued in a self-fulfilling manner until generational characteristics and differences became commonly accepted stereotypes.

Despite the labels and stereotypical characteristics, a consensus is emerging that, instead of being thought of as discrete, age-delimited cohorts, generations are better described as social constructions. The social constructionist perspective proposes that there are two self-reinforcing social processes that contribute to the construction of generations: Pervasive knowledge and beliefs about generational characteristics are formed and popularized, which in turn lead to socially sanctioned generational stereotypes (Rudolph & Zacher, 2015). There are several additional characteristics of the social constructionist perspective on generations that are relevant to the formation of generations.

Specifically, this approach proposes that: (1) generations are social constructs that are "willed into being," (2) generations serve an individual and societal sensemaking function, and (3) the social construction and sensemaking aspects explain the ubiquity and persistence of beliefs about generations. These processes contribute to the social construction of generations as distinct cohorts despite a lack of clear delineation among them. Because human development and aging are complex multidimensional processes, people may be more likely to create and accept constructs such as generations as they offer a simplistic, concrete explanation for the stereotyped characteristics.

Why Do Generational Stereotypes Persist?

Stereotypes regarding generations and the differences among them have similarities to those attached to gender, race, or culture in terms of formation, reinforcement, and persistence. Taking a social-cognitive perspective to stereotype persistence, human survival may depend on quick and efficient judgments that influence subsequent perceiver actions (Bodenhausen & Hugenberg, 2009). This sometimes overly efficient process acts as a heuristic—or a cognitive shortcut—that people use to make quick judgments that are not necessarily based on rational or conscious thought (Bodenhausen & Hugenberg, 2009). Once someone adopts stereotypes about a group of people, it can be difficult to override this heuristic shortcut. One difficulty with challenging stereotypes is that people tend to notice aspects that are consistent with their schema and ignore or make exceptions for characteristics or behaviors that do not align with the stereotype (Queller &

Smith, 2002). Hence, information that could disabuse the stereotyper of their expectations is missed, ignored, or rejected.

An example of this process in a generational context: Assume a younger applicant's resume shows multiple jobs within the past two years. Because a common, although inaccurate, stereotype of younger generations is that they job hop more than older generations (e.g., Waikar et al., 2016), the employer may use the stereotype and assume they possess other negative traits such as narcissism, laziness, and a lack of commitment. This in turn might lead to a poor decision based on societally reinforced heuristics rather than on actual applicant characteristics. In reality, there may be many other explanations for changing jobs, and it goes without saying that displaying one common stereotypical characteristic does not mean that other common stereotypical characteristics apply.

What Are the Effects of Using Stereotypes to Make Decisions?

Beyond heuristic errors, adhering to generational stereotypes may cause problems for organizations. First, using generational stereotypes can hinder performance of individuals and the organization. Generalizing characteristics to a large group of people can demotivate individual employees who feel that their leadership has already developed a schema of who they are and how they work. Taking from the previous example, a young employee who feels stereotyped as narcissistic or lazy may not be motivated to increase performance if they think their boss will still see them through a stereotyped lens. This idea has been explored and supported in research on age-based stereotype threat. When people are faced specifically with stereotype-based rather than fact-based manipulations, they tend to underperform on multiple cognitive and physical tasks (Lamont et al., 2015). Specifically, regarding the workplace, age-based stereotype threat has been associated with lower engagement, adjustment, organizational involvement, and flourishing (Manzi et al., 2019).

Second, generational stereotypes can lead to ineffective and unfair HR decisions and policies. When it comes to support and reinforcement from managers, making group-based (i.e., generational) decisions and assuming those decisions will affect all individuals of that group similarly will lead to incorrect assumptions and suboptimal practices and policies. A company utilizing different recruitment policies, feedback systems, or retention strategies based on group-based stereotypes, such as gender or race, would be viewed as impractical and nonsensical. Doing the same for generational groups should be viewed as equally problematic. Managers should recognize strengths and weaknesses of individuals rather than assuming strengths and weaknesses based on generational stereotypes.

Lastly, using generations and generational stereotypes can place organizations at legal risk. The Age Discrimination in Employment Act of 1967 (90–202 [S. 830] (29 U.S.C., Chapter 14) protects workers aged 40 and over from differential treatment based on age. That means that everyone born before 1980, approximately 60% of the workforce and including the oldest members of a generational cohort typically assumed to be "young," falls under ADEA. The European Union has similar legislation (Directive 2000/78/EC) that prohibits employment discrimination based on disability, sexual orientation, religion, or age (Lahey, 2010). Consequently, an organization using generational stereotypes to guide human resource policies or procedures is at risk of legal challenge from much of their workforce.

Although generations are stereotyped social constructs lacking scientific validity, the components of generations, age and period, have been researched extensively, and important relationships have been found. Next, we briefly review what we know about age and period effects in relation to work and work outcomes.

Age Effects

When discussing age effects, we focus on chronological age, defined as the amount of time passed since birth (Bohlmann et al., 2018). Researchers have drawn on chronological age to predict a number of work outcomes, including work attitudes (Kooij et al., 2010; Ng & Feldman, 2010), responses to conflict (Davis et al., 2009), positive and negative affect (Scheibe et al., 2018), technology use, work motivation, job satisfaction (Elias et al., 2012), job performance (Ng & Feldman, 2008), and career adaptability (Zacher & Griffin, 2015). (See Chapter 1 for an in-depth summary of research on age and work outcomes.) Although chronological age is a component of generation conceptualizations, it is a separate and distinct construct, with its own body of literature in regard to work outcomes.

Age Research is Based in Testable Theory

In the past, age was typically used as a demographic or control variable, but as age research "aged," it developed into a substantive area of its own, drawing from sound, testable theories (Rhodes, 1983; Rudolph et al., 2020; Bohlmann et al., 2018). That said, chronological age is rarely the direct cause of psychosocial workplace variables it predicts (e.g., ability, experience, motivation), and as such has been criticized as an "empty" variable (Bohlmann et al., 2018). However, age holds value, both as a key part of other theories and as a measure of the passage of time necessary for studying longer-term changes in outcomes.

Alternative conceptualizations of age have been proposed and studied to address the "emptiness" of chronological age (Kooij et al., 2008; Schwall, 2012). For example, researchers have proposed functional age (cognitive/physical abilities), psychosocial age (self and social perception of age), and organizational age (career stage) (Kooij et al., 2008) as more meaningful age-related constructs. The most common approaches used to guide age research, though, are lifespan developmental theories (P. B. Baltes, 1987; Zacher et al., 2019). The general framework for lifespan development theories is guided by the principle that human development is a flexible, continuous process that is individually based and lifelong (Rudolph, 2016; P. B. Baltes, 1987).

Researchers have used lifespan development as an umbrella theory to advance more specific models and perspectives. Some examples include the resource approach, the model of selective optimization and compensation, a motivational theory of lifespan development, and the model of assimilative and accommodative coping (for a review of these theories, see Rudolph & Zacher, 2017, and also Chapter 7 of this book). More recently, researchers have turned to looking at age through a social identity approach, which proposes that individuals socially identify with certain age groups (i.e., I am a young employee) and allow this to influence affect, behavior, cognition, and motivation (Zacher et al., 2019; Hornsey, 2008).

Statistical Advantages of Age

One major difference between age and generational cohorts as variables is that age is continuous and generational cohorts are categorical. There is more precision in using the continuous variable of age rather than some small set of generational cohorts (Bohlmann et al., 2018). Age can capture subtle effects, like work experience differences, between those just a few years apart in age, while generational cohorts might lump them together into the same group. Regardless of the purpose of the study, using a continuous variable (age) to represent a continuous phenomenon (change over time) is both statistically and conceptually more sound.

In terms of analyzing differences, using age in research is straightforward while generations are impossible to analyze. Age, period, and cohort effects are statistically inseparable, and the use of different analytical techniques to study generations provides different results and conclusions even when using the same data sets (Costanza et al., 2017). Most analytical techniques used in generations research control for one variable and confound the other two. For example, cross-sectional studies control for period but confound age and cohort. Thus, when effects are observed, it is impossible to know whether they are generational effects or if any differences that are found are attributable to age, period, or some combination (Costanza et al., 2017).

Although it is apparent that age is an important variable to consider, it is not the only time-related variable that plays a role in people's identities in the workplace. Contemporaneous period effects are also important to consider on their own, as events that are happening at a certain period in time likely have an impact on organizational and workplace outcomes.

Period Effects

Period effects refer to significant historical or cultural events that impact those who experience them. The general definition of generations is a group of similar-aged people experiencing the same events at critical, developmental life stages (Costanza et al., 2012). For instance, some suggest that people who grew up during the Great Depression had hard work and frugality instilled in them. Similar claims about recent generations include that growing up with advancements in hand-held technologies and helicopter parents have resulted in a socially conscious but narcissistic generation (Costanza & Finkelstein, 2015; Strauss & Howe, 1991; see Costanza et al., 2021, for evidence refuting this particular claim).

First, it is important to be able to define period as a meaningful variable in order to further research that intends to use it. Period effects are usually measured by year of data collection, which, similar to chronological age as a variable, has been criticized for characterizing an empty or meaningless variable (Rudolph & Zacher, 2017). Period effects refer to historical and cultural events that occurred at the point of time in question, and research being conducted should have a theory as to why a certain experience at a specific period of time (e.g., war, natural disaster, revolution) would result in the hypothesized outcome. Developed theory as to why a defining event results in specific outcomes helps to combat the "emptiness" commonly attributed to using time as a proxy measure.

There is little question that period effects are important, but the way that generations are conceptualized makes the faulty assumption that period effects only impact a single group in time. Did the Great Depression only affect those in their childhood and adolescence? Is it only young people today who are glued to their phones? These historical, cultural, and social events affect everyone who experiences them. The idea that period effects create generational cohorts absurdly assumes that such effects only create identities for those who do not yet have them.

Research exploring contemporaneous period effects shows that critical events (economic conditions, natural disasters, war) do have effects on important work outcomes. From 2004–2005, six major hurricanes devastated the south of the United States causing thousands of casualties, economic problems, property damage, and loss of resources. Hochwarter et al. (2007) studied the effects these hurricanes had and found that stress resulting from the hurricanes was significantly related to higher job tension and contributed to lower job satisfaction. Additionally, Reade and Lee (2011) found that, in times of war, sensitivity to the ethnopolitical conflict was significantly related to decreased organizational commitment.

To further illustrate this point, media reports and academic papers are already claiming that COVID-19 will be the defining event for the next generation, with names such as Generation C, Coronials, and the Quaranteens (Yancey-Bragg, 2020). This occurs despite the complete lack of evidence or reason to expect that there will be a COVID-19 generation (Rudolph & Zacher, 2020). This mentality is attempting to create new cohort identities, but the pandemic is not just affecting younger people. Almost every person experienced increasing unemployment, economic downturn, stress, and decreases in hope for the future, and these will likely impact everyone in some way, not just those in key developmental stages.

The difference between studying generations and studying period effects is that generations assume that critical events impact people of a certain age range, creating lasting cohorts with similar personality traits, attitudes, and values, whereas research on period effects examines how events affect *everyone experiencing them*. This is not to say that everyone experiences these events in the same way, and people do not react and process the information exactly the same. This is why the age by period interaction is still potentially important to understand.

Interactions with Age

Because age has been shown to be a meaningful variable for work-related outcomes, it is reasonable to expect that it also interacts with other relevant variables. The Age × Period interaction is part of the conceptualization of generations, but we argue that the interaction does not lead to lasting cohort effects for one specific age group as generation theory would suggest. Rather, those of all ages will experience period effects, but the perception of the period and reaction to it may differ between different age groups or life stages in that moment in time.

Age × Period

Although it is reasonable to say that almost everyone who experiences global events may have shared experiences, it is not reasonable to say that they processed or reacted to them in a similar way. The age by period interaction is one way to demonstrate that people of certain ages may perceive contemporaneous period effects differently than those of other ages. P. B. Baltes and colleagues (1980) outlined this possibility, theorizing that period influences may be particularly strong for those in adolescence and young adulthood. They also discuss, though, that these effects that we typically characterize as "cohort" effects (period effects creating lasting generational cohorts) do not only occur in a specific age group but rather in all age groups who experience them (P. B. Baltes et al., 1980). While this may seem as though Baltes and colleagues support generations theory, it is important to note that they recognize that age and period interact and affect *all age groups* who experience them. This example highlights that those in adolescence and young adulthood might experience period effects differently than other ages, but there is still no argument for these differences creating *lasting cohort effects* as generations theory would suggest.

As Costanza et al. (2017) explain, different outcomes based on age and period interactions cannot be used to define a generational cohort, as the differences found could be due to either the age of respondents at that point in time or the specific time period in which the data was collected. There is no evidence, though, that these differences actually create lasting effects on that "cohort," and we might really be seeing temporal effects that affect varying ages differently at that particular moment in time.

Reevaluating Generations Research and Recommendations for the Future

Because of all the problems associated with studying generational differences discussed previously, it makes sense to move away from focusing on whether generations exist and instead to turn toward studying the different conceptualizations of age and interactions with other important factors that may explain more variance in work-related outcomes than generations would. As we regrettably do not anticipate the idea of generations going away anytime soon, we go into detail as to how generations can be conceptualized and studied differently in the future, along with other variables that may provide more information and explanation for phenomena previously attributed to generational differences.

It is clear that the manner by which generations are currently conceptualized and studied must be reevaluated. The current age-period-cohort (APC) conceptualization of generations is neither supported by theory nor evidence. Given these serious concerns, we echo the recent recommendations by Rudolph and Zacher (2017) and Rudolph et al. (2020) calling for "a moratorium on time-based operationalizations of generations as units for understanding complex dynamics in organizational behavior" (p. 125). In the following sections, we offer several alternative avenues and recommendations for understanding and thinking about generations and generational differences.

Viewing Generations as a Social Construct

Despite the lack of evidence for the existence of distinct generational cohorts or meaningful generational differences, people believe that generations are real, and to this extent, generations *are* real insomuch as such constructions are reflexive of our attempts to "build out" our social realities (Berger & Luckmann, 1991). Well studied are the ways that stereotypes and situational expectations affect subsequent perceptions, cognitions, attitudes, and behaviors (e.g., Hogan, 1987; Spencer et al., 2016; Rosenhan, 1973). The idea of generations as a useful tool for understanding individuals has been widely promulgated by the popular press, industry advisors and gurus, and some groups of academics (for a critical review, see Rudolph et al., 2020). Although there is little value in further research aimed at identifying generationally based differences (i.e., differences caused by Age × Period interactions that create lasting cohorts), there is indeed value in research aimed at better understanding the emergence, ubiquity, and social acceptance of shared assumptions about generational differences and the effects of these assumptions on individuals.

The social constructionist approach offers a viable alternative to traditional approaches to studying generations. This perspective focuses on understanding the nature of the shared assumptions that people hold about reality through understanding the ways in which meanings develop in coordination with others and how such meanings are attached to lived experiences, social structures, and entities (Leeds-Hurwitz, 2009). According to this approach, generations exist and persist because they offer individuals a way to make sense of the complex, multi-directional, multidimensional process of human development, especially within the context of rapidly changing societies. In this way, generations can be viewed as "willed" into being (Rudolph et al., 2020).

Taking a social constructionist approach to generations research means a transition from research aimed at identifying generational differences toward research focused on understanding why social constructions emerge and the consequences of such constructions (e.g., self-fulfilling prophecies). For instance, Lyons et al. (2019) developed a dynamic social-ecological model of generational identity that takes into account how different levels of environmental influences individually and interactionally may explain the manifestation of generational identity in the workplace. North and Shakeri (2019) proposed the generation, age, tenure, and education (GATE) model, which suggests that generational identity is an important component that shapes one's subjective age. Recent empirical work supports the idea that generations as social constructs have meaningful effects on how individuals perceive themselves and others. For instance, recent work has found that individuals simultaneously categorize themselves and others based on age *and* based on generation and hold differing views of these two social identities (Weiss & Zhang, 2020; see also Chapter 3 herein).

As Rudolph and colleagues (2020) note, the social constructionist perspective is less about gathering evidence against the null hypothesis that generational differences do not exist and

> more about understanding, phenomenologically, the various processes that give rise to people's subjective construction of generations, the systems that facilitate attaching meaning to generational labels, and the structures that support our continued reliance on generations as a sensemaking tool in spite of logical and empirical arguments against doing so.
>
> *(p. 17)*

Thus, researchers who take a social constructionist perspective to the study of generations are able to approach generations as a meaningful social construct with measurable effects without relying on broad generalizations or stereotypes about the ways that generational membership influences individual-level attitudes, values, and behaviors.

The Lifespan Development Approach

The lifespan development approach (P. B. Baltes, 1987) focuses on continuous developmental trajectories in multiple domains and has been applied to age-related differences and changes in work contexts (Rudolph et al., 2020; see also

Chapter 7). According to the lifespan perspective, aging is a multidimensional and multidirectional process that is accompanied by individual and contextual developments over time (i.e., increases, decreases, maintenance, nonlinear changes), which, in turn, influence a person's experiences and behaviors. P. B. Baltes (1987) outlined seven principles to guide thinking about human development from a lifespan perspective. More specially, human development is (1) a lifelong process that involves (2) stability, multidimensional changes, and (3) gains and losses in experience and functioning. Additionally, human development is (4) modifiable at any point in one's life and (5) embedded within social, cultural, and historical context, (6) determined by both normative and nonnormative age and history-graded contexts, and (7) best studied through an interdisciplinary lens.

With respect to how the lifespan approach is relevant to generational research, it does take into account both historical and sociocultural impacts on individuals (Rudolph & Zacher, 2017). Rather than impacting a cohort of people similarly, though, the lifespan approach focuses solely on the individual level. It defines period effects as "normative," in that a group of people can experience the same historical events, but it does not go further to say that these experiences create group-level or collective experiences that then define a specific cohort of people. These events can affect all individuals who experience them, but not necessarily in the same ways as to create a lasting cohort. Experiences can instead interact with both age-graded and nonnormative factors (Rudolph & Zacher, 2017). Rudolph and Zacher (2017) provide specific propositions of generational research from a lifespan development approach along with specific ways this theory could be tested in future studies. They go on to define period effects in terms of intraindividual changes (within-person changes over time) and cohort effects as interindividual differences.

Exploration of Period Effects: Trend Creation, Acceleration, and Reversal

Strauss and Howe (1991) describe generations in terms of "age location" or experiencing epochal, significant events during youth and young adulthood, producing a set of collective behaviors, traits, and attitudes, or cohort effects. Although there is no actual evidence that epochal events spur the formation of distinct generations, macrolevel events and trends certainly have the potential to affect the attitudes and behaviors of working individuals of all ages. The 9/11 attacks, for example, spurred a period of heightened patriotism and national identification in the United States (Li & Brewer, 2004). Evidence suggests that economic conditions affect a host of work-related attitudes and behaviors (e.g., turnover intentions, job search behaviors; Harter et al., 2020; Manroop & Richardson, 2015; Hulin & Judge, 2003), and trends in technology and microcomputing have altered the way that individuals of all ages engage with and perform their work. Importantly, distinct from traditional generations research, there is no assumption that a given epochal event will have any permanent effect on individuals or that an individual's age is particularly likely to interact with these period effects, especially once more meaningful individual differences (e.g., socioeconomic status, career stage) are accounted for.

Although there is little evidence for Strauss and Howe's (1991) conceptualization of repetitive cycles of dominant and recessive generations, an interesting avenue for future research involves the investigation of cycles of trend-creating, trend-accelerating, and trend-reversing epochal events. In the context of work, trend-creating events are those epochal events that spur novel work-related trends; trend-accelerating events are those epochal events that accelerate work-related trends that were already occurring; and trend-reversing events are those epochal events that halt or reverse a work-related trend. To illustrate such a cycle of events, one can look to legislation designed to curtail workplace discrimination and promote workplace diversity enacted in the second half of the twentieth century in the United States.

Coming on the heels of the Civil Rights movement and a time when overt discrimination and segregated workforces were a norm, the Civil Rights Act of 1964 (CRA 1964) began a trend in federal legislation geared toward prohibiting discriminatory practices and increasing diversity within organizations. In the decades following CRA 1964, a number of notable legislative pieces (e.g., the Age Discrimination in Employment Act, 1969; the Rehabilitation Act of 1973; the Pregnancy Discrimination Act of 1978; the Americans with Disabilities Act of 1990) and precedent-setting court cases (e.g., Regents of the University of California v Bakke, 1978; United Steel Workers of America v Weber, 1979; Sheet Metal Workers' International Association v EEOC, 1986) accelerated this trend. Finally, the Civil Rights Act of 1991 (CRA 1991) might be viewed as a trend-reversing or trend-halting epochal event. Although CRA 1991 expanded aspects of the CRA, it also banned practices such as race norming, score adjustments, differential cutoffs, or other workplace practices used to ensure that workplaces had a minimum number of minority employees. Some studies have suggested that employers with greater susceptibility to employment discrimination litigation may have decreased their hiring of protected workers in response to the passage of the legislation (Fink, 2008).

Exploring epochal trends (as opposed to generations) as dynamic and cyclical may be a valuable way to apply a systems perspective (Katz & Kahn, 1978) to period effects. That is, there is value in exploring the way that epochal events may spur cycles of work trends that differentiate individuals across time. In doing so, researchers can steer away from simplistic APC explanations for why individuals today differ from those of the past and toward a more sophisticated understanding of how systems of people, organizations, and environments are continuously shaping and being shaped by one another.

The broad mandate for industrial and organizational psychologists is to find ways to increase the fit between the workforce and the workplace among a backdrop in which the composition of both workers and work are constantly changing (Muchinsky & Howes, 2019). There is no evidence that relying on stereotypes about broad swaths of individuals grouped by birth year contributes to this mission in any way.

Conclusion

There is no dispute that values, attitudes, and preferences of people today differ from those of the past. It is also true that people change over the course of their lifespan and that these changes occur within and in response to broader environmental, geopolitical, social, economic, technological, and organizational shifts, both sudden and gradual. Effective human resource management includes monitoring all of these changes and tailoring policies and practices best to accommodate the individual and collective needs of workers. However, as discussed in this chapter, there is no evidence that any of these changes are attributable to generational effects or that generations as currently conceptualized have any functional utility in research or practice.

References

Baltes, P. B. (1987). Theoretical propositions of life-span developmental psychology: On the dynamics between growth and decline. *Developmental Psychology, 23*(5), 611–626. https://doi.org/10.1037/0012-1649.23.5.611

Baltes, P. B., Reese, H. W., & Lipsitt, L. P. (1980). Life-span developmental psychology, *Annual Review of Psychology, 31,* 65–110. https://doi.org/10.1146/annurev.ps.31.020180.000433

Berger, P. L., & Luckmann, T. (1991). *The social construction of reality: A treatise in the sociology of knowledge.* Penguin UK.

Bodenhausen, G. V., & Hugenberg, K. (2009). Attention, perception, and social cognition. In F. Strack & J. Forster (Eds.), *Social cognition: The basis of human interaction* (pp. 1–22). Psychology Press.

Bohlmann, C., Rudolph, C. W., & Zacher, H. (2018). Methodological recommendations to move research on work and aging forward. *Work, Aging, and Retirement, 4*(3), 225–237. https://doi.org/10.1093/workar/wax023

Clark, K. R. (2017). Managing multiple generations in the workplace. *Radiologic Technology, 88*(4), 379–398.

Costanza, D. P., Badger, J. M., Fraser, R. L., Severt, J. B., & Gade, P. A. (2012). Generational differences in work-related attitudes: A meta-analysis. *Journal of Business and Psychology, 27*(4), 375–394. https://doi.org/10.1007/s10869-012-9259-4

Costanza, D. P., Darrow, J. B., Yost, A. B., & Severt, J. B. (2017). A review of analytical methods used to study generational differences: Strengths and limitations. *Work, Aging, and Retirement, 3*(2), 149–165. https://doi.org/10.1093/workar/wax002

Costanza, D. P., & Finkelstein, L. (2015). Generationally based differences in the workplace: Is there a there there? *Industrial and Organizational Psychology, 8*(3), 1–16. https://doi.org/10.1017/iop.2015.15

Costanza, D. P., Ravid, D. M., & Slaughter, A. (2021). A distributional approach to identifying generational differences: What do you mean they vary? *Journal of Vocational Behavior*. https://doi.org/10.31234/osf.io/kzcmg

Davis, M. H., Kraus, L. A., & Capobianco, S. (2009). Age differences in response to conflict in the workplace. *International Journal of Aging and Human Development, 68*(4), 339–355. https://doi.org/10.2190/AG.68.4.d

Elias, S. M., Smith, W. L., & Barney, C. E. (2012). Age as a moderator of attitude towards technology in the workplace: Work motivation and overall job satisfaction. *Behaviour & Information Technology, 31*(5), 453–467. https://doi.org/10.1080/01449 29X.2010.513419

Fink, J. (2008). Unintended consequences: How antidiscrimination litigation increases group bias in employer-defendants. *New Mexico Law Review, 38*(2), 333–372.

Fry, R. (2018, April 11). *Millennials are the largest generation in the U.S. labor force.* Pew Research Center. www.pewresearch.org/fact-tank/2018/04/11/millennials-largest-generation-us-labor-force/

Harter, J. K., Schmidt, F. L., Agrawal, S., Plowman, S. K., & Blue, A. T. (2020). Increased business value for positive job attitudes during economic recessions: A meta-analysis and SEM analysis. *Human Performance, 33*, 307–330. https://doi.org/10.1080/08959 285.2020.1758702

Hochwarter, W. A., Laird, M. D., & Brouer, R. L. (2007). Board up the windows: The interactive effects of hurricane-induced job stress and perceived resources on work outcomes. *Journal of Management, 34*(2), 263–289. https://doi.org/10.1177/0149206307309264

Hogan, E. A. (1987). Effects of prior expectations on performance ratings: A longitudinal study. *Academy of Management Journal, 30*(2), 354–368. https://doi.org/10.5465/256279

Hornsey, M. J. (2008). Social identity theory and self-categorization theory: A historical review. *Social and Personality Psychology Compass, 2*(1), 204–222. https://doi.org/10.1111/j.1751-9004.2007.00066.x

Hulin, C. L., & Judge, T. A. (2003). Job attitudes. In W. C. Borman, D. R. Ilgen, & R. J. Klimoski (Eds.), *Handbook of psychology: Industrial and organizational psychology* (Vol. 12, pp. 255–276). John Wiley & Sons Inc.

Katz, D., & Kahn, R. L. (1978). *The social psychology of organizations.* John Wiley & Sons.

Knight, R. (2014, September 25). *Managing people from 5 generations.* Harvard Business Review Digital Articles. https://hbr.org/2014/09/managing-people-from-5-generations

Kooij, D., de Lange, A., Jansen, P., & Dikkers, J. (2008). Older workers motivation to continue to work: Five meanings of age: A conceptual review. *Journal of Managerial Psychology, 24*(4), 364–394. https://doi.org/10.1108/02683940810869015

Kooij, D., Jansen, P., Dikkers, J., & de Lange, A. (2010). The influence of age on the associations between HR practices and both affective commitment and job satisfaction: A meta-analysis. *Journal of Organizational Behavior, 31*(8), 1111–1136. https://doi.org/10.1002/job.666

Lahey, J. N. (2010). International comparison of age discrimination laws. *Research on Aging, 32*(6), 679–697. https://doi.org/10.1177/0164027510379348

Lamont, R. A., Swift, H. J., & Abrams, D. (2015). A review and meta-analysis of age-based stereotype threat: Negative stereotypes, not facts, do the damage. *Psychology and Aging, 30*(1), 180–193. https://doi.org/10.1037/a0038586

Leeds-Hurwitz, W. (2009). Social construction of reality. In S. W. Littlejohn & K. A. Foss (Eds.), *Encyclopedia of communication theory* (pp. 892–895). Sage Publications.

Li, Q., & Brewer, M. B. (2004). What does it mean to be an American? Patriotism, nationalism, and American identity after 9/11. *Political Psychology, 25*(5), 727–739. https://doi.org/10.1111/j.1467-9221.2004.00395.x

Lyons, S. T., Schweitzer, L., Urick, M. J., & Kuron, L. (2019). A dynamic social-ecological model of generational identity in the workplace. *Journal of Intergenerational Relationships, 17*(1), 1–24. https://doi.org/10.1080/15350770.2018.1500332

Manroop, L., & Richardson, J. (2015). Job search: A multidisciplinary review and research agenda. *International Journal of Management Reviews, 18*(2), 206–227. https://doi.org/10.1111/ijmr.12066

Manzi, C., Paderi, F., Benet-Martínez, V., & Coen, S. (2019). Age-based stereotype threat and negative outcomes in the workplace: Exploring the role of identity integration. *European Journal of Social Psychology, 49*(4), 705–716. https://doi.org/10.1002/ejsp.2533

Muchinsky, P. M., & Howes, S. S. (2019). *Psychology applied to work: An introduction to industrial and organizational psychology* (12th ed.). Hypergraphic Press.

National Academies of Sciences, Engineering, and Medicine. (2020). *Are generational categories meaningful distinctions for workplace management?* The National Academies Press.

Ng, T. W. H., & Feldman, D. C. (2008). The relationship of age to ten dimensions of job performance. *Journal of Applied Psychology, 93*(2), 392–423. https://doi.org/10.1037/0021-9010.93.2.392

Ng, T. W. H., & Feldman, D. C. (2010). The relationship of age with job attitudes: A meta-analysis. *Personnel Psychology, 63*(3), 677–718. https://doi.org/10.1111/j.1744-6570.2010.01184.x

North, M. S., & Shakeri, A. (2019). Workplace subjective age multidimensionality: Generation, age, tenure, experience (GATE). *Work, Aging and Retirement, 5*(4), 281–286. https://doi.org/10.1093/workar/waz020

Queller, S., & Smith, E. R. (2002). Subtyping versus bookkeeping in stereotype learning and change: Connectionist stimulations and empirical findings. *Journal of Personality and Social Psychology, 82*(3), 300–313. https://doi.org/10.1037/0022-3514.82.3.300

Rauvola, R. S., Rudolph, C. W., & Zacher, H. (2019). Generationalism: Problems and implications. *Organizational Dynamics, 48*(4), 100664. https://doi.org/10.1016/j.orgdyn.2018.05.006

Reade, C., & Lee, H. (2012). Organizational commitment in time of war: Assessing the impact and attenuation of employee sensitivity to ethnopolitical conflict. *Journal of International Management, 18*(1), 85–101. https://doi.org/10.1016/j.intman.2011.09.002

Rhodes, S. R. (1983). Age-related differences in work attitudes and behavior: A review and conceptual analysis. *Psychological Bulletin, 93*(2), 328–367. https://doi.org/10.1037/0033-2909.93.2.328

Rosenhan, D. L. (1973). On being sane in insane places. *Science, 179*(4070), 250–258. https://doi.org/10.1126/science.179.4070.250

Rudolph, C. W. (2016). Lifespan developmental perspectives on working: A literature review of motivational theories. *Work, Aging, and Retirement, 2*(2), 130–158. https://doi.org/10.1093/workar/waw012

Rudolph, C. W., Allan, B., Clark, M., Hertel, G., Hirschi, A., Kunze, F., & Zacher, H. (2020). Pandemics: Implications for research and practice in industrial and organizational psychology [Special Issue]. *Industrial and Organizational Psychology: Perspectives on Science and Practice, 14*(1–2). https://doi.org/10.1017/iop.2020.48

Rudolph, C. W., Rauvola, R. S., Costanza, D. P., & Zacher, H. (2020). Generations and generational differences: Debunking myths in organizational science and practice. *Journal of Business and Psychology*, 1–23. https://doi.org/10.1007/s10869-020-09715-2

Rudolph, C. W., & Zacher, H. (2015). Intergenerational perceptions and conflicts in multi-age and multigenerational work environments. In L. M. Finkelstein, D. M. Truxillo, F. Fraccaroli, & R. Kanfer (Eds.), *SIOP organizational frontiers series: Facing the challenges of a multi-age workforce: A use-inspired approach* (pp. 253–282). Routledge/Taylor & Francis Group.

Rudolph, C. W., & Zacher, H. (2017). Considering generations from a lifespan developmental perspective. *Work, Aging, and Retirement*, 3(2), 113–129. https://doi.org/10.1093/workar/waw019

Rudolph, C. W., & Zacher, H. (2020). "The COVID-19 generation": A cautionary note. *Work, Aging, and Retirement*, 6(3), 139–145. https://doi.org/10.1093/workar/waaa009

Scheibe, S., Yeung, D. Y., & Doerwald, F. (2018). Age-related differences in levels and dynamics of workplace affect. *Psychology and Aging*, 34(1), 106–123. https://doi.org/10.1037/pag0000305

Schwall, A. R. (2012). Defining age, and using age-relevant constructs. In J. W. Hedge & W. C. Borman (Eds.), *Oxford library of psychology: The Oxford handbook of work and aging* (pp. 169–186). Oxford University Press.

Spencer, S. J., Logel, C., & Davies, P. G. (2016). Stereotype threat. *Annual Review of Psychology*, 67, 415–437. https://doi.org/10.1146/annurev-psych-073115-103235

Strauss, W., & Howe, N. (1991). *Generations: The history of America's future, 1584–2069*. William Morrow.

Twenge, J. M., Campbell, S. M., Hoffman, B. J., & Lance, C. E. (2010). Generational differences in work values: Leisure and extrinsic values increasing, social and intrinsic values decreasing. *Journal of Management*, 36(5), 1117–1142. https://doi.org/10.1177/0149206309352246

Waikar, A., Sweet, T., & Morgan, Y. C. (2016). Millennials and job hopping—myth or reality? Implications for organizational management. *Leadership & Organizational Management Journal*, 2016(1), 90–100.

Weiss, D., & Zhang, X. (2020). Multiple sources of aging attitudes: Perceptions of age groups and generations from adolescence to old age across China, Germany, and the United States. *Journal of Cross-Cultural Psychology*, 51(6), 407–423. https://doi.org/10.1177/0022022120925904

Yancey-Bragg, N. (2020, May 1). Coronavirus will define the next generation: What experts are predicting about 'Generation C.' *USA Today*. https://eu.usatoday.com/story/news/nation/2020/05/01/gen-c-coronavirus-covid-19-may-define-next-generation/3046809001/

Zacher, H., Esser, L., Bohlmann, C., & Rudolph, C. W. (2019). Age, social identity and identification, and work outcomes: A conceptual model, literature review, and future research directions. *Work, Aging and Retirement*, 5(1), 24–43. https://doi.org/10.1093/workar/way005

Zacher, H., & Griffin, B. (2015). Older workers' age as a moderator of the relationship between career adaptability and job satisfaction. *Work Aging and Retirement*, 1(2), 227–236. https://doi.org/10.1093/workar/wau009

7

INTEGRATING LIFESPAN DEVELOPMENT THEORIES

Implications for the Study of Age(ing) and Work

Rachel S. Rauvola and Cort W. Rudolph

Researchers studying the aging workforce often draw upon the lifespan development literature, in some form or another, in designing and interpreting their work (see Table 7.1). This is especially true of studies concerning how workers maintain (or even show improvements in) well-being and functioning as they age. Theoretical abundance in this literature bears advantages, providing authors with their choice of mechanisms, systems, and structures to contextualize and test in age or aging research. However, the theories have a great deal in common, and this fact is often disregarded or goes undiscussed in the literature; that is to say, variety does not always translate into uniqueness and differentiation, particularly when applied to the same, specific context (e.g., the workplace).

The purpose of this chapter is threefold. First, we introduce a novel conceptual integration between and extension of lifespan theories, organized in terms of mechanisms, predictions, and guiding principles. Second, we delve into the hallmark characteristics of lifespan development theories in the work and aging literature, placing particular focus on convergent theoretical components. Third, we discuss how our integration can be applied and how applications to the work context can mutually inform and benefit lifespan theories.

Proposed Lifespan Theory Integration

Our integration focuses on mechanisms, predictions, and guiding principles derived broadly from the lifespan perspective and how their mutual consideration can be used to improve understanding of age(ing) and work. This is not meant to be a new theory, per se. Instead, we treat this integration as a broader operating framework and structure—a set of fundamental assumptions and attributes of "lifespan thinking"—upon which each theory is built and from which future

DOI: 10.4324/9781003089674-9

TABLE 7.1 Overview of Lifespan Development Theories: Mechanisms and Key References

Theory	Focal Mechanisms	Key References and Measurement Scales
Dual-process model of assimilative and accommodative coping	Tenacious goal pursuit, flexible goal adjustment	Theory: Brandtstädter and Renner (1990) Measurement: TEN and FLEX scales from Brandtstädter and Renner (1990)
Model of selection, optimization, and compensation	Elective selection, loss-based selection, optimization, compensation	Theory: Baltes and Baltes (1990) Measurement: SOC scale from Baltes et al. (1999)
Motivational theory of lifespan development	Optimization, selective primary control, selective secondary control, compensatory primary control, compensatory secondary control	Theory: Heckhausen et al. (2010) Measurement: Optimization of Primary and Secondary Control scales from Heckhausen et al. (1998)
Socioemotional selectivity theory	Future time perspective (focus on opportunities, limitations; perceived remaining time)	Theory: Carstensen (1991) Measurement: Future Time Perspective scale from Carstensen and Lang (1996)
Strength and vulnerability integration model	Regulatory strengths and vulnerabilities as they relate to emotion regulation and health	Theory: Charles (2010) Measurement: N/A
Model of selection, optimization, and compensation with emotion regulation	Selection, optimization, and compensation in regulating exposure and responses to affective events	Theory: Urry and Gross (2010) Measurement: N/A

research can draw in selecting constructs, forming predictions, and interpreting findings. Through more integrative thinking, knowledge of age(ing) and work can become more interpretable, unified, and useful.

The three sections of our operating framework—lifespan mechanisms, predictions, and guiding principles (see Figure 7.1)—are explored in the following sections. These three categories are interrelated yet represent distinct contributions of the lifespan literature to understanding motivation, functioning, and development in context.

Mechanisms

The first, most granular section of our model concerns the theoretical mechanisms that overlap across the covered lifespan theories. The construct space covered by lifespan theories is concentrated: Each theory's mechanisms fall into one of three broader groupings. Specifically, each theory has some representation of (1) goal engagement and disengagement (including goal selection, commitment,

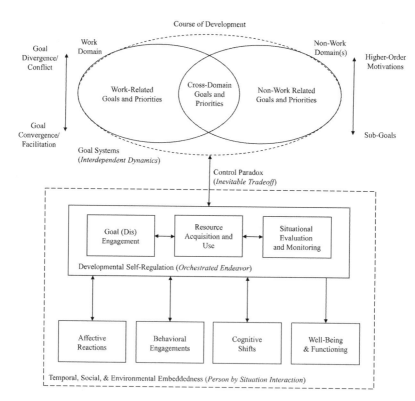

FIGURE 7.1   Integrated model of lifespan development theories

reprioritization, etc.), (2) resource acquisition and use, and (3) situational evaluation and monitoring. In developmental self-regulatory theories, these classes are discussed in detail as either core constructs to measure directly (e.g., primary and secondary selective and compensatory control) or core functions of other theoretical mechanisms (e.g., goal (dis)engagement resulting from the process of socioemotional selectivity). In concert, individuals leverage these mechanisms to appraise themselves and their environment (i.e., with respect to resources and constraints and especially time and social influences), using this information in turn to engage in motivational efforts that will help them minimize losses and maximize gains as they age.

Predictions

The second section of our model pertains to the form and content of predictions, both theoretical and empirical in nature, from the lifespan perspective. These predictions are shared across theories or are complementary to one another, linking mechanisms to their most salient outcomes and relevant boundary conditions in and outside of the workplace. Specifically, across the theories, well-being and functioning are bolstered when an individual selects and strives toward goals that are congruent with their circumstances, needs, and abilities (e.g., person–environment fit). That is to say, the adaptiveness of certain goal pursuits and behaviors is contingent upon context, other domains, and other aspects of an individual's goal system. This suggests that, among other sources of variability, age differences will emerge both between- and within-person in the relative utility and impact of developmental self-regulation on outcomes.

Additionally, each theory makes predictions about functioning and well-being (e.g., subjective, psychological, physiological) as well as cognitive, affective, and behavioral consequences of certain mechanisms. For example, affect serves as a form of feedback in some theories, and different affective experiences, cognitive shifts (e.g., reappraisals), and behavioral engagements (e.g., seeking out new goal-relevant means) are implied to follow from strategy enactment. These, in turn, interact with and influence concurrent and future motivational strategy use; indeed, affect, cognition, and behavior serve as part of the self-regulatory process.

One important caveat and limitation of the current lifespan literature, especially as it is applied to the work context, must be noted. Specifically, holistic developmental self-regulation relative to one's life context is theoretically linked to well-being and effective functioning, not individual strategies measured as general tendencies (e.g., to engage vs. disengage from goals, in general) or their individual affective, behavioral, or cognitive outcroppings. The former entails consideration of developmental self-regulation as an orchestrated entity with well-being and functioning implications, while the latter tests these propositions in a more piecemeal and less theoretically consistent way. Still, this is how much of the literature assesses lifespan developmental concepts. This practice makes it seem, on the surface, that mechanisms can be adaptive in and of themselves, while theory would not suggest this is the case. This point will be discussed further with respect to measurement in our integration application section, but it is an important distinction that is frequently overlooked in the literature.

Guiding Principles

The third and final section of our model concerns the general principles that underlie the lifespan approach—principles that should similarly guide the study of age(ing) and work in the coming years. In other words, these principles provide context for research findings and should shape their interpretation and implications. Each of these principles aligns with the mechanisms and predictions just discussed but bear explicit mention here to emphasize their integrative importance. First, aside from the guiding principles of the lifespan development perspective discussed by P. B. Baltes (1987), each of these theories also features the fundamental roles that time and timing, context, social groups and influences, and various forms of feedback play in the process of development. Most broadly, this can be thought of as a "person by situation interaction" principle—one that highlights the situational, temporal, and social embeddedness of development, with various boundary conditions and processes of comparison and adjustment at play. Thus, while we discussed congruence in prediction earlier, this principle is more generally about the "situatedness" of all aspects of these models.

The remaining three principles featured in Figure 7.1 are (1) the inherent variability in and tradeoffs among intentionality, activity, and consciousness of regulation; (2) the existence of interconnected goal systems, with alignment (and conflict) across multiple levels, domains, and the course of development; and (c) the assumption that a latent entity of developmental self-regulation spans and underlies lifespan mechanisms. The "inevitable tradeoff" principle refers not only to the dually expansive (i.e., opportunities, gains) and limited (i.e., constraints, losses) nature of development but also to the varying ways and levels at which goal striving can be prompted (e.g., proactively vs. reactively) and how these by definition come at the expense of other goals. Indeed, acceptance of the prospect of control relinquishment in some areas so as to gain control in others—of the mutual exclusivities and paradoxes inherent to development (see Chapter 5 of this volume)—would seem to be a part of successful aging and control perception itself.

The "interdependent dynamics" principle is a natural offshoot of this idea, with individuals' goal selection and striving in a given domain (e.g., at work) existing within the larger motivational scope of their life: nonwork domains (e.g., family, leisure), needs, and priorities shift and intersect over time (see Chapter 16 of this volume), and goals exist at multiple levels of specificity and awareness (e.g., subgoals, higher-order motivations). Developmental self-regulation, which according to the "orchestrated endeavor" principle is a domain-and mechanism-spanning ability set, pervades and manages these various layers, optimizing convergence and synergy and minimizing divergence, resource waste, and conflict—in multiple senses—across the lifespan.

With our proposed integration introduced, we next present a discussion of predominant lifespan development theories. We focus on their areas of overlap, emphasizing our integration mechanisms, predictions, and principles in the process.

Predominant Lifespan Development Theories

Each of the specific lifespan theories reviewed next originated from the same metatheoretical lifespan development perspective. This broad perspective on human development treats aging as a continuous, modifiable, and lifelong process of stability and change: As individuals age, they experience both gains and losses within and across life domains, and they exert influence while also being embedded in a system of interacting contextual and developmental influences (P. B. Baltes, 1987).

Developmental Self-Regulatory Theories

The four theories comprising our first lifespan perspective category include Brandtstädter and Renner's (1990) dual-process model of assimilative and accommodative coping; P. B. Baltes and M. M. Baltes' (1990) model of selection, optimization, and compensation; Heckhausen et al.'s (2010) motivational theory of lifespan development; and Carstensen's (1987, 1991) socioemotional selectivity theory. These theories are broadly oriented, seeking to explain how individuals maintain well-being and functioning with age through adaptive goal selection and striving within and across life domains. The motivational mechanisms in this category of theories are largely conceptualized within and between individuals (see discussion of higher-level selection, optimization, and compensation, such as adaptation at the societal level in P. B. Baltes, 1997). Individuals developmentally self-regulate: That is, they leverage different motivational strategies, resulting in affective, behavioral, and cognitive changes or efforts, in the service of their priorities, resources, and opportunities. Through this process, they work to maximize gains and minimize losses as they age, such that gains can offset or even exceed losses.

In the dual-process model of assimilative and accommodative coping, motivational mechanisms take the form of two main constructs: tenacious goal pursuit (assimilative coping) and flexible goal adjustment (accommodative coping; Brandtstädter & Renner, 1990). With tenacious goal pursuit, individuals actively adjust their capacities, circumstances, and resources to facilitate goal attainment through different behavioral engagements. Flexible goal adjustment, conversely, entails the adjustment of goals to fit an individual's (perceived) goal-relevant capacities, circumstances, and resources.

Whether individuals initiate coping behaviors and which of these two coping methods an individual engages depends on goal-specific feedback processes and affective experiences. Individuals assess the magnitude of the "gap" between their current state and desired state (i.e., the product of goal attainment): The larger the perceived discrepancy, the more likely an individual will engage in coping behaviors. Moreover, which coping behaviors are engaged depends on various factors (e.g., goal challenge attributes, behavioral tendencies). If a discrepancy is perceived as manageable, individuals will initially leverage assimilative coping. If these efforts fail or if the discrepancy is perceived to be impractical and insurmountable, individuals will turn to accommodative coping tactics. These strategies are engaged in the service of maintaining self-consistency and congruence (i.e., between actual and goal states), which in turn bolsters well-being and functioning across the lifespan.

P. B. Baltes and M. M. Baltes' (1990) model of selection, optimization, and compensation, especially the prominent and related action-theory framework (Freund & Baltes, 2000; Moghimi et al., 2017), presents a set of four developmental self-regulatory mechanisms that bear many similarities to other theories' constructs. These are elective and loss-based selection, optimization, and compensation. From an individual action regulation perspective (Freund & P. B. Baltes, 2000), both elective and loss-based selection are goal-setting functions, wherein individuals identify and commit to "desired state" or "maintenance" goals, respectively. Optimization entails the acquisition and application of existing and available means for goal striving, and compensation entails the acquisition and application of alternative (i.e., new and/or previously untapped) means for goal striving.

Selection, optimization, and compensation are all treated as adaptive in a variety of combinations relative to the individual and their context. P. B. Baltes and M. M. Baltes (1990), for example, offer that individuals have unique mechanism "patterning, which may vary according to health, preferences, and resources. In each case of successful aging, there is likely to be a creative, individualized, and societally appropriate combination of selection, optimization, and compensation" (p. 24). These regulatory mechanisms are leveraged in the context of age-related gains and losses, with individuals working to maximize gains and minimize losses and thereby bolster their functioning and well-being. Freund and P. B. Baltes (2000) underline the importance of realistic and responsive regulatory feedback for (re)constructing and monitoring meaningful goal hierarchies, allocating resources to attainable goals, framing goals in positive affect-boosting terms, and monitoring the effectiveness of goal striving methods, among others.

Heckhausen and colleagues' (2010) motivational theory of lifespan development is a product of many years of theoretical revision and iteration (e.g., Heckhausen & Schulz, 1993, 1995; Wrosch & Heckhausen, 1999) and presents five core mechanisms: Selective and compensatory forms of primary and secondary control as well as a metaregulative optimization mechanism.

Optimization refers to a cross domain regulatory function, through which individuals select goals that promote goal diversity, are congruent with opportunities and constraints, and stand to positively affect (or at least not interfere with) other current and future goals. After selecting goals, individuals use different control strategies for (dis)engagement. These fall into selective and compensatory categories, which entail efforts to change the external environment to support one's goals and efforts to change oneself to support goal striving in a given context, respectively.

The motivational theory of lifespan development presents two main challenges in development for which control mechanisms are relevant: Selectivity and compensation. Because individuals can only invest resources in some subset of goals at any given time, they must be selective in their allocation of resources to particular goals (e.g., those that are most meaningful and attainable). Individuals also face losses and challenges across the lifespan, for which they must compensate by adjusting priorities and buffering their sense of self. An individual's engagement of different control strategies—their efforts to strengthen goal commitment or to free resources for reallocation—is thus a product of balancing interests and abilities with limitations and gaps and is informed by regulatory feedback and affective experiences. When deadlines have passed and goals no longer seem tenable, for instance, goal disengagement is the adaptive option—just as accommodative coping was in the dual-process model.

The final developmental self-regulatory theory discussed in this chapter appears to be a departure from these tenets but, in fact, tends to the same theoretical space. Socioemotional selectivity theory (Carstensen, 1987, 1991; Carstensen et al., 1999) centers on the idea that people temporally self-contextualize their development, and this has an impact on the types of goals they select and strive toward. As individuals age, their perceptions of remaining opportunities, limitations, and time shift, transitioning from an expansive and open-ended orientation to a more restricted or constrained perspective. This perspective is referred to as *future time perspective*, which has most recently been described as possessing three dimensions: focus on opportunities, perceived remaining time, and focus on limitations (e.g., Rohr et al., 2017; Zacher, 2013).

Future time perspective serves as a mechanism for self-contextualizing regulatory decision-making and is contextually impactful. Having a realistic perception of opportunities, limitations, and time at one's disposal and striving toward goals congruent with these attributes is viewed as adaptive. Socioemotional selectivity theory predicts that the nature of these goals—specifically, their content and intended timing—will differ based upon an individual's future time perspective, with relatively older adults prioritizing shorter-term, emotionally meaningful goals, and relatively younger adults prioritizing longer-term, knowledge acquisition-related goals. Such goals, when aligned with perceived time, opportunities, and limitations, can enhance functioning and address the challenges of aging (i.e., anticipated and actual loss) as well as both proactively and reactively result in surprising improvements in emotional trajectories as adults age (Carstensen et al., 1999).

There is nuance to unpack regarding the adaptiveness of congruence between goals and an individual's personal, social, and temporal context, which is illuminative for our integration more generally. The model of selection, optimization, and compensation mentions the importance of orchestration and strategic balance in goal processes across levels, goals, and time, not just the appropriateness or frequency of an individual's strategy use relative to specific motivational pursuits. Both the motivational theory of lifespan development and the dual-process model emphasize holistic developmental regulation relative to multigoal systems, affective experiences, and an individual's sense of control and self, not simply how differential engagement or disengagement tactics aid in addressing particular objectives. Socioemotional selectivity theory, too, describes developmental self-regulation in terms of the balance or relative prioritization of different goal types, emotional regulation and functioning outcomes, and self-contextualization, rather than simply focusing on the utility of emotional versus instrumental goals or of open-ended versus constrained time perspective.

This means that having future time perspective and goals fit with one's circumstances is not only important to improve well-being and functioning on a goal-by-goal basis but also that the nature of one's future time perspective is adaptive at a broader level, helping to reframe one's outlook, priorities (e.g., for desired and current selves or states), and perceived capacities as bearing opportunities rather than limitations. These are not theories focused on singular, intractable tensions between future preparedness and present emotional satisfaction (Lang & Carstensen, 2002), goal engagement or disengagement, accommodative or assimilative coping, or selection, optimization, and compensation. Rather, they are theories about how these forces work together in complex and dynamic individual goal systems across development.

Lifespan Emotion Regulation Theories

There are two primary theories that relate developmental self-regulatory mechanisms to emotion regulation and age: Charles' (2010) strength and vulnerability integration model, and Urry and Gross' (2010) selection, optimization, and compensation with emotion regulation model. Both theories build upon the propositions discussed previously, translating socioemotional selectivity theory and the model of selection, optimization, and compensation into understanding affective experiences and functioning with age.

Charles' (2010) model is built upon socioemotional selectivity theory, as well as the integrality of time to emotional experiences and effective functioning across the lifespan. The core premise of the model is that individuals experience affective events and regulate emotions differently with age, which translates into distinct emotional trajectories associated with one's place in life. Specifically, based in socioemotional selectivity theory, relatively older adults experience distinct emotional benefits as a function of their temporal orientation, as well as the experience and knowledge that they have accumulated over their lifespan. Those adults who, in alignment with a more constrained future time perspective, focus more on present strengths and states also possess the ability to appraise their current life status favorably relative to goals and other individuals. Additionally, as a function of their greater emotional goal orientation, older adults benefit from smaller, more meaningful social networks that allow them to experience positive emotions, avoid negative emotions in the first place, and adapt to recognized loss. Still, they have vulnerabilities in certain situations where they cannot leverage appropriate regulatory tactics or down-regulate their physiological responses to stress.

Again, the themes of multiple domains and systems are pertinent to discuss, as these strategies and experiences must be considered within the broader scope of an individual's priorities, capacities, and challenges. Time, energy, and attention are limited resources. This means that different goals and strategies can facilitate or oppose one another, within and across domains. Charles' model underlines the idea that individuals' strengths and vulnerabilities, in regulating emotion and in regulating development more generally, are a product of and influence on other areas of their life. Some things become less "worth" the time and effort with age, and individuals can—figuratively and literally—not have the time to deal with some grievances that previously may have been more consequential. Regulatory efforts are shaped by the present and future as well as the past: Individuals deliberately cultivate social systems as they age, curating their experiences and developing areas of expertise and ability while eschewing others, and these influences accrue over time and persist in their effects.

Urry and Gross' (2010) expansion of the model of selection, optimization, and compensation to focus on emotion regulation seeks to explain similar phenomena regarding well-being and functioning with age. It parallels Baltes and colleagues' original model, applying each self-regulatory mechanism to emotional experiences. In particular, the model suggests that different forms of well-being (e.g., negative and positive affect, subjective well-being) improve with age as a result of enhanced emotion regulation. These emotion regulation improvements manifest in both emotion resource allocation increases, as well as more efficient and effective regulatory strategy usage (e.g., relative to the situation and available resources).

The model specifically proposes that adults select and optimize forms of emotion regulation (e.g., situation selection, attentional deployment) that compensate for age-related resource changes and losses, such as cognitive control deficits. As in its source model, compensatory strategies include resources that are gained or maintained with age: These include accrued resources such as close, intentional, meaningful social networks and situational knowledge (e.g., as in Charles', 2010, model) or pertain to sustained resources like response modulation capacity (i.e., emotional expression and experience control).

Applying the Lifespan Integration to Work: Implications and Recommendations

We now turn our attention to a final matter: How can this integration be optimally applied to research on age(ing) and work? We have nine mechanism-, prediction-, and principle-relevant recommendations for implementing this integration and how it stands to impact research and practice (see Table 7.2).

Mechanism Recommendations

This integration should be used as a starting point for research on age(ing) and work among experienced and new scholars alike. It is challenging to assess the areas of commonality and divergence in this literature when referencing theory papers that largely do not converse with one another in a common, formalized vocabulary. Our chapter provides a guide to the fundamentals of each theory and the lifespan perspective that orient researchers toward the types of mechanisms and predictions they can (and should) make and the principles that contextualize a lifespan approach. We recommend greater standardization of language around these concepts in the age(ing) and work literature and greater consistency of conceptual representation and testing in research. One relatively straightforward application of this would be to consistently adopt the terminology presented herein (see Table 7.2).

In addition, we recommend that scholars refer to our model's key tenets, in their entirety, as they theorize, conduct research, and interpret their findings. Because this is a prescriptive integration, researchers still have much flexibility in their work while also coalescing toward semantic and structural standards that will ultimately codify research and practice. There are a number of disconnects, for example, between what lifespan theory would predict and what relationships are actually tested in research, and construct choices are often made out of convenience or atheoretical precedent. The majority of work studies leveraging the lifespan perspective either (1) use adapted lifespan theory to justify studies that do not involve or directly study lifespan mechanisms or (2) measure a subsample of lifespan mechanisms without using findings to further theory. To bridge this divide, there are a wealth of assumptions and principles that should be formally included in study designs (e.g., contextual boundary conditions) and interpretations of empirical findings (e.g., discussing the nature and source of possible underlying developmental self-regulatory ability). By continuing to omit (or reimagine) core aspects that structure, translate, and unite the lifespan perspective from studies in the work context, research risks misrepresenting the experience of the age-diverse workforce and misidentifying how best to support it.

Prediction Recommendations

In line with our focus on functioning and affect, behavior, and cognition predictions, our first prediction-relevant recommendation is to expand lifespan theory

TABLE 7.2 Integrative Lifespan Terminology, Theories, Integrative Propositions, and Future Research Applications at Work

Integrative Terminology	Example Theories and Concepts	Integrative Propositions	Selected Research Applications
Mechanisms			
Goal (dis) engagement	MTLD: Selective and compensatory primary and secondary control	Developmental self-regulation is captured by three categories of motivational processes, and these take the form of core constructs to directly measure or are focal functions of other theoretical processes	Standardize terminology
Resource acquisition and use	SOC: Optimization, compensation		Refer to entire models and not just to specific strategies in theorizing/ hypothesis development, research design and execution, and finding interpretation
Situational evaluation and monitoring	SST: Future time perspective		
Predictions			
Well-being and functioning	AAC: Self-consistency and well-being/functioning improvements through realistic goal striving and attainment	Well-being and functioning are boosted when an individual selects and strives toward goals that are congruent with their circumstances	Expand occupational health- and emotion-focused research to examine developmental self-regulation and motivation in relation to stressor appraisal and strain processes, coping responses, and work design utility
Affect, behavior, cognition	SOC–ER: Distinct, age-adaptive emotion regulatory responses in the form of cognition and behavior	Affective reactions, behavioral engagements, and cognitive shifts are implied to result from, interact with, and influence concurrent and future self-regulatory strategy enactment	Refine existing and create new measures to accurately reflect mechanisms and assumptions, including a shift toward capturing affect, behaviors, and cognition in lieu of general regulatory tendencies
	SAVI: Emotional well-being advantages and vulnerabilities as a product of past and present social behaviors and cognitive appraisals		

(Continued)

TABLE 7.2 (Continued)

Integrative Terminology	Example Theories and Concepts	Integrative Propositions	Selected Research Applications
Guiding Principles			
Person by situation interaction	SST: Self-contextualization of development as a function of perceived time and corresponding socioemotional priorities	Development is situationally, temporally, and socially embedded, with various boundary conditions and processes of comparison and adjustment at play	Consider intersections of work motivation and lifespan theories (vocational decision-making, goal timing and discounting)
Inevitable trade-off	AAC: Recursive patterns of losses/failures and gains/successes that shape individual agency and functioning, reactively and/or proactively	Aging is defined by both opportunities and constraints, and individuals must relinquish control or goals in some areas in order to gain control and strive toward goals in others	Study multidomain influences on work motivation, especially pertaining to multiple goal systems, temporal perceptions (e.g., deadlines, urgency), and social influences (e.g., feedback, normative societal standards, nonwork forces)
Interdependent dynamics	SOC: Individuals construct and monitor goal hierarchies, allocating resources to goals within an individualized context	Goals exist in the broader motivational context of individuals' lives, with alignment and conflict across levels, domains, and the course of development	Investigate how individuals appraise various types of "fit" and their age-contingent effects
Orchestrated endeavor	MTLD: Goal processes are meta-regulated through optimization, whereby individuals choose and schedule motivational pursuits geared for success with respect to time, opportunities, and control costs and benefits	Mechanisms do not function in isolation but exist as part of a domain- and mechanism-spanning ability set (developmental self-regulation), optimizing motivational convergence and synergy and minimizing divergence, resource waste, and conflict—in multiple senses—across the lifespan.	Apply principles (as well as mechanisms and predictions) at the within-domain level (e.g., socialization and relationship cultivation within a work role, leadership development); Investigate the existence of a general factor of developmental self-regulation and develop a single measure of this as appropriate

Note: "AAC" = dual-process model of assimilative and accommodative coping. "MTLD" = the motivational theory of lifespan development. "SOC" = the model of selection, optimization, and compensation. "SST" = socioemotional selectivity theory. "SAVI" = the strength and vulnerability integration model. "SOC-ER" = the model of selection, optimization, and compensation with emotion regulation applications and research in the areas of occupational health and emotion regulation at work. Health is often a focal component of studies of age(ing) and work, yet this does not mean that theories of occupational health and emotional demands at work have been integrated with lifespan theories. Past work has drawn on work such as job demands-resources theory (e.g., Liebermann et al., 2013; Sonnega et al., 2018) or the emotional labor literature (e.g., Dahling & Perez, 2010; Toomey et al., 2020). However, more formal incorporation of the motivational underpinnings of lifespan development into workplace health promotion and maintenance, as well as emotion regulation and well-being, is needed.

The mechanisms, predictions, and principles presented in this chapter can readily be applied to health- and emotion-focused research. This could be accomplished in line with the selection, optimization, and compensation in emotion regulation and strength and vulnerabilities integration models. New integrative conceptualizations, such as advances in theory and research on health and stress monitoring or socioemotional feedback processes in relationships and interactions, could be beneficial as well. There are many important points to investigate therefrom, including how lifespan developmental self-regulatory processes may intercede upon or interact with stressor appraisal processes, strain outcomes, coping responses, the work-life interface, and the desirability and impact of certain work design features on aging employees' health.

Second and relatedly, our integration has important implications and applications to how aging-relevant constructs are measured in the work context: in particular, developmental self-regulatory mechanisms and "successful aging" outcomes. Issues with predominant developmental self-regulatory measurement tools have been noted in past work (e.g., unreliability, inconsistent usage and factor structures; Rudolph, 2016), and study paradigms rely almost exclusively on self-report measures that ask individuals about their domain-general or workplace-specific motivational and behavioral tendencies (see Chapter 8 of this volume). These present notable limitations to research findings, which we recommend be addressed through scale revisions and alternative measurement approaches (e.g., capturing affect, behaviors, and cognition). Aside from the "what," "how" constructs are measured will also need to be addressed: Alternative paradigms and measurement methods are advisable, including other-report, experimental, and varying time-scale designs for capturing self-regulatory behaviors and perceptions (see Chapters 10 and 11 of this volume).

Guiding Principles

In line with our guiding principles, a few remaining research recommendations can be made. First, our integration highlights the need for more work on where prominent theories of work motivation intersect with and inform lifespan development theories, including work concerning vocational decision-making and retirement intentions, control beliefs, identity and needs, goal timing and discounting, and differential goal strategy engagement. Second, attention to multidomain influences on work motivation is needed. In particular, much stands to be learned about individuals' experiences and behaviors within multi-goal systems that are temporally bound and both socially influenced and constructed. This perspective is in contrast to three common but incomplete approaches used at present: (1) viewing workplace decisions of aging workers in isolation from other intersecting life spheres, (2) treating decisions as a pure function of personal, age-related gains and losses or structural aspects of one's job, or (3) assuming that goal-directed behavioral tendencies necessarily apply across domains and goals rather than having more context- and goal-specific effects.

As such, there are potentially fruitful syntheses to be had between lifespan developmental concepts and work on multiple goal systems in the work psychology and motivation literatures. Efforts in these areas will lead to more informative nuance around employee life management and success with age. More work on aspects of regulation as they relate to employees could prove useful as well. In particular, continued research on sources of feedback (e.g., informal and formal performance feedback, goal discrepancy judgements and processes) as well as deadline setting and effects (e.g., work task and career timing, subjective experiences of time pressure and urgency) in relation to aging employees and motivation would move the field forward (see also Dello Russo et al., 2017; Tang et al., 2020; Wang et al., 2015).

Third, we recommend more research on individual by context interactions and development over time. "Fit" was discussed throughout this chapter as a component of developmental self-regulation (e.g., person-environment, uncertainty congruence, goal and resource matching), and it has been studied with respect to age and well-being outcomes in recent years (see Krumm et al., 2013; Rauvola et al., 2020; Zacher et al., 2014). Our integration highlights the need for more work on both how individuals of different ages appraise various types of "fit" and how these fit perceptions may have age- or other identity-contingent effects on outcomes of interest. Given the influence of context on developmental self-regulation, social partners may shape or factor into the "fitting" process as well, which bears more exploration (e.g., the idea of "co-developing individuals"; Baltes, 1987, p. 621; see also Salmela-Aro, 2009).

More generally, although much research tends to focus its applications toward relatively older or younger employees, our fourth recommendation is to consider age and developmental processes across a complete continuum. Research must prioritize the needs of employees of all ages, and lifespan mechanisms, predictions, and principles could be applied to within-context "aging" and development. For example, leadership development, socialization, and relationship growth within one's organizational "lifespan" and gain and loss cycles as one matures in a given role or set of roles could be fruitful areas for integration and innovation. Outside of measurement modifications to concern the work domain specifically (e.g., occupational future time perspective, Zacher & Frese, 2009), such principles have not been extended in this way (see also Chapter 9 of this volume).

Finally, our integration highlights a number of fundamental overlaps across lifespan development theories, as well as the potential for these theories to share an underlying regulatory ability. The potential existence of a general factor of developmental self-regulation should be investigated to this end, which would help theoretically and operationally represent and further integrate mechanisms into the "orchestrated endeavor" within which they operate. Based on this, research should explore whether a single measure of developmental self-regulation can be developed (e.g., representing the three main mechanism categories above). This could be used alongside refined and multidomain versions of other scales and theoretical components (e.g., time perspective, affective reactions, cognitive shifts, behavioral engagements) recommended earlier.

Conclusion

Lifespan perspectives comprise a large share of the age(ing) and work literature, and there is no shortage of theory to draw upon in this area of research. At the same time, however, it can prove difficult to differentiate or select between these theories, as well as to holistically interpret the body of research based upon them. The present chapter sought to highlight the shared aspects of predominant theories of lifespan development and to propose a conceptual integration of these perspectives, particularly so as to pave a path toward synthesis and utility. It is our hope that the components highlighted in our chapter give new and experienced scholars alike new ways to engage in "lifespan thinking," through more attention to the commonalities spanning lifespan mechanisms, predictions, and guiding principles as well as these parallel aspects of the work context. In this way, the field can move closer to an understanding of how individuals age successfully, recognizing the commonalities and distinctions across theories as well as the populations whose development and functioning they seek to describe.

References

Baltes, P. B. (1987). Theoretical propositions of life-span developmental psychology: On the dynamics between growth and decline. *Developmental Psychology, 23*, 611–626. doi:10.1037/0012-1649.23.5.611

Baltes, P. B. (1997). On the incomplete architecture of human ontogeny: Selection, optimization, and compensation as foundation of developmental theory. *American Psychologist, 52*, 366–380. doi:10.1037/0003-066x.52.4.366

Baltes, P. B., & Baltes, M. M. (1990). Psychological perspectives on successful aging: The model of selective optimization with compensation. In P. B. Baltes & M. M. Baltes (Eds.), *Successful aging: Perspectives from the behavioral sciences* (pp. 1–34). Cambridge University Press.

Baltes, P. B., Baltes, M. M., Freund, A. M., & Lang, F. (1999). *The measurement of selection, optimization, and compensation (SOC) by self report.* Max Planck Institute for Human Development.

Brandtstädter, J., & Renner, G. (1990). Tenacious goal pursuit and flexible goal adjustment: Explication and age-related analysis of assimilative and accommodative strategies of coping. *Psychology and Aging, 5,* 58–67. doi:10.1037/0882-7974.5.1.58

Carstensen, L. L. (1987). Age-related changes in social activity. In L. L. Carstensen & B. A. Edelstein (Eds.), *Handbook of clinical gerontology* (pp. 222–237). Pergamon Press.

Carstensen, L. L. (1991). Socioemotional selectivity theory: Social activity in life-span context. In K. W. Schaie (Ed.), *Annual review of gerontology & geriatrics* (Vol. 11, pp. 195–217). Springer.

Carstensen, L. L., Isaacowitz, D. M., & Charles, S. T. (1999). Taking time seriously: A theory of socioemotional selectivity. *American Psychologist, 54,* 165–181. doi:10.1037/0003-066x.54.3.165

Carstensen, L. L., & Lang, F. R. (1996). *Future time perspective scale.* Stanford University Press.

Charles, S. T. (2010). Strength and vulnerability integration (SAVI): A model of emotional well-being across adulthood. *Psychological Bulletin, 136,* 1068–1091. doi:10.1037/a0021232

Dahling, J. J., & Perez, L. A. (2010). Older worker, different actor? Linking age and emotional labor strategies. *Personality and Individual Differences, 48,* 574–578. doi:10.1016/j.paid.2009.12.009

Dello Russo, S., Miraglia, M., & Borgogni, L. (2017). Reducing organizational politics in performance appraisal: The role of coaching leaders for age-diverse employees. *Human Resource Management, 56,* 769–783. doi:10.1002/hrm.21799

Freund, A. M., & Baltes, P. B. (2000). The orchestration of selection, optimization and compensation: An action-theoretical conceptualization of a theory of developmental regulation. In W. J. Perrig & A. Grob (Eds.), *Control of human behavior, mental processes, and consciousness* (pp. 35–58). Lawrance Erlbaum & Associates.

Heckhausen, J., & Schulz, R. (1993). Optimization by selection and compensation: Balancing primary and secondary control in life span development. *International Journal of Behavioral Development, 16,* 287–303. doi:10.1177/016502549301600210

Heckhausen, J., & Schulz, R. (1995). A life-span theory of control. *Psychological Review, 102,* 284–304. doi:10.1037/0033-295x.102.2.284

Heckhausen, J., Schulz, R., & Wrosch, C. (1998). *Developmental regulation in adulthood: Optimization in primary and secondary control-A multiscale questionnaire (OPS-Scales).* Max Planck Institute for Human Development.

Heckhausen, J., Wrosch, C., & Schulz, R. (2010). A motivational theory of life-span development. *Psychological Review, 117,* 32–60. doi:10.1037/a0017668

Krumm, S., Grube, A., & Hertel, G. (2013). No time for compromises: Age as a moderator of the relation between needs-supply fit and job satisfaction. *European Journal of Work and Organizational Psychology, 22,* 547–562. doi:10.1080/1359432X.2012.676248

Lang, F. R., & Carstensen, L. L. (2002). Time counts: Future time perspective, goals, and social relationships. *Psychology and Aging, 17,* 125–139. doi:10.1037/0882-7974.17.1.125

Liebermann, S. C., Wegge, J., & Müller, A. (2013). Drivers of the expectation of remaining in the same job until retirement age: A working life span demands-resources model. *European Journal of Work and Organizational Psychology, 22,* 347–361. doi:10.10 80/1359432X.2012.753878

Moghimi, D., Zacher, H., Scheibe, S., & Van Yperen, N. W. (2017). The selection, optimization, and compensation model in the work context: A systematic review and meta-analysis of two decades of research. *Journal of Organizational Behavior, 38*, 247–275. doi:10.1002/job.2108

Rauvola, R. S., Rudolph, C. W., Ebbert, L. K., & Zacher, H. (2020). Person-environment fit and work satisfaction: Exploring the conditional effects of age. *Work, Aging and Retirement, 6*, 101–117. doi:10.1093/workar/waz011

Rohr, M. K., John, D. T., Fung, H. H., & Lang, F. R. (2017). A three-component model of future time perspective across adulthood. *Psychology and Aging, 32*, 597–607. doi:10.1037/pag0000191

Rudolph, C. W. (2016). Lifespan developmental perspectives on working: A literature review of motivational theories. *Work, Aging and Retirement, 2*, 130–158. doi:10.1093/workar/waw012

Salmela-Aro, K. (2009). Personal goals and well-being during critical life transitions: The four C's-Channelling, choice, co-agency and compensation. *Advances in Life Course Research, 14*, 63–73. doi:10.1016/j.alcr.2009.03.003

Sonnega, A., Helppie-McFall, B., Hudomiet, P., Willis, R. J., & Fisher, G. G. (2018). A comparison of subjective and objective job demands and fit with personal resources as predictors of retirement timing in a national US sample. *Work, Aging and Retirement, 4*, 37–51. doi:10.1093/workar/wax016

Tang, S., Richter, A. W., & Nadkarni, S. (2020). Subjective time in organizations: Conceptual clarification, integration, and implications for future research. *Journal of Organizational Behavior, 41*, 210–234. doi:10.1002/job.2421

Toomey, E. C., Rudolph, C. W., & Zacher, H. (2020). Age-conditional effects of political skill and empathy on emotional labor: An experience sampling study. *Work, Aging and Retirement, 7*, 46–60. doi:10.1093/workar/waaa004

Urry, H. L., & Gross, J. J. (2010). Emotion regulation in older age. *Current Directions in Psychological Science, 19*, 352–357. doi:10.1177/0963721410388395

Wang, M., Burlacu, G., Truxillo, D., James, K., & Yao, X. (2015). Age differences in feedback reactions: The roles of employee feedback orientation on social awareness and utility. *Journal of Applied Psychology, 100*, 1296–1308. doi:10.1037/a0038334

Wrosch, C., & Heckhausen, J. (1999). Control processes before and after passing a developmental deadline: Activation and deactivation of intimate relationship goals. *Journal of Personality and Social Psychology, 77*, 415–427. doi:10.1037/0022-3514.77.2.415

Zacher, H. (2013). Older job seekers' job search intensity: The interplay of proactive personality, age and occupational future time perspective. *Ageing & Society, 33*, 1139–1166. doi:10.1017/S0144686X12000451

Zacher, H., Feldman, D. C., & Schulz, H. (2014). Age, occupational strain, and well-being: A person-environment fit perspective. In P. L. Perrewé, C. C. Rosen, & J. R. B. Halbesleben (Eds.), *The role of demographics in occupational health and well being* (pp. 83–111). Emerald Group Publishing. doi:10.1108/S1479-355520140000012002

Zacher, H., & Frese, M. (2009). Remaining time and opportunities at work: Relationships between age, work characteristics, and occupational future time perspective. *Psychology and Aging, 24*, 487–493. doi:10.1037/a0015425

SECTION III

Advances in Methods to Study Age and Work

8

PERCEIVED AND ACTUAL BEHAVIORS IN RESEARCH ON AGE AND WORK

Fabiola H. Gerpott and Nale Lehmann-Willenbrock

> *It has been well documented that people change physically and psychologically with age. Some of these changes are demonstrated through people's behaviors at work.*
>
> —(*Taneva et al., 2016, p. 397*)

The Goal: Studying Actual Behavior

The opening quote mentions a fact that motivates many age and work scholars to engage in research that aims to understand the antecedents, changes, and consequences of younger and older employees' behaviors at work. However, the field so far largely studies *perceptions* of behavior. To explain this statement, it is worth pondering on what we mean when we refer to the study of behavior. We define *behavior* as any observable action (verbal statement, movement, emotional expression, and so forth) performed by a person that is socially meaningful in the present moment (e.g., Gerpott et al., 2020; Uher, 2016).

Our definition of behavior has two important components that deserve further elaboration. First, the definition focuses on observable actions. As such, we exclude internal bodily functions as they are not directly observable and are not under the control of the individual (Aron, 2010). Second, the notion that behavior must be socially meaningful means that we are interested in behavior as a transmitter of social information. This does not mean that socially meaningful behavior is necessarily logically comprehensible, intentional, or completely self-determined. Rather, behavior can include unconsciously guided acts, occur in highly interdependent contexts, or be enacted thoughtlessly. It also does not necessarily require the physical presence of other people (e.g., a person who

DOI: 10.4324/9781003089674-11

composes an email to their team when working by themselves in the office shows a socially meaningful behavior although no one is watching). What our definition of behavior does require is that the behavior can at least potentially trigger reactions by another individual (i.e., the definition does not include biomarkers such as heartbeats or fMRI activation patterns that cannot be observed by others).

To qualify as a study of behavior, the behavior itself must be the focal act of interest. For example, whereas completing a questionnaire is a behavioral response shown by an individual (i.e., a scholar can observe that a participant is ticking certain answer boxes), we would only consider this a socially meaningful act in a behavior-focused research design if the ticking behavior itself is investigated. However, in most research designs on age and work, this has not been the case as scholars are typically interested in the content that is conveyed through the response behavior (i.e., perceived behaviors, inner convictions, attitudes, etc.) but not the response behavior itself.

Our definition of behavior further implies that we differentiate between research based on "actual behavior" and empirical work that relies on "perceptions of behavior." Studies investigating perceptions of the acts that a focal person engages in use self-reports or other-reports of involved individuals (e.g., peers, supervisors, employees). In contrast, studies that employ measures of actual behavior rely on technology-based behavior tracking (e.g., automatic speech detection, eye tracking) or systematic annotation or coding of behavior by outside observers according to reproducible observation procedures and coding rules (e.g., a researcher classifying the verbal behavior exhibited by participants who were observed during a social interaction). Broadly speaking, this entails that we differentiate survey-based research from research designs that capture behaviors (i.e., the focus of the present chapter), manipulate behaviors (see Chapter 11), or train/develop actual behaviors (see Chapter 14).

The purpose of our chapter is to convince scholars that the time is ripe for age research to combine questionnaire-focused research practices with behavior-based research designs, such as those put forward in this chapter and in the next chapters on methodological advances. Such an enrichment of our methodological toolbox can be used to triangulate results across different methodologies, as well as help to expand theories to explain why there are systematic differences in what people think or perceive they or others do and what they actually do. To preview the structure of this chapter, we begin with a short recap of the problem (i.e., research is often not studying actual behavior) and provide a disclaimer (i.e., studying actual behavior is not a silver bullet). Based on this foundation, we provide an overview of prevalent tools to capture behavior and delineate a conceptual framework for selecting an appropriate time-theoretical scope in behavior research. We end with some future research inspiration that hopefully motivates scholars in the field of age and work to develop more concrete ideas on how their future work could profit from data triangulation by incorporating behavioral measures in their research designs.

The Problem: Not Studying Behavior

Recognizing that people act upon their perceptions and, in doing so, create a rather objective reflection of the world (Gerpott et al., 2018), one may wonder why scholars should even bother about actual behavior. Indeed, the "cognitive revolution" with its focus on inner psychological processes quickly ousted behaviorism with its exclusive focus on observable behavior (Baumeister et al., 2007). And there are many advantages of using questionnaires to capture perceptions of behavior: Scholars can, for example, easily ask about everyday work activities that are difficult to capture via behavioral observation, filling in surveys is often cheaper and requires less data collection effort than obtaining behavioral data, and self-reports are more easily approved by companies and Institutional Review Boards as data security concerns are lower (after all, people can easily lie when they do not want to report about a certain behavior). Considering these exemplary advantages (and there are many more), the laborious path of capturing, manipulating, or training/developing behavior in studies on younger and/or older study participants' behaviors at work may seem like an unnecessary scholarly effort.

However, most scholars will agree that individuals' perceptions can differ substantially from what is happening in organizational reality. Behavioral measures and self-reports often capture different aspects of work-related phenomena, which is also reflected in the empirical finding that self-reports and behavioral measures tend to be only weakly correlated (Dang et al., 2020). The weak correlation between survey-based proxies and observations of actual behavior concerns people's reporting of both their own and others' behavior in hypothetical as well as already experienced situations. Such discrepancies are often driven by a social desirability bias and could, for example, mean that employees drastically overreport their willingness to share knowledge with an older/younger colleague—a prosocial behavior typically captured with survey designs in age and work research (see Chapter 15). This tendency may become even stronger for older employees, because—in line with socioemotional selectivity theory (Carstensen et al., 1999)—with increasing age, people tend to remember situations with a higher self-serving bias (Mezulis et al., 2004). Lastly, employees' actual knowledge-sharing behavior may be more strongly influenced by bodily cues of attractiveness and youthfulness than they would admit (or could imagine; see also Tsay, 2020) because people underestimate the degree to which biases influence their behavior. If the age and work field derives practical implications based only on potentially biased survey reports without ever verifying them with studies of actual behavior, this carries the serious risk of designing training and intervention programs that do not work—or, even worse, that systematically discriminate against younger and/or older employees.

Disclaimer

In positioning this chapter, we want to emphasize that our intention is by no means to completely replace survey research with unobtrusive behavioral measurements.

The choice of an appropriate design and measurement tool always depends on the research question that should be answered and the focal variables of interest. For instance, regarding attitudes as focal variables, asking participants to report about their own attitudes in a survey is often an adequate approach. Furthermore, when using behavior-focused measurement tools, scholars need to be aware that they come with their own challenges. While a discussion of these challenges could certainly fill another book chapter or even book, we highlight three key issues. First, behavioral measurement tools may not be as objective as scholars often claim. To illustrate, scholars who annotate the verbal or nonverbal behavior of participants while observing a workplace interaction need to interpret the behavior. Even when using a standardized coding scheme for this task and ensuring inter-rater reliability, the annotation of the data is still bound to the cultural context and the accompanying translation of meaning. Second, although research shows that employees quickly forget about the fact that they are observed and behave as they normally would (e.g., Kauffeld & Lehmann-Willenbrock, 2012), one can nevertheless raise concerns about behavioral data being subject to biases that are imposed via the process of observation. A classic example in that regard is the Hawthorne effect, which refers to the idea that people behave differently just because they know they are the subject of research (for criticism questioning the existence of this effect see Jones, 1992; Wickström & Bendix, 2000). Third, considering that behavior is often assessed in specific social interactions, the retest reliability (and thus predictive validity) can be lower than for survey instruments that ask participants to report general perceptions. For example, when asking an older employee about their general tendency to share knowledge with younger employees at work, they may respond consistently in a survey over several measurement points. However, when observing and coding two concrete incidents of knowledge sharing with two different younger colleagues, the behavior of the very same person may show high variability depending for example on how much they like each of the two younger colleagues or whether there are differences in the intellectual capability of the two knowledge receivers. Accordingly, the focus in behavior studies lies often on the behavior itself, instead of between-person differences (Dang et al., 2020).

Recognizing that both survey- and behavior-based research has shortcomings, the purpose of our chapter is to increase methodological diversity in research regarding age and work by encouraging the field to combine both data collection approaches to ultimately gain a richer conceptual understanding of how perceptions and behavior are connected (Gerpott et al., 2020). The almost exclusive focus on survey designs puts age-and-work research at risk of falling behind technological solutions for capturing behavioral data to understand younger and older employees' activities at work. For example, computer scientists have established models that can automatically analyze online interactions to recognize when a person may have trouble learning shared knowledge, without requiring the knowledge receiver to explicitly express their learning difficulties (Soller &

Lesgold, 2003). Moreover, eye-tracking software can be utilized to warn leaders when they are not behaving inclusively (Shim et al., 2020) and thus serve as another tool in a comprehensive corporate diversity strategy to fight age discrimination without requiring younger or older employees to explicitly express that they feel left out. While ethical considerations (e.g., algorithmic biases, data access, data collection purpose) in the utilization of such user data need to be discussed, smartphones and Artificial Intelligence (AI) have the potential to capture behavior more objectively than self-reports of activities (Ellis, 2019). Given the ongoing, fast-paced development of AI-based technologies (notwithstanding all their ethical challenges), we believe that age-and-work scholars will miss an opportunity if they neglect being involved in interdisciplinary collaborations to shape relevant AI developments in a way that benefit an inclusive, age-diverse workforce. As Chaffin et al. (2017) have noted, a "wait and see" attitude is inacceptable as the expertise of organizational scholars is needed to avoid construct proliferation that may occur if IT specialists try to find names for the phenomena they are investigating, which may already be well established in the social science literature. To provide some inspiration on measurement options when moving in this direction, we next provide an overview of the advantages and disadvantages of tools that can be used to capture behavior in the laboratory and/or field. The overview is not intended to be comprehensive; in line with the purpose of this chapter, it instead aims to provide a brief introduction to the most prevalent measurement approaches.

Prevalent Tools to Capture Behavior at Different Temporal Scopes

Measurement means the attachment of quantitative labels to describe and differentiate natural events such as behavioral incidents (Cooper et al., 2007). When capturing behavior, scholars need to (1) define the type of behavior, (2) identify specific behaviors of interest, and (3) decide on the temporal resolution (i.e., the temporal scope or time frame across which the behavior should be measured).

Types of Behavior and Behavioral Categorization

To support steps 1 and 2 in the previous section, Table 8.1 provides an overview of prevalent measurement tools to capture different types of behavior. For each type of behavior listed in Table 8.1, several categorization systems exist to further differentiate specific behaviors. For example, when pursuing a *verbal interaction coding* approach using human annotators or raters, a scholar could decide to use a fine-grained behavioral coding system such as act4teams with its 44 observation categories (Kauffeld & Lehmann-Willenbrock, 2012) or to focus their coding efforts on a specific behavior such as respectful inquiry (e.g., asking open questions and listening attentively; Van Quaquebeke & Felps, 2018).

Beyond the scope of this chapter, many resources can help interested scholars to find an appropriate coding scheme (e.g., Brauner et al., 2018) and learn how to conduct systematic behavioral observations of interactions at work (e.g., Waller & Kaplan, 2018). In addition to different categorization systems, there are also several analytical options once the behavioral data is coded. For instance, scholars can use coded verbal interaction data to investigate the absolute frequency of behaviors to predict outcomes (e.g., Schulte et al., 2013), but they can also analyze more fine-grained interaction dynamics such as studying how younger and older employees react to certain behaviors (for an overview of methods see Klonek et al., 2016; Lehmann-Willenbrock & Allen, 2018) or investigating language style matching between younger and older employees as a measure of cohesion (e.g., Meinecke & Kauffeld, 2019).

Verbal behavior can be extracted from written communication such as emails, chat-logs, social media posts, intranet communication, or communication app protocols, too. *Text-based behavior coding* has bloomed in recent years due to the advancements of AI-based text mining tools (Oswald et al., 2020). Age and work scholars who want to move in this direction are referred to Speer (2020) for natural language processing, Hickman et al. (2020) for text preprocessing for data mining, and Banks et al. (2018) for text analysis in R.

Nonverbal behavior coding (i.e., coding of nonverbal acts from videos or in live observations through human coders) resembles verbal behavior coding in many steps as scholars also need to decide how they define a sense unit, which coding scheme (i.e., level of granularity of behaviors of interest) they would like to use, and how they want to train coders to ensure reliability (for an overview, see Harrigan, 2013). Researchers have noted that the abilities to receive and send spontaneous and posed nonverbal messages develop throughout the lifespan (Halberstadt et al., 2013), which indicates that there is much to be gained from an age-specific perspective on nonverbal communication in the workplace.

Table 8.1 further outlines several ways to collect nonverbal behavior via electronic devices. *Eye tracking* (for more information see Meißner & Oll, 2019) may become more interesting for age-and-work scholars who want to collect data in field settings due to improvements in mobile eye-tracking devices and software solutions to analyze gaze patterns in meetings (Shim et al., 2020) or from recorded web-based video conferences and the like (e.g., Park et al., 2020). A related opportunity arises when using video-recordings for *automatic emotion recognition* with software such as iMotions or the Noldus FaceReader that allow researchers to automatically collect the frequency and type of facial display measurement (for an exemplary application, see Jiang et al., 2019). While eye tracking and emotion detection focus on facial expressions, *movement detection via sociometric badges/wearable sensors* or *Smartphone/Bluetooth detection* are appropriate tools to capture body movements and movement profiles (for case studies and guidelines using sociometric sensors/wearables, see Chaffin et al., 2017). Furthermore, when collaborating with computer scientists, age-and-work scholars can utilize

TABLE 8.1 Overview of Prevalent Methods to Capture Behavior

Method	Description	Strengths	Weaknesses	Exemplary Application
Verbal interaction coding	Analysis of spoken behavior by cutting communication into sense units and assigning a code to each sense unit	• Existence of several validated tools (e.g., software, coding schemes, statistical methods) to analyze verbal interactions • Can be relatively easily connected to "perceived behavior" measures (e.g., questionnaire scales on knowledge sharing behavior, inclusive behavior etc.)	• Coding behaviors requires at least some interpretation (i.e., risk of rater biases) • Labor intensive (if conducted by human coders) • Still error-prone (if conducted by algorithms, so far most suitable for calculating speaking time) • Data security concerns in field settings are high (→ difficult to get access) • So far more suitable for episodic research questions than for the study of developmental phenomena	Observing meetings of age–diverse dyads/teams (either live or based on transcripts, audio recordings, or videos) to then apply a communication coding scheme to classify verbal statements
Text-based behavior coding	Analysis of written behavior by cutting communication into sense units and assigning a code to each sense unit	• Many organizations already have a system that "records" text-based behaviors (e.g., emails, intranet, virtual collaboration spaces) • Text-based behavior can also be collected "in hindsight" • Aspiring field due to the increase of AI-supported classification approaches (e.g., topic modeling, text mining with R)	• Labor intensive (if conducted by human coders) • When using automatic word detection/classification software, some behavior (e.g., ironic statements) is often wrongly classified • Written communication is often less spontaneous and more planned than "live" interactions • Not possible to combine with nonverbal data (e.g., voice pitch, facial expressions)	Analysis of chat logs, emails, intranet or social media posts, official communication to uncover communication patterns of age–diverse dyads/teams

(Continued)

TABLE 8.1 (Continued)

Method	Description	Strengths	Weaknesses	Exemplary Application
Nonverbal behavior coding	Analysis of nonverbal behavior (e.g., voice tone, pitch, emotional expressions, hand gestures etc.)	• Existence of several validated tools (e.g., software, coding schemes, statistical methods) to analyze nonverbal interactions • Recent technological advances also allow to combine several nonverbal signals (i.e., multimodal interaction coding)	• Coding behaviors requires at least some interpretation (i.e., risk of rater biases) • Labor intensive (if conducted by human coders)	Observing meetings of age-diverse dyads/teams (either live or based on transcripts, audio-recordings or videos) to then apply a nonverbal behavior coding scheme to classify nonverbal expressions
Eye tracking	Analysis of gaze movements and gaze duration via eye trackers or cameras	• Objective data collection • Gaze patterns are important cues in social interaction that are observable by others • Smallest shifts in social attention can be captured	• Requires high expertise for data collection and analysis • Considerable financial investments necessary • Analytical decisions (e.g., threshold values) strongly influence results • So far, limited to nano-, milli-, and micro-levels	Tracking gaze patterns with mobile eye trackers or high-resolution cameras during an interaction between age-diverse coworkers to measure inclusion behavior
Automatic emotion recognition	Automatic extraction and analysis of facial expression via software tool	• Objective data collection • Allows to analyze larger amounts of data than when using human coders • Sensitive to very small facial changes	• Questions about construct validity of measures remain and are subject to software/device updates etc. • Considerable financial investments necessary	Analysis of younger and older workers' usage of different types of smiles (affiliative, dominant, reward) as facilitators of knowledge-sharing efforts

	Description	Advantages	Challenges/Limitations	Example
Movement detection via sociometric badges/wearable sensors	Data collection via devices with sensors (infrared and/or microphone and/or Bluetooth) that are worn by participants	• Objective data collection • Sensitivity of sensors can be adapted to the research question of interest	• Considerable financial investments necessary • Questions about construct validity of measures (e.g., how to deal with "natural noise" remain and are also subject to software/device updates etc.	Analysis of infrared data to gain information about orientation of individuals toward one another (i.e., approach vs. avoidance reactions), kinematic detection to analyze behavioral mimicry in interactions between younger and older employees
Smartphone/Bluetooth Tracking	Data collection via the Bluetooth function of smartphones and/or observation apps	• Objective data collection • Participants can use their "normal" devices	• Risk of over-detection (e.g., people may not interact even when sitting at opposite desks for a day)	Similar to the functionality of tracing apps during the Corona pandemic: Analysis of Bluetooth data to gain information about interaction frequencies of age-diverse coworkers or boundary-spanning behaviors

Source: Adapted from Hemshorn de Sanchez et al. (2021)

wearable technology to explore social dynamics among interacting individuals (e.g., capturing cohesion through paralinguistic features; Nanninga et al., 2017). Scholars can of course also combine several (non)verbal measures of behavior (so-called multimodal investigations; see Tsay, 2020).

Time and Temporal Resolution Levels

Behavior-based studies vary widely with respect to levels of *temporal resolution*, defined as the number of repeated measurements captured for a specific observation period (Klonek et al., 2019). To decide on the appropriate temporal resolution for capturing a particular behavior, one can differentiate between two broad temporal models, namely the *episodic model* and the *developmental model* (see Table 8.2, column 1). Episodic models focus on specific episodes of concrete work activities during which a younger and an older employee work toward a common goal, for example. Developmental models specify how relationships between (age-diverse) employees mature over time and/or proceed through different qualitative stages. Both time-theoretical levels are closely connected, such that episodes are often nested within the developmental (i.e., long-term) life-cycle of age-diverse coworker interactions (Klonek et al., 2019). For example, from an episodic model perspective, a younger and an older employee may engage in dynamic interactions during a single knowledge sharing incident, which constitutes an episode of micro-dynamic interactions. From a developmental model perspective, the same age-diverse coworker dyad may also experience dynamic changes over multiple weeks/operations, thus offering an opportunity to study long-term relational dynamics and emergent constructs such as their performance outputs over time.

Building on these two broad temporal models (episodic vs. developmental), Klonek et al. (2019) suggested a more fine-grained conceptualization of levels of time theory that can help scholars to pinpoint the temporal scope of the respective behavioral phenomenon of interest. Episodic models require more fine-grained time-theoretical levels (i.e., nano-, micro-, or milli-time) than developmental models. A nano-time level captures interaction process dynamics occurring within seconds (or less), a micro-time level reflects dynamics occurring within minutes, and a milli-time level captures dynamics occurring over hours. For example, analyzing counteractive behaviors in an age-diverse work group meeting might focus on eye gaze behavior (i.e., nano-level), the approach vs. avoidance reactions of age-similar and age-diverse coworkers (i.e., micro-level), or the overall effect of age-diversity on counteractive statements during the meeting and its outcomes (i.e., nano-level; see Schulte et al., 2013). In contrast, developmental perspectives use broader time-theoretical levels that reflect how interaction dynamics can unfold over days (meso-time), weeks (macro-time), months (mega-time), or even years (giga-time).

TABLE 8.2 Temporal scopes of (behavior-focused) research

Temporal model	Level of temporal theory	Example construct	Level of measurements	Possible data sources and methods to capture behavior
EPISODIC	Nano-time	Emotional mimicry	Seconds (or less)	Automatic emotion recognition, eye tracking
	Micro-time	Approach vs. avoidance reactions	Minutes	Sociometric badges (movement coding)
	Milli-time	Counteractive behavior	Hours	Video data, instant messaging (interaction coding)
	Meso-time	Knowledge sharing	Days	Electronic activities in virtual teams (interaction coding)
DEVELOPMENTAL	Macro-time	Interaction frequency	Weeks	Smartphone/Bluetooth data (analysis of all contact points)
	Mega-time	Team innovativeness	Months	Product success
	Giga-time	Collective burnout	Years	Yearly performance measures from HR records

Source: Adapted from Klonek et al. (2019)

Note: Most data sources and methods can also be applied to the other temporal levels by splitting up and/or aggregating the collected data to a lower or higher degree of temporal granularity, respectively

The phenomenon of interest (which operates on a specific time-theory level) determines the level of measurement resolution (Klein et al., 1994). To illustrate, emotional contagion between age-diverse coworkers can unfold in seconds or minutes (see Lehmann-Willenbrock et al., 2017). To align theory and methods, a scholar may decide to investigate the dynamics of these phenomena on a nano- or micro-time theoretical level. However, negative affect can also be operationalized at a higher time-theoretical level, such as the affective tone manifesting in several interactions between age-diverse coworkers. This construct changes at a slower pace (e.g., at a macro-time level, that is, displaying weekly or monthly dynamics; Paulsen et al., 2016). Finally, affective phenomena can also be characterized by mega- or giga-temporal dynamics (e.g., collective burn-out, González-Morales et al., 2012) that change over months or years.

Importantly, while it is usually possible to aggregate data collected at a very high temporal resolution (e.g., nano- or micro-level) to a broader level (e.g., milli- or meso-level), the opposite is considerably more difficult (and requires a recoding of the data) or impossible. Hence, when in doubt about the most appropriate time-theoretical choice, we recommend opting for a higher resolution as this offers more opportunities for different data aggregation approaches later on. As a rule of thumb, manual coding approaches (i.e., those that involve human annotators) are more suitable for episodic research questions, whereas recent technological advances in mobile computing can be leveraged for identifying developmental patterns. This is because high-resolution data characterized by high sampling rates related to written text, movement patterns, or physiological measures can now be collected in unrestricted space over extended periods (Chaffin et al., 2017; Klonek et al., 2019).

Future Research Inspiration

An emphasis should be placed on investigating the similarities and differences between self- and other-reports of behavior in the age and work field and the processes that can explain how these differences come about. A lifespan perspective (see Chapter 7) can certainly help in that regard as it points to several age-specific emotions and motives that may influence how younger versus older employees interpret certain behaviors they or others show. For example, given that older employees tend to pay more attention to the positive rather than the negative aspects of a situation (Reed et al., 2014), have a stronger self-serving bias (Mezulis et al., 2004), and experience a higher generativity motive (i.e., striving to pass on knowledge to the next generation; Kooij et al., 2011) in comparison to their younger counterparts, they may tend to overreport their knowledge-sharing behavior and perceive younger persons as more happy and open knowledge receivers than they actually are. This may further be exacerbated by organizational norms (Burmeister et al., 2018), leading to an inaccurate reporting situation in which self-reports vary considerably from objective measures of knowledge sharing. To move the literature on organizational knowledge flows forward (Chapter 15), survey measures of knowledge sharing need to be combined with more objective measures of the very same construct. For example, verbal interaction coding of the knowledge-sharing and receiving behavior occurring in a workplace meeting between a younger and an older employee could be compared against perceptions of those behaviors collected after the workplace meeting. Alternatively, scholars may want to track knowledge sharing in day-to-day electronic communication and combine these time-stamped data with a diary study design (see Chapter 10) in which participants report on their perceptions of knowledge sharing (or broader prosocial behavior) from themselves and their colleagues repeatedly over several days or weeks.

Although knowledge-sharing research is a rather mature field, similar research designs as the one just discussed would also be suitable to advance the field's conceptual understanding of newer research areas such as paradoxical age-related actions at work (Chapter 5). Scholars could for example observe paradoxical behavior using objective indicators of person-job fit and combine this with rich interview data to dive deeper into people's explanations for these objectively captured behaviors. Alternatively, scholars could select a behavioral observation strategy based on Table 8.1 and track how paradoxical behaviors between younger and older employees coevolve over time (for potential developmental patterns, see McClean et al., 2019).

Lastly, objective behavioral indicators can also help move intersectionality research forward (i.e., studies on the combined influence of several diversity characteristics). Marcus (Chapter 4) outlines the importance of differentiating self- and other-perspectives on outcomes in the context of intersectionality theory. Pointing to the importance of considering actual behavior, Schlamp et al. (2021) demonstrate that the same behavior of an actor is perceived differently by others depending on the age and gender of the actor. Specifically, female managers displaying leadership claiming behaviors in workplace meetings who are significantly older than their employees are endorsed in their leader role by their employees just as much as younger and older men. In contrast, female leaders who are younger than their employees are endorsed less in their leader role when claiming leadership—an indicator for the double jeopardy that younger female managers face.

A common question when implementing behavioral research designs relates to the topic of data access. When trying to collect field data, scholars may recognize that not only data protection laws must be considered, but that practitioners are also (and often even more) worried about access to sensitive company-internal information. From our experience with gathering behavioral interaction data in the field, it helps to provide maximum transparency about how the data will be saved (e.g., password-protected and on separate servers), who has access to it (ideally only the personally identifiable research team), how participants can intervene in the event that they have concerns while the data gathering is under way (i.e., retaining the right to stop the behavioral recording and the right to have their data deleted within a specific period of time, prior to anonymizing the data), and how the data will be analyzed—not in abstract terms, but by showing an example analysis so that company representatives can see what it means when scholars say that "data will be reported on an aggregated level only." Furthermore, although the COVID-19 pandemic came with many challenges for the workplace in general and aging workers in particular (see *Work, Aging and Retirement* Special Issue October 2020), it also brought about a new openness and access to virtual tools that can be used for behavioral data collection purposes. Age-and-work scholars who want to contribute to creating better workplaces can embrace the data collection opportunities provided by technologies used when working from home. Moreover, research framed in the context of new technologies may offer a foot into the door of data collection opportunities. For example, provided of course that the data gathering has received ethical and company approval and that all participants consent, online meetings via video software such as Zoom or Microsoft teams can be recorded with a click on a built-in button, thus allowing scholars to easily collect rich behavioral data from tools that employees use in their daily lives anyway.

Conclusion

We hope that, after reading this chapter, age-and-work scholars are motivated to break new ground by more closely aligning the development of novel and useful theory with rigorous research designs that combine both perception-based and behavioral research methods. This is particularly important against the backdrop that several perceptual biases related to different life stages are well known, but we do not know yet what this means for the difference between what people report they do and what they actually do. When keeping up with recent technological advancements in data collection devices (either through self-learning approaches or by partnering up with computer scientists), age-and-work scholars may not only gain access to exiting new testing ground for their theories. Instead, they can also create opportunities to shape the increasingly data-driven economic world with evidence of what works to design age-inclusive organizational environments.

References

Aron, A. (2010). Behavior, the brain, and the social psychology of close relationships. In C. R. Agnew, D. E. Carlston, W. G. Graziano, & J. R. Kelly (Eds.), *Then a miracle occurs: Focusing on behavior in social psychological theory and research* (pp. 283–299). Oxford University Press.

Banks, G. C., Woznyj, H. M., Wesslen, R. S., & Ross, R. L. (2018). A review of best practice recommendations for text analysis in R (and a user-friendly app). *Journal of Business and Psychology, 33*(4), 445–459. https://doi.org/10.1007/s10869-017-9528-3

Baumeister, R. F., Vohs, K. D., & Funder, D. C. (2007). Psychology as the science of self-reports and finger movements: Whatever happened to actual behavior? *Perspectives on Psychological Science*, *2*(4), 396–403. https://doi.org/10.1111/j.1745-6916.2007.00051.x

Brauner, E., Boos, M., & Kolbe, M. (Eds.). (2018). *The Cambridge handbook of group interaction analysis*. Cambridge University Press.

Burmeister, A., Fasbender, U., & Deller, J. (2018). Being perceived as a knowledge sender or knowledge receiver: A multistudy investigation of the effect of age on knowledge transfer. *Journal of Occupational and Organizational Psychology*, *91*(3), 518–545. https://doi.org/10.1111/joop.12208

Carstensen, L. L., Isaacowitz, D. M., & Charles, S. T. (1999). Taking time seriously: A theory of socioemotional selectivity. *American Psychologist*, *54*(3), 165–181. https://doi.org/10.1037/0003-066X.54.3.165

Chaffin, D., Heidl, R., Hollenbeck, J. R., Howe, M., Yu, A., Voorhees, C., & Calantone, R. (2017). The promise and perils of wearable sensors in organizational research. *Organizational Research Methods*, *20*(1), 3–31. https://doi.org/10.1177/1094428115617004

Cooper, J. O., Heron, T. E., & Heward, W. L. (2007). *Applied behavior analysis*. Pearson.

Dang, J., King, K. M., & Inzlicht, M. (2020). Why are self-report and behavioral measures weakly correlated? *Trends in Cognitive Sciences*, *24*(4), 267–269. https://doi.org/10.1016/j.tics.2020.01.007

Ellis, D. A. (2019). Are smartphones really that bad? Improving the psychological measurement of technology-related behaviors. *Computers in Human Behavior*, *97*, 60–66. https://doi.org/10.1016/j.chb.2019.03.006

Gerpott, F. H., Balliet, D., Columbus, S., Molho, C., & de Vries, R. E. (2018). How do people think about interdependence? A multidimensional model of subjective outcome interdependence. *Journal of Personality and Social Psychology*, *115*(4), 716–742. https://doi.org/10.1037/pspp0000166

Gerpott, F. H., Lehmann-Willenbrock, N., & Scheibe, S. (2020). Is work and aging research a science of questionnaires? Moving the field forward by considering perceived versus actual behaviors. *Work, Aging and Retirement*, *6*(2), 65–70. https://doi.org/10.1093/workar/waaa002

González-Morales, M. G., Peiró, J. M., Rodríguez, I., & Bliese, P. D. (2012). Perceived collective burnout: A multilevel explanation of burnout. *Anxiety, Stress & Coping*, *25*(1), 43–61. https://doi.org/10.1080/10615806.2010.542808

Halberstadt, A. G., Parker, A. E., & Castro, V. L. (2013). Nonverbal communication: Developmental perspectives. In J. A. Hall & M. L. Knapp (Eds.), *Handbooks of communication science: Nonverbal communication* (pp. 93–127). De Gruyter Mouton. https://doi.org/10.1515/9783110238150.93

Harrigan, J. A. (2013). Methodology: Coding and studying nonverbal behavior. In J. A. Hall & M. L. Knapp (Eds.), *Handbooks of communication science: Nonverbal communication* (pp. 35–68). De Gruyter Mouton. https://doi.org/10.1515/9783110238150.35

Hemshorn de Sanchez, C. S., Gerpott, F. H., & Lehmann-Willenbrock, N. (in press). A review and future agenda for behavioral research on leader–follower interactions at different temporal scopes. *Journal of Organizational Behavior*. https://doi.org/10.1002/job.2583

Hickman, L., Thapa, S., Tay, L., Cao, M., & Srinivasan, P. (2020). Text preprocessing for text mining in organizational research: Review and recommendations. *Organizational Research Methods*. Advanced online publication. https://doi.org/10.1177/1094428120971683

Jiang, L., Yin, D., & Liu, D. (2019). Can joy buy you money? The impact of the strength, duration, and phases of an entrepreneur's peak displayed joy on funding performance. *Academy of Management Journal, 62*(6), 1848–1871. https://doi.org/10.5465/amj.2017.1423

Jones, S. R. (1992). Was there a Hawthorne effect? *American Journal of Sociology, 98*(3), 451–468. https://doi.org/10.1086/230046

Kauffeld, S., & Lehmann-Willenbrock, N. (2012). Meetings matter: Effects of team meetings on team and organizational success. *Small Group Research, 43*(2), 130–158. https://doi.org/10.1177/1046496411429599

Klein, K. J., Dansereau, F., & Hall, R. J. (1994). Levels issues in theory development, data collection, and analysis. *Academy of Management Review, 19*(2), 195–229. https://doi.org/10.2307/258703

Klonek, F. E., Gerpott, F. H., Lehmann-Willenbrock, N., & Parker, S. K. (2019). Time to go wild: How to conceptualize and measure process dynamics in real teams with high-resolution. *Organizational Psychology Review, 9*(4), 245–275. https://doi.org/10.1177/2041386619886674

Klonek, F. E., Quera, V., Burba, M., & Kauffeld, S. (2016). Group interactions and time: Using sequential analysis to study group dynamics in project meetings. *Group Dynamics: Theory, Research, and Practice, 20*(3), 209–222. https://doi.org/10.1037/gdn0000052

Kooij, D. T., De Lange, A. H., Jansen, P. G., Kanfer, R., & Dikkers, J. S. (2011). Age and work-related motives: Results of a meta-analysis. *Journal of Organizational Behavior, 32*(2), 197–225. https://doi.org/10.1002/job.665

Lehmann-Willenbrock, N., & Allen, J. A. (2018). Modeling temporal interaction dynamics in organizational settings. *Journal of Business and Psychology, 33*(3), 325–344. https://doi.org/10.1007/s10869-017-9506-9

Lehmann-Willenbrock, N., Chiu, M. M., Lei, Z., & Kauffeld, S. (2017). Understanding positivity within dynamic team interactions: A statistical discourse analysis. *Group & Organization Management, 42*(1), 39–78. doi:10.1177/1059601116628720

McClean, S. T., Barnes, C. M., Courtright, S. H., & Johnson, R. E. (2019). Resetting the clock on dynamic leader behaviors: A conceptual integration and agenda for future research. *Academy of Management Annals, 13*(2), 479–508. https://doi.org/10.5465/annals.2017.0081

Meißner, M., & Oll, J. (2019). The promise of eye-tracking methodology in organizational research: A taxonomy, review, and future avenues. *Organizational Research Methods, 22*(2), 590–617. https://doi.org/10.1177/1094428117744882

Meinecke, A. L., & Kauffeld, S. (2019). Engaging the hearts and minds of followers: Leader empathy and language style matching during appraisal interviews. *Journal of Business and Psychology, 34*(4), 485–501. https://doi.org/10.1007/s10869-018-9554-9

Mezulis, A. H., Abramson, L. Y., Hyde, J. S., & Hankin, B. L. (2004). Is there a universal positivity bias in attributions? A meta-analytic review of individual, developmental, and cultural differences in the self-serving attributional bias. *Psychological Bulletin, 130*(5), 711–747. https://doi.org/10.1037/0033-2909.130.5.711

Nanninga, M., Zhang, Y., Lehmann-Willenbrock, N., Szlávik, Z., & Hung, H. (2017). Estimating verbal expressions of task and social cohesion in meetings by quantifying paralinguistic mimicry. In *Proceedings of 19th ACM International Conference on multimodal interaction (ICMI'17)* (pp. 206–215). https://doi.org/10.1145/3136755.3136811

Oswald, F. L., Behrend, T. S., Putka, D. J., & Sinar, E. (2020). Big data in industrial-organizational psychology and human resource management: Forward progress for organizational research and practice. *Annual Review of Organizational Psychology and Organizational Behavior, 7*(1), 505–533. https://doi.org/10.1146/annurev-orgpsych-032117-104553

Park, S., Aksan, E., Zhang, X., & Hilliges, O. (2020, August). Towards end-to-end video-based eye-tracking. In *European Conference on computer vision* (pp. 747–763). Springer, Cham.

Paulsen, H. F. K., Klonek, F. E., Schneider, K., & Kauffeld, S. (2016). Group affective tone and team performance: A week-level study in project teams. *Frontiers in Communication*, *1*(7), 1–10. https://doi.org/10.3389/fcomm.2016.00007

Reed, A. E., Chan, L., & Mikels, J. A. (2014). Meta-analysis of the age-related positivity effect: Age differences in preferences for positive over negative information. *Psychology and Aging*, *29*(1), 1–15. https://doi.org/10.1037/a0035194

Schlamp, S., Gerpott, F. H., Hentschel, T., & Van Quaquebeke, N. (2021). *Young female managers are less endorsed as leaders when claiming leadership in interactions: A conceptual account of their double-burden* (Manuscript submitted for the Academy of Management Conference).

Schulte, E. M., Lehmann-Willenbrock, N., & Kauffeld, S. (2013). Age, forgiveness, and meeting behavior: A multilevel study. *Journal of Managerial Psychology*, *28*(7–8), 928–949. https://doi.org/10.1108/JMP-06-2013-0193

Shim, S. H., Livingston, R., Phillips, K. W., & Lam, S. S. (2020). The impact of leader eye gaze on disparity in member influence: Implications for process and performance in diverse groups. *Academy of Management Journal*. Advanced online publication. https://doi.org/10.5465/amj.2017.1507

Soller, A., & Lesgold, A. (2003). A computational approach to analyzing online knowledge sharing interaction. *Artificial Intelligence in Education: Shaping the Future of Learning Through Intelligent Technologies*, *922*(6389), 253.

Speer, A. B. (2021). Scoring dimension-level job performance from narrative comments: Validity and generalizability when using natural language processing. *Organizational Research Methods, 24*(3), 572–594. https://doi.org/10.1177/1094428120930815

Taneva, S. K., Arnold, J., & Nicolson, R. (2016). The experience of being an older worker in an organization: A qualitative analysis. *Work, Aging and Retirement*, *2*(4), 396–414. https://doi.org/10.1093/workar/waw011

Tsay, C. J. (2020). Visuals dominate investor decisions about entrepreneurial pitches. *Academy of Management Discoveries*. Advanced online publication. https://doi.org/10.5465/amd.2019.0234

Uher, J. (2016). What is behavior? And (when) is language behavior? A metatheoretical definition. *Journal for the Theory of Social Behavior*, *46*(4), 475–501. https://doi.org/10.1111/jtsb.12104

Van Quaquebeke, N., & Felps, W. (2018). Respectful inquiry: A motivational account of leading through asking questions and listening. *Academy of Management Review*, *43*(1), 5–27. https://doi.org/10.5465/amr.2014.0537

Waller, M. J., & Kaplan, S. A. (2018). Systematic behavioral observation for emergent team phenomena: Key considerations for quantitative video-based approaches. *Organizational Research Methods*, *21*(2), 500–515. https://doi.org/10.1177/1094428116647785

Wickström, G., & Bendix, T. (2000). The "Hawthorne effect" - What did the original Hawthorne studies actually show? *Scandinavian Journal of Work, Environment & Health*, *26*(4), 363–367. https://doi.org/10.5271/sjweh.555

9

AGE AT THE TEAM AND ORGANIZATIONAL LEVELS

Florian Kunze and Kilian Hampel

Demographic change has been observed in almost all western-industrialized economies (Daniele et al., 2019). In Germany, for example, the number of people aged 67 years and older has increased by 54% between 1990 and 2018 (BPB, 2019). This aging of societies has immense implications for organizations and the nature of work, where the average employee is older and teams and organizations are more age-diverse than ever before (Kunze & Menges, 2017).

Following this societal trend, the literature on aging in the workplace has considerably increased over the past two decades. The research focus in this area, with contributions from I/O psychologists, management researchers, and gerontologists, has been mainly on the individual level of analysis to understand how successful individual aging manifests at work (e.g., Zacher, 2015). In practice, the demographic change also results in implications for organizations, beyond individual employees, especially in terms of rising workforce age diversity (i.e., the distribution of different age groups within the workplace; Wang & Fang, 2020). In the current literature, this perspective is far less discussed.

Still, the last 15 years have seen an increase in studies that consider age diversity effects in organizations. Especially in organizational behavior (e.g., Kunze et al., 2011, 2013) and economics research (e.g., Grund & Westergaard-Nielsen, 2008; P. Ilmakunnas & S. Ilmakunnas, 2011), research has focused on the effects of age diversity on both team and organizational outcomes. Other studies have started to consider the tailoring of human resource (HR) practices to an increasingly age-diverse workforce (Boehm et al., 2014) or the evolvement of an organizational climate for successful aging at work for all employees (Zacher & Yang, 2016). Therefore, the present chapter's first aim is to summarize the development of the empirical literature on age as a collective phenomenon in teams and organizations with a particular focus on age diversity research. Beyond this summary,

DOI: 10.4324/9781003089674-12

our second contribution is to offer a guide for theoretical and methodological advancement in this field of research and concrete ideas on how practitioners can manage age diversity in teams and organizations.

Age Diversity Research at the Team Level

When dealing with age-related factors at the team level of analysis, it is helpful to briefly describe the various social processes that underlie teams and their members when confronted with high or low levels of age diversity or "age heterogeneity." In general, *age diversity* can be defined as "age distribution differences among a group of employees either in specific organizational workgroups or the organization" (Paoletti et al., 2020, p. 5). Conceptually, two opposing theoretical perspectives exist to explain compositional age-structures' effects on team processes and outcomes:

First, the *"information/decision-making perspective"* (Van Knippenberg et al., 2004, p. 1009) sees (age) diversity as an opportunity to seize the various skillsets and complementary resources of team members and achieve better results than homogeneous teams. Furthermore, heterogeneous teams are likely to be less vulnerable to biased group think behaviors (Janis, 1972), as heterogeneous teams test to exhibit higher levels of creativity and innovation-related processes (e.g., Kurtzberg, 2005).

Second, contrary to the information/decision-making perspective, a *social identity approach* or *social-categorization perspective* (Tajfel & Turner, 1986) proposes an adverse effect of age-diversity on team processes and outcomes. Based on social-linking and similarity-attraction processes (Byrne, 1971), individuals tend to classify themselves among salient demographic characteristics, such as age. This can lead quickly to in- and out-group formations, followed by negative consequences, such as mutual stereotyping and discrimination (Kunze et al., 2011), all adversely affecting team processes and outcomes. Based on these opposing theoretical accounts, both positive and negative effects of age diversity within teams are imaginable. In the following sections, we will summarize the empirical literature on such phenomena, starting with research on team performance, followed by a summary of comparable research conducted at the organizational level of analysis.

Age Diversity and Team Performance

Team performance is the most often studied outcome variable in research on age diversity, both in primary studies that aim to study age effects and in many team-level studies that only considered age diversity as a covariate. These results have been summarized in multiple reviews and meta-analyses. First, Bell et al. (2011) did not find a significant meta-analytic association between age diversity and workgroup performance. However, Joshi and Roh (2009) observed a negative effect of age heterogeneity on team performance in a meta-analysis conducted across 8,757 teams in 39 studies. In another meta-analysis, Van Dijk et al. (2012) found age diversity to be negatively related to subjective performance but did not find evidence for this effect when referring to objectively assessed performance criteria. Furthermore, Schneid et al. (2016) also quantitatively reviewed existing research on age diversity and team outcomes and did not find statistical evidence for a positive or negative relationship between age diversity and performance.

These mixed findings from meta-analyses are also mirrored in primary empirical research studies that have looked at age diversity and team performance. This literature shows heterogeneous relationships ranging from negative effects (Jehn & Bezrukova, 2004), to curvilinear relationships (Seong & Hong, 2018), to null findings (Pelled et al., 1999). Similarly, inconsistent results are reported for research on top management teams (TMTs) age diversity for both team as well as organizational performance outcomes, with studies reporting either null findings (Bunderson & Sutcliffe, 2002), positive relationships with corporate performance (Ferrero-Ferrero et al., 2015), or negative relationships with objective company performance (Tanikawa et al., 2017).

Context Factors of Age Diversity and Team Performance

One explanation for the inconsistency in the simple effects of age diversity on team and organizational performance outcomes may be that there are boundary conditions, in the form of contextual factors, that affect the nature of these relationships. Indeed, several studies have investigated potential context effects that might help to explain the strength and direction/form of the relationship between age diversity and team performance. First, age diversity is more beneficial for complex rather than simple tasks, as reported by Bowers et al. (2000); although meta-analytic findings are not consistent in this regard (see Schneid et al., 2016). Second, leadership behavior might play an essential role in the relationship between age diversity and team performance. Hoch et al. (2010) found age-diverse teams to perform better with low shared leadership than with high shared leadership.

Interestingly, for age-homogenous groups, there seemed to be the opposite effect. Kearney and Gebert (2009) and Kunze and Bruch (2010) found transformational leadership to moderate the relationship between age diversity and team performance. In the study by Kearney and Gebert (2009), age diversity was not related to team performance when transformational leadership was high, while it was negatively associated with team performance when transformational leadership was low. Kunze and Bruch (2010) found age diversity measured in combination with gender and tenure to be positively related to perceived productive energy in teams with high transformational leadership, whereas the relationship was strongly negative for teams with low transformational leadership. More recently, Seong and Hong (2018) found charismatic leadership to moderate this relationship such that higher charismatic leadership weakened the negative effect of high age diversity on team performance.

Third, other research has investigated team processes as potential contextual boundary conditions that affect the age diversity–team performance relationship. Such research suggests, for example, that the quality of team processes, cooperation, and teamwork suppress the information/decision-making perspective advantages and hinder the exchange of critical discussions about decisions in age-diverse teams (Ely, 2004). In contrast, Choi and Rainey (2010) also investigated team processes (i.e., cooperation, communication) and did not find a significant moderation effect. Other studies found need for cognition—the extent to which the team enjoys being thoughtful—to be a positive boundary condition for the age diversity–performance relationship (Kearney et al., 2009). Accordingly, high need for cognition leads to a positive indirect effect of age diversity and team performance, whereas low need for cognition has the opposite contextual effect (Kearney et al., 2009). Finally, Scheuer and Loughlin (2018) found age diversity to be positively related to team performance under high levels of status congruity—defined as a high degree of perceived status legitimacy—and under high levels of cognition-based trust.

Age Diversity and Other Team-Level Outcomes

Beyond the extensively researched relationship between age diversity and team performance, scholars have also investigated other potential outcome variables that may be associated with team age diversity, which we shortly summarize here. First, meta-analytic evidence suggests weak relationships between age diversity and both team-level *turnover* and *innovation behaviors* (the findings are inconclusive as to the meta-analysis by Schneid et al., 2016). However, in one more recent study, Shuying and Shuijuan (2017) found that age diversity in TMTs was negatively related to innovation.

Other research has investigated relationships between team age diversity and *communication* and *information-sharing behavior*. While Kearney et al. (2009) and Kearney and Gebert (2009) did not find a direct effect of age diversity on the elaboration of task-relevant information, they found transformational leadership (Kearney & Gebert, 2009) as well as the need for cognition (Kearney et al., 2009) to each moderate the relationship. On the other hand, Zenger and Lawrence (1989) reported a negative effect of age diversity in teams on the frequency of technical communication, such that teams with more age-homogenous members were likely to communicate more frequently than groups with age-dissimilar members. For the relationship between age diversity and *emotion regulation*, Kim et al. (2013) found age diversity to be positively related to employees' emotional regulation in 246 workgroups.

Other research has considered *team conflict* as an outcome and found null (Jehn et al., 1997), negative (Pelled et al., 1999), and positive effects (Pelled et al., 2001) on *relationship conflict*, while not reporting any substantial effect in *task conflict* (e.g., Pelled et al., 2001). For the relationship between workgroup age diversity and *wellbeing*, Liebermann et al. (2013) found an adverse effect of team age diversity on employees' health. Interestingly, this effect was shown to be significantly stronger for younger and older individuals. Simultaneously, for middle-aged employees, their health did not seem to be negatively affected by age diversity. Furthermore, Wegge et al. (2008) found age diversity to be positively correlated with health disorders; however, this effect was only observed within groups that worked on routine decision-making tasks.

In summary, research on age diversity at the team level has intensified in recent decades. Additionally, performance is the most often studied outcome variable of team age diversity, but there has also been a focus on other outcome variables like innovation, health, turnover, and conflict. This review highlights a large degree of inconclusiveness in the results of studies in this domain, as for most outcome variables no clear unilateral effect of age diversity can be observed. Moreover, results differ when differentiating between "normal" teams and top management teams. Next, we examine existing research on age diversity at the organizational level of analysis.

Age Diversity Research at the Organizational Level

For the relationship between age diversity and firm performance, two studies by Kunze and colleagues (Kunze et al., 2013, 2011) did not find a direct relationship between age diversity and firm performance but rather an indirect route via the perception of age discrimination in organizations. In both studies age diversity increased collective perceptions of age diversity among all age groups, and Kunze et al. (2013) found that this process can be mitigated through low levels of age stereotypes of the organization's top management and high levels of pro-diversity practices and trainings. This indicates that social-categorization processes are also important for understanding age diversity effects in organizations. Other research has similarly not found direct effects of age diversity on firm performance (e.g., Ilmakunnas et al., 2004; Buche et al., 2013). On the other hand, a positive effect of age diversity on firm performance was found by Li et al. (2011) and as well as by P. Ilmakunnas and S. Ilmakunnas (2011). Similarly, De Meulenaere et al. (2016) measure labor productivity (i.e., dividing the firms' gross added value by the number of employees) and find age diversity operationalized as variety (i.e., hetereogeneity as a maximum number of represented age groups) to positively affect productivity, while age diversity measured as age polarization (i.e., few, large, homogeneous subgroups that widely differ in average age) did negatively affect labor productivity. Grund and Westergaard-Nielsen (2008) find both mean age and age diversity in firms to have an inverse U-shaped relationship with company performance. Thus, similar to the review at the team level, the age diversity-performance relationship results are generally ambiguous, with results variously suggesting null, positive, negative, or potentially nonlinear as well as indirect relationships.

Context Factors of Age Diversity and Organizational Performance

Much like with team performance outcomes, research has also considered various contextual factors as moderators of the relationship between age diversity and organizational performance. First, Backes-Gellner and Veen (2013) found task type to be a relevant contextual factor that helps to explain age diversity—organizational performance relationships. For companies who tend to engage in more creative tasks (e.g., companies that are innovative and develop a certain amount of new products over time), there was a positive relationship between age diversity and company-level productivity (i.e., defined as companies' "sales minus input costs per employee" (Backes-Gellner & Veen, 2013, p. 286), whereas a negative relationship between age diversity and productivity was observed for companies with more standardized, routine tasks (e.g., firms with fewer innovations and more standardized tasks).

De Meulenaere et al. (2016) showed that the positive relationship between age variety and labor productivity was stronger in larger firms and those with higher levels of job security. Moreover, there was a negative relationship between age polarization and productivity, and this negative relationship was again more relevant for larger firms than for small firms, whereas job security did not seem to have a moderating effect. De Meulenaere and Kunze (2020) similarly investigated the contextual influence of age distance (i.e., measured by the standard deviation of age in firms) in a longitudinal study. Results suggest that age diversity is negatively related to labor productivity, defined in terms of a firm's gross added value divided by the number of employees only for firms with larger age distances in their workforce.

Research has also addressed the importance of age diversity management and its impact on organizational performance. For example, Kunze et al. (2013) showed that diversity-friendly HR practices can mitigate the negative impact of age diversity on age discrimination climate and have positive indirect implications for organizational performance. Furthermore, they found negative age stereotypes held by TMTs to exacerbate the negative effect of age diversity on age discrimination climate and firm performance (Kunze et al., 2013). Choi and Rainey (2010) did not find diversity management to moderate the age diversity-organizational performance relationship but observed that age diversity is negatively linked to organizational performance under conditions of complaints about nonsufficient diversity management at the firm. Boehm et al. (2014) also show that age-inclusive HR practices can lead to stronger age diversity climates, defined as "perceptions of the fair and nondiscriminatory treatment of employees of all age groups" (2014, p. 671), which is positively associated with collective perceptions of social exchange and firm performance and negatively associated with turnover intentions. Ali and French (2019) reported age diversity management to be positively related to firms' intentions to extend their CSR practices, while no association with performance was found. Most recently, Rudolph and Zacher (2020) support the positive impact of age-inclusive human resource practices and show it to indirectly lead to increased workability through more positive age diversity climate.

Age Diversity and Other Organizational-Level Outcomes

Other studies have also considered outcomes beyond organizational performance. For example, Lee and Kim (2020) find that age diversity is associated with lower levels of relational coordination and that this negative association was exacerbated when structural empowerment levels were low. Relational coordination, furthermore, had a positive impact on firm performance. Østergaard et al. (2011) investigated firm diversity and organizational innovation. Although educational and gender diversity positively affected innovation, age diversity was negatively related to innovative performance. Contrary to this finding, Sung and Choi (2019) found age diversity to increase firm innovation among high-tech firms. Rabl and Triana (2014) investigated the potential effect of organizational age diversity and organizational age diversity management practices on organizational attractiveness to potential applicants in an experimental survey study. They found age diversity to be positively related to attractiveness to potential applicants and to be negatively related to age discrimination in the organization expected by the applicants. Additionally, age diversity management practices were positively associated with organizational attractiveness and negatively associated with applicants' expected age discrimination (Rabl & Triana, 2014).

In summary, this review shows the increased interest that research on age diversity at the organizational level has experienced in recent years. More specifically, there is emerging evidence to support the moderating effect of age-inclusive HR-practices and other diversity-related initiatives (e.g., trainings and workshops to promote a diversity-friendly culture within the organization) on the relationship between age diversity and organizational performance. This is important both theoretically and practically and has distinct implications for the continued study of age diversity structures at the organizational level. The following section aims to make helpful suggestions for future research of age diversity at the team and organizational levels and outlines the core practical implications of these lines of research.

Ideas for Future Research on Age at the Team and Organizational Levels

Although there is a considerable development in aging research in teams and organizations, as shown previously, there is still immense potential for further developing the field in different and innovative directions. In the following sections we will first introduce four research areas where we see potential for theoretical and methodological advances, followed by a concluding section discussing key practical implications.

Interrelation of Age with Other (Perceptual) Diversity Dimensions in Organizations

Age is not the only diversity facet that drives social-categorization or information-sharing processes in teams and organizations. Consequently, a broader intersectionality perspective (see Chapter 4 in this volume) or, more specifically, "faultline" concept might help integrate age diversity research with research on other surface-level (i.e., gender, tenure, ethnicity) and deep-level (i.e., personality, attitudes, values) criteria. Faultlines are hypothetical dividing lines that split a group into subgroups based on several demographic criteria aligned with one another (Lau & Murnighan, 1998). For example, a four-person team might have strong faultlines if age and gender attributes (two younger women vs. two older men) are aligned. In contrast, weak faultlines might exist in a team if gender functions as a bridging factor in an age-diverse team (two younger women vs. two older women). There are several methodological options available to calculate such faultline measures, for example, the average silhouette width (ASW) approach by Meyer and Glenz (2013). We would thus encourage the development of more research on team faultlines, including age at the team level of analysis, to supplement and extend the limited number of existing studies that have used this approach (e.g., Kunze & Bruch, 2010; Van Knippenberg et al., 2011; Valls et al., 2020). Importantly, too, at the organizational level of analysis, we are not aware of any study that examines the combination of age with other diversity facets on organizational performance and outcomes.

Conceptually, empirical research in this area might also profit from the conceptual ideas in the recent paper by Wegge and Meyer (2020). The authors propose that the individual perception of diversity differences is key for both age diversity and faultline research. Only if employees perceive themselves to be different from others may diversity-related processes play out in teams and organizations. We would extend this argumentation even further and argue that research should also consider the age perception or subjective age (i.e., how old or young individuals feel compared to their chronological age; see also Chapter 3 in this volume) as a base for age diversity processes. Recent research in gerontology (e.g., Montepare, 2009) and organizational behavior (e.g., Kunze et al., 2015; Rudolph et al., 2019) has conceptualized and shown that age perceptions can relate to general and work-related behaviors. Recently, diary studies have reported that work events, such as stress perceptions, drive daily fluctuation of subjective age (Armenta et al., 2018; Goecke & Kunze, 2020). We would speculate that employees' differing chronological and subjective age perceptions are also relevant for diversity processes in teams and organizations. Suppose, for example, in a chronologically age-diverse team, the older team members have notably different perceptions of their age. In that case, similar subjective age perceptions can function as a bridge function that hinders age-based subgroup formation in the team. Additionally, chronologically older employees are likely to possess different levels and types of experience-based knowledge compared to chronologically younger employees, which might present an advantage stemming from the age-diverse composition. In consequence, we would strongly encourage researchers to integrate multifaceted perceptions of age (e.g., Kooij et al., 2013) into future studies on age at both the team and organizational levels. As a first recent example, Kunze et al. (2021) have shown that subjective age diversity affects social processes and individual outcomes beyond chronological age diversity. Testing the interrelation of perceptual and objective age measures in one measure or model might be the next logical step in this research area.

Testing More Complex Measures and Dynamic Theories for Age in Teams and Organizations

As the empirical literature reviewed previously shows, there is minimal evidence that supports the direction and unconditional relationship between age diversity on collective processes and outcomes. Only when considered at the organizational level of analysis is there some consistent evidence to indicate a positive relationship between age diversity and performance, and this is especially true when considering more complex operationalizations of age diversity (i.e., differentiating between age heterogeneity as a diversity and separation measure; De Meulenaere & Kunze, 2020; De Meulenaere et al., 2016). We strongly encourage more research on such complex operationalizations of age diversity, taking the influential framework for diversity operationalization by Harrison and Klein (2007) into account, especially at the team level of analysis. One valuable avenue here might be to consider perceptions of separation vs. variety (age) diversity in teams and organizations to gain more insights as to "when" age diversity can increase performance.

Another fruitful avenue for future age diversity research can incorporate recent empirical advancements borrowed from the general diversity literature. One example is the recent paper by Van Dijk et al. (2017) on microfoundations of diversity research, which argues that stereotypes play a dynamic role in diversity processes. Also, for the case of age diversity, it is unclear if negative mutual stereotypes diminish in their prevalence and impact over time, as the intergroup contact theory would suggest (Pettigrew, 1998). Also, recent empirical research has shown that being in a minority position has long-lasting negative consequences over time (Reinwald & Kunze, 2020). Thus, we would encourage more research on the dynamic effects of team and organizational diversity (e.g., Li et al., 2018), especially focusing on interventions (e.g., employee training, leadership development) to help mitigate the accumulation of and impact of negative age-related stereotypes in age-diverse settings.

Such a dynamic perspective (see also Chapter 10 in this volume) might also help researchers better understand how workforce age structures (e.g., mean age and age diversity) affect organizational productivity over time. Research might use secondary data pools of companies (i.e., the IAB establishment panel in Germany; Ellguth et al., 2014) and observe if stability and/or dynamics in the workforce mean age affects workforce productivity differently. If, for example, a sudden downsizing via early retirement schemes happens in companies, does that affect productivity?; or if a former start-up company acquires a more established firm and has a sudden shift in the workforce age structure, how does that relate to productivity? Discontinuous growth models could be applied to test such dynamic models (Bliese & Lang, 2016).

Age and the Digital Divide in Organizations

An additional relevant issue for age processes and management in organizations is the increasing role of digitalization. Over the last decade, information and communication technologies have transformed the task and work processes in many industries (Colbert et al., 2016). Most jobs require at least a certain amount of digital communication and application. At least stereotypically, there is a potential digital divide between younger workers who were socialized with modern technologies and older workers who may have a less intuitive knowledge of digital competencies (e.g., Colbert et al., 2016). This digital divide increases the potential for age-based categorization in teams and organizations from an age-diversity perspective. Digital competencies, both self-perceived and stereotypically ascribed, can function as another category that divides age groups and spurs stereotypes and discriminatory behavior. Therefore, we would argue that it is a key imperative for organizations to reduce technologically related stereotypes against aging employees and invest continuously in all age groups' digital competencies. This seems relevant, as empirical research does not support a strong digital divide between members of different age groups (Guo et al., 2008). Thus, both research and practical HR-related interventions on digital training (Fenech et al., 2019) should be valuable endeavors for future research on age in organizations.

Age and Status in Organizations

Factors that are often closely related to age structures in organizations are status and hierarchy. In many organizations, age is a status indicator, and traditionally the most experienced employees should receive the highest pay and hierarchical rank. If companies move away from such seniority-based reward systems, traditional age (Lawrence, 1988) and status norms (Erickson & Grove, 2007) might be violated. Especially if companies move to less hierarchical structures, such as shared leadership approaches and self-managed teams, they need to be aware that these new structures often violate classical age and status norms. In age-diverse team and organizational settings, a transformation toward such a flexible structure needs to be closely evaluated—with constant assessment of workforces' perceptions through employee surveys—and might be an interesting avenue for future research. Also, evaluation studies that assess how sudden shifts in structures affect behaviors and productivity of age-diverse workforces are interesting avenues for future research.

Implications for Practitioners Dealing with Age Diversity in Teams and Organizations

Beyond the potential future research agenda, we also want to discuss the critical practical implications of age in teams and organizations. First and foremost, the current empirical research indicates that age and team composition need to be actively addressed by organizations and executives. If age diversity increases without special attention by critical stakeholders in organizations, it can adversely affect collective processes and outcomes. As such, the common myth that (age) diversity just needs to be expanded for the good of the employees and the organizations is not correct.

Companies should regularly evaluate their workforce's age structure and project future developments to manage age diversity. Such monitoring through process-generated HR data will allow them to identify those teams and areas that require the most attention in terms of age-diversity management. Beyond age, companies should also track other surface-level (ethnicity or race) or deep-level (subjective age, personality traits) diversity facets to assess if potential age subgroups can be aligned with other potential faultline activation characteristics. This is particularly relevant if companies try to increase the female workforce participation in formerly male-dominated areas (i.e., engineering teams, top management teams).

Additionally, we would encourage companies to invest in training and development activities that increase a prodiversity culture in organizations. As research shows that general diversity training can buffer negative effects of age diversity at the firm level (Kunze et al., 2013) and age-specific HR-practices increase a positive age-diversity climate in organizations, there is a clear business case for such training investments. Thus, HR should evaluate whether they invest enough resources in training their workforce and executives in working toward a positive age culture in their organizations.

Furthermore, at the team level, tailored leadership behavior might help to prevent negative consequences of age diversity. Multiple studies (e.g., Kearney & Gebert, 2009; Kunze & Bruch, 2010) have shown that transformational leadership behaviors buffer adverse effects of age diversity on team performance. Fostering a shared vision, charismatic communication, intellectual stimulation, and individualized consideration as the core facets of transformational leadership can lower negative age stereotyping and subgrouping behaviors in teams. At the organizational level, research has also shown that top management has an essential impact on the occurrence of age-based subgrouping processes in organizations. As a consequence, companies would be well advised to train and sensitize their top-ranked executives for their role-modeling behaviors.

Finally, despite limited empirical research to date, we would also recommend that companies consider the role of age diversity with respect to the increasing digitalization and other technological advancements at the workplace. Especially given common stereotypes of aging employees' lower technological skills, companies should actively work against turning these stereotypes into self-fulfilling prophecies. If companies can prevent a technology-related age gap from occurring, this may benefit their overall adaptiveness to technological change and also help them to avoid technology from being a further layer for developing age-related categorization and subgrouping processes.

References

Ali, M., & French, E. (2019). Age diversity management and organisational outcomes: The role of diversity perspectives. *Human Resource Management Journal, 29*(2), 287–307. https://doi.org/10.1111/1748-8583.12225

Armenta, B. M., Scheibe, S., Stroebe, K., Postmes, T., & Van Yperen, N. W. (2018). Dynamic, not stable: Daily variations in subjective age bias and age group identification predict daily well-being in older workers. *Psychology and Aging, 33*(4), 559. https://doi.org/10.1037/pag0000263

Backes-Gellner, U., & Veen, S. (2013). Positive effects of ageing and age diversity in innovative companies-large-scale empirical evidence on company productivity. *Human Resource Management Journal, 23*(3), 279–295. https://doi.org/10.1111/1748-8583.12011

Bell, S. T., Villado, A. J., Lukasik, M. A., Belau, L., & Briggs, A. L. (2011). Getting specific about demographic diversity variable and team performance relationships: A meta-analysis. *Journal of Management, 37*(3), 709–743. https://doi.org/10.1177/0149206310365001

Bliese, P. D., & Lang, J. W. (2016). Understanding relative and absolute change in discontinuous growth models: Coding alternatives and implications for hypothesis testing. *Organizational Research Methods, 19*(4), 562–592. https://doi.org/10.1177/1094428116633502

Boehm, S. A., Kunze, F., & Bruch, H. (2014). Spotlight on age-diversity climate: The impact of age-inclusive HR practices on firm-level outcomes. *Personnel Psychology, 67*(3), 667–704. https://doi.org/10.1111/peps.12047

Bowers, C. A., Pharmer, J. A., & Salas, E. (2000). When member homogeneity is needed in work teams: A meta-analysis. *Small Group Research, 31*(3), 305–327. https://doi.org/10.1177/104649640003100303

BPB. (2019). *Bevölkerungsentwicklung und Altersstruktur.* www.bpb.de/nachschlagen/zahlen-und-fakten/soziale-situation-in-deutschland/61541/altersstruktur#:~:text=Die%20Zahl%20der%20Menschen%20im,4%25%20auf%202015%2C9%20Millionen.&text=Die%20Bevölkerungszahl%20ist%20seit%202014,2018%20bei%2082%2C9%20Millionen

Buche, A., Jungbauer-Gans, M., Niebuhr, A., & Peters, C. (2013). Diversität und Erfolg von Organisationen/Diversity and Organizational Performance. *Zeitschrift für Soziologie, 42*(6), 483–501. https://doi.org/10.1515/zfsoz-2013-0604

Bunderson, J. S., & Sutcliffe, K. M. (2002). Comparing alternative conceptualizations of functional diversity in management teams: Process and performance effects. *Academy of Management Journal, 45*(5), 875–893. https://doi.org/10.2307/3069319

Byrne, D. E. (1971). *The attraction paradigm* (Vol. 462). Academic Press.

Choi, S., & Rainey, H. G. (2010). Managing diversity in US federal agencies: Effects of diversity and diversity management on employee perceptions of organizational performance. *Public Administration Review, 70*(1), 109–121. https://doi.org/10.1111/j.1540-6210.2009.02115.x

Colbert, A., Yee, N., & George, G. (2016). The digital workforce and the workplace of the future. *Academy of Management Journal, 59*(3), 731–739. https://doi.org/10.5465/amj.2016.4003

Daniele, F., Honiden, T., & Lembcke, A. C. (2019). Ageing and productivity growth in OECD regions: Combatting the economic impact of ageing through productivity growth? *OECD Regional Development Working Papers, 2019*(8), 1–58.

De Meulenaere, K., Boone, C., & Buyl, T. (2016). Unraveling the impact of workforce age diversity on labor productivity: The moderating role of firm size and job security. *Journal of Organizational Behavior, 37*(2), 193–212. https://doi.org/10.1002/job.2036

De Meulenaere, K., & Kunze, F. (2020). Distance matters! The role of employees' age distance on the effects of workforce age heterogeneity on firm performance. *Human Resource Management, 60*(2), 499–516. https://doi.org/10.1002/hrm.22031

Ellguth, P., Kohaut, S., & Möller, I. (2014). The IAB Establishment Panel—methodological essentials and data quality. *Journal for Labour Market Research, 47*(1–2), 27–41. https://doi.org/10.1007/s12651-013-0151-0

Ely, R. J. (2004). A field study of group diversity, participation in diversity education programs, and performance. *Journal of Organizational Behavior, 25*(6), 755–780. https://doi.org/10.1002/job.268

Erickson, R., & Grove, W. (2007). Why emotions matter: Age, agitation, and burnout among registered nurses. *Online Journal of Issues in Nursing, 13*(1), 1–13. https://doi.org/10.3912/OJIN.Vol13No01PPT01

Fenech, R., Baguant, P., & Ivanov, D. (2019). The changing role of human resource management in an era of digital transformation. *Journal of Management Information and Decision Sciences, 22*(2), 166–175.

Ferrero-Ferrero, I., Fernández-Izquierdo, M. Á., & Muñoz-Torres, M. J. (2015). Age diversity: An empirical study in the board of directors. *Cybernetics and Systems, 46*(3–4), 249–270. https://doi.org/10.1080/01969722.2015.1012894

Goecke, T., & Kunze, F. (2020). "How old do you feel today at work?" Work-related drivers of subjective age in the workplace. *European Journal of Work and Organizational Psychology, 29*(3), 462–476. https://doi.org/10.1080/1359432X.2020.1724098

Grund, C., & Westergaard-Nielsen, N. (2008). Age structure of the workforce and firm performance. *International Journal of Manpower, 29*(5), 410–422. https://doi.org/10.1108/01437720810888553

Guo, R. X., Dobson, T., & Petrina, S. (2008). Digital natives, digital immigrants: An analysis of age and ICT competency in teacher education. *Journal of Educational Computing Research, 38*(3), 235–254. https://doi.org/10.2190/ec.38.3.a

Harrison, D. A., & Klein, K. J. (2007). What's the difference? Diversity constructs as separation, variety, or disparity in organizations. *Academy of Management Review, 32*(4), 1199–1228. https://doi.org/10.5465/amr.2007.26586096

Hoch, J. E., Pearce, C. L., & Welzel, L. (2010). Is the most effective team leadership shared? The impact of shared leadership, age diversity, and coordination on team performance. *Journal of Personnel Psychology, 9*(3), 105. https://doi.org/10.1027/1866-5888/a000020

Ilmakunnas, P., & Ilmakunnas, S. (2011). Diversity at the workplace: Whom does it benefit? *De Economist, 159*(2), 223–255. https://doi.org/10.1007/s10645-011-9161-x

Ilmakunnas, P., Maliranta, M., & Vainiomäki, J. (2004). The roles of employer and employee characteristics for plant productivity. *Journal of Productivity Analysis, 21*(3), 249–276. https://doi.org/10.1023/B:PROD.0000022093.59352.5e

Janis, I. L. (1972). *Victims of groupthink: A psychological study of foreign-policy decisions and fiascoes.* Houghton Mifflin.

Jehn, K. A., & Bezrukova, K. (2004). A field study of group diversity, workgroup context, and performance. *Journal of Organizational Behavior, 25*(6), 703–729. https://doi.org/10.1002/job.257

Jehn, K. A., Chadwick, C., & Thatcher, S. M. (1997). To agree or not to agree: The effects of value congruence, individual demographic dissimilarity, and conflict on workgroup outcomes. *International Journal of Conflict Management, 8*(4), 287–305. https://doi.org/10.1108/eb022799

Joshi, A., & Roh, H. (2009). The role of context in work team diversity research: A meta-analytic review. *Academy of Management Journal, 52*(3), 599–627. https://doi.org/10.5465/AMJ.2009.41331491

Kearney, E., & Gebert, D. (2009). Managing diversity and enhancing team outcomes: The promise of transformational leadership. *Journal of Applied Psychology, 94*(1), 77–89. https://doi.org/10.1037/a0013077

Kearney, E., Gebert, D., & Voelpel, S. C. (2009). When and how diversity benefits teams: The importance of team members' need for cognition. *Academy of Management Journal, 52*(3), 581–598. https://doi.org/10.5465/AMJ.2009.41331431

Kim, E., Bhave, D. P., & Glomb, T. M. (2013). Emotion regulation in workgroups: The roles of demographic diversity and relational work context. *Personnel Psychology, 66*(3), 613–644. https://doi.org/10.1111/peps.12028

Kooij, D. T., de Lange, A. H., Jansen, P. G., & Dikkers, J. S. (2013). Beyond chronological age: Examining perceived future time and subjective health as age-related mediators in relation to work-related motivations and well-being. *Work & Stress, 27*(1), 88–105. https://doi.org/10.1080/02678373.2013.769328

Kunze, F., Boehm, S. A., & Bruch, H. (2011). Age diversity, age discrimination climate and performance consequences - A cross organizational study. *Journal of Organizational Behavior, 32*(2), 264–290. https://doi.org/10.1002/job.698

Kunze, F., Boehm, S. A., & Bruch, H. (2013). Organizational performance consequences of age diversity: Inspecting the role of diversity-friendly HR policies and top managers' negative age stereotypes. *Journal of Management Studies, 50*(3), 413–442. https://doi.org/10.1111/joms.12016

Kunze, F., Boehm, S. A., & Bruch, H. (2021). It matters how old we feel in organizations: Testing a multilevel model of organizational subjective-age diversity on employee outcomes. *Journal of Organizational Behavior, 42*(4), 448–463. https://doi.org/10.1002/job.2505

Kunze, F., & Bruch, H. (2010). Age-based faultlines and perceived productive energy: The moderation of transformational leadership. *Small Group Research, 41*(5), 593–620. https://doi.org/10.1177/1046496410366307

Kunze, F., & Menges, J. I. (2017). Younger supervisors, older subordinates: An organizational-level study of age differences, emotions, and performance. *Journal of Organizational Behavior, 38*(4), 461–486. https://doi.org/10.1002/job.2129

Kunze, F., Raes, A. M., & Bruch, H. (2015). It matters how old you feel: Antecedents and performance consequences of average relative subjective age in organizations. *Journal of Applied Psychology, 100*(5), 1511–1526. https://doi.org/10.1037/a0038909

Kurtzberg, T. R. (2005). Feeling creative, being creative: An empirical study of diversity and creativity in teams. *Creativity Research Journal, 17*(1), 51–65. https://doi.org/10.1207/s15326934crj1701_5

Lau, D. C., & Murnighan, J. K. (1998). Demographic diversity and faultlines: The compositional dynamics of organizational groups. *Academy of Management Review, 23*(2), 325–340. https://doi.org/10.5465/amr.1998.533229

Lawrence, B. S. (1988). New wrinkles in the theory of age: Demography, norms, and performance ratings. *Academy of Management Journal, 31*(2), 309–337. https://doi.org/10.2307/256550

Lee, H. W., & Kim, E. (2020). Workforce diversity and firm performance: Relational coordination as a mediator and structural empowerment and multisource feedback as moderators. *Human Resource Management, 59*(1), 5–23. https://doi.org/10.1002/hrm.21970

Li, J., Chu, C. W. L., Lam, K. C., & Liao, S. (2011). Age diversity and firm performance in an emerging economy: Implications for cross-cultural human resource management. *Human Resource Management, 50*(2), 247–270. https://doi.org/10.1002/hrm.20416

Li, J., Meyer, B., Shimla, M., & Wegge, J. (2018). From being diverse to becoming diverse: A dynamic team diversity theory. *Journal of Organizational Behavior, 39*(8), 956–970. https://doi.org/10.1002/job.2272

Liebermann, S. C., Wegge, J., Jungmann, F., & Schmidt, K. H. (2013). Age diversity and individual team member health: The moderating role of age and age stereotypes. *Journal of Occupational and Organizational psychology, 86*(2), 184–202. https://doi.org/10.1111/joop.12016

Meyer, B., & Glenz, A. (2013). Team faultline measures: A computational comparison and a new approach to multiple subgroups. *Organizational Research Methods, 16*(3), 393–424. https://doi.org/10.1177/1094428113484970

Montepare, J. M. (2009). Subjective age: Toward a guiding lifespan framework. *International Journal of Behavioral Development, 33*(1), 42–46. https://doi.org/10.1177/0165025408095551

Østergaard, C. R., Timmermans, B., & Kristinsson, K. (2011). Does a different view create something new? The effect of employee diversity on innovation. *Research Policy, 40*(3), 500–509. https://doi.org/10.1016/j.respol.2010.11.004

Paoletti, J., Gilberto, J. M., Beier, M. E., & Salas, E. (2020). The role of aging, age diversity, and age heterogeneity within teams. In S. J. Czaja, J. Sharit, & J. B. James (Eds.), *Current and emerging trends in aging and work* (pp. 319–336). Springer.

Pelled, L. H., Eisenhardt, K. M., & Xin, K. R. (1999). Exploring the black box: An analysis of work group diversity, conflict and performance. *Administrative Science Quarterly, 44*(1), 1–28. https://doi.org/10.2307/2667029

Pelled, L. H., Xin, K. R., & Weiss, A. M. (2001). No es como mi: Relational demography and conflict in a Mexican production facility. *Journal of Occupational and Organizational Psychology, 74*(1), 63–84. https://doi.org/10.1348/096317901167235

Pettigrew, T. F. (1998). Intergroup contact theory. *Annual Review of Psychology*, *49*(1), 65–85. https://doi.org/10.1146/annurev.psych.49.1.65

Rabl, T., & Triana, M. (2014). Organizational value for age diversity and potential applicants' organizational attraction: Individual attitudes matter. *Journal of Business Ethics*, *121*(3), 403–417. https://doi.org/10.1007/s10551-013-1729-8

Reinwald, M., & Kunze, F. (2020). Being different, being absent? A dynamic perspective on demographic dissimilarity and absenteeism in blue-collar teams. *Academy of Management Journal*, *63*(3), 660–684. https://doi.org/10.5465/amj.2018.0290

Rudolph, C. W., Kunze, F., & Zacher, H. (2019). Getting objective about subjective age: Introduction to a special issue. *Work, Aging and Retirement*, *5*(4), 265–272. https://doi.org/10.1093/workar/waz019

Rudolph, C. W., & Zacher, H. (2020). Age inclusive human resource practices, age diversity climate, and work ability: Exploring between- and within-person indirect effects. *Work, Aging and Retirement*, *5*(4), 265–272. https://doi.org/10.1093/workar/waaa008

Scheuer, C.-L., & Loughlin, C. (2018). The moderating effects of status and trust on the performance of age-diverse work groups. *Evidence-Based HRM: A Global Forum for Empirical Scholarship*, *7*(1), 56–74. https://doi.org/10.1108/ebhrm-01-2018-0008

Schneid, M., Isidor, R., Steinmetz, H., & Kabst, R. (2016). Age diversity and team outcomes: A quantitative review. *Journal of Managerial Psychology*, *31*(1), 2–17. https://doi.org/10.1108/JMP-07-2012-0228

Seong, J. Y., & Hong, D. S. (2018). Age diversity, group organisational citizenship behaviour, and group performance: Exploring the moderating role of charismatic leadership and participation in decision-making. *Human Resource Management Journal*, *28*(4), 621–640. https://doi.org/10.1111/1748-8583.12197

Shuying, W., & Shuijuan, Z. (2017). Effect of diversity on top management team to the bank's innovation ability-based on the nature of ownership perspective. *Procedia Engineering*, *174*, 240–245. https://doi.org/10.1016/j.proeng.2017.01.126

Sung, S. Y., & Choi, J. N. (2019). Contingent effects of workforce diversity on firm innovation: High-tech industry and market turbulence as critical environmental contingencies. *The International Journal of Human Resource Management*, *32*(9), 1986–2021. https://doi.org/10.1080/09585192.2019.1579243

Tajfel, H., & Turner, J. (1986). The social identity theory of intergroup behavior. In S. Worchel & W. G. Austin (Eds.), *Psychology of intergroup relations* (pp. 7–24). Hall Publishers.

Tanikawa, T., Kim, S., & Jung, Y. (2017). Top management team diversity and firm performance: Exploring a function of age. *Team Performance Management: An International Journal*, *23*(3-4), 156–170. https://doi.org/10.1108/TPM-06-2016-0027

Valls, V., Tomás, I., González-Romá, V., & Rico, R. (2020). The influence of age-based faultlines on team performance: Examining mediational paths. *European Management Journal*, *39*(4), 456–466. https://doi.org/10.1016/j.emj.2020.10.008

Van Dijk, H., Meyer, B., Van Engen, M., & Loyd, D. L. (2017). Microdynamics in diverse teams: A review and integration of the diversity and stereotyping literatures. *Academy of Management Annals*, *11*(1), 517–557. https://doi.org/10.5465/annals.2014.0046

Van Dijk, H., Van Engen, M. L., & Van Knippenberg, D. (2012). Defying conventional wisdom: A meta-analytical examination of the differences between demographic and job-related diversity relationships with performance. *Organizational Behavior and Human Decision Processes*, *119*(1), 38–53. https://doi.org/10.1016/j.obhdp.2012.06.003

Van Knippenberg, D., Dawson, J. F., West, M. A., & Homan, A. C. (2011). Diversity faultlines, shared objectives, and top management team performance. *Human Relations, 64*(3), 307–336. https://doi.org/10.1177/0018726710378384

Van Knippenberg, D., De Dreu, C. K., & Homan, A. C. (2004). Work group diversity and group performance: An integrative model and research agenda. *Journal of Applied Psychology, 89*(6), 1008–1022. https://doi.org/10.1037/0021-9010.89.6.1008

Wang, M., & Fang, Y. (2020). Age diversity in the workplace: Facilitating opportunities with organizational practices. *Public Policy & Aging Report, 30*(3), 119–123. https://doi.org/10.1093/ppar/praa015

Wegge, J., & Meyer, B. (2020). Age diversity and age-based faultlines in teams: Understanding a Brezel phenomenon requires a Brezel theory. *Work, Aging and Retirement, 6*(1), 8–14. https://doi.org/10.1093/workar/waz017

Wegge, J., Roth, C., Neubach, B., Schmidt, K.-H., & Kanfer, R. (2008). Age and gender diversity as determinants of performance and health in a public organization: The role of task complexity and group size. *Journal of Applied Psychology, 93*(6), 1301–1313. https://doi.org/10.1037/a0012680

Zacher, H. (2015). Successful aging at work. *Work, Aging and Retirement, 1*(1), 4–25. https://doi.org/10.1093/workar/wau006

Zacher, H., & Yang, J. (2016). Organizational climate for successful aging. *Frontiers in Psychology, 7*, 1007. https://doi.org/10.3389/fpsyg.2016.01007

Zenger, T. R., & Lawrence, B. S. (1989). Organizational demography: The differential effects of age and tenure distributions on technical communication. *Academy of Management Journal, 32*(2), 353–376. https://doi.org/10.2307/256366

10
LONGITUDINAL AND DIARY METHODS TO STUDY AGE AND WORK

Mo Wang and Yanran Fang

Over the last few decades, the age distribution of the labor force in many countries has shifted toward older workers. For instance, in the United States, the median age of the labor force was 39.3 years in 2000, and it increased to 42.0 years in 2020 (U.S. Bureau of Labor Statistics, 2021). In Europe and Central Asia, populations are growing older as well, and the average age of the labor force was projected to reach 42.6 years by 2030, which was believed to be the highest of any region (International Labour Organization, 2018). Accompanying this trend of aging workforces (which is also described as the *Silver Tsunami*), considerable scholarly attention has been devoted to studying age and work.

In studying age and work, two research questions are particularly of interest. The first type of research question focuses on the main effects of age. Research models specified to answer this type of research question typically aim to investigate the impacts of age-related developmental changes on work outcomes. In addressing this type of research question, the goal is to understand how psychological, physiological, and behavioral phenomena evolve over time along with people's aging process. Notably, the concept of "aging" itself inherently involves the nature of dynamic change at the within-person level. That is, the theoretical content of "aging" involves one's physical and psychological *changes* over the life course. As such, in understanding the main effects of age at a within-person level, the role of age often overlaps with that of time, warranting the adoption of longitudinal designs to track participants for a relatively long period to capture within-person variations in the studied variables (Wang et al., 2016). It is important to note that cross-sectional designs are of little help for addressing this type of research question. When using a cross-sectional design to collect data, all data are obtained by assessing participants at only one point in time. As such, changes in the substantive variables cannot be captured and reflected in the data. Hence, any

DOI: 10.4324/9781003089674-13

research question that is associated with *prospective prediction* (e.g., how the studied variables grow or change over time or over the aging process) cannot be addressed by using cross-sectional data.

The second research question in the area of age and work focuses on the moderation effects of age, which attempts to reveal how the relations among the variables of interest differ across people in different age groups or at different developmental stages. Research models specified to answer this type of research question often aim to understand how day-to-day psychological and/or behavioral processes unfold as a function of age. In this type of research question, age serves as a between-person-level moderator that shapes the relationships at the within-person level. Therefore, multilevel modeling investigating cross-level moderation effects of age is required to address this type of research question. To study the cross-level moderating role of age on the psychological and/or behavioral processes that function at the within-person level, one needs to collect data across multiple timepoints (e.g., longitudinal or diary methods) so as to examine how the interested relations among studied variables may depend on age or different developmental stages.

Given the drawbacks associated with using cross-sectional designs for studying age and work, this chapter aims to provide an overview of longitudinal and diary methods in age and work research. In particular, we summarize different types of research designs for studying age and work. Following that, we offer practical recommendations for research designs and data collection in conducting longitudinal and diary research. We also provide a summary of related statistical methods (i.e., latent growth modeling, growth mixture modeling, and multilevel modeling) that fulfill the purpose of longitudinal and diary research. Limitations of longitudinal and diary designs as well as future directions in studying age and work are discussed at the end of this chapter.

Different Types of Research Design

Serving as an alternative to cross-sectional designs, longitudinal designs emphasize investigating changes over time and require data collected from the same sample repeatedly (Ployhart & Vandenberg, 2010; Wang et al., 2017). Longitudinal designs can be broadly categorized into three types: (1) the *longitudinal panel design* contains relatively fewer measurement occasions with relatively longer time intervals (e.g., months or years) in between, (2) the *intensive longitudinal design* contains more frequent measurement occasions with relatively shorter time intervals (e.g., hours or days) in between, and (3) the combination of the previous two (i.e., the *measurement burst design*), which involves intensive measurements embedded in a longitudinal study over a relatively longer time span (Bohlmann et al., 2018; Sliwinski, 2008).

Although all three forms of longitudinal designs can be used to capture and study change and variability that manifest at the within-person level, they have different emphases. The longitudinal panel design can better capture progressive changes over a relatively long time period, rendering it more appropriate to study age's main effect in terms of the aging process. For example, the Health and Retirement Study (HRS; Fisher & Ryan, 2018) employed a longitudinal panel design to track a representative sample of older workers and retirees from 1992, with a measurement interval of two years between consecutive data collection waves. This dataset allows the investigation of various aging and retirement-related phenomena over time (e.g., Wan et al., 2018; Wang, 2007; Wang & Chan, 2011).

The intensive longitudinal design focuses more on rapid fluctuations, such as one's psychological states or processes. Such intensive longitudinal designs often manifest as the experience sampling method (ESM) and diary-based procedure, wherein participants provide frequent reports regarding events or their experiences of their daily lives (Bolger et al., 2003; Zhou et al., 2021). An example of adopting the intensive longitudinal approach to examine an age-related research question is Finkelstein et al.'s (2020) daily diary study, which studied employees' experience of and reaction to age meta-stereotypes in the workplace.

The measurement burst design lends itself to not only modeling more fine-grained observations within each "burst" but also assessing the progressive change in both average levels of variables and within-person relationships across bursts (Sliwinski, 2008). As illustrated in Figure 10.1, the measurement burst design can be understood as a complex version of the longitudinal study design, with intensive longitudinal data collection being conducted within each measurement occasion. An example of adopting the measurement burst approach to study age and work is Sliwinski et al. (2009), which focused on understanding age-related changes in people's emotional responses to negative events. As the measurement burst design is a combination of the longitudinal panel design and the intensive longitudinal design, in the subsequent sections we only focus our review on the two more foundational design types.

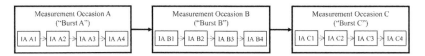

FIGURE 10.1   Measurement burst design (the hybrid approach of longitudinal panel and intensive longitudinal design)

Note: IA = intensive assessments. Solid arrows connecting every two adjacent measurement occasions (or every two "bursts") denote the relatively longer (e.g., months, years) equally spaced time interval in a typical longitudinal panel data. Dash arrows connecting every two adjacent intensive assessments denote the relatively shorter (e.g., seconds, minutes, days) equally spaced time interval in a typical intensive longitudinal data

Recommendations for Data Collection

As compared to collecting cross-sectional data, conducting longitudinal and/ or diary studies is usually more complicated and requires more sophisticated planning and data collection procedures. Especially in studying age and work, researchers need to make a series of decisions to appropriately determine the targeted sample, to plan for and ensure the required sample size, as well as to determine the appropriate number of measurement occasions, the length of time intervals, and the length of the total studied period. These decisions are essential for ensuring data quality (e.g., ensuring the capture of sizable and meaningful variances in the studied variables and reducing the potential systematic errors caused by participants' fatigue), which would directly impact the internal and external validity of research findings. In the following sections, we provide a brief summary of practical recommendations for collecting longitudinal and diary data to study age and work.

Determine the Targeted Sample

Similar to conducting research in any other field, relevance (i.e., the extent to which characteristics of the sample are aligned with the research question) serves as one of the prerequisites of sample selection in studying age and work. It is critical for researchers to identify appropriate sample(s) to address their research questions. Whether the nature of the sample can truly reflect or reveal the phenomena of interest can significantly impact the internal validity of the research findings. For example, when studying the relationship between taking up bridge employment and health status (e.g., Zhan et al., 2009), researchers need to specify prospective or current retirees, rather than general working employees or older workers, as their targeted sample.

Another related issue about sample selection is representativeness. Collecting data from a representative sample helps strengthen the research findings' external validity so that the findings can be applied to a relatively wide range of situations and the contribution of the research can therefore be strengthened. Importantly, although researchers are encouraged to employ random sampling and avoid convenience samples whenever possible (Ployhart & Vandenberg, 2010), it is not surprising that such a design is not always achievable for researchers who study age and work. As such, it would be valuable to conduct cross-validation with multiple samples to ensure generalizability of research findings (Wang & Hanges, 2011).

Determine the Sample Size

Researchers studying age and work need to carefully plan required sample size to ensure sufficient statistical power to test their hypotheses. In particular, when conducting longitudinal panel studies to investigate age's main effects, within-person-level effects are of interest, which renders the premium of ensuring sufficient sample size at the within-person level (i.e., having a sufficient number of within-person observations). When it comes to studying age's moderation effects on the random relationships between studied variables at the within-person level, researchers often face the challenge of ensuring sufficient sample size at both within-person and between-person levels of analysis. This is because a sufficient average number of within-person observations is necessary to estimate the random effects among studied variables at the within-person level, and a sufficient number of participants is necessary to detect how the within-person-level relations among studied variables differ as a function of age.

In practice, factors such as the effect size of the parameter of interest and the probability of Type I and Type II error can still serve as useful criteria in determining sample size at both the within-person and/or the between-person levels, as they are determinants of a study's statistical power (Bliese & Wang, 2020). Moreover, when it comes to collecting multilevel data to test cross-level moderation effects (e.g., studying age's cross-level moderation effects), a practical recommendation from Mathieu et al. (2012) is that the average within-person level sample size should "have a relative premium of about 3:2" as compared to the between-person level sample size (p. 959). Nevertheless, estimating statistical power based on simulations (see a tutorial by Arend & Schäfer, 2019) would be more accurate than simply following rules of thumb.

Be Prepared for the Sample Attrition

Collecting longitudinal data requires tracking participants over time, rendering sample attrition an inevitable issue. Thus, it is important for researchers to plan ahead and make sure that the final sample size (i.e., after attrition) is sufficient to address their research questions. Alternatively, planned missing data designs can be employed to increase cost effectiveness and design efficiency (Graham et al., 2006). Further, multiple imputation (MI) and maximum likelihood (ML) missingness modeling methods can be adopted to address the attrition or the associated missing value issues (Graham, 2009).

Moreover, researchers need to pay attention to the potential impacts of selective attrition on their research findings. That is, it is possible that participants with certain characteristics are more likely to drop out during the data collection process, leaving the remaining sample unrepresentative (assuming it was representative in the first place), which may result in biased research findings (Bohlmann et al., 2018; Goodman & Blum, 1996). To address this issue, researchers are well advised to assess the presence and the potential impacts of sample attrition. For example, researchers can examine the potential effects of nonrandom sampling on means and/or variances of studied variables, as well as the potential effects of nonrandom sampling on the relationships among the studied variables (see the review by Goodman & Blum, 1996).

Determine the Number of Measurement Occasions, the Length of Time Interval, and the Length of the Total Study Period

Determining the number of measurement occasions is to decide how many waves of data will be collected. Determining the length of the time interval is to decide the length of the time lag between two adjacent measurement occasions. Usually, the length of the total study period will be determined when the number of measurement occasions and the length of the time interval are specified. These decisions should be made based on the focal research question and/or the phenomena of interest.

In studying the impacts of age-related developmental changes using a longitudinal panel study (i.e., estimating age's main effects by considering time as a proxy of age), a practical recommendation for determining the number of measurement occasions is to collect at least three waves of data (Ployhart & Vandenberg, 2010; Wang et al., 2017). This is because three waves of data are required to detect and examine the form of change trends (i.e., slopes) in the studied variables, which is inherently embedded in one's aging process (Wang et al., 2017). In particular, measuring the same variable at least three times provides the possibility for the researcher to estimate the intercept along with the slope of the change (Bohlmann et al., 2018; Wang et al., 2017), which may not be linear in nature.

Deciding the length of the time interval is also critical in studying age's main effects. In particular, the length of time interval for data collection should be determined to facilitate the capturing of the true change in the substantive variables or the processes of interest. Although no generalized recommendation could be made regarding the optimal length of time interval, "a rule of thumb has emerged suggesting that effects decline as time lags become longer" (Dormann & Griffin, 2015, p. 490). Additionally, researchers are advised to make their decisions regarding time interval on the basis of prior empirical research, discussions with subject-matter experts, consultation with the methodology literature, and/or statistical estimation derived from existing data or pilot studies (e.g., see procedures recommended by Dormann & Griffin, 2015; Zhou et al., 2021). We note that, when it comes to studying age's main effects, it is possible that one's age-related development may take a relatively longer time to manifest meaningful change (e.g., one's intention to retire may stay relatively stable for years; Wang et al., 2017). Therefore, it could be necessary to employ a relatively long-term longitudinal design to allow the researchers to comprehensively capture and examine the meaningful changes in the studied variables.

When it comes to conducting intensive longitudinal studies wherein a diary-based procedure is employed to examine age's cross-level moderation effects, researchers need to track and assess participants in a relatively frequent manner during the study period. Researchers should be aware that, when doing so, decisions regarding the number of measurement occasions and the length of time interval should be made so as to strike a balance between the frequency of assessments (thereby ensuring the capture of meaningful changes in the variables of interest) and the disturbance that the data collection process may impose on the participants. To partly address the drawbacks associated with frequent data assessments, researchers can adopt online surveys or use mobile/wearable devices to increase data collection efficiency. However, a potential drawback of using online surveys and mobile/wearable devices in data collection is that such approaches can largely limit the social interaction between researchers and participants, which may result in the reduction in participants' personal accountability for their survey responses (Zhou, Song, et al., 2019).

Summary of Related Statistical Methods

In this section, we provide a brief introduction of related statistical methods that are typically used to examine within-person-level changes and cross-level moderation effects. In particular, we introduce latent growth modeling and growth mixture modeling for researchers to address research questions associated with age's main effects and multilevel modeling for researchers to investigate how the within-person-level relations may differ across people in different age groups. It should be noted that latent growth modeling can be done in a mixed effects/multilevel modeling framework as well (Curran, 2003).

Latent Growth Modeling

Latent growth modeling can be employed to assess features of change (e.g., the form of change such as linear or nonlinear, and/or the rate of change), thereby lending itself well to modeling aging processes in key variables. In particular, adopting the latent growth modeling approach, researchers can assess the focal construct's mean of the latent intercept, as well as the mean of the latent slope. The mean of the latent intercept reflects the initial state of the studied variable, whereas the mean of the latent slope reflects the rate of change in the construct. Given the initial state and the rate of change, researchers can estimate and predict changing trajectory of the focal construct over time.

A latent growth model specifying a linear growth trend of the studied variable is illustrated in Figure 10.2. As shown in Figure 10.2, when specifying a linear change in the construct, factor loadings of the latent intercept on each observed variable are set to be 1.0, and the factor loadings of the latent slope are set as 0.0 for the first observation, 1.0 for the second observation, 2.0 for the third observation, . . . , and n-1 for the N observation. To test different research questions or different forms of change (e.g., monotonic or piecewise change), researchers can alter factor loadings of the latent slope on each observation to other numbers or specify additional latent factors (e.g., latent quadratic term) accordingly. Notably, model comparisons among different models are necessary to determine

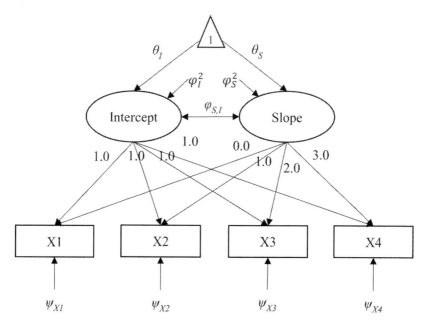

FIGURE 10.2 Latent growth model

Note: This figure illustrates the linear growth trend of a hypothetical variable X. Variable X was measured at four time points, and X1–X4 represent the four observed values obtained at each measurement occasion. θ_I = mean of the latent intercept factor; θ_S = mean of the latent slope factor; φ_I^2 = variance of the latent intercept factor; φ_S^2 = variance of the latent slope factor; $\varphi_{S,I}$ = covariance between the latent intercept factor and the latent slope factor; ψ_{X1}-ψ_{X1} = time-specific errors of each observed value of X

the model that fits the data best. Detailed model specification procedures can be found in Y. Liu et al. (2016).

Latent growth modeling can be applied to multivariate situations. That is, researchers can estimate changing trajectories of different constructs simultaneously. On the basis of the estimated change trajectories of the studied variables, relationships among the change factors (i.e., intercepts, slopes, and/or quadratic terms if available) can be estimated to further examine the interconnections among the change trends of different variables.

Growth Mixture Modeling

In studying age's main effects, recent scholarly attention has been paid to not only within-person changes over time but also the between-person differences in the trajectories of changes. In particular, within-person changes of the studied variable can be well-specified in a latent growth model, and on the basis of the latent growth model, a growth mixture model can be applied to identify unobserved longitudinal change patterns among participants (Wang, 2007; Wang & Bodner, 2007; Wang & Hanges, 2011).

A typical growth mixture model is depicted in Figure 10.3. As shown in Figure 10.3, a growth mixture model can be specified on the basis of a conventional latent growth model, with another latent categorial variable (i.e., the latent class variable c in Figure 10.3) representing the unobserved subpopulation membership of each subject specified to both the latent intercept and the latent slope. In practice, researchers may want to specify the number of latent classes based on their theory and then conduct model comparisons to determine the optimal number of latent classes. In each latent class (subpopulation), a distinct latent growth model can be estimated (i.e., distinct estimation of the latent intercept and the latent slope for each latent class), thereby allowing researchers to observe different patterns of change trajectories that coexist in the sample.

Similar to latent growth modeling, latent factors estimated by growth mixture modeling can also predict or be predicted by other studied variables. Specifically,

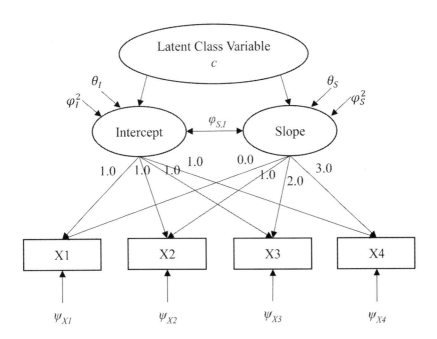

FIGURE 10.3 Growth mixture modeling

Note: This figure illustrates a growth mixture model specified on the basis of the latent growth model depicting in Figure 10.2. A latent categorical variable (i.e., the latent class variable c) is specified to both the latent intercept factor and the latent slope factor. θ_I = mean of the latent intercept factor; θ_S = mean of the latent slope factor; φ_I^2 = variance of the latent intercept factor; φ_S^2 = variance of the latent slope factor; $\varphi_{S,I}$ = covariance between the latent intercept factor and the latent slope factor; ψ_{XI}-ψ_{XI} = time-specific errors of each observed value of X based on the findings of a given growth mixture model, a probability-based latent class membership can be assigned to each subject in the sample, thereby allowing researchers to investigate the unique characteristics of each subpopulation and/or investigate the antecedents and/or the consequences of latent class membership. As such, growth mixture modeling offers a useful approach to understand "the interrelatedness between or among substantive variables as a function of the unobserved heterogeneity of the population" (Wang & Hanges, 2011, p. 24).

Growth mixture modeling has been applied to studying age and work. For example, adopting growth mixture modeling, Wang (2007) found that there were three different latent growth patterns of psychological well-being coexisting in the retiree population, and the three patterns correspond to the predictions made by role theory, continuity theory, and life course perspective, respectively.

Multilevel Modeling

Conducting longitudinal and/or diary studies inherently involves the need to articulate the hierarchically nested data structure, as there are multiple observations embedded in each participant. Specifying a multilevel model is particularly relevant when the research question is about age's cross-level moderation effects on the within-person-level relations among studied variables, as variables at both the within-person level and the between-person level are of interest. A basic multilevel model can be specified as:

Level 1 Model: $Y_{ti} = \beta_{0i} + \beta_{1i} X_{ti} + e_{ti}$
Level 2 Model: $\beta_{0i} = \gamma_{00} + u_{0i}$
$\beta_{1i} = \gamma_{10} + u_{1i}$

The equation and its parameters at Level 1 (within-person level) reflect the within-person linear relationship between participant i's observation of the outcome variable at measurement t (Y_{ti}) and the same participant's observation of the predictor at the time of measurement t (X_{ti}). Specifically, this equation denotes that this linear relationship is determined by the participant i's intercept (β_{0i}) and slope (β_{1i}). Furthermore, the variance of e_{ti} (σ^2) quantifies the magnitude of the deviation from X_{ti}-based prediction. Equations and parameters at Level 2 (between-person level) reflect functions that can be applied to all the participants. Specifically, γ_{00} represents the average intercept from the Level-1 model, and γ_{10} represents the average linear effect of X_{ti} on Y_{ti} across all participants. Moreover, the variances of u_{0i} (τ_{00}) and u_{1i} (τ_{11}) reflect the amount of the variations around Level-1 intercept and predictive effect across all participants in the dataset.

Similar to applying multilevel modeling in other organizational research, when applying multilevel modeling to studying age and work, predictors at both the within-person level and the between-person level can be included to account for the outcome variable's variances at the respective level (i.e., explain σ^2 when a within-person-level predictor is included and explain τ_{00} when a between-person level predictor is included). In particular, when the predictor at the between-person level is included, the fixed effect of the entered predictor on the outcome variable will be estimated so that the effect will be homogenous for all participants in the sample. However, when the predictor at the within-person level is entered, researchers can determine whether to estimate a fixed effect or a random effect of the entered predictor on the outcome variable based on the focal research question.

The cross-level moderation effects of between-person-level characteristics can be further specified in a multilevel model if the within-person-level relation between the predictor and the outcome variable is theorized and specified to be random (i.e., the relation between the within-person predictor and the outcome variable can be different for different participants). In such situations, predictors entered at the between-person level (e.g., age) can be specified to account for variances in the random effect between the two within-person-level variables (i.e., explain τ_{11}), and this is indeed how researchers examine age's cross-level moderation effects on the within-person-level processes.

Finally, another issue closely related to multilevel modeling is the centering strategy. In particular, researchers are well advised that when the "pure" within-subject effects or the cross-level moderation effects are of interest, the person-mean centering approach for within-person predictors is recommended. This is because the person-mean centering approach can partial out the predictors' variances at the between-person level, producing within-person-level coefficients that unambiguously reflect the pooled within-cluster regressions of outcome variables on predictors and generate more accurate estimations of variance components (Enders & Tofighi, 2007; D. Liu et al., 2012).

Limitations and Future Directions

Limitations of Longitudinal and Diary Methods

Although longitudinal and diary methods show great advantages in studying age and work, they have their own limitations. The first limitation of the longitudinal design is that it may not be able to directly test the impacts of age (i.e., developmental change that are associated with particular age in the life course). This is because, when studying the impacts of age, taking a conventional longitudinal design cannot rule out the alternative explanation of period effects (Bohlmann et al., 2018; Fosse & Winship, 2019). In other words, in a conventional longitudinal study, it is very difficult, if not impossible, for researchers to identify whether the observed changes are the results of age-related developments or the results of historical events or social phenomena (such as a global pandemic) that occur to people in all age groups during the data collection period. This could be an impactful drawback for conventional longitudinal studies, as prior research has provided a set of evidence for the contemporaneous period effects on work outcomes (see a review by Rudolph & Zacher, 2017). To more rigorously test the "pure" age-related developmental changes, researchers need to turn to more complex longitudinal designs (e.g., collecting multiple sets of longitudinal data at multiple time periods and from participants at different cohorts). Needless to say, implementing such approaches is a costly endeavor, which would further exacerbate the second drawback of longitudinal study.

The second drawback of conducting a longitudinal study speaks to the time-consuming and costly nature of tracing and assessing participants over time (Bohlmann et al., 2018). As mentioned earlier, this drawback can even be more salient when the study design is quite complex, such as when the researchers need to frequently collect data, when completing the survey/interview questions takes a relatively long period of time or requires the participants to invest more effort to respond (e.g., frequently recall memory, ask colleagues/supervisors/family members to assist with responding), or when additional tools, such as certain online platforms or devices, are required. In such situations, researchers may have to allocate a large budget to compensate participants and/or purchase additional equipment to obtain sufficient sample size and secure data quality. All of these can dramatically increase the costs associated with data collection.

The third prominent drawback of employing a longitudinal design to study age and work is that it can take a relatively longer period of time for the researchers to observe and capture meaningful age-related developmental changes in the studied variable(s). Therefore, the study design, the tools used in assessing participants, and sometimes even the entire research model may need to be updated and kept up with the societal trends and research advancements. For example, it is possible that researchers may need to update their survey measures during the data collection process, as the growing scholarship in the field of age and work may offer more appropriate metrics to capture the variable(s) of interest, even after the data collection process has been launched.

Implementing the diary-based approach to investigate age's cross-level moderating roles also has its limitations. First, a unique feature of the diary-based approach is that each participant is assessed repetitively on the same set of studied variables. As such, errors associated with participants' fatigue, practice effects, and/or testing effects may emerge, and/or the potential communications among participants about the study (such as the purpose of study manipulation or different interventions employed in the study) may arise, which may contaminate their responses and subsequently bias research findings (Bohlmann et al., 2018; Wang et al., 2017). All these potential biases warrant the necessity of determining the "optimal design elements" before data collection (Wang et al., 2017; Zhou et al., 2021).

Second, in some circumstances, nuances of within-person-level fluctuations might not be fully captured in a diary-based study. This limitation is more salient if the time intervals between two measurement occasions are set to be longer.

Particularly when studying age and work, some phenomena or studied variables (e.g., mood, blood pressure, work events) could change in a more frequent manner, rendering assessing these data on a daily basis insufficient to fully capture the nuanced information and reflect the whole picture.

Third, we note that employing diary methods does not necessarily mean that reliable causal inferences among studied variables can be made based on the research findings. This is because when the within-person-level relations among studied variables are of interest, the predictors and the outcome variables can still be assessed at the same measurement point from the same participant (e.g., using a variable measured in the morning survey to predict another variable measured in the same survey), rendering the estimated within-person-level relations prone to common method bias (Podsakoff et al., 2003; Wang et al., 2013). This issue, however, can be partly addressed if time points are lagged (e.g., using a variable measured in the morning survey to predict a variable measured in the afternoon survey, Song et al., 2018) based on the focal research question.

Future Directions

We propose several future directions to help guide further investigations on age and work. First, computational modeling can be applied to advance theory building in the field of age and work (Vancouver et al., 2020; Wang et al., 2017). Computational modeling shows great advantages as a theory-building tool, and it can be employed to generate formal theories that reflect the dynamic processes of interest when relatively little empirical data is available (Wang et al., 2016). When establishing computational models, a set of transition rules, including age-related developmental changes (the impacts of time), can be theorized and specified, rendering the computational model as a mathematic portrait of the age-related theory that explains the phenomena of interest. In recent years, studies employing computational models to assess theory have emerged in many organizational fields (e.g., dynamics of team cognition, Grand et al., 2016; work motivation, Vancouver et al., 2020; leadership goal striving, Zhou, Wang, et al., 2019). As people's age-related developmental changes can unfold and manifest over a relatively longer period and collecting certain long-term longitudinal panel and/or intensive longitudinal data can be difficult, implementing computational modeling in studying age and work offers researchers advantages to enhance theory development in this field (Wang et al., 2017).

Second, when analyzing longitudinal or diary data, a potential issue embedded in research design is that the potential changes in the studied variable(s) and/or process(es) may not necessarily be linear or monotonic. For example, people's aging effects can be shaped by one or multiple planned or unplanned discontinuities (events). Discontinuous growth model can therefore be employed, wherein multiple time-related variables are specified to model the within-person-level transition processes over time (e.g., the slope of the trajectory before/without the occurrence of the event, the occurrence of the event that alters the intercept and/ or the slope of the trajectory afterward). Examples of the coding of these time-related variables are provided in prior methodological literature (e.g., Bliese & Lang, 2016), and, based on the estimated parameters of these time-related variables, researchers can further examine the roles of between-person-level differences (including age) in shaping the within-person-level transition processes (e.g., Lang & Bliese, 2009).

Third, measurement burst designs can be employed as a hybrid approach of longitudinal and diary methods to study age and work. Adopting the measurement burst design, researchers can investigate how the rapid fluctuations of studied variables at the within-person level change as a function of the aging process. When doing so, we note that the aging effects can manifest through various mechanisms, including the potential increase in skills/experience (e.g., effects of tenure), the biological factors or maturation (e.g., physical- and/or cognitive-related changes), the motivational-related changes (i.e., socioemotional selectivity theory, Carstensen, 1992), the acculturation processes (e.g., through intra- or inter-group interactions), and other time-dependent processes. Although some of the potential mechanisms may synergize with one another to shape the within-person trajectories of studied variables, some may function in competing directions and therefore offset each other's impacts. We therefore recommend future studies to further unveil the underlying mechanisms of age in impacting the variables or phenomena of interest (Bohlmann et al., 2018; Gielnik et al., 2018)

References

Arend, M. G., & Schäfer, T. (2019). Statistical power in two-level models: A tutorial based on Monte Carlo simulation. *Psychological Methods*, *24*(1), 1–19. https://doi.org/10.1037/met0000195

Bliese, P. D., & Lang, J. W. (2016). Understanding relative and absolute change in discontinuous growth models: Coding alternatives and implications for hypothesis testing. *Organizational Research Methods*, *19*(4), 562–592. https://doi.org/10.1177/1094428116633502

Bliese, P. D., & Wang, M. (2020). Results provide information about cumulative probabilities of finding significance: Let's report this information. *Journal of Management*, *46*(7), 1275–1288. https://doi.org/10.1177/0149206319886909

Bohlmann, C., Rudolph, C. W., & Zacher, H. (2018). Methodological recommendations to move research on work and aging forward. *Work, Aging and Retirement*, *4*(3), 225–237. https://doi.org/10.1093/workar/wax023

Bolger, N., Davis, A., & Rafaeli, E. (2003). Diary methods: Capturing life as it is lived. *Annual Review of Psychology*, *54*, 579–616. https://doi.org/10.1146/annurev.psych.54.101601.145030

Carstensen, L. L. (1992). Social and emotional patterns in adulthood: Support for socioemotional selectivity theory. *Psychology and Aging*, *7*(3), 331–338. https://doi.org/10.1037/0882-7974.7.3.331

Curran, P. J. (2003). Have multilevel models been structural equation models all along? *Multivariate Behavioral Research*, *38*(4), 529–569. https://doi.org/10.1207/s15327906mbr3804_5

Dormann, C., & Griffin, M. A. (2015). Optimal time lags in panel studies. *Psychological Methods*, *20*(4), 489–505. https://doi.org/10.1037/met0000041

Enders, C. K., & Tofighi, D. (2007). Centering predictor variables in cross-sectional multi-level models: A new look at an old issue. *Psychological Methods*, *12*(2), 121–138. https://doi.org/10.1037/1082-989X.12.2.121

Finkelstein, L. M., Voyles, E. C., Thomas, C. L., & Zacher, H. (2020). A daily diary study of responses to age meta-stereotypes. *Work, Aging and Retirement*, *6*(1), 28–45. https://doi.org/10.1093/workar/waz005

Fisher, G. G., & Ryan, L. H. (2018). Overview of the health and retirement study and introduction to the special issue. *Work, Aging and Retirement*, *4*(1), 1–9. https://doi.org/10.1093/workar/wax032

Fosse, E., & Winship, C. (2019). Analyzing age-period-cohort data: A review and critique. *Annual Review of Sociology*, *45*, 467–492. https://doi.org/10.1146/annurev-soc-073018-022616

Gielnik, M. M., Zacher, H., & Wang, M. (2018). Age in the entrepreneurial process: The role of future time perspective and prior entrepreneurial experience. *Journal of Applied Psychology*, *103*(10), 1067–1085. https://doi.org/10.1037/apl0000322

Goodman, J. S., & Blum, T. C. (1996). Assessing the non-random sampling effects of subject attrition in longitudinal research. *Journal of Management*, *22*(4), 627–652. https://doi.org/10.1177/014920639602200405

Graham, J. W. (2009). Missing data analysis: Making it work in the real world. *Annual Review of Psychology*, *60*, 549–576. https://doi.org/10.1146/annurev.psych.58.110405.085530

Graham, J. W., Taylor, B. J., Olchowski, A. E., & Cumsille, P. E. (2006). Planned missing data designs in psychological research. *Psychological Methods*, *11*(4), 323–343. https://doi.org/10.1037/1082-989X.11.4.323

Grand, J. A., Braun, M. T., Kuljanin, G., Kozlowski, S. W. J., & Chao, G. T. (2016). The dynamics of team cognition: A process-oriented theory of knowledge emergence in teams. *Journal of Applied Psychology*, *101*(10), 1353–1385. https://doi.org/10.1037/apl0000136

International Labour Organization. (2018, October 1). *Europe's ageing population comes with a silver lining*. www.ilo.org/brussels/information-resources/news/WCMS_645926/lang--en/index.htm

Lang, J. W. B., & Bliese, P. D. (2009). General mental ability and two types of adaptation to unforeseen change: Applying discontinuous growth models to the task-change paradigm. *Journal of Applied Psychology*, *94*(2), 411–428. https://doi.org/10.1037/a0013803

Liu, D., Zhang, Z., & Wang, M. (2012). Mono-level and multilevel mediated moderation and moderated mediation: Theorizing and test. In X. Chen, A. Tsui, & L. Farh (Eds.), *Empirical methods in organization and management research* (2nd ed., pp. 545–579). Peking University Press.

Liu, Y., Mo, S., Song, Y., & Wang, M. (2016). Longitudinal analysis in occupational health psychology: A review and tutorial of three longitudinal modeling techniques. *Applied Psychology*, *65*(2), 379–411. https://doi.org/10.1111/apps.12055

Mathieu, J. E., Aguinis, H., Culpepper, S. A., & Chen, G. (2012). Understanding and estimating the power to detect cross-level interaction effects in multilevel modeling. *Journal of Applied Psychology*, *97*(5), 951–966. https://doi.org/10.1037/a0028380

Ployhart, R. E., & Vandenberg, R. J. (2010). Longitudinal research: The theory, design, and analysis of change. *Journal of Management*, *36*(1), 94–120. https://doi.org/10.1177/0149206309352110

Podsakoff, P. M., MacKenzie, S. B., Lee, J.-Y., & Podsakoff, N. P. (2003). Common method biases in behavioral research: A critical review of the literature and recommended remedies. *Journal of Applied Psychology*, *88*(5), 879–903. https://doi.org/10.1037/0021-9010.88.5.879

Rudolph, C. W., & Zacher, H. (2017). Considering generations from a lifespan developmental perspective. *Work, Aging and Retirement*, *3*(2), 113–129. https://doi.org/10.1093/workar/waw019

Sliwinski, M. J. (2008). Measurement-burst designs for social health research. *Social and Personality Psychology Compass*, *2*(1), 245–261. https://doi.org/10.1111/j.1751-9004.2007.00043.x

Sliwinski, M. J., Almeida, D. M., Smyth, J., & Stawski, R. S. (2009). Intraindividual change and variability in daily stress processes: Findings from two measurement-burst diary studies. *Psychology and Aging*, *24*(4), 828–840. https://doi.org/10.1037/a0017925

Song, Y., Liu, Y., Wang, M., Lanaj, K., Johnson, R. E., & Shi, J. (2018). A social mindfulness approach to understanding experienced customer mistreatment: A within-person field experiment. *Academy of Management Journal*, *61*(3), 994–1020. https://doi.org/10.5465/amj.2016.0448

U.S. Bureau of Labor Statistics. (2021, September 8). *Median age of the labor force, by sex, race, and ethnicity*. www.bls.gov/emp/tables/median-age-labor-force.htm

Vancouver, J. B., Wang, M., & Li, X. (2020). Translating informal theories into formal theories: The case of the dynamic computational model of the integrated model of work motivation. *Organizational Research Methods*, *23*(2), 238–274. https://doi.org/10.1177/1094428118780308

Wan, W. H., Antonucci, T. C., Birditt, K. S., & Smith, J. (2018). Work-hour trajectories and depressive symptoms among midlife and older married couples. *Work, Aging and Retirement*, *4*(1), 108–122. https://doi.org/10.1093/workar/wax028

Wang, M. (2007). Profiling retirees in the retirement transition and adjustment process: Examining the longitudinal change patterns of retirees' psychological well-being. *Journal of Applied Psychology*, *92*(2), 455–474. https://doi.org/10.1037/0021-9010.92.2.455

Wang, M., Beal, D. J., Chan, D., Newman, D. A., Vancouver, J. B., & Vandenberg, R. J. (2017). Longitudinal research: A panel discussion on conceptual issues, research design, and statistical techniques. *Work, Aging and Retirement*, *3*(1), 1–24. https://doi.org/10.1093/workar/waw033

Wang, M., & Bodner, T. E. (2007). Growth mixture modeling: Identifying and predicting unobserved subpopulations with longitudinal data. *Organizational Research Methods*, *10*(4), 635–656. https://doi.org/10.1177/1094428106289397

Wang, M., & Chan, D. (2011). Mixture latent Markov modeling: Identifying and predicting unobserved heterogeneity in longitudinal qualitative status change. *Organizational Research Methods*, *14*(3), 411–431. https://doi.org/10.1177/1094428109357107

Wang, M., & Hanges, P. J. (2011). Latent class procedures: Applications to organizational research. *Organizational Research Methods*, *14*(1), 24–31. https://doi.org/10.1177/1094428110383988

Wang, M., Liu, S., Liao, H., Gong, Y., Kammeyer-Mueller, J. D., & Shi, J. (2013). Can't get it out of my mind: Employee rumination after customer mistreatment and negative mood in the next morning. *Journal of Applied Psychology*, *98*(6), 989–1004. https://doi.org/10.1037/a0033656

Wang, M., Zhou, L., & Zhang, Z. (2016). Dynamic modeling. *Annual Review of Organizational Psychology and Organizational Behavior, 3*, 241–266. https://doi.org/10.1146/annurev-orgpsych-041015-062553

Zhan, Y., Wang, M., Liu, S., & Shultz, K. S. (2009). Bridge employment and retirees' health: A longitudinal investigation. *Journal of Occupational Health Psychology, 14*(4), 374–389. https://doi.org/10.1037/a0015285

Zhou, L., Song, Y., Alterman, V., Liu, Y., & Wang, M. (2019). Introduction to data collection in multilevel research. In S. E. Humphrey & J. M. LeBreton (Eds.), *The handbook of multilevel theory, measurement, and analysis* (pp. 225–252). American Psychological Association.

Zhou, L., Wang, M., & Vancouver, J. B. (2019). A formal model of leadership goal striving: Development of core process mechanisms and extensions to action team context. *Journal of Applied Psychology, 104*(3), 388–410. https://doi.org/10.1037/apl0000370

Zhou, L., Wang, M., & Zhang, Z. (2021). Intensive longitudinal data analyses with dynamic structural equation modeling. *Organizational Research Methods, 24*(2), 219–250. https://doi.org/10.1177/1094428119833164

11

CONDUCTING EXPERIMENTS AND INTERVENTION STUDIES TO UNDERSTAND AGE AND WORK

Sabine Hommelhoff and Susanne Scheibe

Most researchers probably agree that experiments and interventions are the methods of choice to test causal relationships and to provide theory-based solutions to practical challenges. It is also well recognized that the study of age and work is a relevant topic of our time. Still, researchers rarely consider these statements in concert: Compared to correlational designs, experimental and intervention research is relatively scarce in the context of age and work (Truxillo et al., 2015). This scarcity also holds true for lifespan developmental psychology in general (Freund & Isaacowitz, 2013).

The major reason for the scarcity of experiments on work and aging probably lies in the fact that researchers cannot randomly assign individuals to different chronological age groups—it is logically impossible to meet this key requirement of experimental designs (Freund & Isaacowitz, 2013). Similar to research on other naturally occurring groups, much of the research on age (and work) therefore remains correlational and quasi-experimental (Truxillo et al., 2015). A further reason for the scarcity of interventions or training studies probably lies in the relatively large amount of time and effort that need to be invested to develop and conduct well-designed interventions, along with the risk of low return on investment (Fernandez et al., 2019; Michie et al., 2011). However, there are still manifold possibilities for conducting true experiments and effective interventions to understand and address age-and-work issues and consequently render age-and-work research more valuable and relevant to nonacademic communities. This chapter outlines how such research can be realized in the future; we also draw on exemplary existing studies (e.g., Burmeister et al., 2020; Gärtner & Hertel, 2017; Hommelhoff et al., 2018; Müller et al., 2016) to illustrate different research approaches.

DOI: 10.4324/9781003089674-14

In the first part of our chapter, we discuss similarities and differences between experiments and interventions. Although both research designs involve the manipulation of certain variables or stimuli, they differ in their primary objective: Experimental research seeks to *understand and explain* causal relationships, while interventions aim to *change* work behavior and outcomes (e.g., workplace well-being and performance) for the better (e.g., Gerrig, 2013).

In the second part of our chapter, we highlight two basic strategies of how researchers can realize experiments on age and work. First, we focus on the experimental *manipulation of participants' internal context*. That is, participants' imagination or perceptions can be experimentally manipulated (e.g., their occupational future time perspective; Hommelhoff et al., 2018). Second, we describe the experimental *manipulation of participants' external context*. That is, outer context conditions can be manipulated in different ways to explain age-related differences in work behavior and outcomes (e.g., certain contexts allow expertise to compensate for declines in perceptual-motor efficiency; Bosman, 1993, 1994; Salthouse, 1984).

In the third part, we present a four-step approach of how interventions on age and work can be designed to maximize their potential effectiveness. This approach involves (1) a systematic problem description, (2) a theory-driven causal analysis to derive a logic model of the problem, (3) the development of the intervention, taking into account the specific implementation context, and (4) the monitoring and evaluation of the intervention (Buunk & Van Vugt, 2013; Fernandez et al., 2019). We will illustrate this systematic approach with examples of work and aging interventions (Burmeister et al., 2020; Müller et al., 2016).

In summary (see also Table 11.1 for an overview), our chapter aims to stimulate more experiments and interventions in the field of age and work. The fourth and final part of this chapter therefore derives practical recommendations for researchers who plan experiments and interventions on work and aging.

TABLE 11.1 Experiments and Interventions to Understand Age and Work

	Experiments	*Interventions*
Commonality	Controlled experimental variation of certain stimuli/conditions	
Differences	• Primary goal is to *understand/ explain* causal relationships • Conducted in different contexts (e.g., lab, field, online) • Assesses short-term differences or changes in outcomes	• Primary goal is to *change* something for the better • Mainly conducted in applied contexts (field), thus randomization and control group not always possible • Strives for long-term changes in outcomes

(Continued)

TABLE 11.1 (Continued)

	Experiments	*Interventions*
Approach	*Two basic strategies* **1) Experimental variation of participants' internal context** *Explanation:* Participants' imagination or perceptions are experimentally manipulated in the context of age and work *Ideas for future research:* a) Further "*Please imagine that you are . . .* "*-experiments:* Participants are asked to imagine different occupational time perspectives, levels of muscular strength, life stages, etc. b) Further "*How do you think about . . .* "*-experiments:* Participants are asked to evaluate different kinds of (fictitious) CVs, employees, jobs, articles etc. with age-relevant content *Goals:* (1) Understanding of age-related mechanisms, age stereotypes, images of aging, and age-related expectations at work; (2) demonstration of how employees envision their own future and aging at work **2) Experimental variation of participants' external context** *Explanation:* Participants' external environment is experimentally manipulated in the context of age and work *Ideas for future research:* Vary external context conditions that should offset the hypothesized processes underlying observable age differences *Goals:* (1) Understanding the interplay of age, skill, prior knowledge, tenure, experience, subjective age, and motivation in different work tasks and contexts. (2) Understanding how older employees maintain functioning and compensate for losses (e.g., in fluid intelligence or sensory acuity) at work	*An approach in four steps* **1) Systematic problem definition** Investigate what the problem is that should be targeted by the intervention, for whom it is a problem, and in which contexts it is a problem. Derive measurable indicators that need to change in the target group. **2) Logic model of the problem** Specify the multilevel factors (e.g., at individual, group, or organizational level) that give rise to the problem. Resort to existing studies and theories and double-check with stakeholders/practitioners. **3) Intervention design** Based on the causal analysis in step 2, develop possible and suitable intervention strategies and policies. Among all suitable interventions, select a feasible intervention and formulate a *theory of change* (which maps intervention activities to desired outcomes). **4) Monitoring and evaluation** Specify how the intervention will be monitored (in terms of participants and intervention activities) and evaluated (in terms of immediate, mid-term and long-term outcomes). Develop a research design and select appropriate measures.

Research Objectives of Experiments and Interventions

Psychological research strives to describe, to understand, and to predict and change human behavior (Gerrig, 2013). Research questions that focus on *describing* human experience and behavior can best be addressed through correlational and descriptive research designs, for example via cross-sectional or longitudinal surveys (i.e., data collections *without* manipulation or design-based control of variables; MacDonald & Stawski, 2016). Even though longitudinal surveys offer some advantages over cross-sectional ones in terms of approaching the question of causality, the experiment remains the ideal and often the only method to conclusively answer causal questions—that is, psychological experiments allow *understanding and explaining* human behavior (Tabachnick & Fidell, 2007). Experiments have at least three specific characteristics, namely random assignment of participants to different levels of the independent variable, manipulation of those levels, and control of potential confounding variables (Tabachnick & Fidell, 2007). Interventions and training studies are special types of experiments (Freund & Isaacowitz, 2013); they are closely related to experiments because they also involve the controlled manipulation of certain variables or stimuli. However, the main objective of an intervention is to *change* human behavior or increase positive outcomes (Robertson et al., 1993; Zabel & Baltes, 2015).

For example, existing experimental research in the context of age and work has looked into *why* employees prefer new versus familiar work teams (Gärtner & Hertel, 2017) or *why* they favor instrumental versus emotional social partners for a lunch break from work (Hommelhoff et al., 2018). Based on socioemotional selectivity theory (Carstensen, 2006) that predicts changes in social motivation when endings come closer, these experiments have explained employees' social preferences by their occupational future time perspective (Zacher & Frese, 2009). When the occupational future appears restricted or limited (e.g., when respondents are asked to imagine being close to retirement), instrumental social partners are preferred less for breaks (Hommelhoff et al., 2018), and familiar teams are preferred over new teams (Gärtner & Hertel, 2017). While these experiments focus on explaining human behavior, existing intervention studies in the context of age and work were designed to change or increase, for example, retirement adjustment (Seiferling & Michel, 2017), life satisfaction and workplace retention (Stevens-Roseman, 2009), or appreciation of team diversity (Jungmann et al., 2020).

More gradual differences between experiments and interventions follow from the difference in their main objective—explaining versus changing human behavior. Experiments are often conducted in the lab or online, while interventions are typically carried out in the field under real-life conditions. Thus, whereas (lab) experiments are commonly internally valid, less applied, more a snapshot in time, and more focused on making a theoretical contribution, interventions tend to be more externally valid, more applied, more long-term focused, and more focused on making a practical contribution (e.g., Schram, 2005). However, some studies illustrate the gradual nature of these differences by combining both approaches; they involve mini-interventions in laboratory experiments. For example, Malinen and Johnston (2013) have shown that a mental imagery intervention changed explicit (but not implicit) attitudes toward older workers in a positive way.

Although this chapter encourages the use of experiments and interventions, we emphasize that the use of these methods is not an end in itself but should depend on the research interest. Most likely it is the *combination* of different methods that allows us to understand aging in the context of work. While interventions can help to improve outcomes for employees and organizations (Zabel & Baltes, 2015) and while (quasi-)experimental studies help us to explain and understand age-related differences in the world of work, longitudinal designs (without manipulation of variables) help us to describe aging-related within-person changes over longer time intervals (MacDonald & Stawski, 2016). Along these lines, it is noteworthy that not all experiments and interventions in the context of age and work fully achieve their research goal of explaining or changing human behavior. Some experimental research in the field of organizational behavior has been criticized as superficial and non-generalizable (Highhouse, 2009); and even well-crafted interventions can fail to produce the desired change or can even have unintended negative effects (e.g., when expectations are disappointed; Aust et al., 2010).

Two Basic Strategies for Conducting Experimental Research on Age and Work

One general strategy to experimentally examine age and work issues is the experimental manipulation of participants' *internal context*. Thus, the experimental stimuli are focused on the participants' inner world, their imagination and perceptions. A second strategy involves the controlled manipulation of participants' *external context* and thus the experimental situation. Usually, only one of the two strategies is applied in a given experiment (e.g., see Gärtner & Hertel, 2017 for the first principle and Bosman, 1993 for the second), although it is theoretically possible to combine them. In the following, we will illustrate these two strategies in more detail by describing typical procedures and main research goals, as well as avenues for future research (for an overview, see Table 11.1).

Experimental Manipulation of Participants' Internal Context

In this experimental framework, participants are typically asked to *imagine* different situations (e.g., being far from or close to retirement; Gärtner & Hertel, 2017; Hommelhoff et al., 2018), or they are asked to *evaluate* or otherwise react to different scenarios or descriptions at hand (e.g., different employee or job descriptions; Bertolino et al., 2013; Gaillard & Desmette, 2010; Hanscom & Cleveland, 2018; Truxillo et al., 2012; Zacher et al., 2017). This experimental approach thus allows random assignment of participants to different stimuli that make age-related processes more or less salient in people's minds. Because participants can be randomized to these different imagination or evaluation tasks irrespective of their age, this experimental principle finds a way around the problem that it is impossible to manipulate chronological age while still investigating age-related phenomena (Freund & Isaacowitz, 2013). Depending on the research question, it is of course possible to include calendar age in the analysis as an additional independent, moderating variable; however, this means that (this part of) the experiment turns into a quasi-experiment (e.g., Bertolino et al., 2013; Truxillo et al., 2012; Zacher et al., 2017).

Besides conducting such experiments online (e.g., Hommelhoff et al., 2018; Rahn et al., 2019; Truxillo et al., 2012), lab and field experiments are also possible. In field experiments, researchers have constructed CVs of fictitious applicants that were identical except for the age of the applicants. These CVs were then randomly assigned to genuine job vacancies in the context of age discrimination research (e.g., Baert et al., 2016). Thus, the use of *fictitious* CVs or persons allows random assignment of different employee ages to different employers who then respond or react to the application. In lab experiments (e.g., Kulik et al., 2000; Malinen & Johnston, 2013), researchers have for example conducted mini-interventions to positively change attitudes or evaluations regarding age-related topics. While some small interventions show positive effects (in explicit attitudes; Malinen & Johnston, 2013), others reveal unintended effects: Kulik and colleagues (2000) demonstrate that those participants randomly assigned to view an age-diversity video asking them to suppress age-related thoughts later evaluated an older applicant less favorably than other raters did.

The *main goals* of studies following this first strategy of experimentation involve the understanding of age-related mechanisms (e.g., Gärtner & Hertel, 2017; Hommelhoff et al., 2018). After all, chronological age is never a causal explanation in itself; rather, it is linked to age-related cognitions, motivations, and capacities that influence behavior (Settersten & Mayer, 1997). This type of experimentation can further be used to understand the social context of aging workers, such as age stereotypes, images of aging, and age-related expectations and norms in the work context (e.g., Bertolino et al., 2013; Hanscom & Cleveland, 2018; Malinen & Johnston, 2013; Truxillo et al., 2012). These studies thus help understand how employees envision their own future and aging at work or how others react to them as a function of their age.

In *future studies*, researchers could ask participants either to imagine further work-related scenarios ("*Please imagine that you are . . .*" experiments) or to evaluate further employees, CVs, articles, jobs, teams, or work situations ("*How do you think about . . .*" experiments, see also Table 11.1). Depending on the research question and theoretical framework, participants' own age can be made more or less salient via age questions with long scroll-down bars (e.g., Rahn et al., 2021), or positive versus negative aspects of aging can be highlighted through a quiz (e.g., Weiss & Lang, 2012). In general, researchers should consider not only calendar age but also other meanings of age (see also Chapter 3) such as subjective age, tenure, or lifespan age (e.g., measured by life stage via instructions like "please imagine that you have a full-time position and two toddlers vs. teenagers vs. an empty nest at home"). As to subjective age, researchers could also think of experiments that involve individuals' subjective or felt age as *dependent* variables (for a non-work-related study with this approach, see Stephan et al., 2013).

Experimental Manipulation of Participants' External Context

Within this approach, the experimenter systematically varies participants' external context and thus the outer experimental situation in ways that are hypothesized to either help or hinder older versus younger workers. If age-related differences in the outcome change in magnitude or even direction across conditions, conclusions can be made about how and why age affects work behavior. Typist studies (Bosman, 1993, 1994; Salthouse, 1984) are a classic and successfully replicated example for this approach from the work domain (other examples come from the field of air traffic control; e.g., Morrow et al., 1994). In these typing experiments, the preview of the text to be typed was manipulated (Bosman, 1993; Salthouse, 1984). This experimental variation allowed for an understanding of how older typists manage to maintain their performance despite declines in perceptual-motor efficiency: Older typists begin keystroke preparation earlier (i.e., they notice characters in advance sooner) than younger typists. In general, in this approach, the experimenter varies conditions in ways that should cancel out hypothesized processes underlying age differences (Freund & Isaacowitz, 2013). However, note that a completely random assignment of participants to different external conditions is not always possible: When calendar age is a prominent independent variable and thus when groups of younger and older workers are compared, the experiment becomes a quasi-experiment (for work-related examples from economics and ergonomics, see Charness & Villeval, 2009; Norheim et al., 2020).

Further examples of this second experimental strategy can be found in the general lifespan psychology literature and can serve as inspiration for age-and-work researchers. For example, Li and colleagues (2001) manipulated task difficulty in memory and walking tasks (via faster presentation rate of words in memory tasks or via higher wooden obstacles in walking tasks) to understand dual task costs in younger and older adults. Lindenberger and colleagues (2001) experimentally decreased participants' visual and/or auditory acuity to understand the relationships between sensory and cognitive functioning.

A special case of the experimental principle of changing external contexts is a natural experiment. For example, pension reforms and changes in statutory retirement ages can be construed as experimental manipulations (although, of course, random assignment is not given). In the Netherlands, for instance, researchers have found that exogenous shocks to pension rights affected the expected retirement age and training participation (Montizaan et al., 2010).

The *main goals* of experiments following from this second strategy involve understanding the interplay of age, skill, prior knowledge, and motivation in different work tasks and environments. In particular, they strive to understand if and how older employees maintain functioning and compensate for losses and reductions (e.g., in fluid intelligence or muscular strength) at work.

In line with the previous experiments and Freund and Isaacowitz (2013, p. 361), *future experiments* could vary further "conditions that should compensate for the hypothesized developmental process underlying observed age differences." For example, information to be learned could be shown to different age, skill, and prior-knowledge groups for longer or shorter periods and in different formats. The lengths of breaks from learning different materials could be varied, as well as public accountability of task performance (Hess et al., 2001). Such experiments could thus address age differences in fluid intelligence, recovery times, and motivation. Future studies should again consider meanings of age beyond chronological age (see Chapter 3). For example, younger workers with longer tenure and older workers with shorter tenure could be in the sample. Even if some future experiments following this principle will turn into quasi-experiments, we think that the strategy of experimentally introducing external changes is promising in the field of age and work.

Four Steps of Designing Interventions to Address Age and Work Challenges

Developing effective interventions requires integrating theoretical and practical knowledge on intervention needs, possibilities, and the specific population and context in which the intervention will be embedded. To master this integration, systematic approaches have been developed in public health and applied social psychology, such as *intervention mapping* (Fernandez et al., 2019), the *behavior change wheel* (Michie et al., 2011), and the *from-problems-to-solutions approach* (Buunk & Van Vugt, 2013). A common feature of these approaches is that they define a number of steps that researchers should follow. We outline four common steps and illustrate these by relating them to two existing intervention studies from the work and aging field (Burmeister et al., 2020; Müller et al., 2016). Table 11.1 shows an overview of these steps.

Step 1: Systematic Problem Definition

Often, the impetus to develop an intervention arises from conversations with practitioners or from noticing unsolved problems in the workplace. For example, an employee survey in a healthcare organization may show that older personnel lack the physical vitality to perform heavy physical tasks (Müller et al., 2016), or organizational leaders may observe that age-diverse teams fail to benefit from their various expertise (Burmeister et al., 2020). The first step of intervention research therefore is to develop a clear problem definition by precisely describing what the problem is, why and for whom it is a problem, and what the key aspects and possible causes are (Buunk & Van Vugt, 2013). Attention should be paid to identify the target group for a possible intervention, that is, the group whose cooperation is essential to solve the problem (Buunk & Van Vugt, 2013). In the examples, these could be older nurses with chronic health conditions or age-diverse coworkers who may give a new impetus to team processes.

The ultimate goal of this step is to derive measurable indicator(s) of the target behaviors or outcomes that would need to change in the target group for an intervention to succeed. The outcome variables thus specify the desirable end situation; they should be relevant to the problem, specific and concrete, and continuous (i.e., can be described as less or more; Buunk & Van Vugt, 2013). In our examples, measurable indicators may be the level of perceived work ability of healthcare employees and the degree of knowledge exchange in age-diverse teams, respectively (Burmeister et al., 2020; Müller et al., 2016).

Step 2: Logic Model of the Problem

Once the problem, target group, and outcome indicators are clearly defined, a systematic causal analysis of the problem is needed to gain leads for the intervention (Buunk & Van Vugt, 2013; Fernandez et al., 2019). Here, it is important to consider potential causes at all organizational levels (Michie et al., 2011). Researchers may consider factors at the level of individuals, the group, leadership, the organization, or the overarching social context (IGLOO; Nielsen et al., 2018). A further framework that can inform the logic model of the problem is the A-M-O model of organizational behavior (Blumberg & Pringle, 1982, see also Michie et al., 2011). Thus, researchers should consider abilities (e.g., skills, knowledge), motivation (e.g., intrinsic or extrinsic), and opportunities (e.g., physical space, social norms) in their search for the most plausible mechanism(s) to address in the intervention.

In the first example, researchers may conclude that the most plausible explanation for a threat to nurses' work ability may lie in their self-regulatory strategies captured by the model of selection, optimization, and compensation (SOC; Müller et al., 2016). In the second example, the most plausible explanation for the scant knowledge exchange between age-diverse coworkers may lie in a lacking awareness of each other's knowledge utility (Burmeister et al., 2020).

Step 3: Intervention Design

Once the causal factors of the target behavior or outcome have been exposed, an intervention can be developed, starting with choosing a general approach and then working out specific intervention modules and activities (Fernandez et al., 2019). For example, the *behavior change wheel* (Michie et al., 2011) maps the causes identified in Step 2 to intervention strategies (at the individual level) and policies (at the organizational level; Michie et al., 2011). Strategies might involve training, education, persuasion, or incentives, while policies can comprise changes of guidelines, regulations, or services. When designing the intervention step by step, including details such as specific modules, materials, communication, timeline, and many more substeps (Fernandez et al., 2019), consideration of the specific context and target group are essential. Among all the possible interventions, only few will be suitable and feasible for the target group in the specific environmental context (Astbury & Leeuw, 2010; Walton & Yeager, 2020).

An important part of this step is an evidence-based *theory of change* underlying the intervention (Astbury & Leeuw, 2010; Fernandez et al., 2019). This theory is best illustrated by a graphical model that links specific intervention activities with immediate, midterm, and longer-term expected outcomes. This theory of change builds on the logic model of the problem and forms the basis for transparency in intervention goals and for monitoring and evaluation. In the first example (Müller et al., 2016), the research group designed a training with six sessions over a period of nine months, mainly grounded in the SOC model (P. B. Baltes & M. M. Baltes, 1990). The theory of change entailed that training nurses in the use of SOC behaviors leads to a more efficient use of their personal resources, which in turn enhances their sense that job demands and resources are in balance, resulting in higher levels of work ability (Müller et al., 2016). In the second example (Burmeister et al., 2020), the researchers designed a half-day training and follow-up call for age-diverse dyads of coworkers grounded in the information/decision-making perspective (Williams & O'Reilly, 1998). The theory of change involved that awareness of knowledge types and exposure of knowledge similarity and differences with older/younger coworkers would increase transactive memory, which in turn enhances knowledge transfer (Burmeister et al., 2020).

Step 4: Monitoring and Evaluation

Monitoring and evaluating an intervention are important to ensure and measure its effectiveness—or to understand why an intervention failed or produced unintended effects (Fernandez et al., 2019). Theoretically, an intervention can fail for two reasons. First, despite the best intentions, an intervention may not have been implemented as planned (indicating *implementation failure*; e.g., when materials were phrased too difficultly for participants). Second, the intervention may have been based on an inaccurate theory of change (indicating *theory failure*; e.g., when assumptions made were invalid, at least in the given context conditions; Walton & Yeager, 2020). For example, training SOC behaviors may only produce enhanced work ability if nurses have sufficient job autonomy to exercise these behaviors (Riedel et al., 2015). Furthermore, increasing knowledge exchange between age-diverse coworkers may produce higher team performance only if teams are facing complex, interdependent tasks (Wegge et al., 2008).

Monitoring and evaluating an intervention is therefore crucial. *Monitoring* entails tracking attendance and immediate reactions to intervention materials and activities (D. L. Kirkpatrick & J. Kirkpatrick, 2006). It allows detecting implementation failure, as well as conducting evaluation analyses with only the subgroup who completed all intervention activities as planned (per-protocol analyses; e.g., Müller et al., 2016). *Evaluation* entails measuring all components of the theory of change in the prespecified temporal order and allows detecting theory failure. The optimal design for intervention evaluation is a longitudinal design with random assignment to intervention and control group (Lipsey & Cordray, 2000). The control group could receive the intervention at a later time point in a waitlist-control design (as in Müller et al., 2016) or receive an alternative intervention (as in Burmeister et al., 2020). The measures and their temporal spacing should be aligned with the theory of change. Typically, a baseline survey would include all outcomes and possible moderators; a post-training survey would include measures of immediate reactions and short-term outcomes, and one or more delayed surveys would include measure of mid- and long-term outcomes (D. L. Kirkpatrick & J. Kirkpatrick, 2006).

Practical Recommendations for Implementation and Data Analysis

This last section of our chapter provides further brief recommendations for planning, conducting, and analyzing data from experiments and interventions in the context of age and work. Some of these recommendations are specific for this context, while others are more generally applicable.

In the *phase of generating ideas and planning a study*, we consider it important to think about both the workplace and the larger social-cultural environment in which workers live (Truxillo et al., 2015). As pointed out before, we also recommend thinking about age beyond calendar age and to bear in mind other meanings such as subjective age, functional age, tenure, or lifespan age (e.g., Chapter 3). We further advise developing hypotheses that are grounded in theory (e.g., P. B. Baltes & M. M. Baltes, 1990; Bakker & Demerouti, 2007; Carstensen, 2006; see also Chapter 7) and suggest not only preregistration of hypotheses (e.g., via OSF.io or aspredicted.org) but also power analyses (e.g., Faul et al., 2007) to determine an appropriate sample size for experimental/intervention and control groups. As for sample composition, it is advisable to avoid extreme-group comparisons (e.g., career starters vs. near-retirees) because of potential overestimation of effects (Freund & Isaacowitz, 2013). Since inferences about causal effects are tentative until the research is successfully replicated (Tabachnick & Fidell, 2007), experiments and interventions that strive to both replicate and extend prior work seem particularly important.

When *designing their study*, researchers could also think of assessments that go beyond self- and other-reports (Gerpott et al., 2020; see also Chapter 8). Furthermore, many scholars have highlighted that experimental stimuli should be as realistic and as externally valid as possible (Freund & Isaacowitz, 2013; Highhouse, 2009). Overly long or tedious tasks (e.g., in within-person designs with many different scenarios that differ only slightly) should be avoided as well; if such tasks are necessary to answer a specific research question, they should at least be tested and adapted in a pilot study.

When designing an invention, we suggest thinking in advance of potential (additional) effects that are not apparent or desirable. Researchers should bear in mind that interventions can have unintended or negative effects despite positive intentions (Aust et al., 2010; Kulik et al., 2000). Although interventions are often time-consuming and resource-intensive, we want to note that there are also small, scalable, and psychologically rich interventions that can have relatively far-reaching benefits (Truxillo et al., 2015; Walton & Yeager, 2020).

As to *data analysis*, researchers have traditionally used GLM approaches (e.g., ANOVA) to analyze data from experiments or interventions (Breitsohl, 2019). When it comes to within-subjects designs (e.g., when ratings of scenarios are nested within participants), current studies have increasingly relied on multilevel and thus GLMM approaches instead of applying ANOVA with repeated measures (for examples, see Gärtner & Hertel, 2017; Zacher et al., 2017). For using structural equation modeling (SEM) to analyze data from experimental designs, a helpful guide is offered by Breitsohl (2019), who points out several advantages of the SEM versus the ANOVA approach, such as control of measurement error, accounting for unequal variances across groups, or the calculation of model fit indices.

In conclusion, we want to emphasize that the field will benefit most from "the right mix" of different research designs and methods to understand aging in the context of work (see also other chapters from Section III in this book). Correlational and descriptive work should be complemented with more (quasi-) experiments and interventions to properly test causal pathways or boundary conditions for age-related effects on work behaviors and outcomes. Whenever we find that age differences disappear after experimental/interventional manipulation (e.g., when the external work context is changed in certain ways or when imagined time perspectives are equated; Carstensen, 2006), researchers have probably tapped into mechanisms that influence age-related differences and changes. Moreover, by engaging in intervention research, despite the high effort and risky return on investment, work and age scholarship will boost its relevance for and impact on nonacademic communities.

References

Astbury, B., & Leeuw, F. L. (2010). Unpacking black boxes: Mechanisms and theory building in evaluation. *American Journal of Evaluation, 31*, 363–381. https://doi. org/10.1177/1098214010371972

Aust, B., Rugulies, R., Finken, A., & Jensen, C. (2010). When workplace interventions lead to negative effects: Learning from failures. *Scandinavian Journal of Public Health, 38*, 106–119. https://doi.org/10.1177/1403494809354362

Baert, S., Norga, J., Thuy, Y., & Van Hecke, M. (2016). Getting grey hairs in the labour market: An alternative experiment on age discrimination. *Journal of Economic Psychology, 57*, 86–101. https://doi.org/10.1016/j.joep.2016.10.002

Bakker, A. B., & Demerouti, E. (2007). The job demands-resources model: State of the art. *Journal of Managerial Psychology, 22*, 309–328. https://doi.org/10.1108/02683940710733115

Baltes, P. B., & Baltes, M. M. (1990). Psychological perspectives on successful aging: The model of selective optimization with compensation. In P. B. Baltes & M. M. Baltes (Eds.), *Successful aging: Perspectives from the behavioral sciences* (pp. 1–34). Cambridge University Press.

Bertolino, M., Truxillo, D. M., & Fraccaroli, F. (2013). Age effects on perceived personality and job performance. *Journal of Managerial Psychology, 28*, 867–885. https://doi.org/10.1108/JMP-07-2013-0222

Blumberg, M., & Pringle, C. D. (1982). The missing opportunity in organizational research: Some implications for a theory of work performance. *The Academy of Management Review, 7*, 560–569. https://doi.org/10.5465/AMR.1982.4285240

Bosman, E. A. (1993). Age-related differences in the motoric aspects of transcription typing skill. *Psychology and Aging, 8*, 87–102. https://doi.org/10.1037/0882-7974.8.1.87

Bosman, E. A. (1994). Age and skill differences in typing related and unrelated reaction time tasks. *Aging, Neuropsychology, and Cognition, 1*, 310–322. https://doi.org/10.1080/13825589408256584

Breitsohl, H. (2019). Beyond ANOVA: An introduction to structural equation models for experimental designs. *Organizational Research Methods, 22*, 649–677. https://doi.org/10.1177/1094428118754988

Burmeister, A., Gerpott, F. H., Hirschi, A., Scheibe, S., Pak, K., & Kooij, D. T. (2020). Reaching the heart or the mind? Test of two theory-based training programs to improve interactions between age-diverse coworkers. *Academy of Management Learning & Education*. Advance online publication. https://doi.org/10.5465/amle.2019.0348

Buunk, A. P., & Van Vugt, M. (2013). *Applying social psychology: From problems to solutions*. Sage.

Carstensen, L. L. (2006). The influence of a sense of time on human development. *Science, 312*, 1913–1915. https://doi.org/10.1126/science.1127488

Charness, G., & Villeval, M. C. (2009). Cooperation and competition in intergenerational experiments in the field and the laboratory. *American Economic Review, 99*, 956–978. https://doi.org/10.1257/aer.99.3.956

Faul, F., Erdfelder, E., Lang, A. G., & Buchner, A. (2007). G*Power 3: A flexible statistical power analysis program for the social, behavioral, and biomedical sciences. *Behavior Research Methods, 39*, 175–191. https://doi.org/10.3758/BF03193146

Fernandez, M. E., Ruiter, R. A., Markham, C. M., & Kok, G. (2019). Intervention mapping: Theory-and evidence-based health promotion program planning: Perspective and examples. *Frontiers in Public Health, 7*, 209. https://doi.org/10.3389/fpubh.2019.00209

Freund, A. M., & Isaacowitz, D. M. (2013). Beyond age comparisons: A plea for the use of a modified Brunswikian approach to experimental designs in the study of adult development and aging. *Human Development, 56*, 351–371. https://doi.org/10.1159/000357177

Gaillard, M., & Desmette, D. (2010). (In) validating stereotypes about older workers influences their intentions to retire early and to learn and develop. *Basic and Applied Social Psychology, 32,* 86–98. https://doi.org/10.1080/01973530903435763

Gärtner, L. U., & Hertel, G. (2017). Future time perspective in occupational teams: Do older workers prefer more familiar teams? *Frontiers in Psychology, 8,* 1639. https://doi.org/10.3389/fpsyg.2017.01639

Gerpott, F. H., Lehmann-Willenbrock, N., & Scheibe, S. (2020). Is work and aging research a science of questionnaires? Moving the field forward by considering perceived versus actual behaviors. *Work, Aging and Retirement, 6,* 65–70. https://doi.org/10.1093/workar/waaa002

Gerrig, R. J. (2013). *Psychology and life.* Pearson.

Hanscom, M. E., & Cleveland, J. N. (2018). The influence of successful aging at work upon simulated performance decisions. *Work, Aging and Retirement, 4,* 129–144. https://doi.org/10.1093/workar/wax021

Hess, T. M., Rosenberg, D. C., & Waters, S. J. (2001). Motivation and representational processes in adulthood: The effects of social accountability and information relevance. *Psychology and Aging, 16,* 629–642. https://doi.org/10.1037/0882-7974.16.4.629

Highhouse, S. (2009). Designing experiments that generalize. *Organizational Research Methods, 12,* 554–566. https://doi.org/10.1177/1094428107300396

Hommelhoff, S., Müller, T., & Scheibe, S. (2018). Experimental evidence for the influence of occupational future time perspective on social preferences during lunch breaks. *Work, Aging and Retirement, 4,* 367–380. https://doi.org/10.1093/workar/wax022

Jungmann, F., Wegge, J., Liebermann, S. C., Ries, B. C., & Schmidt, K. H. (2020). Improving team functioning and performance in age-diverse teams: Evaluation of a leadership training. *Work, Aging and Retirement, 6,* 175–194. https://doi.org/10.1093/workar/waaa003

Kirkpatrick, D. L., & Kirkpatrick, J. (2006). *Evaluating training programs: The four levels.* Berrett-Koehler Publishers.

Kulik, C. T., Perry, E. L., & Bourhis, A. C. (2000). Ironic evaluation processes: Effects of thought suppression on evaluations of older job applicants. *Journal of Organizational Behavior, 21,* 689–711. https://doi.org/10.1002/1099-1379(200009)21:6 < 689::AID-JOB52 > 3.0.CO;2-W

Li, K. Z., Lindenberger, U., Freund, A. M., & Baltes, P. B. (2001). Walking while memorizing: Age-related differences in compensatory behavior. *Psychological Science, 12,* 230–237. https://doi.org/10.1111/1467-9280.00341

Lindenberger, U., Scherer, H., & Baltes, P. B. (2001). The strong connection between sensory and cognitive performance in old age: Not due to sensory acuity reductions operating during cognitive assessment. *Psychology and Aging, 16,* 196–205. https://doi.org/10.1037/0882-7974.16.2.196

Lipsey, M. W., & Cordray, D. S. (2000). Evaluation methods for social intervention. *Annual Review of Psychology, 51,* 345–375. https://doi.org/10.1146/annurev.psych.51.1.345

MacDonald, S. W., & Stawski, R. S. (2016). Methodological considerations for the study of adult development and aging. In K. W. Schaie & S. L. Willis (Eds.), *Handbook of the psychology of aging* (pp. 15–40). Academic Press. https://doi.org/10.1016/B978-0-12-411469-2.00002-9

Malinen, S., & Johnston, L. (2013). Workplace ageism: Discovering hidden bias. *Experimental Aging Research, 39,* 445–465. https://doi.org/10.1080/0361073X.2013.808111

Michie, S., Van Stralen, M. M., & West, R. (2011). The behaviour change wheel: A new method for characterising and designing behaviour change interventions. *Implementation Science*, *6*, 1–12. https://doi.org/10.1186/1748-5908-6-42

Montizaan, R., Cörvers, F., & De Grip, A. (2010). The effects of pension rights and retirement age on training participation: Evidence from a natural experiment. *Labour Economics*, *17*, 240–247. https://doi.org/10.1016/j.labeco.2009.10.004

Morrow, D., Leirer, V., Altiteri, P., & Fitzsimmons, C. (1994). When expertise reduces age differences in performance. *Psychology and Aging*, *9*, 134–148. https://doi.org/10.1037/0882-7974.9.1.134

Müller, A., Heiden, B., Herbig, B., Poppe, F., & Angerer, P. (2016). Improving well-being at work: A randomized controlled intervention based on selection, optimization, and compensation. *Journal of Occupational Health Psychology*, *21*, 169–181. http://dx.doi.org/10.1037/a0039676

Nielsen, K., Yarker, J., Munir, F., & Bültmann, U. (2018). IGLOO: An integrated framework for sustainable return to work in workers with common mental disorders. *Work & Stress*, *32*, 400–417. https://doi.org/10.1080/02678373.2018.1438536

Norheim, K. L., Samani, A., & Madeleine, P. (2020). The effects of age on response time, accuracy, and shoulder/arm kinematics during hammering. *Applied Ergonomics*, *90*, 103157. https://doi.org/10.1016/j.apergo.2020.103157

Rahn, G., Martiny, S. E., & Nikitin, J. (2021). Feeling out of place: Internalized age stereotypes are associated with older employees' sense of belonging and social motivation. *Work, Aging and Retirement*. Advance online publication. https://doi.org/10.1093/workar/waaa005

Riedel, N., Müller, A., & Ebener, M. (2015). Applying strategies of selection, optimization, and compensation to maintain work ability–A psychosocial resource complementing the job demand–control model? Results from the representative lidA cohort study on work, age, and health in Germany. *Journal of Occupational and Environmental Medicine*, *57*, 552–561. https://doi.org/10.1097/jom.0000000000000402

Robertson, P. J., Roberts, D. R., & Porras, J. I. (1993). Dynamics of planned organizational change: Assessing empirical support for a theoretical model. *Academy of Management Journal*, *36*, 619–634. https://doi.org/10.5465/256595

Salthouse, T. A. (1984). Effects of age and skill in typing. *Journal of Experimental Psychology: General*, *113*, 345–371. https://doi.org/10.1037/0096-3445.113.3.345

Schram, A. (2005). Artificiality: The tension between internal and external validity in economic experiments. *Journal of Economic Methodology*, *12*, 225–237. https://doi.org/10.1080/13501780500086081

Seiferling, N., & Michel, A. (2017). Building resources for retirement transition: Effects of a resource-oriented group intervention on retirement cognitions and emotions. *Work, Aging and Retirement*, *3*, 325–342. https://doi.org/10.1093/workar/wax011

Settersten Jr, R. A., & Mayer, K. U. (1997). The measurement of age, age structuring, and the life course. *Annual Review of Sociology*, *23*, 233–261. https://doi.org/10.1146/annurev.soc.23.1.233

Stephan, Y., Chalabaev, A., Kotter-Grühn, D., & Jaconelli, A. (2013). "Feeling younger, being stronger": An experimental study of subjective age and physical functioning among older adults. *Journals of Gerontology Series B*, *68*, 1–7. https://doi.org/10.1093/geronb/gbs037

Stevens-Roseman, E. S. (2009). Older mentors for newer workers: Impact of a worker-driven intervention on later life satisfaction. *Journal of Workplace Behavioral Health*, *24*, 419–426. https://doi.org/10.1080/15555240903358652

Tabachnick, B. G., & Fidell, L. S. (2007). *Experimental designs using ANOVA*. Duxbury.

Truxillo, D. M., Cadiz, D. M., & Hammer, L. B. (2015). Supporting the aging workforce: A review and recommendations for workplace intervention research. *Annual Review of Organizational Psychology and Organizational Behavior, 2*, 351–381. https://doi.org/10.1146/annurev-orgpsych-032414-111435

Truxillo, D. M., McCune, E. A., Bertolino, M., & Fraccaroli, F. (2012). Perceptions of older versus younger workers in terms of big five facets, proactive personality, cognitive ability, and job performance. *Journal of Applied Social Psychology, 42*, 2607–2639. https://doi.org/10.1111/j.1559-1816.2012.00954.x

Walton, G. M., & Yeager, D. S. (2020). Seed and soil: Psychological affordances in contexts help to explain where wise interventions succeed or fail. *Current Directions in Psychological Science, 29*, 219–226. https://doi.org/10.1177/0963721420904453

Wegge, J., Roth, C., Neubach, B., Schmidt, K.-H., & Kanfer, R. (2008). Age and gender diversity as determinants of performance and health in a public organization: The role of task complexity and group size. *Journal of Applied Psychology, 93*, 1301–1313. https://doi.org/10.1037/a0012680

Weiss, D., & Lang, F. R. (2012). "They" are old but "I" feel younger: Age-group dissociation as a self-protective strategy in old age. *Psychology and Aging, 27*, 153–163. https://doi.org/10.1037/a0024887

Williams, K. Y., & O'Reilly III, C. A. (1998). Demography and diversity in organizations: A review of 40 years of research. *Research in Organizational Behavior, 20*, 77–140.

Zabel, K. L., & Baltes, B. B. (2015). Workplace intervention effectiveness across the lifespan. In L. Finkelstein, D. Truxillo, F. Fraccaroli, & R. Kanfer (Eds.), *Facing the challenges of a multi-age workforce: A use-inspired approach* (pp. 209–229). Routledge.

Zacher, H., Dirkers, B. T., Korek, S., & Hughes, B. (2017). Age-differential effects of job characteristics on job attraction: A policy-capturing study. *Frontiers in Psychology, 8*, 1124. https://doi.org/10.3389/fpsyg.2017.01124

Zacher, H., & Frese, M. (2009). Remaining time and opportunities at work: Relationships between age, work characteristics, and occupational future time perspective. *Psychology and Aging, 24*, 487–493. https://doi.org/10.1037/a0015425

12

QUALITATIVE METHODS FOR STUDYING AGE AND WORK[1]

Annika Wilhelmy, Guido Hertel and Tine Köhler

Research on aging and age-related differences at work is still a new field in psychology (see Chapter 1 of this volume). Driven by increasing life expectancies and ongoing demographic changes worldwide, organizations and societies are faced with new challenges but also interesting opportunities (see Chapter 18 of this volume for examples). However, established models and frameworks in work and organizational psychology are often not sufficiently sensitive for the specifics of older workers. Moreover, the high (and so far largely unseen) level of demographic changes might have initiated entirely new processes and reactions at work that are not captured by existing frameworks and related measures. In this chapter, we argue that qualitative research methods offer novel avenues for understanding age at work, affiliated processes (e.g., retirement), and the mechanisms through which age influences other relevant organizational variables. Qualitative research methods allow researchers to explore aging processes, aging experiences, and interactions between individuals of different age groups, which can lead to novel theorizing on age and a more nuanced conceptualization of how age impacts work experiences and outcomes. However, age researchers have not yet taken full advantage of the various possibilities that qualitative research methods offer (Amabile, 2019).

This chapter serves as an introduction for scholars and students who have no or only a rudimentary familiarity with qualitative research. Our aim is to inspire researchers in the domain of age and work to explore how qualitative research methods may allow them to address research questions that they have so far been unable to examine using quantitative methods alone. In the first part of this chapter, we outline core characteristics of qualitative research methods, opportunities they afford, and challenges researchers need to manage, as well as recommendations for their application. In the second part of this chapter, we introduce a

DOI: 10.4324/9781003089674-15

taxonomy connecting key dimensions of aging research with core aims of qualitative research. We further develop specific research questions that emerge from this taxonomy and provide concrete illustrations of how research might be advanced using specific qualitative methods.

An Introduction to Qualitative Research Methods

Defining Features of Qualitative Research

Qualitative research constitutes a broad umbrella of various perspectives, practices, and methods. It can be defined as a set of methods that "seek to describe, decode, translate, and otherwise come to terms with the meaning, not the frequency, of certain more or less naturally occurring phenomena in the social world" (Van Maanen, 1979, p. 520). Qualitative research uses interpretive, naturalistic approaches and social actors' meanings to study processes and phenomena in the environment in which they naturally occur (Gephart, 2004). As such, qualitative research is grounded in the idea that knowledge is subjective, and that access to knowledge must consider human examination and sense-making.

Qualitative research most commonly is inductive (i.e., making an inference based on observations) and/or abductive (i.e., inferring an explanation for an observation by drawing a probable conclusion from existing knowledge). It uses a bottom-up approach to theorizing by systematically analyzing observations that capture the participants' perspective and experiences, and by developing insights from these data (i.e., inductive reasoning). It then uses subsequent abductive reasoning about the nature of the observed phenomenon and the underlying mechanisms that create the observations. Qualitative research comprises an investigative and adaptive process in which researchers gradually make sense of what is studied, for example, by immersing themselves in the natural setting chosen for the study, entering participants' worlds, and exploring their perspectives through interaction. It also involves cataloguing and classifying information about the phenomenon of interest and potentially collecting additional data to extend and clarify conclusions drawn from the data (Creswell & Creswell, 2018). Along similar lines, qualitative research is flexible to match evolving demands of the research process, adapting the research approach as researchers learn more about their phenomenon of interest so that ensuing data collection can be targeted at theory clarification and consolidation (Lee et al., 1999).

Like quantitative methods, qualitative methods are grounded in the researcher's ontological (i.e., what a researcher perceives as knowledge) and epistemological position (i.e., what a researcher perceives as the best way to understand and learn about the nature of a phenomenon) (Rheinhardt et al., 2018). For instance, an interpretivist stance emphasizes that knowledge is a subjective and contextually mediated account of the lives of those who are studied. This is relevant for aging research because individuals' experiences differ across their lifespan, and the field would benefit from deeper insights into age-related changes and the meaning individuals attribute to age and aging (Locke & Golden-Biddle, 2002). "Retirement age," for instance, may harbor a threatening meaning for some people but invoke images of a work-life well lived for others. In contrast, a postmodernist stance emphasizes the political dimension inherent in knowledge, which creates and maintains power relations in society. In aging research, terminology can, for example, reinforce or buffer discrimination against older workers (for a comprehensive overview of epistemological paradigms, see Locke & Golden-Biddle, 2002).

Importantly, the distinction between qualitative and quantitative research refers to more than "no numbers vs. numbers." For example, consider differences in the understanding of a specific survey item between younger and older workers that might lead to the same ratings even though the item is interpreted quite differently. From a quantitative research perspective, these differences would be considered a source of error variance. From a qualitative research perspective, however, these different interpretations are interesting and potentially meaningful observations that could contribute to insights into the phenomenon of interest and, subsequently, to theorizing. Thus, qualitative research focuses on participants' unique and idiosyncratic realities rather than on what is common across larger groups of people (Creswell & Creswell, 2018). Likewise, qualitative research considers extreme cases or participants with highly unique experiences as potentially important for theoretical insight and for the exploration of phenomenon boundaries (Murphy et al., 2017).

Goals and Typical Designs of Qualitative Research

A central purpose of qualitative research is to understand a particular social phenomenon, situation, role, event, or interaction. With respect to age and work, we differentiate four main goals or purposes related to qualitative research in this chapter: (1) understanding meaning and sense-making, (2) capturing lived experiences and differences in life/career courses and narratives, (3) determining processes and dynamics, and (4) exploring context influences (see Table 12.1 for an overview). Typical research questions addressed with qualitative methods often start with "how," "why," "when," and "what" (Pratt & Bonaccio, 2016) and explore reasons, conditions, or mechanisms over the course of the qualitative study, rather than testing predetermined reasons, conditions, or mechanisms as would be the case in quantitative research. Therefore, qualitative approaches are often described as hypothesis *generating*, as compared to hypothesis *testing* quantitative research.

To provide answers to "how," "why," "when," and "what" questions, a vast range of designs, approaches, methods, and techniques can be used in qualitative research. Lê and Schmid (2019) differentiated three families of qualitative designs: Post-positivist (e.g., comparative case studies, extended case method), interpretive

TABLE 12.1 How Can Qualitative Methods Be Used to Advance Our Understanding of Age and Work?

Foci of aging research	Goals of qualitative research	Examples of relevant questions	Example approaches
Experience of age-related changes at work	Understanding meaning and sense-making	How do workers perceive and make sense of their own aging processes? How do bodily changes affect the understanding and identity of one's role as an employee, manager, etc.?	Narrative analysis Grounded theory (interpretivism) Ethnography and autoethnography (phenomenological) Thematic analysis Open content analysis
	Capturing lived experiences and differences in life/career courses and narratives	When and how does one's understanding of age and aging change in the course of one's work life?	
	Determining processes and dynamics	How are workers' team roles shaped by age-related physiological indicators? How do coworkers perceive and interact with older workers?	Process analysis
	Exploring context influences	What conditions help or impede positive experiences of age-related changes?	
Reactions to cope with age-related changes at work	Understanding meaning and sense-making	How do older workers understand, frame, and reframe work-related challenges? How do people manage age-related cognitive changes?	Observations Grounded theory Thematic analysis Narrative analysis
	Capturing lived experiences and differences in life/career courses and narratives	How do people deal with transitioning from work to retirement?	Case study analysis Action research
	Determining processes and dynamics	How do coworkers react to older workers and vice versa?	Appreciative inquiry Ethnography and autoethnography
	Exploring context influences	How do different organizational events influence the coping strategies of older workers?	

(Continued)

TABLE 12.1 (Continued)

Foci of aging research	Goals of qualitative research	Examples of relevant questions	Example approaches
Interaction with others in an age-heterogenous workforce	Understanding meaning and sense-making	How are relationships experienced between leaders and followers as a function of age diversity?	Discourse analysis Thematic analysis Open content coding Linguistic style analysis Grounded theory (symbolic interactionism) Observations
	Capturing lived experiences and differences in life/career courses and narratives	How do work–related friendships develop or change across people's career course?	
	Determining processes and dynamics	How are workers' team roles shaped through interactions with older and younger workers? Why and how do age-heterogeneous friendships at work develop and last?	
	Exploring context influences	When and how do different organizational contexts impede or provide opportunities for older and younger workers to interact?	

(e.g., grounded theory, action research), and critical designs (e.g., discourse analysis). Within these various qualitative designs, different data collection and analysis procedures can be employed. Data collection techniques include semistructured interviews (i.e., using a predefined set of questions but also new questions as a result of what the interviewee says; for an overview see e.g. Brinkmann & Kvale, 2015), focus groups (i.e., a group of people assembled to participate in a discussion on predefined questions), open-ended questions in questionnaires (e.g. Salmon, 2016), systematic observations, and diary events method (i.e., reporting on events during a specified time period and with a short time span between occurrence and reporting). Data analysis methods include thematic analysis (e.g., Braun & Clarke, 2006), content analysis (e.g., Neuendorf, 2017), narrative analysis (e.g., Riessman, 2008), grounded theory coding (e.g., Locke, 2001), discourse analysis (e.g., Vaara et al., 2016), and template analysis (e.g., Brooks et al., 2015), among many others. Comprehensive overviews of qualitative research designs, approaches, methods, and techniques are provided by Lee et al. (1999) and Locke and Golden-Biddle (2002). Different qualitative methods and techniques (and even elements of these) can and should be flexibly combined as long as they are nested within the same research paradigm (e.g., interpretivism, post-positivism, critical realism, or phenomenology). This is referred to as the bricolage approach (Pratt, Sonenshein, et al., 2020). When using bricolage, researchers mindfully pick and choose methodological elements and explain each decision made and how it fits the purpose of their study (e.g., Grodal et al., 2020).

Importantly, qualitative methods are not opponents of—but rather are complementary to—quantitative methods. An example of combining qualitative and quantitative research across publications would be a qualitative study that seeks to refresh a mature and predominantly quantitatively studied field by questioning well-trodden paths of that field (Edmundson & McManus, 2007). Qualitative and quantitative research methods can also be combined in a multistudy paper (e.g., a quantitative study might reveal a group difference and a qualitative study might seek to examine what the reasons for these differences may be). In addition, mixed methods research involves collecting and analyzing qualitative and quantitative data in a single study and integrating the different approaches to achieve a more comprehensive examination of a research question (Gibson, 2017).

Common Challenges and Recommendations for Qualitative Research

Conducting qualitative research is challenging, and resulting publications are judged based on the fit between research methods and research questions, extent of theoretical and practical contributions, and transparency about the methods used (Harley & Cornelissen, 2020). Due to their different goals, quality criteria for qualitative research and quantitative research differ, which often poses a challenge for scholars who are new to qualitative research (Wilhelmy & Köhler, in press). Thus, our first and foremost recommendation is to seek training in the specific literature of the qualitative method to be employed (see previous suggestions) and to collaborate with researchers experienced in these methods.

Our second recommendation is not to blindly follow templates, checklists, or reporting guides such as the journal article reporting standards for qualitative research of the American Psychological Association (Levitt et al., 2018), the author guidelines for qualitative research by the Journal of Occupational and Organizational Psychology ("Qualitative Guidelines"), or checklists created for specific qualitative research methods (e.g., Tong et al., 2007). While these checklists and templates might provide an informative starting point, there are many disciplinary standards and traditions as well as epistemological considerations directing how qualitative methods get employed that these checklists often do not fully acknowledge. Thus, checklists may be too simple or even misleading for employing a specific qualitative method. Furthermore, they pose the risk of putting qualitative research into a "methodological straightjacket" (Corley et al., 2020, p. 161) that restricts its core potential and capacities. Qualitative research lives from flexibility and innovativeness. Authors and reviewers should critically evaluate the applicability of reporting standards and guidelines related to the specific research project, the background, purpose, and context of the respective study. Standards may need to be modified or abandoned when not useful for examining the study in question (Köhler et al., 2019; Wilhelmy, 2016).

There are many helpful and comprehensive frameworks on how to achieve rigor when using qualitative methods (e.g., Harley & Cornelissen, 2020). Criteria for rigor in qualitative research include *methodological coherence* (i.e., the chosen methods need to match the study's purpose and the researcher's ontological and epistemological assumptions), *consistency* (i.e., applying the chosen method to its full intent), *logical consistency* (i.e., the links between data, steps of data analysis, and theoretical conclusions that are logical and explicitly expressed), and *inference to the best explanation* (i.e., not accepting the most likely explanation but instead questioning one's findings and considering alternative explanations).

Challenges arise when qualitative work is inappropriately judged against criteria that stem from quantitative research. For example, during a study's ethics approval process an internal/institutional review board (IRB) may request the study protocol to be fully formed and strictly carried out as approved. Because of the iterative nature of qualitative research, the sampling strategy, interview questions, and even research questions may change as a result of learning more about the phenomenon and its context. This is considered good practice as long as such key decisions are well described and justified. A solution can be to explain to the IRB that qualitative research needs to be adaptive, to submit a study protocol about the initial focus and to add updates throughout the course of the study, or to acknowledge in the protocol that specific content may be adjusted.

Similar problems arise when trying to integrate qualitative research into the Open Science framework. Whereas some Open Science movements seem compatible with qualitative research, such as Open Access (i.e., making research publications widely available to the public) or Open Peer Review (allowing for identification of authors and reviewers and/or publishing the reviewer comments alongside a scientific article, e.g., Ross-Hellauer, 2017), other Open Science movements are not. For example, preregistration of hypotheses is impossible for studies that are not following the hypothetico-deductive method of theory testing. Furthermore, making raw data available in online repositories (i.e., Open Data) would cause severe ethical problems for most qualitative studies because the very detailed data often cannot be sufficiently anonymized. Removing names from an interview transcript does not protect confidentiality when the specific details reported and the jargon of the interviewee enable identification by colleagues or supervisors. Informing participants that their information would become part of Open Data might affect their openness and their responses. Similarly, organizations may no longer be willing to support such research or share organizational documents with researchers. Finally, while qualitative research is committed to transparently disclosing how data were collected and analyzed, it is not assumed that another researcher would come to the same conclusions if they followed the same steps. Far from being seen as a methodological flaw, though, qualitative research acknowledges that researchers have unique backgrounds, knowledge, skills, and experiences that are an important part of the data collection and analysis process (e.g., Pratt, Kaplan, et al., 2020). While specifics of the compatibility of qualitative research and Open Science are still being debated, we sincerely hope that future institutional solutions will be more forthcoming in their acknowledgement and acceptance of different methodological approaches and view them as a strength for holistic scientific knowledge generation.

Potential Contributions of Qualitative Research Methods for Studying Age and Work

Ongoing demographic changes in most industrialized countries (and beyond) affect the workforce in many ways. For instance, the life expectancy of humans has increased by at least 20 years in the last 100 years due to advances in technologies, medicine, and nutrition. At the same time, birthrates have decreased in most industrialized countries for various reasons (e.g., Chapters 1 and 2 of this volume). As a consequence, the average age of the workforce increases, requiring adaptations of human resource management strategies (see Chapter 18 of this volume). Empirical research is mandatory to enable evidence-based adaptations rather than mere intuitive behavior, the latter often being negatively biased by preassumptions and age stereotypes. However, although research on age differences at work has grown in the last years (e.g., Hertel & Zacher, 2018), many age-related processes are not fully explored but rather extrapolated from generalizations based on research with younger workers (see also Chapter 1 of this volume). Moreover, the level of life expectancy and the size of the human population worldwide are entirely new in human history, so researchers lack experience with such an increasingly large population of older people (and workers). Systematic exploration is warranted to better understand the experiences and behaviors of older workers, both with respect to within-person processes and inter-individual interactions (see also Chapter 9 of this volume).

Age differences and their impact in work contexts can be explored from different perspectives (employees vs. supervisors, customer, or clients, etc.). Moreover, aging itself is a complex process, including changes of the biological system, cognitive processes, emotional reactions, and motivational needs, as well as interactions between these systems and processes (e.g., Hertel & Zacher, 2018, for a review). These changes can result in declines of certain capacities but also in increases in skills and competencies and in changes in priorities and orientations toward work (e.g., Kanfer & Ackerman, 2004). However, existing research on age and work is often based on theories, concept specifications, and measures that have been developed with rather young participants (often college students). These existing taxonomies can neglect constructs that are more relevant for older workers. Moreover, transformations that happen as part of the aging process can be overlooked because they are not captured by existing category systems and quantitative measures.

For instance, initial studies on age differences in work values used established concepts from general motivation research, such as the distinction between intrinsic and extrinsic motives; between growth, social, and security needs; or the components of expectancy models (Gärtner et al., 2019; Kanfer & Ackerman, 2004; Rudolph et al., 2013). However, values particularly relevant for older workers, such as generativity motives (e.g., Hertel et al., 2013; Kooij et al., 2011), were rarely considered in early empirical studies and thus overlooked as potential motivators of older workers (see Krumm et al., 2013 for an extended measure of work values). As another example, research on age differences in cognitive capacities suggests a decline of fluid intelligence after the mid-20s or even earlier (e.g., Salthouse, 2012). However, empirical studies usually applied established intelligence tests, which have been originally developed to predict performance in school. Therefore, their items resemble typical school tasks, for which younger persons are better trained than older persons. When adapting test items to contexts that are equally familiar to participants, older persons show considerable competencies in their current fields, such as job-related tasks or recreational activities (e.g., Ackerman, 1996). These examples illustrate that overgeneralizing established epistemic structures and related measures might neglect factors relevant for older workers and might fall short in capturing dynamic aging processes. One fruitful way to address this problem is to adopt insights and models from lifespan research (see Chapter 7 of this volume for a recent review). However, these models are not always specific enough for work-related processes. Qualitative research methods offer important means to extend and complement existing epistemic structures to advance both practical and scientific purposes.

In the following sections, we develop specific goals and opportunities for qualitative research on age differences and aging-related phenomena at work. These are suggested with respect to three foci of aging-related research: (1) *experience* of age-related changes at work, (2) *reactions*, such as behavior and strategies, to cope with age-related changes at work, and (3) *interaction with others* in an age-heterogeneous workforce.

Experience of Age-Related Changes at Work

One major aspect of age-related changes at work is the individual's subjective experience of these changes. For instance, bodily changes, such as a decrease of agility and muscle strength or changes in eyesight, require adaptations in work routines, tasks, and goals but also provide challenges for workers' self-esteem and well-being (e.g., Kanfer & Ackerman, 2004). At the same time, gains in skills and expertise, such as work routines, job knowledge, or stress management strategies (e.g., Hertel et al., 2015), enable further career advancement and adoption of new roles and responsibilities (see Chapter 5 of this volume). Moreover, changes in job-related motives and priorities might prompt reorientation in occupational plans and activities. Yet, how aging individuals experience these changes is not well understood, partly because existing theoretical models and empirical measures neglect the perspective of older persons.

Potential research questions in this field that would be well addressed with qualitative methods include how workers perceive and make sense of their own aging processes. For instance, what do older workers consider to be major achievements and insights (lessons learned) in their career? What are qualifying conditions that help or impede positive experiences of age-related changes? Individual and contextual demands and resources, such as personal dispositions and skills, education and training, coworkers and supervisors, and organizational culture might provide opportunities to better understand these processes but also to plan intervention strategies. Finally, it would be fruitful to explore how older workers are perceived by others. Given that the prevalence of older workers has significantly changed in the last decades, the related perceptions of older workers might be quite different as compared to 20 or 40 years ago and will continue to change (see also Chapter 6 of this volume).

A range of qualitative approaches would be useful to study questions as they relate to individuals' perceptions, interpretations, sense-making, or identity construction and lived experiences, among other topics. For example, narrative analysis or narrative inquiry are frequently used to draw out how people see themselves, process their experiences, and construct meaning from these experiences (Riessman, 2008). Sparkes and Smith (Sparkes & Smith, 2008, p. 295) state that: "Epistemologically, narratives have emerged as both a *way* of telling about our lives and a *method* or *means* of knowing." A narrative analysis conducted with older workers, for example, on how organizational communications, decision-making, or policies affect sense-making of their role in the organization and subsequently their job identity could be an interesting endeavor to uncover whether organizations should take age differences into account in their decision-making. Similarly, interpretivist approaches that specifically focus on how individuals interpret their experiences and their environments around them (e.g., Myers, 2020) could help find mechanisms that explain how and why older workers experience and understand age-related phenomena differently from other workers. Approaches that can be used in an interpretive epistemological stance are grounded theory, thematic analysis, and open content analysis, among many others.

Going one step further, ethnographies and autoethnographies of older workers in organizations can reveal how older workers experience their working life and the organizational context around them (Myers, 2020; Spradley, 2016). Organizational ethnographies are commonly set in a phenomenological epistemology in which it is most important to obtain a rich understanding of how a phenomenon and context are experienced by the informants. The researcher uses informants' and their own lived experiences in the specific context to generate deep insight about the underlying dynamics at work in the given context. An ethnographic study could, for example, be useful in uncovering issues with discrimination of older workers, especially issues that relate to systematic forms of discrimination built into organizational structures.

Finally, qualitative process studies (Langley, 1999) can explore the change processes workers go through as they are aging and explore mechanisms underlying different trajectories of changes. Using process research, aging researchers can explore at which times or occasions bodily changes matter in a worker's career and initiate shifts in sense-making, perceptions of adequacy, and job or role identity, among other things. Indeed, workers may "age differently," that is, their experiences and sense-making processes might change differently and at different velocities, for instance, as a function of profession, organizational climate, personal dispositions, or ethnicity (see also Chapter 4 of this volume). Qualitative process studies can advance aging research and theorizing about the construct of aging to assess how and why underlying experiences of aging differ.

Reactions to Cope with Age-Related Changes at Work

The second major focus contains the behavioral reactions of individuals to aging processes at work. For instance, how do workers cope with expected and unexpected changes of bodily, cognitive, and socioemotional capacities? How do they navigate their work life across larger time intervals? Again, approaching these questions with category systems and measures from research with younger persons might obscure unique coping strategies of older persons. Integrating models from lifespan research is fruitful, and quantitative research using such models has revealed strengths of older workers, for instance, with respect to socioemotional or self-regulation skills (e.g., Blanchard-Fields, 2007; Scheibe & Zacher, 2013) or active stress management strategies (e.g., Hertel et al., 2015; see also Chapter 7 of this volume). However, lifespan models are often not very specific with respect to work-related processes and contexts. Thus, additional creative and unique behavior strategies of older workers might still be discovered. For example, qualitative research on workers' post-retirement career planning (Wöhrmann et al., 2014) has revealed facilitating factors that might have been overlooked with a deductive approach. Finally, behavioral reactions from persons interacting with older workers are also worth considering, such as reactions from coworkers, supervisors, and customers.

Qualitative methods are particularly useful for studying actual behaviors, which is still rare in research on age and work (see Chapter 8 of this volume). Data collection methods include observations, collections of email correspondences, or considerations of organizational data. Different from interviews or surveys, these methods allow a direct assessment of behavioral reactions that older workers choose in response to their environment or to their own sense-making processes. When these methods are used in conjunction with methods that focus on introspection, sense-making, or rationalization, such as interviews or narrative approaches, researchers can then trace how behavioral expression and choices are influenced by and correspond to the informant's internal processes.

This could be interesting, for example, when comparing age-related differences in behavioral choices at work. For instance, there could be situations in which younger and older workers both feel apprehensive about certain managerial decisions (e.g., company lay-offs). Yet, their behavioral reactions might be quite different because older workers have a more varied toolbox of behavioral reactions and coping mechanisms or different rationalizations of the underlying organizational events, which in turn make them choose more effective behavioral reactions. These sense-making processes and associated behavioral reactions can be studied through an interpretivist lens, using an approach such as grounded theory or thematic analysis.

Other useful qualitative approaches include the case-study approach. In a case-study approach, researchers can examine the interaction between the context and the individual by contrasting behaviors, experiences, and individual interpretations across different individuals, work groups, or organizations (i.e., Myers, 2020). For example, researchers might explore in depth how certain older workers act differently from other older workers in the same organizational context. A case-study approach could also be used to study differences between organizations or different industries. For example, it might be interesting to learn how older employees are treated differently in a variety of organizations and how this influences older employees' commitment to the organization. Companies have different training or benefit programs for older employees, and researchers can compare these organizations to explore how older employees make use of these programs and why.

Interaction with Others in an Age-Heterogenous Workforce

Finally, whereas the first two foci address age-related changes at the level of the individual person, age and aging phenomena are certainly also relevant at the level of more complex social systems, such as worker–supervisor relationships, team dynamics, or the climate and culture within organizations. Indeed, age-related diversity has evolved as a popular research field in the last years, but the complexity of this phenomenon limits the insights of a purely quantitative approach (see also Chapter 9 of this volume). For instance, meta-analyses on age-diversity in teams (Joshi & Roh, 2009; Schneid et al., 2016) revealed only small or even no overall effects of age diversity on team outcomes, although considerable effects of age diversity would be predicted by theoretical approaches (e.g., van Knippenberg et al., 2004). Therefore, more in-depth analyses are desirable to better understand facilitating and impeding processes of age diversity in teams, also considering subjective perceptions of involved team members in addition to demographic data (e.g., Wegge & Meyer, 2020). Qualitative approaches can be helpful to navigate through the multiplicity of conditions. In addition, qualitative approaches can facilitate the study of phenomena at different levels of analysis (e.g., individual, team, organization, industry). Promising research questions are, for example, how relationships and conflicts between leaders and their followers—or within teams—are experienced as a function of age diversity and how individual roles are shaped in these contexts and across time.

Several qualitative approaches have been specifically designed to capture interactions between individuals or dynamic interactions within context. One of these approaches is discourse analysis. In discourse analysis, the researcher studies characteristics of communications and discourse around specific topics or phenomena of interest (e.g., O'Reilly & Kiyimba, 2015). As Potter and Hepburn (Potter & Hepburn, 2008, p. 275) state: "For social scientists working with DC [discursive constructionism], the study of discourse becomes the central way of studying mind, social processes, organizations, and events as they are continually made live in human affairs." Among other things, the researcher pays specific attention, often using conversation analysis (e.g., based on email protocols), to how such discourse and communication patterns reveal underlying dynamics and structures of the relationship between different participants in the discourse (such as power differentials or differences in experiences). Discourse analysis could, for example, be used to understand how certain policies concerning older workers were created in an organization and how they affect the communication and sense-making processes of leaders and their employees. Discourse analysis could also assess underlying power differentials or stereotypes between older and younger workers that elicit conflicts in daily work-life. Along similar lines, alternative qualitative approaches can incorporate an analysis of linguistic features when analyzing communications between people to uncover how communication affects other outcome variables, such as leadership effectiveness or team functioning.

These techniques include grounded theory, thematic analysis, open content coding, linguistic style analysis, and several others.

Another interesting lens through which to explore the effects of aging in the workplace could be symbolic interactionism (O'Reilly & Kiyimba, 2015). In this tradition, researchers observe how individuals interact with objects, the context, or others in the context to interpret from these interactions the meaning and sense-making that these individuals attach to the objects, context, others, or themselves. For example, it may be interesting for organizations to analyze how older workers use a workspace differently from younger workers, for instance, when designing assembly areas or activity-based flexible offices. By interacting with objects and others in the workspace and by charting movement through the workspace, researchers could draw conclusions about beneficial workspace design to increase wanted interaction between coworkers, decrease conflict or communication breakdowns, and increase knowledge sharing (see also Chapter 14 and 15). Similarly, research could focus on how older workers interact with their team members or supervisors differently than younger workers, for example, to obtain a richer understanding of how older workers interpret their roles and responsibilities in the organization and in their team. As previously suggested, a conjoint application of observation methods and methods to elicit perceptions, experiences, and sense-making processes would be most useful here.

All in all, with these examples, we are just scratching the surface of potential research questions for a better understanding of age and work. We encourage readers to look deeper into the types of questions they would like to ask with regard to age-related individual experiences, behavioral reactions, and interactions but have not yet been able to do so with quantitative methods and to explore suitable qualitative methods to pursue them.

Note

1 The second and third authors contributed equally to the work.

References

Ackerman, P. L. (1996). A theory of adult intellectual development: Process, personality, interest, and knowledge. *Intelligence, 22*(2), 227–257. https://doi.org/10.1016/S0160-2896(96)90016-1

Amabile, T. M. (2019). Understanding retirement requires getting inside people's stories: A call for more qualitative research. *Work, Aging and Retirement, 5*(3), 207–211. https://doi.org/10.1093/workar/waz007

Blanchard-Fields, F. (2007). Everyday problem solving and emotion: An adult developmental perspective. *Current Directions in Psychological Science, 16*(1), 26–31. https://doi.org/10.1111/j.1467-8721.2007.00469.x

Braun, V., & Clarke, V. (2006). Using thematic analysis in psychology. *Qualitative Research in Psychology, 3*(2), 77–101. https://doi.org/10.1191/1478088706qp063oa

Brinkmann, S., & Kvale, S. (2015). *InterViews: Learning the craft of qualitative research interviewing*. Sage.

Brooks, J., McCluskey, S., Turley, E., & King, N. (2015). The utility of template analysis in qualitative psychology research. *Qualitative Research in Psychology*, *12*(2), 202–222. https://doi.org/10.1080/14780887.2014.955224

Corley, K., Bansal, P., & Yu, H. (2020). An editorial perspective on judging the quality of inductive research when the methodological straightjacket is loosened. *Strategic Organization*. Advance online publication. https://doi.org/10.1177/1476127020968180

Creswell, J. W., & Creswell, J. D. (2018). *Research design: Qualitative, quantitative, and mixed methods approaches*. Sage.

Edmundson, A. C., & McManus, S. E. (2007). Methodological fit in management field research. *Academy of Management Review*, *32*(4), 1155–1179. https://doi.org/10.5465/amr.2007.26586086

Gärtner, L. U. A., Nohe, C., & Hertel, G. (2019). Lifespan perspectives on individuals' effort in work teams. In B. B. Baltes, C. W. Rudolph, & H. Zacher (Eds.), *Work across the lifespan* (pp. 437–454). Academic Press.

Gephart, R. P., Jr. (2004). Qualitative research and the Academy of Management Journal. *Academy of Management Journal*, *47*(4), 454–462. https://doi.org/10.5465/amj.2004.14438580

Gibson, C. B. (2017). Elaboration, generalization, triangulation, and interpretation: On enhancing the value of mixed method research. *Organizational Research Methods*, *20*(2), 193–223. https://doi.org/10.1177/1094428116639133

Grodal, S., Anteby, M., & Holm, A. L. (2020). Achieving rigor in qualitative analysis: The role of active categorization in theory building. *Academy of Management Review*. Advance online publication. https://doi.org/10.5465/amr.2018.0482

Harley, B., & Cornelissen, J. (2020). Rigor with or without templates? The pursuit of methodological rigor in qualitative research. *Organizational Research Methods*. Advance online publication. https://doi.org/10.1177/1094428120937786

Hertel, G., Rauschenbach, C., Thielgen, M., & Krumm, S. (2015). Are older workers more active copers? Longitudinal effects of age-contingent coping on strain at work. *Journal of Organizational Behavior*, *36*(4), 514–537. https://doi.org/10.1002/job.1995

Hertel, G., Thielgen, M., Rauschenbach, C., Grube, A., Stamov-Roßnagel, C., & Krumm, S. (2013). Age differences in motivation and stress at work. In C. Schlick, E. Frieling, & J. Wegge (Eds.), *Age-differentiated work systems* (pp. 119–147). Springer.

Hertel, G., & Zacher, H. (2018). Managing the aging workforce. In D. S. Ones, N. Anderson, C. Viswesvaran, & H. K. Sinangil (Eds.), *The SAGE handbook of industrial, work, & organizational psychology* (Vol. 3, pp. 396–428). Sage.

Joshi, A., & Roh, H. (2009). The role of context in work team diversity research: A meta-analytic review. *Academy of Management Journal*, *52*(3), 599–627. https://doi.org/10.5465/AMJ.2009.41331491

Kanfer, R., & Ackerman, P. L. (2004). Aging, adult development, and work motivation. *Academy of Management Review*, *29*(3), 440–458. https://doi.org/10.5465/AMR.2004.13670969

Köhler, T., Smith, A., & Bhakoo, V. (2019). Feature topic for ORM: Templates in qualitative research methods. *Organizational Research Methods*, *22*(1), 3–5. https://doi.org/10.1177/1094428118805165

Kooij, D. T. A. M., De Lange, A. H., Jansen, P. G. W., Kanfer, R., & Dikkers, J. S. E. (2011). Age and work-related motives: Results of a meta-analysis. *Journal of Organizational Behavior*, *32*(2), 197–225. https://doi.org/10.1002/job.665

Krumm, S., Grube, A., & Hertel, G. (2013). The Munster work value measure. *Journal of Managerial Psychology*, *28*(5), 532–560. https://doi.org/10.1108/JMP-07-2011-0023

Langley, A. (1999). Strategies for theorizing from process data. *Academy of Management Review*, *24*(4), 691–710. https://doi.org/10.5465/AMR.1999.2553248

Lê, J. K., & Schmid, T. (2019). An integrative review of qualitative strategy reserach: Presenting 12 "designs-in-use". In *Research methodology in strategy and management: Standing on the shoulders of giants* (Vol. 11, pp. 115–154). Emerald. https://doi.org/10.1108/S1479-838720190000011009

Lee, T. W., Mitchell, T. R., & Sablynski, C. J. (1999). Qualitative research in organizational and vocational psychology, 1979–1999. *Journal of Vocational Behavior*, *55*(2), 161–187. https://doi.org/10.1006/jvbe.1999.1707

Levitt, H. M., Bamberg, M., Creswell, J. W., Frost, D. M., Josselson, R., & Suárez-Orozco, C. (2018). Journal article reporting standards for qualitative primary, qualitative meta-analytic, and mixed methods research in psychology: The APA publications and communications board task force report. *American Psychologist*, *73*(1), 26–46. https://doi.org/10.1037/amp0000151

Locke, K. (2001). *Grounded theory in management research*. Sage.

Locke, L., & Golden-Biddle, K. (2002). An introduction to qualitative research: Its potential for industrial and organizational psychology. In S. G. Rogelberg (Ed.), *Handbook of research methods in industrial and organizational psychology* (pp. 99–118). Blackwell.

Murphy, C., Klotz, A. C., & Kreiner, G. E. (2017). Blue skies and black boxes: The promise (and practice) of grounded theory in human resource management research. *Human Resource Management Review*, *27*(2), 291–305. https://doi.org/doi.org/10.1016/j.hrmr.2016.08.006

Myers, M. D. (2020). *Qualitative research in business and management*. Sage.

Neuendorf, K. A. (2017). *The content analysis guidebook*. Sage.

O'Reilly, M., & Kiyimba, N. (2015). *Advanced qualitative research: A guide to using theory*. Sage.

Potter, J., & Hepburn, A. (2008). Discursive constructionism. In J. A. Holstein & J. F. Gubrium (Eds.), *Handbook of constructionist research* (pp. 275–293). Guilford.

Pratt, M. G., & Bonaccio, S. (2016). Qualitative research in I-O psychology: Maps, myths, and moving forward. *Industrial and Organizational Psychology: Perspectives on Science and Practice*, *9*(4), 693–715. https://doi.org/10.1017/iop.2016.92

Pratt, M. G., Kaplan, S., & Whittington, R. (2020). Editorial essay: The tumult over transparency: Decoupling transparency from replication in establishing trustworthy qualitative research. *Administrative Science Quarterly*, *65*(1), 1–19. https://doi.org/10.1177/0001839219887663

Pratt, M. G., Sonenshein, S., & Feldman, M. S. (2020). Moving beyond templates: A bricolage approach to conducting trustworthy qualitative research. *Organizational Research Methods*. Advance online publication. https://doi.org/10.1177/1094428120927466

Rheinhardt, A., Kreiner, G. E., Gioia, D. A., & Corley, K. G. (2018). Conducting and publishing rigorous qualitative research. In C. Cassell, A. L. Cunliffe, & G. Grandy (Eds.), *The SAGE handbook of qualitative business and management research methods: History and traditions*. Sage.

Riessman, C. K. (2008). *Narrative methods for the human sciences*. Sage.

Ross-Hellauer, T. (2017). What is open peer review? A systematic review [version 1; referees: 1 approved, 2 approved with reservations]. *F1000Research*, *6*, 588. https://doi.org/10.12688/f1000research.11369.1

Rudolph, C., Baltes, B. B., & Zabel, K. L. (2013). Age and work motives. In J. Field, R. J. Burke, & C. L. Cooper (Eds.), *The SAGE handbook of aging, work and society* (pp. 118–140). Sage.

Salmon, J. (2016). *Doing qualitative research online.* Sage.

Salthouse, T. (2012). Consequences of age-related cognitive declines. *Annual Review of Psychology, 63,* 201–226. https://doi.org/10.1146/annurev-psych-120710-100328

Scheibe, S., & Zacher, H. (2013). A lifespan perspective on emotion regulation, stress, and well-being in the workplace. In P. L. Perrewé, J. Halbesleben, & C. C. Rosen (Eds.), *Research in occupational stress and well-being* (Vol. 11, pp. 167–197). Emerald.

Schneid, M., Isidor, R., Steinmetz, H., & Kabst, R. (2016). Age diversity and team outcomes: A quantitative review. *Journal of Managerial Psychology, 31*(1), 2–17. https://doi.org/10.1108/JMP-07-2012-0228

Sparkes, A. C., & Smith, B. (2008). Narrative constructionist inquiry. In A. Holstein & J. F. Gubrium (Eds.), *Handbook of constructionist research* (pp. 295–314). Guilford.

Spradley, J. P. (2016). *Participant observation.* Waveland Press.

Tong, A., Sainsbury, P., & Craig, J. (2007). Consolidated criteria for reporting qualitative research (COREQ): A 32-item checklist for interviews and focus groups. *International Journal for Quality in Health Care, 19*(6), 349–357. https://doi.org/10.1093/intqhc/mzm042

Vaara, E., Sonenshein, S., & Boje, D. (2016). Narratives as sources of stability and change in organizations: Approaches and directions for future research. *The Academy of Mangement Annals, 10*(1), 495–560. https://doi.org/10.1080/19416520.2016.1120963

van Knippenberg, D., de Dreu, C. K. W., & Homan, A. C. (2004). Work group diversity and group performance: An integrative model and research agenda. *Journal of Applied Psychology, 89*(6), 1008–1022. https://doi.org/10.1037/0021-9010.89.6.1008

Van Maanen, J. (1979). Reclaiming qualitative methods for organizational research: A preface. *Administrative Science Quarterly, 24*(4), 520–526. https://doi.org/10.2307/2392358

Wegge, J., & Meyer, B. (2020). Age diversity and age-based faultlines in teams: Understanding a Brezel phenomenon requires a Brezel theory. *Work, Aging and Retirement, 6*(1), 8–14. https://doi.org/10.1093/workar/waz017

Wilhelmy, A., & Köhler, T. (in press). Qualitative research in work and organizational psychology journals: Practices and future opportunities. *European Journal of Work and Organizational Psychology.*

Wilhelmy, A. (2016). Journal guidelines for qualitative research? A balancing act that might be worth it. *Industrial and Organizational Psychology: Perspectives on Science and Practice, 9*(4), 726–732. https://doi.org/10.1017/iop.2016.80

Wöhrmann, A. M., Deller, J., & Wang, M. (2014). A mixed-method approach to post-retirement career planning. *Journal of Vocational Behavior, 84,* 307–317. https://doi.org/10.1016/j.jvb.2014.02.003

13

USING ARCHIVAL DATA TO RESEARCH AGE AND WORK

Gwenith G. Fisher, Janet L. Barnes-Farrell, Julia L. Beckel and Kenneth S. Shultz

Archival data is data that already exists, such as observations, texts, survey responses, or other information that pre-date a planned research project versus data that is expressly collected for the primary purposes of a particular research project (Fisher & Shultz, 2006; Fisher & Barnes-Farrell, 2013; Shultz & Fisher, 2016). Although primary data collection and analysis are commonplace and fundamental to psychological researchers' training, analysis of secondary data is relatively new to most psychology and management researchers (Trzesniewski et al., 2011). Archival data is frequently used for secondary data analysis in which researchers across many disciplines (e.g., criminal justice, economics, sociology, gerontology) conduct specific analyses after primary data collection has been completed. Secondary data analyses may represent a re-examination of data for their originally intended purposes using new or more sophisticated analytical strategies, or they may be conducted to address questions that are unrelated to the purposes for which the data were originally collected. Many archival data sources are of special value for research examining age-and-work phenomena because they constitute longitudinal and/or large-scale repeated cohort research projects that can be especially useful for taking a lifespan perspective (see Table 13.1). Furthermore, the open-science movement that has begun to gain traction in the research community continues to increase the number of primary data sources that are being made available for secondary analysis by other researchers (Bauer, 2021).

In this chapter we discuss the benefits and challenges of using archival data, with a focus on methodological issues associated with using archival data for research relevant to aging and work. Potential sources of archival data for age and work research are outlined, as are possible supplemental datasets (e.g., O*NET, Census records) that can be linked to existing archival data sources, which allow for an even richer and more comprehensive exploration of age and work from

DOI: 10.4324/9781003089674-16

TABLE 13.1 Prominent Archival Data Sources for Age-and-Work Research

Name of Archival Database	Geographic Source	URL	Citation
45 and up Study collaborators	Australia	www.saxinstitute.org.au/our-work/45-up-study/	Griffin et al. (2016)
Americans' Changing Lives (ACL) study	USA	www.isr.umich.edu/acl/	Zacher and Griffin (2015); National longitudinal panel survey to study middle and later life among Black and white Americans on a variety of social science issues
Australian National Survey of Mental Health and Wellbeing (NSMHWB)	Australia	www.abs.gov.au/statistics/health/mental-health/national-survey-mental-health-and-wellbeing-summary-results/2007	Forbes et al. (2015)
British Household Panel Survey (BHPS)	UK	www.iser.essex.ac.uk/bhps	Lux and Scherger (2018)
Canadian Census	Canada	www.statcan.gc.ca/eng/census?MM=1	Curtis and McMullin (2016)
Canadian Work, Stress, and Health Study (CAN-WSH)	Canada	https://workandhealth.ca/2020/09/21/can-wsh/	Silver et al. (2019)
Current Population Survey (CPS)	USA	www.census.gov/programs-surveys/cps.html	
Current Population Survey prepared by IPUMS	USA	https://cps.ipums.org/cps/	Moen et al. (2020)
English Longitudinal Study of Ageing (ELSA)	UK	www.elsa-project.ac.uk	van der Horst et al. (2017)
Family Survey Dutch Population (FSDP)	Netherlands	www.ru.nl/sociology/research/family-survey-dutch/	Visser et al. (2018)
Finnish Linked Employer Employee Data (FLEED)	Finland	www.stat.fi/tup/mikroaineistot/aineistot_en.html	Riekhoff et al. (2020)

Data source	Country	Website	Notes	References
Gateway to Global Aging Data		https://g2aging.org/	Provides detailed information about 11 different national longitudinal studies (sister studies of the HRS)	Costanza et al. (2017)
General Social Survey (GSS) conducted by the National Opinion Research Center (NORC)	USA	www.gss.norc.org		
German Socio-Economic Panel (SOEP)	Germany	www.eui.eu/Research/Library/ResearchGuides/Economics/Statistics/DataPortal/GSOEP		Heisig and Radl (2017), Lux and Scherger (2018)
Health and Retirement Study (HRS)	USA	https://hrs.isr.umich.edu/		Barnes-Farrell and Petery (2018), Burgard and Sonnega (2018), Cahill et al. (2015), (2018), Fisher et al. (2014), Fisher et al. (2016), Ghilarducci and Webb (2018), Hudomiet et al. (2018), Infurna and Andel (2018), Liu et al. (2018), Marchiondo et al. (2020), von Bonsdorff et al. (2017), Voss et al. (2020)
Health, Ageing and Retirement Transitions in Sweden (HEARTS) study	Sweden	www.gu.se/en/research/hearts		Hansson et al. (2018), Henning et al. (2019)
Household Income and Labour Dynamics in Australia (HILDA) Survey	Australia	https://melbourneinstitute.unimelb.edu.au/hilda		Warren (2015)

(Continued)

TABLE 13.1 (Continued)

Name of Archival Database	Geographic Source	URL	Citation
Inter-university Consortium for Political and Social Research (ICPSR)	USA	www.icpsr.umich.edu/web/pages/	Data archive. Gateway to search and access multiple datasets that available for download or online analysis
Midlife in the United States National Study of Health and Well-Being (MIDUS)	USA	midus.wisc.edu/data/index.php	Grzywacz et al. (2016) Vélez-Coto et al. (2021)
Monitoring the Future Survey	USA	www.monitoringthefuture.org	Campbell et al. (2017)
National Food Survey (NFS)	UK	www.herc.ox.ac.uk/downloads/health_datasets/browse-data-sets/national-food-survey-nfs	Parry and Urwin (2017)
National Longitudinal Studies	USA	www.bls.gov/iif/oshcfoi1.htm	Longitudinal surveys of men and women that include work history and other life events
National Social Life, Health, and Aging Project (NSHAP)	USA	www.norc.org/Research/Projects/Pages/national-social-life-health-and-aging-project.aspx	Settels and Schafer (2018)
New Zealand Health, Work and Retirement Study	New Zealand	www.massey.ac.nz/massey/learning/departments/school-of-psychology/research/hart/new-zealand-health-work-and-retirement-study/new-zealand-health-work-and-retirement-study_home.cfm	www.massey.ac.nz/massey/learning/departments/school-of-psychology/research/hart/new-zealand-health-work-and-retirement-study/nzhwr-journal-articles.cfm
NIDI Pension Panel	Netherlands	https://nidi.nl/project/nppo/	van Solinge and Henkens (2017)

Name	Country	URL	References
Occupational Information Network (O★NET)	USA	www.onetonline.org/	Beier et al. (2020) Fisher et al. (2014) Grzywacz et al. (2016)
RAND HRS Data	USA	www.rand.org/well-being/social-and-behavioral-policy/centers/aging/dataprod.html	Hudomiet et al. (2018)
Research Data Center of the German Federal Employment Agency	Germany	https://fdz.iab.de/en.aspx	Brussig (2016)
Study of Cognition and Aging in the USA (CogUSA)	USA	www.icpsr.umich.edu/web/NACDA/studies/36053	Beier et al. (2020)
Survey of Health Ageing and Retirement in Europe (SHARE)	EU	www.share-project.org/home0.html	Madero-Cabib et al. (2016); Hyde and Dingemans (2017); Hoven et al. (2018); Litwin and Tur-Sinai (2015); Segel-Karpas (2015)
The Irish Longitudinal Study on Ageing (TILDA)	Ireland	www.ucd.ie/tssda/data/tilda/wave1/#d.en.379719	Heraty and McCarthy (2015)
Transitions and Old Age Potential (TOP)	Germany	www.bib.bund.de/EN/Research/Surveys/TOP/transitions-and-old-age-potential.html	Fasbender et al. (2016)
Work and Retirement Panel from Netherlands Interdisciplinary Demographic Institute (NIDI)	Netherland	https://nidi.nl/en/research/themegroups/work-retirement/	Damman and van Duijn (2017) van den Bogaard (2017)
Work, Family, and Health Study (WFHS)	USA	www.icpsr.umich.edu/web/DSDR/studies/36158	Moen et al. (2016)

a lifespan and life course perspective. We provide several examples of empirical research on topics of age and work that used archival data. We conclude with directions for future research and recommendations for using archival data to address pressing theoretical and practical issues in aging and work.

Benefits and Challenges of Using Archival Data

The strongest benefit of archival data is that they already exist. In other words, rather than needing to design a study and collect data, archival data are typically readily accessible (i.e., downloadable from the internet with various data security measures) and can be used for analyses rather expediently. This is particularly important for longitudinal and lifespan research because it is especially time-consuming and arduous to collect longitudinal data. In addition, archival datasets may also offer other specific sampling (e.g., nationally representative samples; large sample sizes; over-samples of participants from underrepresented groups or populations that are more difficult to reach) or other special design characteristics (e.g., cross-national harmonized datasets; cross-lagged research designs) to facilitate age-and-work research.

For example, the Health and Retirement Study (HRS) conducted in the United States began in 1992. The initial 1992 sample consisted of a nationally representative sample of people ages 51–61. In 1998 a new cohort (ages 51–56) was added to the sample, and older samples from the related AHEAD study were added so that the resulting sample became representative of U.S. adults ages 51 and older. Newer cohorts are added every six years (see Figure 13.1). Biennial interviews of over 18,000 people are conducted, and the survey covers a broad array of topics (https://hrs.isr.umich.edu/data-products/collection-path) to facilitate multidisciplinary research. For a more detailed summary and description of the HRS origins and evolution of the data collection process and sampling, see Fisher and Ryan (2018).

As another example, the Survey of Health, Ageing, and Retirement in Europe (SHARE) began in 2004 and has collected data across 28 countries in Europe and Israel from more than 140,000 people (see *https://g2aging.org/?section=surveyOverview* to compare 11 such studies). The SHARE dataset allows for both longitudinal analysis and cross-national comparisons when addressing age- and work-related research questions. At a practical level, obtaining access to readily-available cross-lagged longitudinal datasets such as the HRS and SHARE may be especially useful when conducting research that is time-sensitive (e.g., student research projects to facilitate timely degree completion) or when financial or human resources to facilitate data collection are limited.

Despite the benefits of using archival data, there are still notable challenges and drawbacks. One of the biggest challenges associated with using these often large and complicated datasets is that it requires strong data management skills and time to learn, navigate, and assemble a dataset for analysis (Trzesniewski et al., 2011). Anecdotally, we have found in our own experiences with archival data, as well as in our experiences with supervising students' master's theses and doctoral

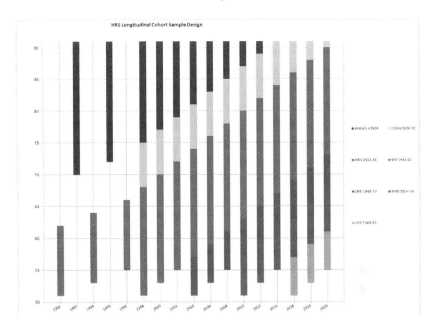

FIGURE 13.1   Health and Retirement Study (HRS) Longitudinal Cohort Sample
Design

Note. Reprinted with permission from HRS. This graphic depicts the longitudinal cohort sample
design of HRS. The initial 1992 HRS cohort consisted of persons born 1931 to 1941—who were
then aged 51 to 61—and their spouses of any age. Members of this first HRS cohort, now in their
70s and 80s, have been interviewed every two years since 1992. A second study was added in 1993,
the Asset and Health Dynamics Among the Oldest Old, or AHEAD, which captured those born
before 1924, who were 70 and older at the time. Then in 1998 the HRS and AHEAD cohorts were
merged, and two new cohorts were enrolled to bridge the study age gaps for Americans 50 and older.
These birth cohorts are the Children of the Depression or CODA for those born 1924 to1930 and
the War Babies for those born 1942 to 1947. HRS now employs a steady-state design, replenishing
the sample every six years with younger cohorts. In 2004 HRS added the Early Baby Boomers, born
1948 to 1953 and in 2010 added the Mid Baby Boomers, born 1954 to 1959. The Late Baby Boomers, born 1960 to 1965, were added in 2016. For all cohorts, both members of a couple are included
in the sample.

dissertations, that it is all too easy to underestimate the time necessary to assemble
a dataset ready for analysis to address research questions of interest. Additionally, similar to the need for strong data management skills, some datasets require
knowledge about complex sample survey designs and how to use sample weights
in statistical analyses. Furthermore, not all datasets are publicly available and may
require special permission and/or additional costs to obtain access. There may also
be ethical issues associated with using certain archival data for research purposes,
depending upon the purpose and manner in which data were originally collected.
Shultz et al. (2005) provided a table outlining numerous benefits and challenges to
using archival data for industrial-organizational psychology research more broadly.

Methodological Issues

One of the advantages of using archival data is the ability to use more sophisticated methodological approaches to answer important research questions, especially when using a lifespan approach to study age and work. For example, having repeated cross-sectional archival data allows researchers to use hierarchical Age-Period-Cohort (APC) models (Yang & Land, 2006) when investigating age- and work-related research questions. Repeated cross-sectional surveys ask the same or similar questions of different samples of respondents over multiple timeframes (e.g., annually or biennially). These designs allow researchers to apply APC models in order to partition variance into various effects associated with respondents' age, birth cohort, and the time period the data was collected, thus providing a clearer understanding of the nature and source of any changes observed over time (Hoffman et al., 2020). The ability to tease apart age (i.e., physiological and developmental changes over time), period (i.e., specific events impacting individuals living at a given point in time), and cohort (i.e., all individuals born around a given time) effects are a distinct advantage of repeated cross-sectional archival data. However, APC models have been scrutinized (Bell & Jones, 2013, 2014). For example, Bell and Jones indicated that it is quite challenging, if not impossible, to statistically separate age, period, and cohort effects because they are mathematically confounded. That is, to hold two effects constant would necessitate also holding the third effect constant (see also Rudolph et al., 2020, Chapter 6 in this volume).

A classic example of a repeated cross-sectional data archive is the General Social Survey (GSS) in the United States. The GSS has been administered by the National Opinion Research Center (NORC) at the University of Chicago since 1972. Although initially administered annually, since 1994 the GSS has been administered biennially. The GSS has investigated a core set of demographic, behavioral, and attitudinal questions, in addition to topics of special interest, such as civil liberties, social mobility, psychological well-being, and stress and trauma. Thus, the GSS consists of nationally representative, large-scale data collections that are ripe for answering questions related to age and work that allow researchers to tease apart age, period, and cohort effects.

For example, Kalleberg and Marsden (2019) used the GSS to examine how processes of aging, generational shifts, and changes over historical time periods shaped differences in work values in the United States. Using hierarchical logistic regression analyses, the authors found that changes over historical time periods are most consistently responsible for temporal differences in work values. In addition, they determined that some differences in work values are also attributable to aging or life course processes, however they found few differences in work values among members of different generations or cohorts. Specifically, the authors found significant overall age differences in the centrality of work within peoples' lives, including a steady decline in work centrality until around age 65 when retirement becomes more prevalent. Their findings also indicated that people in their prime working ages place greater importance on income and security, while younger people are most apt to value interesting work. Thus, Kalleberg and Marsden's analysis of archival repeated cohort GSS data provide important insights into how the factors of aging, generational shifts, and time periods ultimately impact work values that would otherwise be impossible in a traditional single-use cross-sectional data collection research design.

Other possible challenges of using archival data concern important methodological and measurement issues. For example, many large-scale surveys tend to emphasize content breadth over measurement precision (Fisher & Barnes-Farrell, 2013). These measurement issues may contribute to poor reliability and questionable construct validity for key psychological measures, specifically criterion deficiency. In addition, in longitudinal datasets, the time lags between measurement occasions may be inconsistent with time lags that make theoretical or conceptual sense. For example, the HRS measures data about psychosocial work factors as part of a leave-behind questionnaire that is administered once every four years rather than every two years like the primary or "core" HRS survey. Changes in variables of interest over age or time may actually occur in less than four years. However, researchers who rely upon the psychosocial survey in the HRS to obtain valuable work-related information do not have the opportunity to analyze data collected with shorter time lags.

For example, in one study by Marchiondo and colleagues (2020) using data from HRS, researchers examined how incivility relates to worker well-being and to spouse/partner well-being over time. Although the HRS was useful for answering this research question about incivility, the four-year time lag and limited number of observations did not allow the researchers to investigate shorter term or autoregressive effects. Results indicated that workplace incivility was related to lower well-being at a later time. However, due to the long time lag between observations, it is also possible that other variables could explain lower levels of well-being found at subsequent time points.

It is also important to recognize the context in which data were originally collected. Cultural context, points in time, and features of the sample and data collection methodologies can have implications for the kinds of questions that can be appropriately asked of the dataset and the proper interpretation of findings (Bauer, 2021).

Finally, there is potential for overuse or saturation within a given prominent dataset such as the HRS when using archival data for studying age and work phenomena. For example, Mroczek et al. (2021) noted that the lack of independence of research findings reported regarding the same associations within the same data source across multiple published papers can lead to accentuating particular biases (e.g., sampling biases) within those well-used data sets. Thus, Mroczek et al. suggested several solutions, including greater use of data sharing, preregistrations, holdout samples, split-sample cross-validation, and coordinated analysis, in order to address the overuse of data from a frequently-used archival data set. These data use safeguards can help to preserve these extraordinary data resources for future generations of researchers.

Taken together, the methodological and measurement challenges associated with using archival data should not be ignored. For anyone considering these data for student research projects or time-sensitive work, it is important to note that archival data may lack suitability for specific projects despite having other strengths. It is ultimately up to the researchers to determine whether the benefits of using archival data outweigh the challenges (Shultz et al., 2005).

How Does Archival Data Advance Age and Work Research?

Our review of *Work, Aging, and Retirement*, a journal exclusively devoted to publishing research related to the topics of age and work, has published 53 articles since 2015 that have used archival data. A wide variety of topics related to age and work have been studied using archival data. Examples include age in relation to work design and job characteristics (Beier et al., 2020; Liu et al., 2018; Moen et al., 2016; Parker et al., 2021; Shultz et al., 2010), job satisfaction and other indicators of well-being (Griffin et al., 2016; Marchiondo et al., 2020; van den Bogaard, 2017; Zacher & Griffin, 2015), retirement (Cahill et al., 2015, 2018; Ghilarducci & Webb, 2018; Hudomiet et al., 2018; Litwin & Tur-Sinai, 2015; van Solinge & Henkens, 2017), financial planning for retirement (Heraty & McCarthy, 2015), unemployment and preretirement (Voss et al., 2020), postretirement work (Fasbender et al., 2016), pensions (Brussig, 2016), health (Beier et al., 2020; Burgard & Sonnega, 2018; Infurna & Andel, 2018; Marchiondo et al., 2020), and methodological issues (Campbell et al., 2017; Costanza et al., 2017).

Although space constraints limit opportunities for a detailed review, we provide a few examples. Shultz et al. (2010) used cross-national data across 15 European countries contained in the Eurobarometer to examine how the job demand–control model of work stress may function differently for older versus younger workers. Their results indicated that different work controls (e.g., job autonomy) may in fact buffer different types of job demands (e.g., time pressures) for younger versus older workers. Further, Shultz et al.'s findings revealed that only the interaction between problem solving and time to complete tasks was significant for younger workers. For older workers, however, the interactions between time deadlines and having sufficient time to complete tasks, autonomy, and the interaction between problem solving and schedule flexibility were all significant predictors of self-reported stress.

As another example, Spiegel and Shultz (2003) used archival longitudinal data from the US Navy *Officer Career Questionnaire* (Time 1) and *Retirement from Navy Life Survey* (Time 2) to determine if preretirement planning and having knowledge, skills, and abilities (KSAs) that were readily transferable to civilian work affect retirement satisfaction and adjustment in retired naval officers. Results from their archival data analyses indicated that both preretirement planning and transferability of KSAs directly influenced the retirement satisfaction and adjustment of naval officers. More specifically, engaging in preretirement planning and having more transferable KSAs to the civilian workforce were associated with higher retirement satisfaction and adjustment. Although at first glance the results may not seem generalizable beyond the military context, the "retirement" of military personnel is in many ways more akin to bridge employment (Beehr & Bennett, 2015) than traditional retirement, and thus their results broadly apply to many contemporary bridge employment situations in which individuals retire from their career jobs in their 50s or early 60s but then continue to engage in paid and volunteer work (often part time and/or seasonal) for years after initial retirement (Sullivan & Al Ariss, 2019).

As a final example, Noone et al. (2021) used three waves (2006, 2008, 2014) from the longitudinal New Zealand Health, Work and Retirement Study (NZ HWRS) to explore how retirement planning may play a mediating role in explaining by what means preretirement antecedents are converted into retirement resources in retirement. Results of their secondary analysis of the archival NZ HWRS data indicated that health, income, and positive retirement attitudes were the most prominent predictors of retirement planning, which in turn predicted health, psychosocial, and financial resources in retirement. Their findings can help to inform policy decision-makers by identifying those older individuals who are at greatest risk of not planning, as well as pinpoint the factors most likely to explain the longer-term effects of retirement planning. In addition, understanding which resources are predicted by different domains of planning will help to inform the targeting of interventions for those most at risk of poor retirement-related outcomes.

Potential Sources of Archival Data for Age-and-Work Research

Fortunately, there are many potential archival data sources to facilitate age-and-work research. Table 13.1 lists possible archival data resources related to age and work that may be useful in future studies. This table includes archival data sources based on our knowledge of age-and work-related archival data resources, our knowledge of age-and work-related research, and our review of studies published in *Work, Aging, and Retirement* since its inception (given its relevance to age-and-work research). It is important to note that this is not necessarily an exhaustive list but includes many valuable resources collected in various countries and covering multiple topics. Other studies have used archival data to study age and work and have been published elsewhere in applied psychology, management, gerontology, sociology, economics, and other social science journals.

Linking Archival Datasets

In addition to main data sources that contain content about age and work (e.g., HRS, SHARE), another viable option is to link archival datasets that contain valuable data about work-related phenomena. For example, some archival datasets may have rich data about work status or employment history, economic status, health, well-being, and other topics but may lack other valuable work-related information such as key information about work or worker requirements for jobs or occupational characteristics. The Occupational Information Network (O★NET; Peterson et al., 2001) contains information about work and worker characteristics for more than 900 unique jobs that can be linked to other archival datasets based on occupation codes.

For example, Fisher et al. (2014) linked data from HRS and O★NET to examine how occupational cognitive job complexity (i.e., mental work demands) is associated with individuals' cognitive functioning while working and after retirement. They concluded that workers in more mentally demanding occupations performed better before and after retirement on cognitive performance tests after adjusting for age, education, socioeconomic status, gender, and other relevant covariates. Beier and colleagues (2020) linked data from O★NET about worker cognitive requirements for various jobs and compared them with results from cognitive performance measures among a middle age and older adult sample in the Study of Cognition and Aging in the USA (CogUSA). Beier and colleagues compared the extent to which congruity between cognitive requirements and cognitive performance related to health and retirement and found that, when cognitive abilities met or exceeded cognitive job requirements, individuals were in better health and retired later than when requirements and performance were incongruent. Parker et al. (2021) reviewed more than 500 articles about work design and cognition to develop and offer a model describing ways in which work design may shape cognitive functioning over short- and longer-term timeframes. Archival datasets will likely be central to being able to test the propositions offered by this model. For example, HRS and SHARE data include measures of cognitive functioning and information about employment and opportunities to link data to O★NET that can be used to examine how work relates to cognition over time.

Despite the O★NET's utility for conducting archival investigations, there are methodological considerations associated with linking datasets with the O★NET over time. Changes across the O★NET databases include updates and additions of occupations, industries, and their respective coding schemes. Since 2000, there have been five major changes to the O★NET occupation classification system, based on the Standardized Occupation Codes. Thus, given code variation of codes across years, researchers may need to identify and crosswalk occupational codes in order to appropriately link archival datasets over time. There are a handful of resources available to facilitate crosswalking and linking O★NET data, such as a valuable resource described by Rauvola and colleagues (2021).

Other examples of datasets that can be linked include organizations' human resources (HR) records, workers compensation claims data, records pertaining to government pension programs (e.g., U.S. Social Security earnings), and information about mortality (e.g., the National Death Index). For example, HR records can yield valuable objective information about employment dates, position title, job level, various HR benefits, and absenteeism. Linking to pension programs can yield valuable information about retirement timing and pension earnings.

Future Directions and Recommendations

Based on our review of archival data relevant to aging and work, we offer some suggestions to advance research on age and work. Consistent with recommendations by Bohlmann et al. (2018), we encourage more research to investigate alternative conceptualizations of age (e.g., psychological age, subjective age, functional age, etc. as explained in Chapter 3) as well as mediators and moderators associated with age and work. For example, how are work factors such as chronic underemployment related to retirement? How do issues related to the future of work, such as automation, changing work arrangements (e.g., contingent work, gig work), and changing work demands relate to employment patterns, health, and well-being across the life course? Many archival datasets may be able to facilitate such research given the breadth of content available.

We also call for more cross-national and cross-cultural research to compare and contrast age-and-work issues across countries and cultures. Cross-national differences in retirement age are influenced by public policy and government pension systems (Fisher et al., 2016). As Rudolph et al. (2019) indicated, there are important global issues related to age and work that sorely need further investigation. For example, demography and workforce aging are both progressing at different rates in various countries. Cross-national data (e.g., SHARE) would be particularly helpful in addressing cross national differences in workforce aging patterns and demographic composition differences across countries. Rudolph et al. (2019) also noted the differences in mortality and morbidity across countries which can be primary drivers of differences in retirement patterns and workforce participation rates at older ages as these health and well-being issues affect not only the older workers themselves but can also affect caregiving demands for aging parents and partners. Another key issue noted by Rudolph et al. concerns cross-cultural and cross-national differences in worker mobility patterns at older ages. Traditionally, workers have found it more difficult to change jobs or careers as they age (Feldman & Shultz, 2019); however, barriers to late life job and career changes can vary dramatically across countries. See also Chapter 10 about diary and longitudinal studies as well as chapters that highlight other methods, including experiments and interventions (Chapter 11) and qualitative research (Chapter 12).

Methodologically, archival data offers many opportunities to follow Bohlmann et al.'s (2018) recommendations by obtaining access to large samples with sufficient numbers of participants across various age groups and being able to operationalize age as a continuous (rather than categorical) variable. To facilitate a lifespan approach to understand age and work, it is important to consider what the appropriate time lag ought to be between measurement occasions (Ford et al., 2014). Finally, we call for more large-scale surveys to incorporate theoretically sound and psychometrically robust indicators of work-related psychosocial constructs to overcome the limitations of the aforementioned measurement issues all too common in many archival datasets. Many existing data sources have not been developed by researchers with expertise about work phenomena (e.g., industrial/organizational psychologists, management scholars, labor economists). As a result, many existing datasets lack detail about individual workers' perceptions of their own jobs, which is important for acknowledging the importance of cognitive appraisal (Lazarus & Folkman, 1984). In other words, workers classified as having the same occupation may have very different work experiences based on between-organization differences and individual worker differences in perceptions as well as important differences in abilities, skills, attitudes, and traits.

Our final recommendation is for researchers to collaborate and plan up front more often to agree upon "best ways" to measure various constructs that are common across multiple surveys. More consistency in the measurement of various constructs (e.g., job characteristics, worker well-being) will facilitate comparisons over time and across different cultural contexts.

To conclude, we suggest that there are many existing archival data sources that will be useful for advancing research on age and work taking a lifespan or life course perspective, particularly given that many archival datasets offer readily available longitudinal data. There are many benefits associated with using archival data for this purpose, although we caution the reader that this method is not without some potential challenges and limitations. There are many important research questions that can and should be answered to advance research on age and work.

References

Barnes-Farrell, J. L., & Petery, G. A. (2018). The moderating role of employment status and gender on relationships between psychological age and health: A two-wave cross-lagged panel analysis of data from the Health and Retirement Study. *Work, Aging, and Retirement, 4*(1), 79–95. https://doi.org/10.1093/workar/wax019

Bauer, P. (2021). Why it is important to know how the sausage is made: Benefits, risks, and responsibilities of using third-party data. *Psychological Science, 32*(6), 861–862. https://doi.org/10.1177/09567976211021594

Beehr, T. A., & Bennett, M. M. (2015). Working after retirement: Features of bridge employment and research directions. *Work, Aging, and Retirement, 1*(1), 112–128. https://doi.org/10.1093/workar/wau007

Beier, M. E., Torres, W. J., Fisher, G. G., & Wallace, L. E. (2020). Age and job fit: The relationship between demands–ability fit and retirement and health. *Journal of Occupational Health Psychology, 25*(4), 227–244. https://doi.org/10.1037/ocp0000164

Bell, A., & Jones, K. (2013). The impossibility of separating age, period and cohort effects. *Social Science & Medicine*, *93*, 163–165. https://doi.org/10.1016/j.socscimed.2013.04.029

Bell, A., & Jones, K. (2014). Another 'futile quest'? A simulation study of Yang and Land's Hierarchical Age-Period-Cohort model. *Demographic Research*, *30*, 333–360. https://doi.org/10.4054/DemRes.2013.30.11

Bohlmann, C., Rudolph, C. W., & Zacher, H. (2018). Methodological recommendations to move research on work and aging forward. *Work, Aging, and Retirement*, *4*(3), 225–237. https://doi.org/10.1093/workar/wax023

Brussig, M. (2016). Working conditions in the last job and transitions into old-age pensions: An analysis of two pension entry cohorts in Germany. *Work, Aging, and Retirement*, *2*(1), 54–64. https://doi.org/10.1093/workar/wav016

Burgard, S. A., & Sonnega, A. (2018). Occupational differences in BMI, BMI trajectories, and implications for employment status among older US workers. *Work, Aging, and Retirement*, *4*(1), 21–36. https://doi.org/10.1093/workar/waw038

Cahill, K. E., Giandrea, M. D., & Quinn, J. F. (2018). Is bridge job activity overstated? *Work, Aging and Retirement*, *4*(4), 330–351. https://doi.org/10.1093/workar/way006

Cahill, K. E., James, J. B., & Pitt-Catsouphes, M. (2015). The impact of a randomly assigned time and place management initiative on work and retirement expectations. *Work, Aging, and Retirement*, *1*(4), 350–368. https://doi.org/10.1093/workar/wav012

Campbell, S. M., Twenge, J. M., & Campbell, W. K. (2017). Fuzzy but useful constructs: Making sense of differences between generations. *Work, Aging, and Retirement*, *3*(2), 130–139. https://doi.org/10.1093/workar/wax001

Costanza, D. P., Darrow, J. B., Yost, A. B., & Severt, J. B. (2017). A review of analytical methods used to study generational differences: Strengths and limitations. *Work, Aging, and Retirement*, *3*(2), 149–165. https://doi.org/10.1093/workar/wax002

Curtis, J., & McMullin, J. (2016). Older workers and the diminishing return of employment: Changes in age-based income inequality in Canada, 1996–2011. *Work, Aging, and Retirement*, *2*(3), 359–371. https://doi.org/10.1093/workar/waw003

Damman, M., & van Duijn, R. (2017). Intergenerational support in the transition from work to retirement. *Work, Aging and Retirement*, *3*(1), 66–76.

Fasbender, U., Wang, M., Voltmer, J. B., & Deller, J. (2016). The meaning of work for post-retirement employment decisions. *Work, Aging and Retirement*, *2*(1), 12–23. https://doi.org/10.1093/workar/wav015

Feldman, D. C., & Shultz, K. S. (2019). Career embeddedness and career crafting among older workers. In K. S. Shultz & G. A. Adams (Eds.), *Aging and work in the 21st century* (pp. 191–212). Routledge.

Fisher, G. G., & Barnes-Farrell, J. L. (2013). Use of archival data in OHP research. In M. Wang, R. R. Sinclair, & L. E. Tetrick (Eds.), *Research methods in occupational health psychology: State of the art in measurement, design, and data analysis* (pp. 290–322). Routledge.

Fisher, G. G., Chaffee, D. S., & Sonnega, A. (2016). Retirement timing: A review and recommendations for future research. *Work, Aging, and Retirement*, *2*(2), 230–261. https://doi.org/10.1093/workar/waw001

Fisher, G. G., & Ryan, L. H. (2018). Overview of the Health and Retirement Study and introduction to the special issue. *Work, Aging, and Retirement*, *4*(1), 1–9. https://doi.org/10.1093/workar/wax032

Fisher, G. G., & Shultz, K. S. (2006). Methodological issues: Using archival data to conduct occupational stress and health research to study older workers. In G. G.

Fisher (Chair), *Using archival data: Research examples studying issues among older workers.* Symposium conducted at the APA/NIOSH Work, Stress, and Health Conference. Orlando, FL.

Fisher, G. G., Stachowski, A., Infurna, F. J., Faul, J. D., Grosch, J., & Tetrick, L. E. (2014). Mental work demands, retirement, and longitudinal trajectories of cognitive functioning. *Journal of Occupational Health Psychology, 19*(2), 231–242. https://doi.org/10.1037/a0035724

Forbes, M. K., Spence, K. M., Wuthrich, V. M., & Rapee, R. M. (2015). Mental health and wellbeing of older workers in Australia. *Work, Aging, and Retirement, 1*(2), 202–213. https://doi.org/10.1093/workar/wav004

Ford, M. T., Matthews, R. A., Wooldridge, J. D., Mishra, V., Kakar, U. M., & Strahan, S. R. (2014). How do occupational stressor-strain effects vary with time? A review and meta-analysis of the relevance of time lags in longitudinal studies. *Work & Stress, 28*(1), 9–30. https://doi.org/10.1080/02678373.2013.877096

Ghilarducci, T., & Webb, A. (2018). The distribution of time in retirement: Evidence from the health and retirement survey. *Work, Aging, and Retirement, 4*(3), 251–261. https://doi.org/10.1093/workar/way001

Griffin, B., Bayl-Smith, P., & Hesketh, B. (2016). The longitudinal effects of perceived age discrimination on the job satisfaction and work withdrawal of older employees. *Work, Aging, and Retirement, 2*(4), 415–427. https://doi.org/10.1093/workar/waw014

Grzywacz, J. G., Segel-Karpas, D., & Lachman, M. E. (2016). Workplace exposures and cognitive function during adulthood: Evidence from National Survey of Midlife Development and the O★ NET. *Journal of Occupational and Environmental Medicine, 58*(6), 535–541. https://doi.org/10.1097/JOM.0000000000000727

Hansson, I., Buratti, S., Thorvaldsson, V., Johansson, B., & Berg, A. I. (2018). Changes in life satisfaction in the retirement transitions: Interaction effects of transition type and individual resources. *Work, Aging, and Retirement, 4*(4), 352–366. https://doi.org/10.1093/workar/wax025

Heisig, J. P., & Radl, J. (2017). Adding scars to wrinkles? Long-run effects of late-career job loss on retirement behavior and personal income. *Work, Aging, and Retirement, 3*(3), 257–272. https://doi.org/10.1093/workar/wax006

Henning, G., Stenling, A., Tafvelin, S., Hansson, I., Kivi, M., Johansson, B., & Lindwall, M. (2019). Preretirement work motivation and subsequent retirement adjustment: A self-determination theory perspective. *Work, Aging and Retirement, 5*(2), 189–203.

Heraty, N., & McCarthy, J. (2015). Unearthing psychological predictors of financial planning for retirement among late career older workers: Do self-perceptions of aging matter? *Work, Aging and Retirement, 1*(3), 274–283. https://doi.org/10.1093/workar/wav008

Hoffman, B. J., Shoss, M. K., & Wegman, L. A. (2020). The changing nature of work and workers: An introduction. In B. J. Hoffman, M. K. Shoss, & L. A. Wegman (Eds.), *The Cambridge handbook of the changing nature of work.* Cambridge University Press.

Hoven, H., Dragano, N., Blane, D., & Wahrendorf, M. (2018). Early adversity and late life employment history—A sequence analysis based on SHARE. *Work, Aging and Retirement, 4*(3), 238–250. https://doi.org/10.1093/workar/wax014

Hudomiet, P., Parker, A. M., & Rohwedder, S. (2018). Cognitive ability, personality, and pathways to retirement: An exploratory study. *Work, Aging, and Retirement, 4*(1), 52–66. https://doi.org/10.1093/workar/wax030

Hyde, M., & Dingemans, E. (2017). Hidden in plain sight? Does stricter employment protection legislation lead to an increased risk of hidden unemployment in later life? *Work, Aging and Retirement, 3*(3), 231–242.

Infurna, F. J., & Andel, R. (2018). The impact of changes in episodic memory surrounding retirement on subsequent risk of disability, cardiovascular disease, and mortality. *Work, Aging, and Retirement*, *4*(1), 10–20. https://doi.org/10.1093/workar/wax020

Kalleberg, A. L., & Marsden, P. V. (2019). Work values in the United States: Age, period, and generational differences. *The ANNALS of the American Academy of Political and Social Science*, *682*(1), 43–59. https://doi.org/10.1177/0002716218822291

Lazarus, R. S., & Folkman, S. (1984). *Stress, appraisal, and coping*. Springer.

Litwin, H., & Tur-Sinai, A. (2015). The role of the social network in early retirement among older Europeans. *Work, Aging and Retirement*, *1*(4), 340–349. https://doi.org/10.1093/workar/wav013

Liu, M., McGonagle, A. K., & Fisher, G. G. (2018). Sense of control, job stressors, and well-being: Inter-relations and reciprocal effects among older US workers. *Work, Aging, and Retirement*, *4*(1), 96–107. https://doi.org/10.1093/workar/waw035

Lux, T., & Scherger, S. (2018). The effects of taking up employment after pension age on self-reated health in Germany and the UK: Evidence based on Fixed Effects Models. *Work, Aging, and Retirement*, *4*(3), 262–273. https://doi.org/10.1093/workar/way003

Madero-Cabib, I., Gauthier, J. A., & Le Goff, J. M. (2016). The influence of interlocked employment–family trajectories on retirement timing. *Work, Aging and Retirement*, *2*(1), 38–53. https://doi.org/10.1093/workar/wav023

Marchiondo, L. A., Fisher, G. G., Cortina, L. M., & Matthews, R. A. (2020). Disrespect at work, distress at home: A longitudinal investigation of incivility spillover and crossover among older workers. *Work, Aging, and Retirement*, *6*(3), 153–164. https://doi.org/10.1093/workar/waaa007

Moen, P., Kojola, E., Kelly, E. L., & Yagmur Karakaya, K. (2016). Men and women expecting to work longer: Do changing work conditions matter? *Work, Aging, and Retirement*, *2*(3), 321–344. https://doi.org/10.1093/workar/waw018

Moen, P., Pedtke, J. H., & Flood, S. (2020). Disparate disruptions: Intersectional COVID-19 employment effects by age, gender, education, and race/ethnicity. *Work, Aging, and Retirement*, *6*(4), 207–228.

Mroczek, D. K., Weston, S. J., Graham, E. K., & Willroth, E. C. (2021, April 29). Data overuse in aging research: Emerging issues and potential solutions. *Psychology and Aging*. Advance online publication. http://dx.doi.org/10.1037/pag0000605

Noone, J., Earl, J., Stephens, C., Rafalski, J., Allen, J., Alpass, F., & Topa, G. (2021). An application of the resource-based dynamic process model in the context of retirement planning. *Work, Aging and Retirement*. Advance online publication. https://doi.org/10.1093/workar/waab006

Parker, S. K., Ward, M. K., & Fisher, G. G. (2021). Can high-quality jobs help adults learn new tricks? A multi-disciplinary review of work design for cognition. *Academy of Management Annals*, *15*. https://doi.org/10.5465/annals.2019.0057

Parry, E., & Urwin, P. (2017). The evidence base for generational differences: Where do we go from here? *Work, Aging, and Retirement*, *3*(2), 140–148. https://doi.org/10.1093/workar/waw037

Peterson, N. G., Mumford, M. D., Borman, W. C., Jeanneret, P. R., Fleishman, E. A., Levin, K. Y., Campion, M. A., Mayfield, M. S., Morgeson, F. P., Pearlman, K., Gowing, M. K., Lancaster, A. R., Silver, M. B., & Dye, D. M. (2001). Understanding work using the Occupational Information Network (O★NET): Implications for practice and research. *Personnel Psychology*, *54*(2), 451–492. https://doi.org/10.1111/j.1744-6570.2001.tb00100.x

Rauvola, R. S., Nyberg, B., Moreno, M. M., & Rudolph, C. W. (2021, April). Putting O★NET back to work: An occupational crosswalk for archival research in I/O. Poster

Presented at the Annual Conference of the Society for Industrial and Organizational Psychology, New Orleans, LA. [Conference Moved Online due to COVID-19]

Riekhoff, A. J., Järnefelt, N., & Laaksonen, M. (2020). Workforce composition and the risk of labor market exit among older workers in Finnish companies. *Work, Aging, and Retirement, 6*(2), 88–100. https://doi.org/10.1093/workar/waz023

Rudolph, C. W., Marcus, J., & Zacher, H. (2019). Global issues in work, aging, and retirement. In K. S. Shultz, & G. A. Adams (Eds.), *Aging and work in the 21st century* (pp. 292–324). Routledge.

Rudolph, C. W., Rauvola, R. S., Costanza, D. P., & Zacher, H. (2020). Generations and generational differences: Debunking myths in organizational science and practice and paving new paths forward. *Journal of Business and Psychology*, 1–23. https://doi.org/10.1007/s10869-020-09715-2

Segel-Karpas, D. (2015). Number of illnesses, self-perceived health, and depressive symptoms: The moderating role of employment in older adulthood and old age. *Work, Aging and Retirement, 1*(4), 382–392.

Settels, J., & Schafer, M. H. (2018). Workforce transitions and social connectedness among older adults in the United States. *Work, Aging, and Retirement, 4*(3), 274–288. https://doi.org/10.1093/workar/wax029

Shultz, K. S., & Fisher, G. G. (2016). Ageing and retirement behaviour. In L. Riby (Ed.), *The handbook of gerontology research methods* (pp. 118–136). Taylor and Francis.

Shultz, K. S., Hoffman, C. C., & Reiter-Palmon, R. (2005). Using archival data for I-O research: Advantages, pitfalls, sources, and examples. *The Industrial-Organizational Psychologist, 42*(3), 31–37. https://doi.org/10.1037/e579182011-004

Shultz, K. S., Wang, M., Crimmins, E., & Fisher, G. G. (2010). Age differences in the Demand-Control Model of work stress: An examination of data from 15 European countries. *Journal of Applied Gerontology, 29*(1), 21–47. https://doi.org/10.1177/0733464809334286

Silver, M. P., Settels, J., Schafer, M. H., & Schieman, S. (2019). Getting the hours you want in preretirement years: Work hour preferences and mismatch among older Canadian workers. *Work, Aging, and Retirement, 5*(2), 175–188. https://doi.org/10.1093/workar/way015

Spiegel, P. E., & Shultz, K. S. (2003). The influence of pre-retirement planning and transferability of skills on naval officers' retirement satisfaction and adjustment. *Military Psychology, 15*(4), 284–306. https://doi.org/10.1207/S15327876MP1504_3

Sullivan, S. E., & Al Ariss, A. (2019). Employment after retirement: A review and framework for future research. *Journal of Management, 45*(1), 262–284. https://doi.org/10.1177/0149206318810411

Trzesniewski, K. H., Donnellan, M. B., & Lucas, R. E. (Eds.). (2011). *Secondary data analysis: An introduction for psychologists*. American Psychological Association.

van den Bogaard, L. (2017). Leaving quietly? A quantitative study of retirement rituals and how they affect life satisfaction. *Work, Aging, and Retirement, 3*(1), 55–65. https://doi.org/10.1093/workar/waw026

van der Horst, M., Vickerstaff, S., Lain, D., Clark, C., & Baumberg Geiger, B. (2017). Pathways of paid work, care provision, and volunteering in later careers: Activity substitution or extension? *Work, Aging, and Retirement, 3*(4), 343–365. https://doi.org/10.1093/workar/waw028

Van Solinge, H., & Henkens, K. (2017). Older workers' emotional reactions to rising retirement age: The case of the Netherlands. *Work, Aging, and Retirement, 3*(3), 273–283. https://doi.org/10.1093/workar/wax010

Vélez-Coto, M., Andel, R., Pérez-García, M., & Caracuel, A. (2021). Complexity of work with people: Associations with cognitive functioning and change after retirement. *Psychology and Aging, 36*(2), 143–157. https://doi.org/10.1037/pag0000584

Visser, M., Gesthuizen, M., Kraaykamp, G., & Wolbers, M. H. (2018). Labor market vulnerability of older workers in the Netherlands and its impact on downward mobility and reduction of working hours. *Work, Aging, and Retirement, 4*(3), 289–299. https://doi.org/10.1093/workar/wax017

von Bonsdorff, M. E., Zhan, Y., Song, Y., & Wang, M. (2017). Examining bridge employment from a self-employment perspective–Evidence from the Health and Retirement Study. *Work, Aging, and Retirement, 3*(3), 298–312. https://doi.org/10.1093/workar/wax012

Voss, M. W., Al Snih, S., Li, W., Hung, M., & Richards, L. G. (2020). Boundaries of the construct of unemployment in the preretirement years: Exploring an expanded measurement of lost-work opportunity. *Work, Aging, and Retirement, 6*(1), 59–63. https://doi.org/10.1093/workar/waz006

Warren, D. A. (2015). Pathways to retirement in Australia: Evidence from the HILDA survey. *Work, Aging, and Retirement, 1*(2), 144–165. https://doi.org/10.1093/workar/wau013

Yang, Y., & Land, K. C. (2006). A mixed models approach to the age-period-cohort analysis of repeated cross-section surveys, with an application to data on treads in verbal test scores. *Sociological Methodology, 36*(1), 75–97. https://doi.org/10.1111/j.1467-9531.2006.00175.x

Zacher, H., & Griffin, B. (2015). Older workers' age as a moderator of the relationship between career adaptability and job satisfaction. *Work, Aging, and Retirement, 1*(2), 227–236. https://doi.org/10.1093/workar/wau009

SECTION IV
Advances in Practice Regarding Age and Work

14

AGE AND JOB CRAFTING

How and Why do Employees of Different Ages Craft Their Job?

Dorien T. A. M. Kooij and Ruth Kanfer

Recent studies on (successful) aging at work have highlighted the benefits of job crafting behavior for older workers (Kooij, 2015; Lichtenthaler & Fischbach, 2016; Vanbelle et al., 2017). Job crafting captures self-initiated changes individuals make in their job to improve their person–job fit (e.g., Wrzesniewski & Dutton, 2001). By crafting their job, older workers can continuously adjust their job to accommodate intrapersonal changes in personal resources (e.g., in physical abilities, motives, and emotion regulation) that relate to the aging process and so promote work motivation and productivity (Kooij et al., 2015; Kooij et al., 2020). Continuous fit is also important for older workers because it leads to the sustainable use of personal resources (Kooij, 2015); maintaining continuous fit means that workers fulfill present needs and optimally use current skills and knowledge without overburdening their personal resources (De Lange et al., 2015). In line with this reasoning, numerous studies demonstrate the positive effects that job crafting has on a range of important job outcomes, such as person–job fit, engagement, employability, and performance (e.g., Petrou et al., 2012; Tims et al., 2016).

Nonetheless, while a meta-analysis of 50 independent samples found only modest correlations (Rudolph et al., 2017), the relationship between age and job crafting was generally not the main focus of these studies—age was assessed as a control variable. Research *focusing* on the relationship between age and job crafting is infrequent, and little is known about how and why employees of different ages craft their jobs. In this chapter we begin with a brief review of the literature on job crafting and age. We then report the results of a qualitative interview study in which we examined job crafting motives and types, how these motives and types interconnect, and how job crafting motives, types, and their interconnections differ between younger and older workers.

DOI: 10.4324/9781003089674-18

Job Crafting Types

Job crafting captures proactive, self-initiated changes employees make in their tasks or in the relational boundaries of their job to improve job fit with changing personal needs and abilities (De Bloom et al., 2020; Wrzesniewski & Dutton, 2001; Tims et al., 2012). Since the introduction of the concept of job crafting in 2001, multiple job crafting dimensions have been proposed. Wrzesniewski and Dutton (2001) distinguish task (i.e., changing the type or number of job tasks), relational (i.e., changing how or with whom one interacts at work), and cognitive crafting (i.e., changing one's view of the job) dimensions. However, many job crafting researchers (e.g., Lichtenthaler & Fischbach, 2019; Nielsen & Abildgaard, 2012; Tims et al., 2012) build on the job demands and resources model (e.g., Demerouti et al., 2001), and have examined job crafting dimensions organized in terms of job resources and job demands. In these studies, job crafting may involve increasing job resources such as autonomy or learning opportunities and/or decreasing job demands, such as work pressure or emotional work (i.e., increasing structural job resources and challenging demands or decreasing hindering job demands).

Recently, Zhang and Parker (2019) integrated these two research streams by building on the distinction between approach vs avoidance goal orientation. Approach-oriented job crafting involves behaviors designed to improve the working experience; avoidance-oriented job crafting behaviors are aimed at reducing negative aspects of the working experience. Accordingly, Zhang and Parker (2019) introduce eight types of job crafting as reported in Table 14.1. At the same time, Bindl et al. (2019) distinguished promotion- (similar to approach) and prevention- (similar to avoidance) oriented task, relationship, and cognitive crafting. Although Bindl et al. (2019) also distinguished skill crafting, which refers to employees' self-initiated efforts to change their skills at work to better carry out their own jobs (Wrzesniewski et al., 2012), this form of crafting does not involve changes to (perceptions of) the job. In this chapter we therefore build on Zhang and Parker's (2019) categorization to distinguish between different types of job crafting behaviors.

Job Crafting Motives

Why employees craft their job is a crucial question for advancing both theory and practice. Wrzesniewski and Dutton (2001) argue that the ultimate goal of job crafting is to experience enhanced meaning of work and a positive work identity, resulting in the fulfillment of basic individual needs for autonomy, competence, and relatedness. Hence, they propose that employees engage in job crafting to (1) increase control over their job and to avoid alienation from work; (2) to create and sustain a positive self-image; and (3) to improve social relations. Supporting this line of reasoning, Niessen et al. (2016) found that a higher need for

TABLE 14.1 Job Crafting Dimensions and Motive Categories

Dimension	Definition
What people do	
Approach Resources Behavioral	Actions to gain positive job resources
Approach Demands Behavioral	Actions to increase one's challenging demands or address hindering demands
Approach Resources Cognitive	Reframing one's job to gain positive job resources
Approach Demands Cognitive	Reframing one's demands as either more challenging or less hindrance
Avoidance Resources Behavioral	Actions to avoid aspects of the job that lack positive resources
Avoidance Demands Behavioral	Actions to avoid hindering demands
Avoidance Resources Cognitive	Reframing one's job to avoid or diminish aspects of the job that lack resources
Avoidance Demands Cognitive	Reframing one's job to avoid the experience of demands
Why people job craft (motives)	
Accommodative	Aimed at regulating losses in personal resources and similar to fulfilling avoidance needs
Utilization	Aimed at using one's current personal resources (e.g., interests, needs, strengths)
Developmental	Aimed at optimizing personal resources through realizing one's growth potential

positive self-image predicted subsequent job crafting. Similarly, in their qualitative study, Baroudi and Khapova (2017) found that the need for control, which arose from the need for work efficiency, and a positive self-image were particularly mentioned as job crafting motives. Also building on the notion that individual needs serve as triggers for job crafting behavior, Bindl et al. (2019) argued and found that the drive to fulfill different needs at work was positively associated with different job crafting types. Similarly, De Bloom et al. (2020) argue that needs discrepancies trigger job crafting behavior. However, rather than detailing different needs, they focus on broader categories of approach and avoidance needs. Approach needs refer to pursuing a positive state centered on growth, enrichment, and the creation of new resources, whereas avoidance needs refer to people's desire to decrease physical and/or mental effort investment, to optimize levels of cognitive stimulation, and to restore homeostatic balance. Finally, Lazazzara et al. (2018) identified proactive and reactive motives to job craft from their review of qualitative job crafting studies. Proactive motives revolve around reaching desirable goals and fulfilling unsatisfied needs, while reactive motives are related to the need to cope with adversity.

In another line of reasoning, Wrzesniewski et al. (2013) emphasized the importance of incorporating employees' motives, strengths, and passions in the job crafting concept and Berg et al. (2013) argued that to create a better person–environment fit employees should focus on their "motives, strengths, and passions" (p. 13) when crafting their jobs. Answering these calls, Kooij et al. (2017) introduced two new job crafting dimensions. Job crafting toward strengths refers to changes employees make to their job to better use their strengths. In contrast, job crafting toward interests refers to actions aimed at making the job more interesting and enjoyable. In 2020, Kuijpers et al. (2020) introduced a third developmental crafting dimension, reflecting actions to reach one's growth potential. Finally, Kooij et al. (2021) build on this work by introducing three job crafting dimensions based on three prominent resource allocation goals of developmental adaptation identified in the literature on lifespan development (i.e., growth, maintenance, and regulation of loss; Baltes et al., 1999; please see also Chapter 7). Development crafting aims to accomplish a higher level of functioning by optimizing personal resources, utilization crafting seeks to maintain one's current level of functioning by using personal resources when faced with aging challenges, and accommodative crafting seeks to regulate and hence minimize personal resources losses. In this chapter, we follow Kooij et al. (2021) in distinguishing these three job crafting motives (see Table 14.1).

Job Crafting and Age

Although previous studies on aging at work have demonstrated that behavior, cognitions, and motives at work differ across the lifespan (Kooij et al., 2011; Yeung & Fung, 2009; please see also Chapter 1), research on how job crafting types and motives change with age is scarce. According to De Bloom et al. (2020), individual factors, such as age, influence the crafting process both directly through their effects on the salience of needs and the degree of perceived needs discrepancy and indirectly, through their effects on the strength of the relationships between needs discrepancy and crafting efforts. Rudolph et al. (2017) found in their meta-analysis that job crafting behavior in terms of changing job demands and job resources is correlated with age. Specifically, older workers engage in less job crafting to increase social job resources and challenging demands and to decrease hindering demands but in more job crafting to increase structural resources. Similarly, Zacher and Kooij (2017) reviewed the literature on age and proactive behavior and found evidence suggesting that older workers engage in less proactive career behavior than younger employees but are more proactive with regard to other forms of proactive work behavior.

Baroudi and Khapova (2017) compared job crafting types and motives of younger and older workers in their qualitative study. They found that both older and younger workers changed the way they performed their jobs and the quality of their interactions. Both younger and older workers increased as well as decreased their number of tasks and interactions with others. Nevertheless, younger workers were more likely to engage in these job crafting behaviors than older workers.

With respect to job crafting motives, Baroudi and Khapova (2017) found that, although the need for control was an important job crafting motive for both older and younger workers, older workers crafted to create and sustain a positive self-image, whereas younger workers crafted to improve their image in the eyes of others. Besides these studies on the direct effect of age on job crafting types and motives, other studies have focused on the indirect effects of age. Findings from an experimental field study by Kooij et al. (2017) show that age moderated the relationship between participating in a job crafting intervention and job crafting behavior. Specifically, they found that participating in a job crafting intervention leads to strengths crafting but only among older workers. Strengths crafting was, in turn, positively associated with demands—abilities and needs—supplies fit.

In summary, although there has been a burgeoning literature on the topic of job crafting, important yet unanswered questions in this area pertain to which job crafting motives are salient, how different job crafting motives and types interconnect (De Bloom et al., 2020), and how this differs with age. Based on previous findings, we would broadly expect that employees engage in approach crafting for developmental and utilization motives and in avoidance crafting for accommodative motives. In addition, based on lifespan theories (P. B. Baltes & M. M. Baltes, 1990; Carstensen, 1995), we anticipate that younger workers engage more in approach crafting for developmental motives, whereas older workers engage more in avoidance crafting for accommodative motives. The following section describes a qualitative study that explores our expectations.

Qualitative Study on Age and Job Crafting

Method

Together with six research assistants, the first author conducted interviews among 80 participants in the Netherlands. We used purposeful sampling (Patton, 1990) to allow a range of participants from different sectors, organizations, jobs, gender, rank, life stages (i.e., age), and career stages (i.e., tenure). Potential participants were contacted through our personal networks. The 80 participants worked in 10 different organizations in different sectors (e.g., in construction, retail, and finance) and in different jobs, such as shop-floor employees, production workers, and managers. Of the participants, 40 were female (50%), with age ranging from 21 to 63 (M = 43.8, SD = 12.0) and organizational tenure ranging from 1 to 40 years (M = 13.9 years, SD = 10.7). Educational level ranged from primary school to master's degree with most participants having obtained a bachelor's degree.

We conducted face-to-face semistructured interviews. In this format, key questions are asked in a similar way in each interview while probing for further information when necessary (Lewis & Ritchie, 2003). We used an existing (Berg et al., 2010) but slightly adjusted interview protocol (e.g., adding alternative clarifications/probes), which we pilot tested before using them in our study. Each interview lasted between 13 and 63 minutes ($M = 36.6$ minutes, $SD = 11.4$). All interviews began with general information questions about the participant's job (e.g., content and dynamics). Next, participants were asked whether they had changed their job out of their own initiative since they started in their job (probing with "to adapt the job to your own needs and abilities" or "to make your job your own"). For each instance, we queried about the motives (goals/why) associated with the job crafting episode. This protocol was followed for every job crafting episode mentioned until the participant could not mention any more job crafting episodes.

Data Analysis

All interviews were recorded and transcribed to enable coding of the material. The first round of coding focused on distinguishing job crafting episodes, using the broad conceptualization of job crafting as "self-initiated changes individual employees make to the tasks, relationships, and cognitions of their job." Next, each job crafting episode was coded for motives, and each episode and motive was aligned to existing job crafting types and motives in the literature based on their content but also identifying potentially new types and motives. Every interview was coded by at least two researchers, and all discrepancies were discussed. The Atlas.ti software program was used by the researchers to code the interview data. We then imported the codes and frequencies into SPSS and conducted correlation analyses to examine relationships among job crafting motives and types, as well as to examine possible age differences in job crafting types and motives and their interconnections.

Results

A total 210 job crafting types and 262 job crafting motives were reported across the 80 participants. Eight participants did not report any job crafting type.

Job Crafting Types

Table 14.2 reports the 20 job crafting types reported, including their frequencies and illustrative quotes. As shown in Table 14.2, taking on additional tasks was by far the most frequent type of crafting. The additional tasks stated were very diverse and ranged from small tasks, such as sweeping the floor, to large tasks, such as initiating and implementing a new project. There was also large variation in how participants changed the way they do their job. For example, some participants set deadlines for themselves, some participants worked extra fast, and some participants made minor or major changes in work procedures. Bruning and Campion (2018) refer to these changes as work organization tactics. Some of the job

TABLE 14.2 Frequency of Reported Behaviors and Examples by Job Crafting Types

Job Crafting Type	N	Behaviors	Example quotes
Approach demands behavioral crafting	73	Take on tasks	"I took on the checkup of all cars. We used to do this separate [for our own cars], but now I organize it. I keep track of when a periodic checkup is needed and try to repair small defects myself"
	16	Change/replace Tasks	"Physically I am not in the store anymore. I decided that the store now is for the employees, the store in one month is for the managers, and for the long term policy it is mine. . . . And that works much better. I have more time to think and make plans . . . to get results"
	5	Take on more responsibility	"I take my own responsibility and decide by myself whether we pay customers back"
	2	Extend the scope of a task	"I can say, this is my assignment, to fix that sewerage system, done. But I can also say, hey, but we should also install drainage and to connect that area where there are troubles and with a small extension of my project we can solve that as well"
Approach resources behavioral crafting	13	Increase number of interactions with coworkers	"I put a lot of energy in that. To drink a cup of coffee, have a chat, how are you?"
	13	Change the way you plan your work	"I planned to leave work at the office and to no longer take it home . . . good is good enough"
	11	Change the way you do your work	"A pack of 40 kilos is much heavier now than when I was 50. I still lift them, but you need to know how to lift them, because then they don't weigh 40 kilos anymore"
	12	Offer advice/ transfer knowledge	"I give advice to the director, I have a new project, who should do it. That is responsibility, from experience, knowing people and who works here"
	9	Increase number of interactions with customers	"When I am talking to someone on the phone a number of times, purely for business, then I tend to make an appointment. That is important to me"

(Continued)

TABLE 1.2 (Continued)

Job Crafting Type	N	Behaviors	Example quotes
	7	Ask for help	"I ask help from coworkers . . . if a role is too heavy we lift it with the two of us"
	5	Offer help to others	"If you see that it is very busy somewhere and you have a spare moment, that you can help, and you do"
	5	Use tools	"I ensured there are three machines to wind up the carpet"
	3	Mentor coworkers	"And you can use your experience to support other people in their job"
	2	Increasing decision-making authority	"Those agreements are not there so I take my own responsibility and if I think it needs to paid we pay"
Approach demands cognitive crafting	5	Increase involvement in work	"And now I think that work is really a part of my life . . . you should have a job that you enjoy"
Approach resources cognitive crafting	5	Finding more purpose in work	"Along the way I also got the drive to produce environmentally friendly products"
Avoidance demands behavioral crafting	6	Delegate tasks/ask others to take over tasks	"We have to put the offers in a certain system. So I asked somebody else to do this for me"
	3	Don't do tasks	"I used to hang the lamps but I am afraid to climb a ladder now"
	3	Don't take on/get rid of extra tasks	"Say no more often and do the things that are part of your job. So prioritize"
	4	Decrease number of interactions with hindering coworkers	"The contacts with her are much less now"
Avoidance demands cognitive crafting	6	Reduce involvement in/ worry less about work	"I used to think I want to improve this and this and used to look at details. . . . So my thoughts shifted from I want to improve something, but now I think it is okay like this"
	2	Less purpose of work	"I've become less idealistic . . . my attitude towards my work has become more work instead of taking it personally"

crafting types mentioned by the participants were particularly interesting as they have not been identified in earlier empirical research on job crafting. For example, some participants reported that they craft their job by offering advice, for example to coworkers or management. Next, we further organized job crafting types by linking them to the job crafting types distinguished by Zhang and Parker (2019). Results of this classification showed that participants engaged mostly in approach demands behavioral crafting and approach resources behavioral crafting. Participants reported surprisingly few instances of avoidance demands behavioral, avoidance demands cognitive, approach demands cognitive, and approach resources cognitive crafting and did not engage in avoidance resources behavioral or avoidance resources cognitive crafting.

Job Crafting Motives

As shown in Table 14.3, participants reported 27 distinct job crafting motives. Table 14.3 also shows that making one's work more enjoyable was the most

TABLE 14.3 Frequency of Reported Motives and Examples by Job Crafting Motive Category

Motive Category	N	Motive	Example quotes
Developmental motives	23	Learn and develop	"I increased contacts with the coworker from technical services . . . to use his knowledge"
	6	More challenge	"Because of my own development, because I want some challenges. I design the brochure every year . . . that is routine now so it is time to do something else"
	3	Broadly/sustainably employable	"The more I know, the more employable I will be".
	4	Accomplish the maximum	"To always try to accomplish new goals, putting your limits further and further, I want to see how far I can go, in everything"
	3	Career development	"I want to advance to sous chef of head chef".
Utilization motives	44	Enjoyable and interesting work	"I have a great interest in cars"
	10	Work in a pleasant way	"That is more pleasant for everybody"

(Continued)

TABLE 14.3 (Continued)

Motive Category	N	Motive	Example quotes
	28	Use knowledge and experience	"My experience plays a big role in this. I used to do fieldwork so when it comes to commercial contacts I have a lot of experience. . . . So give all the angry customers to me"
	8	Good at	"I am good at system technical things, such as Excel and Access. I work pretty structured, so I can find information easily . . . and you use that"
	5	Make work more varied	"I like to be able and do everything. So that I can help everywhere, the variation that it brings".
	10	Increase meaning of work	"You notice the impact it has on people"
Social motives	2	Increase number of contacts with others	"More contacts with other airlines"
	5	Increase the network/ get to know other people	"And also because I like to know other people within the organization, it is fun when you see people again"
	3	Social cohesion	"The social aspect is so important in a company"
	8	Personal contact with people you like	"We get along very well"
	2	Accommodate coworkers	"If he is under time pressure . . . I make some time, . . . I don't have to do that. That is accommodating each other"
Add value motives	10	To keep busy	"Now I keep track of that . . . not really nice work, but it is pleasant to do something when it is quiet"
	20	Make work easier	"If there is a complaint and the customer threw the ticket away, and that happens a lot, very often, then I have the ticket and it is much more easy to solve the complaint"
	3	Nobody else does it	"I took on operational management and making their reports . . . because nobody did it"
	3	To keep the overview/control	"We get so much, otherwise it is not manageable"
	5	More efficient	"I am not going to do six steps when I can do the work in two steps"

Motive Category	N	Motive	Example quotes
	12	Company performance	"I thought it was an opportunity to diversify ourselves from competitors and to develop a good reputation"
	13	Customer satisfaction	"I try to remember what customers tell me. They tell me lots of private stuff. I try to remember that so that I can ask them about it . . . and the customers like that"
Accommodative motives	17	Decrease physical demands	"I organized work in such a way that I don't have to make the old line of machines anymore . . . because that is pretty demanding"
	3	Not capable anymore	"Something I am not capable of doing, I want to, but I can't, that goes to the youngsters"
	3	Reduce work pressure and stress	"That change has taken some pressure of me"
	9	Cope with work pressure	"If the work pressure has increased by 20% you need to get it somewhere", "In the morning I take it easy . . . I know I will have to work hard in the afternoon"

frequently mentioned motive. Other important reasons to job craft are to use their knowledge and experience, to learn and develop, to make work easier or simpler, to decrease physical demands, to increase customer satisfaction, to improve company performance, to stay busy, to work in a pleasant way, and to increase the meaningfulness of their work. Participants often mentioned multiple job crafting motives for the same job crafting type. For example, a manager of customer services mentioned: "My experience plays a big role in this. I used to do fieldwork so when it comes to commercial contacts I have a lot of experience. My goal is always a happy customer. . . . So give all angry customers to me, I love it." His motive to craft his job by taking on this additional task was to use his experience, to increase customer satisfaction, and to make his work more enjoyable.

Next, we further categorized the job crafting motives by linking them to the job crafting motives distinguished by Kooij et al. (2021). Results of this classification showed that employees particularly craft their job for utilization motives and to a lesser extent to develop and accommodate themselves. However, this classification also revealed two additional motives for job crafting. First, employees also craft to work with and help other people. This overarching job crafting motive includes five specific motives (i.e., increase number of contacts with others, increase one's network, social cohesion, increase personal contacts, and accommodate coworkers) and relates to satisfying socials needs of connecting to others (Wrzesniewski & Dutton, 2001; Bindl et al., 2019). Second, employees craft to add value to the organization as indicated by seven specific job crafting motives (i.e., to keep busy, to make work easier, nobody else does it, to keep in control, to work more efficiently, to increase company performance and to increase customer satisfaction; see also Lyons, 2008) and relates to satisfying the need for a positive self-image (Baroudi & Khapova, 2017; Lazazzara et al., 2018; Wrzesniewski & Dutton, 2001).

Job Crafting Types and Motives: Why Do Employees Engage in Job Crafting Types

Table 14.4 shows the correlations between job crafting types and motives. This table reveals that employees mention multiple motives for the same job crafting type. Participants engage in job crafting to increase challenging demands or resolve hindering demands (approach demands behavioral crafting) for utilization motives, to add value and to develop themselves. Participants engage in crafting behaviors to gain positive job resources (approach resources behavioral crafting) for accommodative motives, to add value, and for utilization motives. Participants engage in approach resources cognitive crafting to add value. Participants engage in avoidance demands behavioral crafting for accommodative motives. Finally, participants engage in avoidance demands cognitive crafting to develop themselves.

Age Differences in Job Crafting Types and Motives

Table 14.4 also shows the correlations between age and job crafting types and motives. This table reveals few age differences in job crafting types and motives. Specifically, only accommodative motives increase with age such that older participants engage more in job crafting to fulfill their avoidance needs. We also

TABLE 14.4 Correlations Between Job Crafting Types and Motives

	Approach demands behavior	Approach resource behavior	Approach demands cognitive	Approach resources cognitive	Avoidance demands behavior	Avoidance demands cognitive	Age
Accommodative	.17	.78*	.06	.00	.34*	.13	.27*
Add value	.33*	.46*	.09	.24*	-.06	-.10	-.18
Develop	.33*	-.05	-.03	.03	.01	.26*	-.08
Social	.17	-.03	-.12	-.10	.10	.08	-.06
Utilization	.57*	.26*	.11	.05	.05	-.05	.07
Age	-.10	.13	-.04	-.05	.20	.18	

Note: * p < .05

TABLE 14.5 Frequencies of and Correlations Between Job Crafting Types and Motives of Younger and Older Participants

	Motive frequency younger/ older	Approach demands behavior	Approach resource behavior	Approach demands cognitive	Approach resources cognitive	Avoidance demands behavior	Avoidance demands cognitive
Type frequency younger/ older		51/45	34/42	3/2	3/2	4/11	2/5
Accommoda- tive	9/22	.14/.26	(.68*/.83*)†	-.13/.18	.05/-.02	(.55*/.23)†	.14/.06
Add value	39/26	.32*/.35*	(.64*/.40*)†	.01/.21	.24/.21	.08/-.18	.10/-.32
Developmental	21/18	.24/.43**	.05/-.09	-.08/.00	-.06/.12	-.01/.03	.17/.37*
Social	10/10	.25/-.04	.02/-.07	-.11/-.13	-.09/-.13	.00/.21	.09/.10
Utilization	51/53	.57*/.57*	.16/.31	.11/.10	-.12/.28	.08/-.01	-.05/-.08

Note: * $p < .05$; Young (≤ 45) ($N = 41$)/old (> 45) ($N = 36$); (.68*/.83*)†: difference between .68 and .83 is significant at $p < .05$ level.

compared the correlations between job crafting types and motives of younger (≤ 45) and older (> 45) participants using dependent correlation tests (see Table 14.5). Similar to other studies (e.g., Kiss et al., 2008), we focused on workers aged 45 and older, since this is the age at which employees start to experience age-related changes (WHO, 1993). These analyses reveal that older participants engage more in approach resources behavioral crafting to accommodate themselves compared to younger participants, whereas younger participants engage more in approach resources behavioral crafting to add value compared to older participants. Younger participants engage in avoidance demands behavioral crafting to accommodate themselves, whereas older participant do not.

Discussion

Job crafting is a process that individuals have long used to improve their working experience. Consistent with recent systematic research findings on job crafting, our findings point to regularities in what employees do to improve their job experience and how these changes relate to age. Specifically, results of our interview study across a range of job levels and types found support for six of the eight job crafting types proposed by Zhang and Parker (2019). We found that most participants reported engaging in approach oriented crafting (i.e., approach resources behavioral and approach demands behavioral crafting) that have been found to have positive effects on worker outcomes (Zhang & Parker, 2019). With respect to job crafting motives, as expected, avoidance needs were all related to accommodative motives (e.g., reducing work pressure). However, our findings also suggest a more nuanced taxonomy with respect to fulfilling approach needs (e.g., De Bloom et al., 2020). Two approach motives, utilization motives and developmental motives, proposed in the literature (Kooij et al., 2021) were further distinguishable from social and adding value motives. Hence, in addition to crafting to use current personal resources and optimize their personal resources through realizing their growth potential, participants also crafted to fulfill social needs and the need for a positive self-image (e.g., Baroudi & Khapova, 2017; Niessen et al., 2016) by adding value to the company.

To our knowledge, this is one of the first chapters to discuss and explore the relationship between job crafting types, motives, and age (see also Bindl et al., 2019). In line with expectations, making job changes to increase positive job resources (approach resources behavioral crafting) and job challenges (approach demands behavioral crafting) appeared to be driven by motives to use one's personal resources (utilization motive), but also to add value to the organization. Similarly, employees who reported making job changes to avoid impeding job demands (avoidance demands behavioral crafting) frequently report these actions taken in response to motives aimed at regulating resource loss (accommodative motive). However, contrary to expectations, employees also reported development motives as the impetus for both actions to increase challenging demands (approach demands behavioral crafting) and to reframing the job to avoid demands (avoidance demands cognitive crafting) and accommodative motives for making job changes to increase positive job resources (approach resources behavioral crafting). Social motives are not strongly related to any specific type of job crafting. It might be that social needs are fulfilled during breaks and not seen as a motive to job craft. Finally, avoidance and cognitive crafting were only associated with one job crafting motive. This finding could indicate that approach and behavioral crafting are more proactive, whereas avoidance and cognitive crafting are more adaptive/reactive. Since job crafting behavior is, by definition, proactive (e.g., De Bloom et al., 2020), avoidance and cognitive crafting might be better conceptualized as coping rather than job crafting.

Surprisingly, job crafting types and motives did not vary by age, although older workers indeed reported more accommodative reasons for job crafting. We also found that interconnections between job crafting types and motives differed somewhat between younger and older workers. Compared to younger workers, older workers engage more in approach resources behavioral crafting to accommodate themselves, whereas younger participants engage more in approach resources behavioral crafting to add value compared to older participants. In addition, younger workers engage in avoidance demands behavioral crafting to regulate losses in personal resources (accommodative motive), whereas older workers reported accommodative motives only in association with approach resources behavioral job crafting. An important question for future research is whether older workers are more reluctant to engage in avoidance demands behavioral job crafting in order to avoid fueling age stereotypes.

In addition to these contributions to the literature, our chapter has some important practical implications. First, the findings from the interview study demonstrate that almost all employees in different jobs, occupations, organizations, and of different ages craft their jobs. Thus, organizational leaders and managers should realize that employees continuously adjust their job to accommodate intrapersonal changes in personal resources that relate to the aging process. Since job crafting and person–job fit have beneficial effects for the employee and the organization, managers should stimulate job crafting behavior among all their workers, for example by investing in interventions that stimulate job crafting behavior (e.g., Kooij et al., 2017). Second, our findings extend understanding about why and how employees change their working experience and show that employees have different motives to engage in particular job crafting types. Since some job crafting types are less beneficial for work outcomes (i.e., avoidance crafting), organizations should try to fulfill the motives related to these job crafting types in different ways.

Conclusion

In order to age successfully at work and adjust their job to changing personal resources, older workers engage in job crafting behavior. Besides job crafting in order to optimize, use, and regulate losses in personal resources, younger and older workers craft to fulfill social needs and the need for a positive self-image. Although older workers engage more in job crafting for accommodative motives and different crafting motives trigger different job crafting types, there seem to be few age differences in job crafting types and motives and their interconnections.

References

Baltes, P. B., & Baltes, M. M. (1990). Psychological perspectives on successful aging: The model of selective optimization with compensation. In P. B. Baltes & M. M. Baltes (Eds.), *Successful aging: Perspectives from the behavioral sciences* (pp. 1–34). Cambridge University Press. https://doi.org/10.1017/cbo9780511665684.003

Baltes, P. B., Staudinger, U. M., & Lindenberger, U. (1999). Lifespan psychology: Theory and application to intellectual functioning. *Annual Review of Psychology, 50*(1), 471–507. https://doi.org/10.1146/annurev.psych.50.1.471

Berg, J. M., Dutton, J. E., & Wrzesniewski, A. (2013). Job crafting and meaningful work. In B. J. Dik, Z. S. Byrne, & M. F. Steger (Eds.), *Purpose and meaning in the workplace* (pp. 81–104). American Psychological Association. https://doi.org/10.1037/14183-005

Berg, J. M., Wrzesniewski, A., & Dutton, J. E. (2010). Perceiving and responding to challenges in job crafting at different ranks: When proactivity requires adaptivity. *Journal of Organizational Behavior, 31*(2–3), 158–186. https://doi.org/10.1002/job.645

Bindl, U. K., Unsworth, K. L., Gibson, C. B., & Stride, C. B. (2019). Job crafting revisited: Implications of an extended framework for active changes at work. *Journal of Applied Psychology, 104*(5), 605–628. https://doi.org/10.1037/apl0000362

Bruning, P. F., & Campion, M. A. (2018). A role–resource approach–avoidance model of job crafting: A multimethod integration and extension of job crafting theory. *Academy of Management Journal*, *61*(2), 499–522. https://doi.org/10.5465/amj.2015.0604

Carstensen, L. L. (1995). Evidence for a life-span theory of socioemotional selectivity. *Current Directions in Psychological Science*, *4*(5), 151–156. https://doi.org/10.1111/1467-8721.ep11512261

De Bloom, J., Vaziri, H., Tay, L., & Kujanpää, M. (2020). An identity-based integrative needs model of crafting: Crafting within and across life domains. *Journal of Applied Psychology*, *105*(12), 1423–1446. https://doi.org/10.1037/apl0000495

De Lange, A. H., Kooij, D. T. A. M., & Van der Heijden, B. I. J. M. (2015). Human resource management and sustainability at work across the lifespan: An integrative perspective. In D. Truxillo, L. Finkelstein, F. Fraccaroli, & R. Kanfer (Eds.), *Facing the challenges of a multiage workforce: A use-inspired approach: SIOP Frontiers Series* (pp. 50–80). Taylor and Francis/Routledge. https://doi.org/10.4324/9780203776322

Demerouti, E., Bakker, A. B., Nachreiner, F., & Schaufeli, W. B. (2001). The job demands–resources model of burnout. *Journal of Applied Psychology*, *86*(3), 499–512. https://doi.org/10.1037/0021-9010.86.3.499

El Baroudi, S., & Khapova, S. N. (2017). The effects of age on job crafting: Exploring the motivations and behavior of younger and older employees in job crafting. In *Leadership, innovation and entrepreneurship as driving forces of the global economy* (pp. 485–505). Springer, Cham. https://doi.org/10.1007/978-3-319-43434-6_42

Kiss, P., De Meester, M., & Braeckman, L. (2008). Differences between younger and older workers in the need for recovery after work. *International Archives of Occupational and Environmental Health*, *81*(3), 311–320. https://doi.org/10.1007/s00420-007-0215-y

Kooij, D. T. A. M. (2015). Successful aging at work: The active role of employees. *Work, Aging and Retirement*, *1*(4), 309–319. https://doi.org/10.1093/workar/wav018

Kooij, D. T. A. M., De Lange, A. H., Jansen, P. G., Kanfer, R., & Dikkers, J. S. (2011). Age and work-related motives: Results of a meta-analysis. *Journal of Organizational Behavior*, *32*(2), 197–225. https://doi.org/10.1002/job.665

Kooij, D. T. A. M., De Lange, A. H., & Van de Voorde, F. C. (2021). Stimulating job crafting behaviors of older workers: The influence of opportunity-enhancing human resource practices and psychological empowerment. *European Journal of Work and Organizational Psychology*. https://doi.org/10.1080/1359432x.2021.1899161

Kooij, D. T. A. M., Tims, M., & Kanfer, R. (2015). Successful aging at work: The role of job crafting. In P. M. Bal, D. T. A. M. Kooij, & D. M. Rousseau (Eds.), *Aging workers and the employee-employer relationship* (pp. 145–161). Springer, Cham. https://doi.org/10.1007/978-3-319-08007-9_9

Kooij, D. T. A. M., van Woerkom, M., Wilkenloh, J., Dorenbosch, L., & Denissen, J. J. (2017). Job crafting towards strengths and interests: The effects of a job crafting intervention on person–job fit and the role of age. *Journal of Applied Psychology*, *102*(6), 971–981. https://doi.org/10.1037/apl0000194

Kooij, D. T. A. M., Zacher, H., Wang, M., & Heckhausen, J. (2020). Successful aging at work: A process model to guide future research and practice. *Industrial and Organizational Psychology*, *13*(3), 345–365. https://doi.org/10.1017/iop.2020.1

Kuijpers, E., Kooij, D. T. A. M., & van Woerkom, M. (2020). Align your job with yourself: The relationship between a job crafting intervention and work engagement, and the role of workload. *Journal of Occupational Health Psychology*, *25*(1), 1–16. https://doi.org/10.1037/ocp0000175

Lazazzara, A., Tims, M., & De Gennaro, D. (2020). The process of reinventing a job: A meta–synthesis of qualitative job crafting research. *Journal of Vocational Behavior, 116*, 103267. https://doi.org/10.1016/j.jvb.2019.01.001

Lewis, J., Ritchie, J., Ormston, R., & Morrell, G. (2003). Generalising from qualitative research. *Qualitative Research Practice: A Guide for Social Science Students and Researchers, 2*, 347–362.

Lichtenthaler, P. W., & Fischbach, A. (2016). Job crafting and motivation to continue working beyond retirement age. *Career Development International, 21*(5), 477–497. https://doi.org/10.1108/cdi-01-2016-0009

Lichtenthaler, P. W., & Fischbach, A. (2019). A meta-analysis on promotion-and prevention-focused job crafting. *European Journal of Work and Organizational Psychology, 28*(1), 30–50. https://doi.org/10.1080/1359432x.2018.1527767

Lyons, P. (2008). The crafting of jobs and individual differences. *Journal of Business and Psychology, 23*(1), 25–36. https://doi.org/10.1007/s10869-008-9080-2

Nielsen, K., & Abildgaard, J. S. (2012). The development and validation of a job crafting measure for use with blue-collar workers. *Work & Stress, 26*(4), 365–384. https://doi.org/10.1080/02678373.2012.733543

Niessen, C., Weseler, D., & Kostova, P. (2016). When and why do individuals craft their jobs? The role of individual motivation and work characteristics for job crafting. *Human Relations, 69*(6), 1287–1313. https://doi.org/10.1177/0018726715610642

Patton, M. Q. (1990). *Qualitative evaluation and research methods.* Sage Publications.

Petrou, P., Demerouti, E., Peeters, M. C., Schaufeli, W. B., & Hetland, J. (2012). Crafting a job on a daily basis: Contextual correlates and the link to work engagement. *Journal of Organizational Behavior, 33*(8), 1120–1141. https://doi.org/10.1002/job.1783

Rudolph, C. W., Katz, I. M., Lavigne, K. N., & Zacher, H. (2017). Job crafting: A meta-analysis of relationships with individual differences, job characteristics, and work outcomes. *Journal of Vocational Behavior, 102*, 112–138. https://doi.org/10.1016/j.jvb.2017.05.008

Tims, M., Bakker, A. B., & Derks, D. (2012). Development and validation of the job crafting scale. *Journal of Vocational Behavior, 80*(1), 173–186. https://doi.org/10.1016/j.jvb.2011.05.009

Tims, M., Derks, D., & Bakker, A. B. (2016). Job crafting and its relationships with person–job fit and meaningfulness: A three-wave study. *Journal of Vocational Behavior, 92*, 44–53. https://doi.org/10.1016/j.jvb.2015.11.007

Vanbelle, E., Van Den Broeck, A., & De Witte, H. (2017). Job crafting: Autonomy and workload as antecedents and the willingness to continue working until retirement age as a positive outcome. *Psihologia Resurselor Umane, 15*(1), 25–41. https://doi.org/10.24837/pru.2017.1.3

World Health Organization. (1993). *Aging and working capacity: Report of a WHO study group* [Meeting held in Helsinki from 11 to 13 December 1991]. World Health Organization.

Wrzesniewski, A., Berg, J. M., Grant, A. M., Kurkoski, J., & Welle, B. (2012, August). Job crafting in motion: Achieving sustainable gains in happiness and performance. In *Annual Meeting of the Academy of Management.* Boston, MA.

Wrzesniewski, A., & Dutton, J. E. (2001). Crafting a job: Revisioning employees as active crafters of their work. *Academy of Management Review, 26*(2), 179–201. https://doi.org/10.5465/amr.2001.4378011

Wrzesniewski, A., LoBuglio, N., Dutton, J. E., & Berg, J. M. (2013). Job crafting and cultivating positive meaning and identity in work. In *Advances in positive*

organizational psychology. Emerald Group Publishing Limited. https://doi.org/10.1108/
s2046-410x(2013)0000001015

Yeung, D. Y., & Fung, H. H. (2009). Aging and work: How do SOC strategies contribute
to job performance across adulthood? *Psychology and Aging, 24*(4), 927–940. https://
doi.org/10.1037/a0017531

Zacher, H., & Kooij, D. T. A. M. (2017). Aging and proactivity. In S. K. Parker & U. K.
Bindl (Eds.), *Proactivity at work: Making things happen in organizations* (Ch. 10, pp. 258–
294). Routledge.

Zhang, F., & Parker, S. K. (2019). Reorienting job crafting research: A hierarchical structure of job crafting concepts and integrative review. *Journal of Organizational Behavior,
40*(2), 126–146. https://doi.org/10.1002/job.2332

15

AGE AND KNOWLEDGE EXCHANGE

Ability, Motivation, and Opportunities

Laura Dietz, Anne Burmeister and Ulrike Fasbender

Introduction

The challenges of the current demographic workforce development in many countries have been described using terms such as *demographic time bomb* and *pension brain drain*. These terms highlight the potential tension between the increasing importance of knowledge as a valuable resource at work and the increasing demographic risk of the aging of workforces (Strack et al., 2008; see also Chapter 2 for an overview on workforce age trends and projections). Employees build up expertise across their lifespan (Mannucci & Yong, 2018), and large numbers of older and retiring employees pose the risk of valuable knowledge getting lost.

Research has started to examine this phenomenon, addressing it from the perspectives of succession management and knowledge retention (Burmeister & Deller, 2016; Rothwell, 2005), as well as intergenerational learning and relational human resources (HR) management practices that enable knowledge-based interactions between older and younger employees (Gerpott & Fasbender, 2020; Moore & Klein, 2020). Initial evidence suggests that focusing on knowledge retention from older employees and facilitating knowledge exchange between older and younger employees benefits organizations as well as employees (Harvey, 2012). Organizations can safeguard valuable expertise and maintain productivity levels (Strack et al., 2008), and age-diverse employees benefit because these knowledge-based interactions are aligned with their age-specific motivational orientations (i.e., generativity striving for older employees and development striving for younger employees; Gerpott & Fasbender, 2020).

It thus seems timely and worthwhile to provide an overview of research on age and knowledge exchange to summarize how, why, and when employees across the lifespan engage in knowledge exchange. More specifically, we use the ability-motivation-opportunity framework (Appelbaum et al., 2000; Blumberg &

DOI: 10.4324/9781003089674-19

Pringle, 1982) to organize this chapter and to highlight which employees, from an age perspective, have the ability, motivation, and opportunities to exchange knowledge. We include insights capturing knowledge exchange experiences for employees across the lifespan and refer to age-diverse knowledge exchange (i.e., between two colleagues of different ages) to explore the role of knowledge exchange against the backdrop of workforce diversity. In doing so, we draw from lifespan psychological theories about ability (e.g., cognitive aging; Cavanaugh & Blanchard-Fields, 2006), motivation (e.g., socioemotional selectivity theory; Carstensen, 1992), and opportunity (e.g., organizational age norm theory; Lawrence, 1988), and we enrich these theoretical foundations with empirical research evidence (see also Chapter 7 for an integration of lifespan theories).

Age and Knowledge Exchange at Work: Central Concepts

Older and younger employees can engage in a variety of knowledge-related behaviors. *Knowledge exchange* (also called knowledge transfer) consists of two components: Knowledge receiving and knowledge sharing (Wang & Noe, 2010). *Knowledge receiving* (also called knowledge seeking, knowledge acquisition) is defined as employees searching for knowledge from their colleagues. *Knowledge sharing* (also called knowledge providing, knowledge donating) refers to the process of making one's knowledge, skills, and abilities available to others. In contrast, *knowledge hiding* goes beyond the absence of knowledge sharing, describing the deliberate attempt to withhold knowledge requested by others (Connelly et al., 2012). While knowledge can be exchanged at higher levels (e.g., between teams, departments, or organizations; please see Chapter 9 for insights on age at higher organizational levels), we focus on knowledge exchange between coworkers to be able to delineate the role of employee age at the individual level.

Past research has used the terms *age-diverse* and *intergenerational* interchangeably when referring to knowledge exchange between coworkers from different age groups. The conceptual and practical difficulty of disentangling age, period, and cohort effects that has been specified in critical reviews of research on generational differences (e.g., Costanza & Finkelstein, 2015; Rudolph et al., 2020; please also see Chapter 6) has been recognized in research on knowledge exchange in the context of aging and age-diverse workforces. For example, researchers acknowledged that the specification of age differences between younger and older study participants (e.g., 10 or 15 years) is arbitrary but allows for the empirical examination of the phenomenon of interest (e.g., Burmeister, Gerpott, et al., in press; Burmeister, Hirschi, et al., in press; Fasbender & Gerpott, 2021). Researchers concluded that at the heart of both perspectives are the potential differences between older and younger employees, regardless of whether these stem from their chronological age or birth cohort (Schmidt & Muehlfeld, 2017). Following this logic, we include research on both intergenerational and age-diverse knowledge exchange in our review, but we adopt theoretical perspectives that explain why, how, and when employee age rather than birth cohort shapes knowledge exchange.

The Ability-Motivation-Opportunity Framework: A Lens to Analyze Factors That Drive Age-Diverse Knowledge Exchange

According to the ability-motivation-opportunity (AMO) framework, work performance (and related behaviors such as knowledge exchange) has three antecedents: Ability, motivation, and opportunity (Appelbaum et al., 2000; Blumberg & Pringle, 1982). *Ability* reflects the physiological and cognitive factors that enable an individual to perform a task (e.g., information processing speed, expertise). *Motivation* refers to psychological and cognitive factors that influence an individual's willingness to perform a task (e.g., goals, values, emotions). *Opportunity* describes environmental factors that promote or hinder the performance of a task (e.g., tools, norms, policies). The AMO framework has been applied to explain various age-related processes and outcomes at work, such as the extension of working lives (Pak et al., 2019) and age-based knowledge management in the healthcare sector (Profili et al., 2019). We use the AMO framework to synthesize the scattered and interdisciplinary research on antecedents of age-diverse knowledge exchange. Table 15.1 provides a schematic overview of the state of research on age and knowledge exchange structured according to the AMO framework.

Who is Able to Exchange Knowledge?

Cognitive Abilities and Expertise

Theories of cognitive aging specify a decrease in fluid cognitive abilities (i.e., innate information processing capacity, such as problem solving) and an increase in crystallized cognitive abilities (i.e., accumulated knowledge and experience, such as verbal skills) across the lifespan (Ackerman, 2011; Cattell, 1971; Cavanaugh & Blanchard-Fields, 2006). Expertise refers the acquisition of the skill(s) of an expert through practice or experience (Ackerman, 2011) and is associated with older age. While acquiring expertise depends on one's level of fluid cognitive abilities for most domains of expertise (i.e., those in which more knowledge leads to increased performance), crystallized cognitive abilities grow increasingly important when becoming an expert because one's existing knowledge serves as the foundation for new knowledge (P. L. Ackerman, 2011).

Knowledge Receiving

Given that fluid cognitive ability, which is associated with learning, declines steadily after young adulthood, older employees may be faced with issues in

TABLE 15.1 Overview of the State of Research on the Relations Between Knowledge–Related Behaviors Within the AMO Framework and Research Gaps

Knowledge-related behaviors			Ability	Motivation	Opportunity		
			Cognitive abilities and expertise	Motives and goals	Age norms	HR[a] practices and organizational culture	Knowledge management technology
Theoretical frameworks			Cognitive aging theory, theory of expertise	Lifespan development (e.g., socioemotional selectivity theory)	Organizational age norm theory, social identity and self-categorization theories, interactional model of cultural diversity, social exchange theory		
Knowledge Exchange	Knowledge Receiving	O	+/-	-	-	?	o
		Y	+/-	+	+/-	?	o
	Knowledge Sharing	O	+/-	+	+/-	+	o
		Y	+/-	-	-	?	o
	Knowledge Hiding	O	?	?	?	?	?
		Y	?	?	?	?	?

Note: O = older age. Y = younger age. Plus sign (+) = positive relation to respective knowledge-related behavior. Minus sign (–) = negative relation to respective knowledge-related behavior. Plus and minus sign (+/–) = mixed findings regarding relation to respective knowledge-related behavior. Circle (o) = no significant relation to respective knowledge-related behavior. Question mark (?) = insufficient amount of research to adequately assess the research state.
[a] HR = human resource.

receiving knowledge. This is supported by findings showing a negative relationship between age and learning outcomes in trainings for older workers (Kubeck et al., 1996). Moreover, research suggests that to support older worker knowledge receiving, certain conditions such as time flexible learning forms (e.g., self-paced and autonomous learning) need to be in place (Zwick, 2015). Research on expertise paints a mixed picture regarding the reception of knowledge. On the one hand, experts have a body of knowledge to which they can link new information (Ackerman, 2011), which can give them an advantage in knowledge receiving (Grand et al., 2016; Fasbender et al., in press). However, research indicates that the success of knowledge receiving for experts depends on how knowledge is shared. Indeed, the expertise reversal effect describes how additional information can have a positive effect on novices' (i.e., individuals with less expertise) knowledge receiving, as it helps them internalize new knowledge but can hinder experts' knowledge receiving if it contradicts their existing knowledge (Kalyuga et al., 2003). Put differently, while older workers and experts need the right conditions to receive knowledge and learn, younger workers and novices might find it easier to receive knowledge due to their fluid cognitive capabilities.

Knowledge Sharing

In contrast, their increased crystallized cognitive abilities should enable older employees to share their accumulated knowledge and experience with others. Having a large amount of knowledge should also make experts ideal knowledge providers. For instance, being an expert in a domain is linked to knowledge-sharing intentions via the expert's perceived importance of their own contribution (Moser, 2017). Research also showed that older workers are perceived as able to share knowledge (Burmeister, Fasbender, et al., 2018) and that younger workers value their unique and highly contextualized company-specific knowledge, which they gained through experience (Gerpott et al., 2019). However, having a lot of knowledge does not necessarily entail being able to share it with others. On the contrary, research indicates that experts may have to deal with cognitive limitations when it comes to estimating the performance of novices (Hinds, 1999). This is due to the increasing abstraction and automation of experts' knowledge, who therefore struggle to relate to and share knowledge with novices (Hinds & Pfeffer, 2003). In contrast, younger workers and novices might have more difficulties sharing knowledge. While younger workers can share their metacognitive knowledge (e.g., strategies for information search and problem solving) with older workers (Gerpott et al., 2019), they tend to be perceived as less able to share knowledge (Burmeister, Fasbender, et al., 2018). Research thus suggests that older workers are better positioned to share their knowledge with others compared to younger workers and novices.

Knowledge Exchange

Research indicates that an individual's amount of knowledge may not necessarily be relevant to knowledge exchange, but instead nonredundant types of knowledge between younger and older colleagues lay the foundation for age-diverse knowledge exchange (Geeraerts et al., 2016). Accordingly, complementarity in age-based cognitive abilities might be crucial to facilitate knowledge exchange between age-diverse coworkers. Regarding reciprocal knowledge exchange in case of expertise differentials, it is assumed that, within the context of a specific domain of expertise, novices are unable to reciprocate an expert's shared knowledge by sharing knowledge on their own (Moser, 2017). Although novices cannot contribute their own knowledge to the knowledge sharing process, findings suggest that the act of knowledge sharing itself may benefit experts (Darnis & Lafont, 2015). Thus, the interplay of knowledge sharing and knowledge receiving in knowledge exchange with novices may lead to experts being able to view their knowledge from a different, more naïve perspective and connect existing knowledge structures in novel ways. Wilkesmann and Wilkesmann (2011) describe how, in practice, knowledge receiving by novices and knowledge sharing by experts can simultaneously foster routines as well as innovation in organizations.

Conclusion

Theories on cognitive aging and expertise present a mixed picture. Changes in fluid and crystallized cognitive abilities across the lifespan suggest that it becomes more difficult to receive novel knowledge with increasing age. In line with this, research on expertise suggests that domain-specific accumulated knowledge supports the acquisition of new knowledge in the same domain. Accordingly, while younger employees are better able to acquire novel knowledge, they are not yet able to draw on the same body of knowledge as older employees, which may inhibit their understanding of knowledge that is shared with them. Regarding knowledge sharing, older as well as younger employees appear to be able to contribute nonredundant knowledge to knowledge exchanges, while older employees can draw on a greater wealth of knowledge due to their crystallized cognitive abilities. Moreover, despite their accumulated expertise, experts may struggle to effectively share their knowledge with novices.

Who is Motivated to Exchange Knowledge?

Motives and Goals

Lifespan development theories address the developmental challenges and opportunities that individuals encounter throughout their lifespan (Baltes, 1987). Socioemotional selectivity theory (Carstensen, 1992) suggests that, due to changes in perceptions of remaining time (i.e., "time left in life" vs "time since birth"), individuals adjust their motivational orientations across the lifespan. Accordingly, older individuals who perceive their remaining time as constrained prioritize socioemotional goals, such as *generativity goals*, over *developmental goals*, which are prioritized at younger ages. Empirical as well as meta-analytic research supports that the prevalence of generativity goals increases with age, whereas the prevalence of developmental goals declines with age in line with the predictions of socioemotional selectivity theory (Doerwald et al., 2021; Penningroth & Scott, 2012).

Knowledge Receiving

Developmental goals are future-oriented and emphasize professional advancement, for instance through knowledge receiving. Employing a need fulfillment perspective, Burmeister et al. (2020) showed that motivational benefits of receiving knowledge are particularly salient for younger employees as they can fulfill their needs for autonomy, competence, and relatedness. As a result, younger employees are particularly motivated to receive knowledge. Further, younger workers tend to perceive themselves as knowledge receivers (Burmeister, Fasbender, et al., 2018) and prefer job characteristics that are associated with gaining new experiences (e.g., Zaniboni et al., 2013), which often entails knowledge receiving. Similarly, individuals' desire for personal growth, which includes the acquisition of new knowledge, declines with increasing age (Inceoglu et al., 2012), suggesting that younger employees are more motivated to receive knowledge compared to their older counterparts.

Knowledge Sharing

Generativity goals fall into the category of socioemotional goals, which in general are present-oriented and emphasize the employee's prompt emotional gratification. At work, generativity goals reflect an employee's intentions to support younger colleagues, for instance by sharing knowledge (e.g., Kooij et al., 2011). Burmeister et al. (2020) showed that knowledge sharing fulfills older workers' needs for autonomy, competence, and relatedness, as it allows them to act out their need for generative activities in the workplace, apply their existing knowledge, and connect with younger colleagues. As a result, older employees are particularly motivated to share knowledge. In addition, the motivation to share knowledge is positively related to the age of the knowledge sender (Prelog et al., 2019), and older employees tend to perceive themselves as knowledge senders (Burmeister, Fasbender, et al., 2018). Doerwald et al. (2021) also list knowledge sharing among the stereotypical work-related generative behaviors for older employees, suggesting that older employees are more motivated to share knowledge compared to their younger counterparts.

Knowledge Exchange

The simultaneous activation of both developmental and generativity goals might be beneficial for age-diverse knowledge exchange (Gerpott & Fasbender, 2020). For instance, in a case study, Gerpott et al. (2017) established how mutual learning and teaching can be enabled in a formalized, age-diverse training setting. They illustrated how, throughout a multiyear course, older and younger participants became aware of their distinct knowledge resources and exchanged knowledge with each other. The roles of knowledge sender and receiver fluctuated depending on the temporal context within the training and the type of knowledge. Fasbender et al. (in press) investigated the age-specific interplay of knowledge sharing and knowledge receiving at a dyadic level and demonstrated that generativity striving as well as development striving account for knowledge exchange behaviors of older and younger colleagues. Specifically, they found that employees' generativity striving was related to their knowledge sharing, which in turn predicted their colleagues' reception of knowledge. A higher score on development striving additionally predicted knowledge receiving for younger employees.

Conclusion

Lifespan development theories, in particular socioemotional selectivity theory, suggest that employees differ in their focus on developmental goals versus socioemotional goals, such as generativity goals. Specifically, higher age is typically associated with a stronger focus on generativity goals, whereas lower age is associated with a stronger focus on developmental goals. Knowledge sharing can satisfy both developmental and generativity goals, while knowledge receiving is predominantly aligned with developmental goals.

Who has the Opportunity to Exchange Knowledge?

Age Norms

Even if employees are able and motivated to share and receive knowledge, knowledge exchange processes rise and fall with environmental factors facilitating or obstructing knowledge-related behaviors (e.g., Siemsen et al., 2008). In this regard, age-related normative beliefs describing who is perceived as a capable knowledge sender or receiver are a central factor influencing the knowledge exchange opportunities the work environment provides to its employees. In particular, *age norms* are defined as widespread assumptions about the typical age of individuals occupying particular organizational roles (Lawrence, 1988).

Knowledge Receiving

Burmeister, Fasbender et al. (2018) revealed the prevalence of age norms concerning the perceived ability and perceived motivation of one's colleagues. They showed that younger employees were perceived as more capable and motivated to receive knowledge in comparison to their older counterparts. These assumptions also translated to the behavioral level, showing that the age of one's colleague was positively related to one's knowledge receiving and negatively related to one's knowledge sharing. Such normative assumptions are also evident in the mentoring literature, in which younger and less-experienced mentees typically receive knowledge (Russell & Adams, 1997). Even when older employees take on the role of mentees, they do not receive certain types of mentoring that younger mentees receive (i.e., career mentoring; Finkelstein et al., 2003), which may be due to the presumption that older employees do not need such knowledge. Moreover, older employees are stereotypically viewed as resistant to change and as having a lower ability to learn (Ng & Feldman, 2012; Posthuma & Campion, 2009) and therefore receive fewer training opportunities (Lazazzara et al., 2013), despite empirical counterevidence (Ng & Feldman, 2012). Accordingly, from a normative point of view, younger employees are perceived as knowledge recipients.

Knowledge Sharing

In contrast to perceptions on knowledge receiving, Burmeister, Fasbender, et al. (2018) reported that older employees were perceived as less able but more motivated to share knowledge compared to younger employees. As a complement to the role of younger employees as mentees, older and more experienced employees are often assumed to be mentors and thus knowledge senders in the mentoring literature (Russell & Adams, 1997). Furthermore, De Blois and Lagacé (2017) revealed older employees perceive themselves as willing to share their knowledge with younger colleagues and that this perception informs older employees' communication patterns in order to accommodate younger employees. Greller and Stroh (2004) indicated that stereotypical beliefs may act like self-fulfilling prophecies, underlining that, from a normative point of view, older employees are seen as knowledge senders.

Knowledge Exchange

Although we have illustrated the prevalence of age norms in identifying who receives the opportunity to receive and share knowledge, organizations are introducing practices to break through these norms and enable bidirectional knowledge exchange where all employees, regardless of age, can share and receive knowledge. For instance, reverse mentoring, which reverses the roles of mentor and mentee, has been identified as an efficient tool for age-diverse knowledge exchange (Gadomska-Lila, 2020). Further, Satterly et al. (2018) propose intergenerational mentoring, in which the positive aspects of reverse mentoring are embraced while overcoming its hierarchical framework. Intergenerational mentoring focuses on the strengths and skills of all employees, regardless of their age, which are examined against the needs of the workforce and matched accordingly to achieve the best possible fit between knowledge resources and knowledge needs.

Age-Inclusive HR Practices and Organizational Culture

Research suggests that characteristics of the organizational environment such as equal access to training and development and age-independent promotions and the promotion of age-inclusive organizational culture can influence employee behavior (i.e., knowledge exchange) because employees interpret these characteristics as signals of what is expected of them (Boehm et al., 2013). Accordingly, employees within an organization create a collective understanding of how to deal with knowledge in an age-diverse context based on the behavioral guidelines they are exposed to.

Knowledge Receiving

Sammarra et al. (2017) list several different approaches organizations can implement to ensure knowledge retention from older and retiring employees to their younger colleagues. In addition to simply writing down existing knowledge, this includes direct contact arrangements with knowledge recipients such as apprentice programs, job shadowing, coaching, and mentoring.

Knowledge Sharing

Gerpott et al. (2019) proposed that organizations can facilitate knowledge sharing by taking steps to create perceptions of psychological safety (i.e., the feeling that knowledge, thoughts, or ideas can be shared within a safe space without having to fear repercussions for expressing them). Further, they suggest that reducing age discrimination and treating all employees equally, regardless of age, should provide a platform for knowledge sharing. In line with this, Fasbender and Gerpott (2021) uncovered that perceptions of age discrimination hinder older employees' knowledge sharing but that HR development practices targeted at older employees (i.e., HR activities that facilitate the professional development of older employees and support lifelong learning) promote their knowledge sharing.

Knowledge Exchange

The previous examples show that organizations can target knowledge receiving and knowledge sharing behaviors specifically, but scholars suggest that knowledge management-related HR practices should be constructed as "bidirectional learning experiences rather than unidirectional teaching activities" (Sammarra et al., 2017, p. 176). Schmidt and Muehlfeld (2017) argued that job autonomy, leadership characteristics, and organizational culture have positive effects on age-diverse knowledge exchange, while age discrimination culture has negative effects. Since then, research showed that age-diversity climate (i.e., shared perceptions regarding age diversity-related policies, practices, and procedures within an organization; Boehm et al., 2013) and age-diverse knowledge exchange are positively related (Lagacé et al., 2019). Further, age-inclusive HR practices can facilitate age-diverse knowledge exchange via an age-diversity climate (Burmeister, van der Heijden, et al., 2018). In addition, Sammarra et al. (2017) argued that organizations could leverage the motivational shift from extrinsic rewards (e.g., bonuses, praise) to intrinsic rewards (e.g., pleasure from performing a task) that occurs with increasing age by implementing reward systems that create opportunities for older and younger employees alike to share and receive knowledge.

Knowledge Management Technology and Systems

Overall, research suggests that, although age-related differences and preferences regarding the use of knowledge management technology and systems (e.g., corporate wikis, expertise locator systems, electronic collaboration systems) exist, their impact at work may be rather limited. Research on the influence of technology on knowledge exchange is still in its early stages. Yet, more general findings provide evidence for age-related differences regarding the general use of technology, suggesting that younger individuals utilize a wider range of technologies overall, but that age differences in use depend strongly on the technology domain (e.g., older individuals prefer telephones vs. younger individuals prefer cellphones; Olson et al., 2011). Oftentimes, younger individuals are classified as digital natives, whereas older individuals are regarded as digital immigrants, hinting at the age groups' levels of familiarity and comfort with the use of technologies. With respect to the learnability of software systems, Arning et al. (2016) emphasized the increasing importance of considering age-related user-specific requirements to ensure optimal learning conditions for new technologies. Referring specifically to the context of knowledge exchange at work, Widen et al. (2020) suggested that, despite the frequently echoed differences in older and younger employees' attitude toward the use of technology, "dynamics and demands for efficient knowledge sharing rather than age dictate how and when employees use technology for knowledge sharing" (p. 846).

Conclusion

There is a wide variety of prevalent normative beliefs about who is suited to share and receive knowledge at work. Beliefs that discourage certain age groups from sharing or receiving knowledge may be particularly damaging to knowledge exchange processes. One reason for this is that normative beliefs translate into HR practices, such as who gets to participate in work-related trainings or how mentoring programs are implemented. To address this, the literature highlights age-inclusive HR practices, which take into account the needs and abilities of employees of different ages and help to create a positive age-diversity climate as one solution to foster knowledge exchange between younger and older employees. Preliminary findings on the role of technology in creating opportunities for knowledge exchange suggest that the age of the employees involved is of limited importance.

Discussion

In this chapter, we adopted the AMO framework to synthesize the literature on age and knowledge exchange related to the three antecedents of ability, motivation, and opportunity. We found that several arguments in the ability and motivation literature suggest that younger employees are more able and motivated to receive knowledge, while older employees are more able and motivated to share knowledge. Regarding opportunities, younger workers are perceived as knowledge receivers and older workers as knowledge senders, which influences the knowledge sharing process. Organizations can intervene and promote knowledge exchange through age-inclusive HR practices and organizational culture. Table 15.1 presents an overview of the current state of research as we have synthesized it in the chapter and offers a starting point for us to specify directions for future research.

Future Research Directions

Overall, we suggest three directions for future research to move the field forward. First, there is a lack of research on age and knowledge hiding, except for research theorizing on the impact of different types of fear on knowledge hiding (Gerpott & Fasbender, 2020). While the antecedents of knowledge hiding have been explored to some extent (e.g., Anand et al., 2020; Fasbender, 2018), we urge future research to additionally consider an age-based perspective to explore knowledge hiding, because it constitutes behavior that may have serious long-term consequences for knowledge retention in organizations.

Second, we suggest that greater attention should be paid to the influence the three factors in the AMO framework exert on each other. For instance, Nguyen et al. (2019) propose that contextual factors shaping the influence of motivation on knowledge sharing remain unclear and emphasize the value of exploring and contrasting online and physical settings. While we argue earlier that technology does not seem to shape the opportunities for employees of different age groups to exchange knowledge, such technological advancements may have an impact on age-related motivation. For instance, age has been identified as a central moderator of the link between attitude toward technology and work motivation (Elias et al., 2012), suggesting that the components of the AMO framework may exert influences on each other. Thus, we encourage future research to take a closer look at the interplay of ability, motivation, and opportunity to exchange knowledge and how it impacts knowledge exchange behaviors.

Third, future research can complement current research by examining how and when knowledge that is shared by one employee is received and used by another employee. Ability, motivation, and opportunity-related factors of both older and younger employees might influence the more dynamic and relational process of responding to each other's knowledge-related behaviors. For example, older employees may respond better to modest and agreeable younger knowledge seekers, whereas expertise and status may be important signs to guide younger employees in their search for knowledge providers. Moreover, situational factors could also be considered, for instance in comparing how the context in which knowledge exchange takes place (e.g., public vs private situations) influences the effectiveness of knowledge exchange and exploring how the age of knowledge sender and receiver respectively plays into this connection.

Practical Implications

Research on age-related knowledge exchange suggests several approaches that organizations can implement. First, evidence suggests that older and younger employees differ in their ability and motivation to adopt the roles of knowledge sender versus receiver, which is further exacerbated by normative beliefs (Finkelstein et al., 2013). To make optimal use of everyone's knowledge in the organization, regardless of age, organizations need to create awareness and implement practices (e.g., age-inclusive climate, reverse mentoring) to counteract these tendencies (Boehm et al., 2013). For example, organizations could implement trainings to reduce identity-related barriers by focusing on commonalities between different age groups. They could furthermore improve age-diverse employees' knowledge-based understanding by raising awareness for the knowledge of one's colleagues and encouraging them to reflect on their own knowledge (Burmeister, Gerpott, et al., in press).

Second, organizations can use employees' age-related motivations and goals as a cue to guide their knowledge-related behaviors. We have highlighted that the generativity motive associated with knowledge sharing increases with age, while the development motive associated with knowledge receiving declines with age (e.g., Kooij et al., 2011). Considering this as a starting point, organizations can activate older employees' developmental motives to foster knowledge behaviors that are not naturally promoted by age-related motives. In this regard, it may be possible to introduce reward systems that take into account age-related reward preferences concerning sharing and receiving knowledge and thus promote behaviors beyond employees' age-related need for generativity and development (Sammarra et al., 2017). For instance, younger employees could be remunerated with extrinsic rewards (e.g., monetary bonuses) for engaging in knowledge exchange, whereas older employees could receive intrinsic rewards (e.g., framing knowledge reception as a social interaction in line with older employees' stronger focus on socioemotional goals).

References

Ackerman, P. L. (2011). Intelligence and expertise. In R. J. Sternberg & S. B. Kaufman (Eds.), *Cambridge handbooks in psychology: The Cambridge handbook of intelligence* (pp. 847–860). Cambridge University Press. https://doi.org/10.1017/CBO9780511977244.042

Anand, A., Centobelli, P., & Cerchione, R. (2020). Why should I share knowledge with others? A review-based framework on events leading to knowledge hiding. *Journal of Organizational Change Management, 33*(2), 379–399. https://doi.org/10.1108/JOCM-06-2019-0174

Appelbaum, E., Bailey, T., Berg, P., & Kalleberg, A. L. (2000). *Manufacturing advantage: Why high-performance work systems pay off.* Cornell University Press.

Arning, K., Himmel, S., & Ziefle, M. (2016). You can('t) teach an old dog new Ttricks: Analyzing the learnability of manufacturing software systems in older users. In J. Zhou & G. Salvendy (Eds.), *Lecture notes in computer science, Vol. 9755. Human aspects of IT for the aged population: Healthy and active aging: ITAP 2016: Lecture notes in computer science* (Vol. 9755, pp. 277–288). Springer. https://doi.org/10.1007/978-3-319-39949-2_27

Baltes, P. B. (1987). Theoretical propositions of life-span developmental psychology: On the dynamics between growth and decline. *Developmental Psychology, 23*(5), 611–626. https://doi.org/10.1037/0012-1649.23.5.611

Blumberg, M., & Pringle, C. D. (1982). The missing opportunity in organizational research: Some implications for a theory of work performance. *Academy of Management Review, 7*(4), 560–569. https://doi.org/10.5465/amr.1982.4285240

Boehm, S. A., Kunze, F., & Bruch, H. (2013). Spotlight on age-diversity climate: The impact of age-inclusive HR practices on firm-level outcomes. *Personnel Psychology.* https://doi.org/10.1111/peps.12047

Burmeister, A., & Deller, J. (2016). Knowledge retention from older and retiring workers: What do we know, and where do we go from here? *Work, Aging and Retirement, 2*(2), 87–104. https://doi.org/10.1093/workar/waw002

Burmeister, A., Fasbender, U., & Deller, J. (2018). Being perceived as a knowledge sender or knowledge receiver: A multistudy investigation of the effect of age on knowledge transfer. *Journal of Occupational and Organizational Psychology, 91*(3), 518–545. https://doi.org/10.1111/joop.12208

Burmeister, A., Gerpott, F. H., Hirschi, A., Scheibe, S., Pak, K., & Kooij, D. T. A. M. (in press). Reaching the heart or the mind? Test of two theory-based training programs to improve interactions between age-diverse coworkers. *Academy of Management Learning & Education.*

Burmeister, A., Hirschi, A., & Zacher, H. (in press). Explaining age differences in the motivating potential of intergenerational contact at work. *Work, Aging and Retirement.* Advance online publication. https://doi.org/10.1093/workar/waab002

Burmeister, A., van der Heijden, B., Yang, J., & Deller, J. (2018). Knowledge transfer in age-diverse coworker dyads in China and Germany: How and when do age-inclusive human resource practices have an effect? *Human Resource Management Journal, 28*(4), 605–620. https://doi.org/10.1111/1748-8583.12207

Burmeister, A., Wang, M., & Hirschi, A. (2020). Understanding the motivational benefits of knowledge transfer for older and younger workers in age-diverse coworker dyads: An actor-partner interdependence model. *The Journal of Applied Psychology, 105*(7), 748–759. https://doi.org/10.1037/apl0000466

Carstensen, L. L. (1992). Social and emotional patterns in adulthood: Support for socioemotional selectivity theory. *Psychology and Aging, 7*(3), 331–338. https://doi.org/10.1037//0882-7974.7.3.331

Cattell, R. B. (1971). *Abilities: Their structure, growth, and action.* Houghton Mifflin.

Cavanaugh, J. C., & Blanchard-Fields, F. (2006). *Adult development and aging* (5th ed., International student ed.). Wadsworth Thomson Learning. www.loc.gov/catdir/enhancements/fy1409/2005922847-d.html

Connelly, C. E., Zweig, D., Webster, J., & Trougakos, J. P. (2012). Knowledge hiding in organizations. *Journal of Organizational Behavior, 33*(1), 64–88. https://doi.org/10.1002/job.737

Costanza, D. P., & Finkelstein, L. M. (2015). Generationally based differences in the workplace: Is there a there there? *Industrial and Organizational Psychology, 8*(3), 308–323. https://doi.org/10.1017/iop.2015.15

Darnis, F., & Lafont, L. (2015). Cooperative learning and dyadic interactions: Two modes of knowledge construction in socio-constructivist settings for team-sport teaching. *Physical Education and Sport Pedagogy, 20*(5), 459–473. https://doi.org/10.1080/17408989.2013.803528

De Blois, S., & Lagacé, M. (2017). Understanding older Canadian workers' perspectives on age and aging in the context of communication and knowledge transfer. *Canadian Journal of Communication, 42*(4). https://doi.org/10.22230/cjc.2017v42n4a3071

Doerwald, F., Zacher, H., van Yperen, N. W., & Scheibe, S. (2021). Generativity at work: A meta-analysis. *Journal of Vocational Behavior, 125*, 103521. https://doi.org/10.1016/j.jvb.2020.103521

Elias, S. M., Smith, W. L., & Barney, C. E. (2012). Age as a moderator of attitude towards technology in the workplace: Work motivation and overall job satisfaction. *Behaviour & Information Technology, 31*(5), 453–467. https://doi.org/10.1080/0144929X.2010.513419

Fasbender, U. (2018). Knowledge retention from older workers. *Academy of Management Proceedings, 2018*(1), 10229. https://doi.org/10.5465/AMBPP.2018.10229abstract

Fasbender, U., & Gerpott, F. H. (2021). To share or not to share: A social-cognitive internalization model to explain how age discrimination impairs older employees' knowledge sharing with younger colleagues. *European Journal of Work and Organizational Psychology, 30*(1), 125–142. https://doi.org/10.1080/1359432X.2020.1839421

Fasbender, U., Gerpott, F. H., & Unger, D. (2021). Give and take? Knowledge exchange between older and younger employees as a function of generativity and development striving. *Journal of Knowledge Management.* Advance online publication. https://doi.org/10.1108/JKM-11-2020-0856

Finkelstein, L. M., Allen, T. D., & Rhoton, L. A. (2003). An examination of the role of age in mentoring relationships. *Group & Organization Management, 28*(2), 249–281. https://doi.org/10.1177/1059601103028002004

Finkelstein, L. M., Ryan, K. M., & King, E. B. (2013). What do the young (old) people think of me? Content and accuracy of age-based metastereotypes. *European Journal of Work and Organizational Psychology, 22*(6), 633–657. https://doi.org/10.1080/1359432X.2012.673279

Gadomska-Lila, K. (2020). Effectiveness of reverse mentoring in creating intergenerational relationships. *Journal of Organizational Change Management, ahead-of-print* (ahead-of-print), 123. https://doi.org/10.1108/jocm-10-2019-0326

Geeraerts, K., Vanhoof, J., & van den Bossche, P. (2016). Teachers' perceptions of intergenerational knowledge flows. *Teaching and Teacher Education, 56*, 150–161. https://doi.org/10.1016/j.tate.2016.01.024

Gerpott, F. H., & Fasbender, U. (2020). Intergenerational learning in age-diverse meetings: A social comparison perspective. In A. L. Meinecke, J. A. Allen, & N. Lehmann-Willenbrock (Eds.), *Research on managing groups and teams, Vol. 20. Managing meetings in organizations* (pp. 185–206). Emerald Publishing. https://doi.org/10.1108/S1534-085620200000020009

Gerpott, F. H., Lehmann-Willenbrock, N., & Voelpel, S. C. (2017). A phase model of intergenerational learning in organizations. *Academy of Management Learning & Education, 16*(2), 193–216. https://doi.org/10.5465/amle.2015.0185

Gerpott, F. H., Lehmann-Willenbrock, N., Wenzel, R., & Voelpel, S. C. (2021). Age diversity and learning outcomes in organizational training groups: The role of knowledge sharing and psychological safety. *The International Journal of Human Resource Management, 32*(18), 3777–3804. https://doi.org/10.1080/09585192.2019.1640763

Grand, J. A., Braun, M. T., Kuljanin, G., Kozlowski, S. W. J., & Chao, G. T. (2016). The dynamics of team cognition: A process-oriented theory of knowledge emergence in teams. *The Journal of Applied Psychology, 101*(10), 1353–1385. https://doi.org/10.1037/apl0000136

Greller, M. M., & Stroh, L. K. (2004). Making the most of "late-career" for employers and workers themselves. *Organizational Dynamics, 33*(2), 202–214. https://doi.org/10.1016/j.orgdyn.2004.01.007

Harvey, J.-F. (2012). Managing organizational memory with intergenerational knowledge transfer. *Journal of Knowledge Management, 16*(3), 400–417. https://doi.org/10.1108/13673271211238733

Hinds, P. J. (1999). The curse of expertise: The effects of expertise and debiasing methods on prediction of novice performance. *Journal of Experimental Psychology: Applied, 5*(2), 205–221. https://doi.org/10.1037/1076-898X.5.2.205

Hinds, P. J., & Pfeffer, J. (2003). Why organizations don't "know what they know": Cognitive and motivational factors affecting the transfer of expertise. In M. Ackerman, V. Pipek, & V. Wulf (Eds.), *Sharing expertise: Beyond knowledge management* (pp. 3–22). Massachusetts Institute of Technology Press.

Inceoglu, I., Segers, J., & Bartram, D. (2012). Age-related differences in work motivation. *Journal of Occupational and Organizational Psychology, 85*(2), 300–329. https://doi.org/10.1111/j.2044-8325.2011.02035.x

Kalyuga, S., Ayres, P., Chandler, P., & Sweller, J. (2003). The expertise reversal effect. *Educational Psychologist, 38*(1), 23–31. https://doi.org/10.1207/S15326985EP3801_4

Kooij, D. T. A. M., Lange, A. H. de, Jansen, P. G. W., Kanfer, R., & Dikkers, J. S. E. (2011). Age and work-related motives: Results of a meta-analysis. *Journal of Organizational Behavior, 32*(2), 197–225. https://doi.org/10.1002/job.665

Kubeck, J. E., Delp, N. D., Haslett, T. K., & McDaniel, M. A. (1996). Does job-related training performance decline with age? *Psychology and Aging, 11*(1), 92–107. https://doi.org/10.1037/0882-7974.11.1.92

Lagacé, M., van de Beeck, L., & Firzly, N. (2019). Building on intergenerational climate to counter ageism in the workplace? A cross-organizational study. *Journal of Intergenerational Relationships, 17*(2), 201–219. https://doi.org/10.1080/15350770.2018.1535346

Lawrence, B. S. (1988). New wrinkles in the theory of age: Demography, norms, and performance ratings. *Academy of Management Journal, 31*(2), 309–337. https://doi.org/10.5465/256550

Lazazzara, A., Karpinska, K., & Henkens, K. (2013). What factors influence training opportunities for older workers? Three factorial surveys exploring the attitudes of HR professionals. *The International Journal of Human Resource Management, 24*(11), 2154–2172. https://doi.org/10.1080/09585192.2012.725077

Mannucci, P. V., & Yong, K. (2018). The differential impact of knowledge depth and knowledge breadth on creativity over individual careers. *Academy of Management Journal, 61*(5), 1741–1763. https://doi.org/10.5465/amj.2016.0529

Moore, A. L., & Klein, J. D. (2020). Facilitating informal learning at work. *TechTrends, 64*(2), 219–228. https://doi.org/10.1007/s11528-019-00458-3

Moser, K. S. (2017). The influence of feedback and expert status in knowledge sharing dilemmas. *Applied Psychology, 66*(4), 674–709. https://doi.org/10.1111/apps.12105

Ng, T. W. H., & Feldman, D. C. (2012). Evaluating six common stereotypes about older workers with meta-analytical data. *Personnel Psychology, 65*(4), 821–858. https://doi.org/10.1111/peps.12003

Nguyen, T.-M., Nham, T. P., Froese, F. J., & Malik, A. (2019). Motivation and knowledge sharing: A meta-analysis of main and moderating effects. *Journal of Knowledge Management, 23*(5), 998–1016. https://doi.org/10.1108/jkm-01-2019-0029

Olson, K. E., O'Brien, M. A., Rogers, W. A., & Charness, N. (2011). Diffusion of technology: Frequency of use for younger and older adults. *Ageing International, 36*(1), 123–145. https://doi.org/10.1007/s12126-010-9077-9

Pak, K., Kooij, D. T. A. M., Lange, A. H. de, & van Veldhoven, M. J. P. M. (2019). Human resource management and the ability, motivation and opportunity to continue working: A review of quantitative studies. *Human Resource Management Review, 29*(3), 336–352. https://doi.org/10.1016/j.hrmr.2018.07.002

Penningroth, S. L., & Scott, W. D. (2012). Age-related differences in goals: Testing predictions from selection, optimization, and compensation theory and socioemotional selectivity theory. *International Journal of Aging & Human Development, 74*(2), 87–111. https://doi.org/10.2190/AG.74.2.a

Posthuma, R. A., & Campion, M. A. (2009). Age stereotypes in the workplace: Common stereotypes, moderators, and future research directions†. *Journal of Management, 35*(1), 158–188. https://doi.org/10.1177/0149206308318617

Prelog, N., Ismagilova, F. S., & Boštjančič, E. (2019). Which employees are most motivated to share knowledge–the role of age-based differentiation in knowledge-sharing motivation. *Changing Societies & Personalities, 3*(1), 52–67. https://doi.org/10.15826/csp.2019.3.1.060

Profili, S., Sammarra, A., Dandi, R., & Mascia, D. (2019). Clinicians' ability, motivation, and opportunity to acquire and transfer knowledge: An age-driven perspective. *Health Care Management Review, 44*(3), 216–223. https://doi.org/10.1097/hmr.0000000000000187

Rothwell, W. J. (2005). *Effective succession planning: Ensuring leadership continuity and building talent from within* (3rd ed.). AMACOM American Management Association.

Rudolph, C. W., Rauvola, R. S., Costanza, D. P., & Zacher, H. (2020). Generations and generational differences: Debunking myths in organizational science and practice and paving new paths forward. *Journal of Business and Psychology*, 1–23. https://doi.org/10.1007/s10869-020-09715-2

Russell, J. E. A., & Adams, D. M. (1997). The changing nature of mentoring in organizations: An introduction to the special issue on mentoring in organizations. *Journal of Vocational Behavior, 51*(1), 1–14. https://doi.org/10.1006/jvbe.1997.1602

Sammarra, A., Profili, S., Maimone, F., & Gabrielli, G. (2017). Enhancing knowledge sharing in age-diverse organizations: The role of HRM practices. In S. Profili, A. Sammarra, & L. Innocenti (Eds.), *Advanced series in management: Age diversity in the workplace* (Vol. 17, pp. 161–187). Emerald Publishing Limited. https://doi.org/10.1108/s1877-636120170000017009

Satterly, B. A., Cullen, J., & Dyson, D. A. (2018). The intergenerational mentoring model: An alternative to traditional and reverse models of mentoring. *Mentoring & Tutoring: Partnership in Learning, 26*(4), 441–454. https://doi.org/10.1080/13611267.2018.1530172

Schmidt, X., & Muehlfeld, K. (2017). What's so special about intergenerational knowledge transfer? Identifying challenges of intergenerational knowledge transfer. *Mrev Management Revue, 28*(4), 375–411. https://doi.org/10.5771/0935-9915-2017-4-375

Siemsen, E., Roth, A. V., & Balasubramanian, S. (2008). How motivation, opportunity, and ability drive knowledge sharing: The constraining-factor model. *Journal of Operations Management, 26*(3), 426–445. https://doi.org/10.1016/j.jom.2007.09.001

Strack, R., Baier, J., & Fahlander, A. (2008). Managing demographic risk. *Harvard Business Review, 86*(2), 119–128, 138.

Wang, S., & Noe, R. A. (2010). Knowledge sharing: A review and directions for future research. *Human Resource Management Review, 20*(2), 115–131. https://doi.org/10.1016/j.hrmr.2009.10.001

Widen, G., Ahmad, F., Siven, T., & Ivantsova, E. (2020). Understanding generational differences in knowledge sharing. In *Proceedings of the European Conference on Knowledge Management* (pp. 841–849). ACIL, Reading. https://doi.org/10.34190/EKM.20.209

Wilkesmann, M., & Wilkesmann, U. (2011). Knowledge transfer as interaction between experts and novices supported by technology. *VINE, 41*(2), 96–112. https://doi.org/10.1108/03055721111134763

Zaniboni, S., Truxillo, D. M., & Fraccaroli, F. (2013). Differential effects of task variety and skill variety on burnout and turnover intentions for older and younger workers. *European Journal of Work and Organizational Psychology, 22*(3), 306–317. https://doi.org/10.1080/1359432X.2013.782288

Zwick, T. (2015). Training older employees: What is effective? *International Journal of Manpower, 36*(2), 136–150. https://doi.org/10.1108/IJM-09-2012-0138

16

AGE AND MANAGING THE WORK–NONWORK INTERFACE

Gregory R. Thrasher, Boris B. Baltes and
Caitlin A. Demsky

Research shows that factors associated with a healthy work–nonwork interface such as social support, quality of social relationships, and marital satisfaction have a positive effect on various indicators of successful aging such as cognitive functioning (Seeman et al., 2001) and life satisfaction (Gow et al., 2007). The work–nonwork interface has been characterized in several ways within the literature, including work–family conflict, work–life balance, and work–family enrichment. Across these various conceptualizations, a common theme is the powerful effect that the interplay between life domains has on a variety of outcomes for older workers. As the future of work becomes increasingly less structured and decentralized through the necessity for remote and hybrid work, the presence of unstructured schedules, and the fact the workers are remaining in the workforce longer, understanding how older workers can effectively manage the work–nonwork interface in the face of a shifting workforce is especially important (see Chapter 2).

In a broad sense, aging has traditionally been defined as a process of resource gains and resource losses (Baltes, 1997)—with successful aging being a function of how effectively one can engage in strategies to manage this process (see Chapters 1 and 7). As an individual goes through the aging process, work–nonwork roles are often an integral focus of one's development, and resource losses and gains are often naturally described within a work–nonwork context and in a domain-integrated manner (e.g., "I lack the energy to work long hours and now am too tired to watch a movie with my spouse" (loss-integrated)). The natural embeddedness of the aging process and the work–nonwork interface is further reflected in the work–nonwork interface literature, which uses similar concepts to describe the roles of resource gains-losses and resource management. The literature on the work–nonwork interface traditionally has applied a demands–resources approach

DOI: 10.4324/9781003089674-20

to explaining the effects of work–nonwork constructs on various outcomes (e.g., Greenhaus & Beutell, 1985)—suggesting that role conflict results from competing role demands depleting finite domain-specific resources.

Empirically, the literature on age and the work–nonwork interface has applied a demands–resources framework with results suggesting three primary themes. First, as age-related demand and resource shifts occur, the relationship between age and aspects of the work–nonwork interface are characterized by mean-level shifts across the lifespan—with some evidence for a nonlinear inverted-U relationship between age and outcomes such as work–family conflict (Allen & Finkelstein, 2014). Second, the work–nonwork interface of older workers is characterized by unique demands across various domains of life. For example, many older workers belong to the "sandwich generation"—defined as individuals who act as caregivers for both their adult children and an older parent (Griggs et al., 2020). Lastly, as individuals age, they experience developmental shifts in goals, motives, and value hierarchies (e.g., increased priority placed on emotional-focused goals; Carstensen, 1992) that are directly related to how one manages domain-specific resources to maintain balance across the work and life arenas (Thrasher et al., 2016).

The conceptualization of the work–nonwork interface as a function of the balance and conflict of demands and resources has clear value in describing how the different domains of life intersect for older individuals; however, this model assumes that roles are largely separate and competing and that individuals are passive within these larger social structures. More recent models have begun to adopt the idea that, within and across the various domains of life, individuals hold agency over the management of cross-domain resources and the pursuit of cross-domain goals (Hirschi et al., 2019). This agency has been specifically described within the work–nonwork literature as a "whole-life" process of action regulation that characterizes the individual as an active actor within their environment—one that sets goals and creates strategies to create and manage resources from a higher level and integrative whole-life perspective (Hirschi et al., 2019, 2021).

In the current chapter, we aim to address the complexity of age and the work–nonwork interface through the integration of life course and lifespan development perspectives to outline a whole-life course perspective with a focus on how individuals can take agency over their environment to foster a healthy work–nonwork interface into later working life. We do this through three primary goals and subsequent sections. First, we synthesize the current understanding of the theoretical and empirical foundation that supports the need for practitioner attention in the area of age and the work–nonwork interface. Second, as the work–nonwork interface is affected by both micro (individual development) and macro (social structure) factors, we discuss both individual and organizational-level strategies for fostering work–nonwork balance for older workers. Third, we discuss characteristics of the future of work that are especially relevant for the work–nonwork interface of older workers.

A Lifespan–Life Course Perspective on the Work–Life Interface

Research on age and the work–nonwork interface has primarily investigated mean level differences in work–family conflict (defined as an incompatibility of demands across the work and nonwork domains; Greenhaus & Beutell, 1985). Across the literature on age and work–family conflict a theme emerges; (1) work–family conflict is low in the early life-career stages, (2) in middle life-career stages work–family conflict rises, and (3) work–family conflict begins to decline to the lowest level toward later life-end of career stages.

On the surface, this broad summary of work–nonwork lifespan trajectories seems to support a rational view (Shockley et al., 2017) or a role-demand hypothesis of work–family conflict. The rational view of the work–nonwork interface proposes that conflict between domains is a direct reflection of demands and resources spent in each domain (i.e., as time spent in Domain A increases, conflict with the time demands of Domain B will increase). From an aging perspective, the rational view would suggest that, as the demands of life and work change (e.g., children moving out, taking on a challenging leadership role), so does one's perception of their work–family conflict. The rational view of work–family conflict offers a concrete way of understanding how work–nonwork role intersections are dynamic and affected by environmental factors (e.g., hours spent at work, number of children). However, this view is necessary but insufficient for capturing the complex way that work and nonwork domains interact across the lifespan for three primary reasons. First, this approach may lead to the interpretation of older workers' thriving across the work–nonwork domains (i.e., they experience decreasing work–family conflict, so they are doing just fine) by minimizing other factors that play a role in the work–nonwork interface of older workers. Second, the work–nonwork interface can be characterized by several other concepts beyond simply the presence or absence of conflict (e.g., work–life balance, work–life synergy, work–life enrichment). Third, the rational view of the work–nonwork interface—conflict equals hours spent in each domain—ignores the inter- and intraindividual variance in age-related changes in role motives, goals, and attitudes.

Considering empirical and theoretical themes within the work–nonwork interface, we can see that the unique work–nonwork experiences of older workers are a result of both (1) changes in social structures that are inherently part of growing older (e.g., children leaving the house, phased retirement, an increased presence of eldercare demands) and (2) intraindividual lifespan developmental changes that are associated with age (e.g., shifts in goals and motives). These parallel processes call for a framework that includes propositions around how individuals experience lifespan development within a macrolevel social context. This complexity can be addressed through the integration of the life course perspective (Elder, 1975; Mayer, 2009) within a traditional lifespan development framework.

The life course perspective draws on sociology, gerontology, and developmental psychology to describe how individuals change over time as a result of transitions between various social structures or roles (e.g., marriage, employment, parenthood). Regarding the dynamic nature of human development, the life course perspective relies on the primary tenets that: (1) changes occur over long periods, (2) changes occur across multiple domains simultaneously (e.g., work and family), and (3) individual change must be viewed through the lens of collective groups (e.g., the family, the marriage, the work-group; Mayer, 2009). The multidomain, extended-time period, and collective focus of the life course perspective make this approach especially well suited for describing the unique work–life challenges of older workers. Although the life course perspective has traditionally been applied to answer broader sociological questions, the relevance of such an approach has begun to be acknowledged by domains of organizational psychology that are "lifelong" by definition (e.g., life course and careers; Zacher & Froidevaux, 2021).

The life course perspective offers a broad framework for understanding how individuals develop through the various courses of life (e.g., early career, marriage, parenthood, empty nesting, leadership roles, retirement) (Mayer, 2009). It is within this broad framework that the integration of specific developmental psychology theories within a life course perspective can offer concrete implications for the successful management of the work and nonwork domains by older workers. For example, several established lifespan development theories (see Chapter 7), such as socioemotional selectivity theory (SST; Carstensen, 1992), selection, optimization, compensation (SOC; P. B. Baltes & M. M. Baltes, 1990), and the dual-process model of coping (Brandtstädter & Renner, 1990) all make specific propositions about how individuals experience shifts in goals and resource management strategies in the face of dynamic environments. By integrating established lifespan development theories within a broader life course perspective, we can begin to develop a model of age and the work–nonwork interface that addresses one's "whole life course" by incorporating transitions through various high-level social structures alongside changes in domain-specific individual motives, goals, and values.

Research on age and the work–nonwork interface does have a history of acknowledging the larger social structures—or life courses—at play (Allen & Finkelstein, 2014; Gutek et al., 1991). For example, early work–family conflict research acknowledged the importance of integrating a rational view (hours equals conflict) with a role norm perspective to understand gender differences in the work-life interface (Gutek et al., 1991). More recently, this model has been extended to other social structures, with Allen and Finkelstein (2014) highlighting larger social structures of age, gender, couple-hood, and life stage in their examination of work–family trajectories in dual-earner couples. The authors found that, while the trajectory of work–family conflict through life-stages (as defined by child age and presence in the home) is represented by a nonlinear inverted-U, gender norms create differences for men and women within various life stages. Although this body of work acknowledges the power of the life course, it largely assumes that individuals within these life courses are homogenous, are influenced by that life course independently, and are passive within that structure. In reality, although various life courses are influential, individuals are defined by multiple life courses simultaneously (parent, leader, child, spouse) while also experiencing age-related individual shifts in attitudes and motivations that cause them to actively change their environment as they progress through those life courses.

Looking to both theoretical and empirical work that has applied lifespan development theories to questions of age-related changes in work and life outcomes (e.g., Baltes & Heydens-Gahir, 2003; Thrasher et al., 2016), we can see that intraindividual developmental shifts and strategies play an important role in how individuals navigate both work and life demands. For example, Thrasher and colleagues (2016) suggest that, although specific work and life demands are an important factor in work–life conflict, developmental shifts in motives across the lifespan play a key role in how older workers perceive, value, and set goals toward engagement in both work and nonwork domains.

Considering both of these perspectives in unison, we can see the role that age plays in how individuals experience the work–nonwork interface is a complex interplay between both macrolevel social structures (e.g., life-stage, gender, and age norms) and developmental shifts and resource maintenance strategies. In summary, the life course perspective suggests that, by engaging in various social roles, individuals "embed" their own lives into broader existing social structures; however, individuals also maintain agency over their own lives and are not simply passive within larger social structures (Mayer, 2003, 2009). The agency individuals hold over their own lives creates an opportunity for the development of interventions that integrate the life course and lifespan perspectives.

A Whole-Life Course Approach to Work-Life Intervention

Lifespan development theories characterize aging as a process of losses and gains (Baltes, 1997). Throughout this process, individuals who maintain and grow resources through various strategies and environmental circumstances are more likely to age adaptively and successfully (Zacher, 2015). The important role that both macrolevel social structures and microlevel individual strategies play in the maintenance of resources across the work–nonwork interface creates opportunities for interventions that target successful aging across both of these levels. To foster a healthy work–nonwork interface, older workers must not only engage in individual strategies that support prioritized work–nonwork goals but also exist within social structures that support those goals. To address these parallel forces, we next outline strategies and programs, at both the individual and organizational level, that offer practical advice and support toward the development of a healthy work–nonwork interface into later working life.

Individual-Level Strategies

At the core of all lifespan development research is the proposition that to age successfully individuals must manage the resource losses associated with the aging process (Baltes, 1997; Zacher, 2015). Recent theoretical advancements in the work–nonwork literature have highlighted the importance of examining multi-domain demand–resource models from an action-regulation perspective (Hirschi et al., 2019). The action-regulation model specifically states that individuals actively manage their environments to pursue valued goals through a process of resource allocation, adapting current resources, and defining and revising relevant goals over time (Hirschi et al., 2019). The lifespan development literature has long defined the aging process as characterized by both resource gains and losses (Baltes, 1997) and shifting goals and motives (Carstensen, 1992; Thrasher et al., 2016). As such, an action-regulation model of the work–nonwork interface is especially relevant for describing individual strategies that, when deployed, may be especially advantageous for older workers in maintaining a healthy work–nonwork interface. We will now highlight two primary sets of strategies that are specific ways that older workers can take agency over their environments to achieve relevant work–nonwork goals through the management of shifting resources: Selection, optimization, and compensation (SOC) and recovery experiences.

Selection, Optimization, Compensation (SOC)

Selection, optimization, and compensation (SOC) is a life-management strategy that comes from the lifespan developmental literature and focuses on how one successfully manages life changes. SOC was originally developed by P. B. Baltes and M. M. Baltes (1990) to describe the coordinated use of three behaviors (selection, optimization, and compensation) that one uses throughout the aging process in the face of resource loss (Freund & P. B. Baltes, 2002)—see Chapter 7. Broadly, SOC describes strategies that individuals engage in to take agency over both shifting resources and the allocation of those resources to life goals (Heckhausen et al., 2019). By engaging in SOC, older individuals can increase resources, help maintain functioning in the face of challenges, and help regulate a loss in resources. While SOC can be applied to all stages of human development, research suggests that the role that SOC plays in taking control over one's environment makes these strategies especially relevant for older workers as they transition through the later stages of life (e.g., Unson et al., 2013).

SOC has been proposed to apply to domains relevant to both work and nonwork (B. B. Baltes & Dickson, 2001). Specifically, the SOC model provides a framework for understanding how certain individuals handle the conflicting demands of work and nonwork better than others. The strategies (i.e., selection, optimization, and compensation) discussed later are theorized to work together as an ensemble and have generally been positively correlated with one another in previous research (e.g., Freund & P. B. Baltes, 2002). Since the introduction of SOC in the work–nonwork domain, a growing number of studies on SOC at work have shown that the SOC model is a valuable framework for explaining successful coping with resource-related changes at work and at home (Moghimi et al., 2017). A consistent finding within SOC research is that SOC use is especially important in the face of work–nonwork demands (Young et al., 2007). As the future of work shifts and creates unique demands around technology and domain integration, older workers who engage in SOC may be better suited to cope with such novel environments.

Selection gives direction to behavior; thus, the primary focus is on identifying and setting goals. According to the SOC model, selection can be elective or loss-based. Individuals may focus their goals at a desired state based on personal preference or social norms (elective selection). For example, as an individual approaches retirement, they may choose to engage in career opportunities that allow for the flexibility necessary for retirement planning. A person may also reconstruct their goals in the face of a loss of goal-relevant means (loss-based selection). For example, an older worker who has health concerns may reduce their overtime hours to ensure they can have the energy necessary to focus on health goals. Optimization involves acquiring, applying, and refining goal-relevant means. Specifically, optimization refers to *how* one goes about accomplishing a higher level of functioning (Freund & P. B. Baltes, 2002). Individuals using optimization might enhance existing skills, learn new skills, invest their time into a goal, or model successful others. For example, an older worker may engage in mentoring roles to apply their expertise toward achieving generative goals. Compensation is the use of alternative means when specific goal-relevant means are no longer available. More specifically with regard to technology adoption, compensation might involve older workers engaging in training surrounding how to effectively use remote work technologies (e.g., Zoom training).

Research suggests that SOC is an effective strategy for managing work–nonwork conflict. One of the first studies to empirically apply the SOC model to the work and family domain was by B. B. Baltes and Heydens-Gahir (2003). Specifically, this study investigated whether one's use of SOC was related to reduced job and stressors and subsequently lower levels of work–family conflict. Indeed, the study did find that the use of SOC strategies was related to lower levels of work–family conflict as mediated by a reduction in domain-specific stressors. Another study found that SOC strategies are especially effective at reducing stressors for people in demanding situations (Young et al., 2007). For example, the results indicated that the use of family-based SOC strategies seems to be more important for individuals with younger (as opposed to older) children at home. In addition, the study found that the use of SOC strategies in both the work and nonwork domains may be most important for individuals in their midlife, most likely due to the large number of demands faced by individuals during this life stage (Young et al., 2007). Although empirical evidence on the efficacy of SOC use for older workers is somewhat mixed, the importance of SOC for managing decreasing resources in the face of demands suggests that SOC may be especially important for older individuals who face unique demands around eldercare, technology use, decreases in health, and the challenges of retirement.

Recovery Experiences

Much of the discussion surrounding the management of the work–nonwork interface for older workers focuses on specific goal-directed strategies. However, one's ability to grow or recover resources is an equally important part of this process. Hirschi and colleagues (2019) define this strategy within an action-regulation framework as *changing* and highlight the importance of this strategy for "strengthening resources (and) creating new resources" (p. 157). Within the literature on the intersection of work–nonwork resources, the concept of recovery from work presents a specific and empirically supported example of how individuals can actively change their existing resources.

Recovery from work demands refers to a process in which individuals' psychophysiological systems can return to baseline after removing demands (Meijman & Mulder, 1998). Given the importance of managing demands and resources for successful aging, the ability to recover from work demands may be particularly important for employees as they age. Sonnentag and Fritz (2007) identified several recovery experiences that facilitate recovery from work, including psychological detachment, relaxation, mastery experiences, and nonwork control. *Psychological detachment* refers to mentally and physically separating oneself from work (Etzion et al., 1998), while relaxation refers to a low activation state characterized by positive affect. Mastery experiences provide opportunities for learning and growth, and lastly *nonwork control* refers to having autonomy over how nonwork time is spent. Additional recovery experiences have been examined, including social activities, physical exercise, and volunteering (Fritz et al., 2013). Research has largely shown positive effects of recovery experiences on employees' health and well-being, including increased positive mood, vitality, and life satisfaction and decreased burnout, disengagement, and negative mood (Steed et al., 2021). Generally, research identifies positive effects of recovery experiences for employees across the lifespan; however, this is an area that warrants further examination.

Notably, recovery researchers have scarcely focused on the intersection of age and recovery experiences. One recent exception to this found that older teachers appeared to benefit more from nonwork control and mastery experiences in terms of vitality as an outcome than younger teachers, who benefited more from relaxation (Virtanen et al., 2020). However, a small but growing body of research has examined changes in individuals' need for recovery—that is, the need to recover from work-induced fatigue—across the lifespan. More specifically, researchers have noted that it is likely that aging workers may need additional time to recover from work-related stress, given age-related reductions in individuals' ability to maintain homeostasis (Charles, 2010). Further, Kiss et al. (2008) and Mohren et al. (2010) found that older workers experienced a higher need for recovery, although the need for recovery began to decrease in employees after the age of 55. Several explanations for this are possible, including that some employees may have begun the process of downshifting their careers or had already established effective compensation strategies (e.g., SOC) or that those with a higher need for recovery may have already left the workforce or switched careers.

Traditionally, recovery has been viewed through a resource-based lens, in which recovery experiences allow individuals to restore and replenish resources that have been lost due to exposure to work-related demands. Given this view, it is likely that recovery continues to remain important as employees age and seek to maintain an optimal balance of demands and resources (Zacher, 2015). Further, habits around the selection and implementation of recovery experiences that are established early in an individual's career may have implications for long-term well-being and career success, making it important that employees across the lifespan are aware of and able to implement recovery experiences. Engaging in optimal recovery experiences throughout the lifespan can also promote longevity in one's career.

In line with a life course perspective, individuals are embedded in contexts that will inherently influence their ability to successfully recover from work. At an individual level, employees can engage in recovery experiences in a variety of ways, although they may need the support of family members to do so (Park & Fritz, 2015). Psychological detachment can be achieved through maintaining a set work schedule and limiting work-related communication to work hours, while relaxation can be created through a variety of activities, including taking walks, reading, or listening to music. Mastery experiences will vary by individual but provide some level of challenge and an opportunity to learn—these may include hobbies such as sports, learning a new language, or practicing an art form. Lastly, nonwork control can be fostered through family and partner support, allowing the individual to self-select how they spend their nonwork hours. For employees across the lifespan, the availability of nonwork control may vary due to a range of life and family-related obligations, such as childcare earlier in one's career and eldercare responsibilities later in one's career.

Organizational-Level Strategies

The way that individuals manage their resources and exert agency over their work–nonwork interface (e.g., SOC, recovery experiences, etc.) is a primary driver of successful aging. However, the broader social structures within which individuals exist create the framework that allows individuals to take agency over their work–nonwork interface. Organizations that offer their employees the autonomy and support to manage their work–nonwork domains set the stage for workers to effectively navigate the complicated transitions associated with the life course. We focus here on autonomy given through flexible work arrangements and leadership support for work–nonwork balance. See Chapter 18 for a broader discussion of organizational practices.

Flexible Work Arrangements

One of the most widely used organizational initiatives to help workers balance their work and nonwork lives are flexible work arrangements (FWAs). FWAs are generally defined as policies that permit flexibility in terms of "where" work is completed (e.g., flexplace) and/or "when" work is completed (e.g., flextime; Rau & Hyland, 2002). Recent research suggests the flexible work arrangements have age-specific benefits for older workers such as reduced sick day use and higher levels of subjective health (Piszczek & Pimputkar, 2020).

Concerning flextime and/or flexible workweeks (B. B. Baltes et al., 1999), this type of schedule grants employees some level of freedom in deciding what time of day they will arrive at and leave from work. For example, an employee may prefer to work from 7:00 a.m. to 3:00 p.m. one day of the week and from 9:00 a.m. to 5:00 p.m. on another day. Another important characteristic that may vary widely among flexible work schedule arrangements concerns the degree of flexibility in the required number of work hours across days, weeks, or even months. Whichever way flextime may be defined, the key to the benefits is in the increased autonomy individuals are given over the hours in their day. More recently, flexplace arrangements (also referred to as remote work) have become an increasingly ubiquitous part of working life and are likely to define many future workplaces. These types of "schedules" could range from working from home a few days a week to working fully remotely. As the nature of work changes, older workers who can balance their schedules in both time and place are likely to be better suited to engage in the strategies need to manage age-related resource losses.

Overall, research has shown that FWAs are associated with many individual as well as organizational benefits. For example, a meta-analysis of the literature found that flexible work schedules have positive effects on employee productivity, job satisfaction, satisfaction with work schedule, and employee absenteeism (B. B. Baltes et al., 1999). However, this quantitative review also found several moderators of the positive impact of flextime schedules. For example, flextime flexibility (measured by core hours) was found to moderate the positive effects of flexible work schedules. Specifically, the positive effects seem to diminish as the number of core hours becomes smaller. One explanation for this finding is that the positive outcomes expected from a highly flexible schedule may be offset when employees have little overlap at work. This is especially the case if the work being performed is one with a high degree of interdependence between employees. With respect to flexplace work arrangements, the results are mixed in terms of their positive impact on work–family conflict (Allen et al., 2013). This may be because working from home may blur both the psychological and the physical boundaries that exist between work and family (Allen & Shockley, 2009). That being said, flexplace work arrangements may be especially useful for older workers as we discuss later.

Although FWAs are normally considered beneficial for employees of all ages, older workers may experience increased benefits as motivational and social role changes occur across the lifespan. For example, as individuals experience motivational shifts from knowledge-focused to emotion-focused goals in later life (Carstensen, 1992), flexible schedules may allow them to tailor their working hours to fit newly prioritized nonwork goals. Furthermore, older workers are more likely to experience issues related to their health as well as the health of those under their care (Griggs et al., 2020). The increased presence of eldercare responsibilities among older workers leaves many individuals with demands that cannot be addressed by common support systems (e.g., childcare). Flexible schedules offer a way for individuals to manage the institutional demands associated with age in a manner that best fits their situations and preferences. With respect to flexplace arrangements, SST (Carstensen, 1992) would suggest that, as individuals age, flexible work arrangements (e.g., flexspace) would be important, because employees will be focused on maintaining their relationships with a small inner circle of friends and relatives (Zabel & B. B. Baltes, 2015). To this end, having geographical flexibility may be very important for retaining older workers. One well-known program is the CVS Snowbird Program. This particular program allows older employees at numerous different organizational levels to move to a different CVS office location for seasonal employment (The Sloan Center on Aging & Work, 2012). Furthermore, the results of this program suggest that CVS has increased its retention rates of older workers.

Leader Support

As individuals are also embedded within workplaces across their lifespan, leaders can support employees' ability to manage the work–nonwork interface in a variety of ways. Specific leadership behaviors have traditionally been described as family-supportive supervisor behaviors (FSSB; Hammer et al., 2009). FSSBs have the potential to create a resource-rich environment that may be especially beneficial for the management of resource losses experienced by older workers. Considering our discussion of individual work–nonwork strategies discussed in earlier sections of this chapter, leaders who offer work–nonwork support have the potential to amplify strategy success in several ways. For example, leaders send important messages about the importance of recovery through their expectations for employees' availability outside of nonwork hours (Bennett et al., 2016). Leaders must avoid making assumptions about employees' nonwork availability based on their career stage or age (e.g., that older "empty nester" employees may have more bandwidth for work that spills into nonwork hours). Clear organizational policies and norms around the availability and use of vacation time and breaks can further ensure appropriate recovery from work for employees of all ages.

More generally, supportive leaders send a clear message that work–nonwork balance is an important part of the organizational culture. Older workers may experience negative stereotypes associated with lower health and decreased job performance (Ng & Feldman, 2012). To counter these stereotypes, older workers may avoid asking for accommodations that would otherwise buffer resource loss. Leaders who engage in work–nonwork supportive behaviors can destigmatize these actions and foster environments that benefit the dynamic needs of older workers.

Future of Age and the Work–Nonwork Interface

There is little debate that sustaining a healthy work–nonwork interface is beneficial for employees of all ages. However, as the nature of work changes, how older workers manage the various domains of life will need to change as well. Researchers and practitioners interested in understanding the future work–nonwork interface of older workers should pay attention to the following trends; the integration of remote work into normal working lives, the increasing age at which individuals are retiring, and increased engagement in both bridge jobs and the gig economy. Pertaining to remote work, older workers are likely to be faced with increasing stereotypes around their abilities to engage in new technology essential for engaging in remote work. Although there is some evidence that older workers are hesitant to adopt new technologies in the short term (Morris & Venkatesh, 2000), this finding was mediated by factors such as perceived norms and behavioral control. As meta-analytic evidence suggests there no age differences in training participation (Ng & Feldman, 2012), organizations should ensure that employees of all ages are trained and familiar with technical competencies, the value in the use of such technologies, as well norms associated with remote work.

With the growing age of the workforce, employees are not only working longer but are also seeking additional employment via bridge jobs (Garcia et al., 2021). While there is a large body of research on the effects of bridge employment for older workers, the participation of older workers within the gig economy—work that is short-term and contract-based (e.g., Uber)—as a type of bridgework has been much less studied. From a work–nonwork interface perspective, participation in gig work has the potential to offer many of the positive factors discussed in this chapter such as flexible schedules. However, gig work also likely adds several stressors and demands such as inconsistent income and the potential for unpredictable work environments (Ashford et al., 2018). Researchers are encouraged to study not only the effects of gig work on older workers but also how various coping strategies (e.g., SOC/recovery) can play a role in how older workers manage their work–nonwork interface during gig employment.

Based on these trends it is apparent that, as individuals approach their later working life, the factors that influence the work–nonwork interface will become increasingly complex. Researchers and practitioners that acknowledge both the intraindividual developmental shifts and the unique social structures experienced by older workers will be able to foster healthy work–nonwork interactions for their employees well into later working life.

References

Allen, T. D., & Finkelstein, L. M. (2014). Work–family conflict among members of full-time dual-earner couples: An examination of family life stage, gender, and age. *Journal of Occupational Health Psychology*, *19*(3), 376–384. https://doi.org/10.1037/a0036941

Allen, T. D., Johnson, R. C., Kiburz, K. M., & Shockley, K. M. (2013). Work–family conflict and flexible work arrangements: Deconstructing flexibility. *Personnel Psychology*, *66*, 345–376. https://doi.org/10.1111/peps.12012

Allen, T. D., & Shockley, K. (2009). Flexible work arrangements: Help or hype? In R. Crane, & J. Hill (Eds.), *Handbook of families and work: Interdisciplinary perspectives* (pp. 265–284). University Press of America.

Ashford, S. J., Caza, B. B., & Reid, E. M. (2018). From surviving to thriving in the gig economy: A research agenda for individuals in the new world of work. *Research in Organizational Behavior*, *38*, 23–41. https://doi.org/10.1016/j.riob.2018.11.001

Baltes, B. B., Briggs, T. E., Huff, J. W., Wright, J. A., & Neuman, G. A. (1999). Flexible and compressed workweek schedules: A meta-analysis of their effects on work related criteria. *Journal of Applied Psychology*, *84*(4), 496–513. https://doi.org/10.1037/0021-9010.84.4.496

Baltes, B. B., & Dickson, M. W. (2001). Using life-span models in industrial-organizational psychology: The theory of selective optimization with compensation. *Applied Developmental Science*, *5*(1), 51–62. https://doi.org/10.1207/S1532480XADS0501_5

Baltes, B. B., & Heydens-Gahir, H. A. (2003). Reduction of work-family conflict through the use of selection, optimization, and compensation behaviors. *Journal of Applied Psychology*, *88*(6), 1005–1018. https://doi.org/10.1037/0021-9010.88.6.1005

Baltes, P. B. (1997). On the incomplete architecture of human ontogeny: Selection, optimization, and compensation as foundation of developmental theory. *American Psychologist*, *52*(4), 366–380. https://doi.org/10.1037/0003-066X.52.4.366

Baltes, P. B., & Baltes, M. M. (1990). Psychological perspectives on successful aging: The model of selective optimization with compensation. In P. B. Baltes, & M. M. Baltes (Eds.), *Successful aging: Perspectives from the behavioral sciences* (pp. 1–34). Cambridge University Press.

Bennett, A. A., Gabriel, A. S., Calderwood, C., Dahling, J. J., & Trougakos, J. P. (2016). Better together? Examining profiles of employee recovery experiences. *Journal of Applied Psychology*, *101*(12), 1635–1654. http://dx.doi.org/10.1037/apl0000157

Brandtstädter, J., & Renner, G. (1990). Tenacious goal pursuit and flexible goal adjustment: Explication and age-related analysis of assimilative and accommodative strategies of coping. *Psychology and Aging*, *5*(1), 58–67. https://doi.org/10.1037//0882-7974.5.1.58

Carstensen, L. L. (1992). Social and emotional patterns in adulthood: Support for socioemotional selectivity theory. *Psychology and Aging*, *7*(3), 331–338. https://doi.org/10.1037//0882-7974.7.3.331

Charles, S. T. (2010). Strength and vulnerability integration (SAVI): A model of emotional well-being across adulthood. *Psychological Bulletin, 136*, 1068–1091. https://doi.org/10.1037/a0021232

Elder, G. H. (1975). Age differentiation and the life course. *Annual Review of Sociology, 1*, 165–190. https://doi.org/10.1146/annurev.so.01.080175.001121

Etzion, D., Eden, D., & Lapidot, Y. (1998). Relief from job stressors and burnout: Reserve service as a respite. *Journal of Applied Psychology, 83*(4), 577–585. https://doi.org/10.1037/0021-9010.83.4.577

Freund, A. M., & Baltes, P. B. (2002). Life-management strategies of selection, optimization and compensation: Measurement by self-report and construct validity. *Journal of Personality and Social Psychology, 82*(4), 642–662. https://doi.org/10.1037/0022-3514.82.4.642

Fritz, C., Ellis, A. M., Demsky, C. A., Lin, B. C., & Guros, F. (2013). Embracing work breaks: Recovering from work stress. *Organizational Dynamics, 42*(4), 274–280. http://dx.doi.org/10.1016/j.orgdyn.2013.07.005

Garcia, P. R. J. M., Amarnani, R. K., Bordia, P., & Restubog, S. L. D. (2021). When support is unwanted: The role of psychological contract type and perceived organizational support in predicting bridge employment intentions. *Journal of Vocational Behavior, 125*, 103525. https://doi.org/10.1016/j.jvb.2020.103525

Gow, A. J., Pattie, A., Whiteman, M. C., Whalley, L. J., & Deary, I. J. (2007). Social support and successful aging: Investigating the relationships between lifetime cognitive change and life satisfaction. *Journal of Individual Differences, 28*(3), 103–115. https://doi.org/10.1027/1614-0001.28.3.103

Greenhaus, J. H., & Beutell, N. J. (1985). Sources of conflict between work and family roles. *Academy of Management Review, 10*(1), 76–88. https://doi.org/10.2307/258214

Griggs, T. L., Lance, C. E., Thrasher, G., Barnes-Farrell, J., & Baltes, B. (2020). Eldercare and the psychology of work behavior in the twenty-first century. *Journal of Business and Psychology, 35*, 1–8. https://doi.org/10.1007/s10869-019-09630-1

Gutek, B. A., Searle, S., & Klepa, L. (1991). Rational versus gender role explanations for work-family conflict. *Journal of Applied Psychology, 76*(4), 560–568. https://doi.org/10.1037/0021-9010.76.4.560

Hammer, L. B., Kossek, E. E., Yragui, N. L., Bodner, T. E., & Hanson, G. C. (2009). Development and validation of a multidimensional measure of family supportive supervisor behaviors (FSSB). *Journal of Management, 35*(4), 837–856. https://doi.org/10.1177/0149206308328510

Heckhausen, J., Wrosch, C., & Schulz, R. (2019). Agency and motivation in adulthood and old age. *Annual Review of Psychology, 70*, 191–217. https://doi.org/10.1146/annurev-psych-010418-103043

Hirschi, A., Shockley, K. M., & Zacher, H. (2019). Achieving work-family balance: An action regulation model. *Academy of Management Review, 44*(1), 150–171. https://doi.org/10.5465/amr.2016.0409.

Hirschi, A., Zacher, H., & Shockley, K. M. (2021). Whole-life career self-management: A conceptual framework. *Journal of Career Development*. https://doi.org/10.1177/0894845320957729

Kiss, P., De Meester, M., & Braeckman, L. (2008). Differences between younger and older workers in the need for recovery after work. *International Archives of Occupational and Environmental Health, 81*, 311–320. https://doi.org/10.1007/s00420-007-0215-y

Mayer, K. U. (2003). The sociology of the life course and lifespan psychology: Diverging or converging pathways? In U. M. Staudinger & U. Lindenberger (Eds.), *Understanding human development: Dialogues with lifespan psychology* (pp. 463–481). Springer.

Mayer, K. U. (2009). New directions in life course research. *Annual Review of Sociology*, *35*, 413–433. https://doi.org/10.1146/annurev.soc.34.040507.134619

Meijman, T. F., & Mulder, G. (1998). Psychological aspects of workload. In P. J. D. Drenth & H. Theirry (Eds.), *Handbook of work and organizational psychology*, Vol. 2. *Work psychology* (pp. 5–33). Psychology Press.

Moghimi, D., Zacher, H., Scheibe, S., & Van Yperen, N. W. (2017). The selection, optimization, and compensation model in the work context: A systematic review and meta-analysis of two decades of research. *Journal of Organizational Behavior*, *38*(2), 247–275. https://doi.org/10.1002/job.2108

Mohren, D. C. L., Jansen, N. W. H., & Kant, I. J. (2010). Need for recovery from work in relation to age: A prospective cohort study. *International Archives of Occupational and Environmental Health*, *83*, 553–561. https://doi.org/10.1007/s00420-009-0491-9

Morris, M. G., & Venkatesh, V. (2000). Age differences in technology adoption decisions: Implications for a changing work force. *Personnel Psychology*, *53*(2), 375–403.

Ng, T. W., & Feldman, D. C. (2012). Evaluating six common stereotypes about older workers with meta-analytical data. *Personnel Psychology*, *65*(4), 821–858. https://doi.org/10.1111/peps.12003

Park, Y., & Fritz, C. (2015). Spousal recovery support, recovery experiences, and life satisfaction among dual-earner couples. *Journal of Applied Psychology*, *100*(2), 557–566. https://doi.org/10.1037/a0037894

Piszczek, M. M., & Pimputkar, A. S. (2020). Flexible schedules across working lives: Age-specific effects on well-being and work. *Journal of Applied Psychology*. Advance online publication. https://doi.org/10.1037/apl0000844

Rau, B. L., & Hyland, M. M. (2002). Role conflict and flexible work arrangements: The effects on applicant attraction. *Personnel Psychology*, *55*(1), 111–136. https://doi.org/10.1111/j.1744-6570.2002.tb00105.x

Seeman, T. E., Lusignolo, T. M., Albert, M., & Berkman, L. (2001). Social relationships, social support, and patterns of cognitive aging in healthy, high-functioning older adults. *MacArthur Studies of Successful Aging: Health Psychology*, *20*(4), 243–255. https://doi.org/10.1037/0278-6133.20.4.243

Shockley, K. M., Shen, W., DeNunzio, M. M., Arvan, M. L., & Knudsen, E. A. (2017). Disentangling the relationship between gender and work–family conflict: An integration of theoretical perspectives using meta-analytic methods. *Journal of Applied Psychology*, *102*(12), 1601–1635. https://doi.org/10.1037/apl0000246

The Sloan Center on Aging & Work. (2012). *CVS caremark snowbird program*. http://capricorn.bc.edu/agingandwork/database/browse/case_study/24047

Sonnentag, S., & Fritz, C. (2007). The recovery experience questionnaire: Development and validation of a measure for assessing recuperation and unwinding from work. *Journal of Occupational Health Psychology*, *12*(3), 204–221. http://dx.doi.org/10.1037/1076-8998.12.3.204

Steed, L. B., Swider, B. W., Keem, S., & Liu, J. T. (2021). Leaving work at work: A meta-analysis on employee recovery from work. *Journal of Management*, *47*, 867–897. http://doi.org/10.1177/0149206319864153

Thrasher, G. R., Zabel, K., Wynne, K., & Baltes, B. B. (2016). The importance of workplace motives in understanding work–family issues for older workers. *Work, Aging and Retirement*, *2*(1), 1–11. https://doi.org/10.1093/workar/wav021

Unson, C., & Richardson, M. (2013). Insights into the experiences of older workers and change: Through the lens of selection, optimization, and compensation. *The Gerontologist*, *53*(3), 484–494. https://doi.org/10.1093/geront/gns095

Virtanen, A., De Bloom, J., & Kinnunen, U. (2020). Relationships between recovery experiences and well-being among younger and older teachers. *International Archives of Occupational and Environmental Health, 93*, 213–227. https://doi.org/10.1007/s00420-019-01475-8

Young, L. M., Baltes, B. B., & Pratt, A. K. (2007). Using selection, optimization, and compensation to reduce job/family stressors: Effective when it matters. *Journal of Business and Psychology, 21*(4), 511–539. https://doi.org/10.1007/s10869-007-9039-8.

Zabel, K., & Baltes, B. B. (2015). Workplace intervention effectiveness across the lifespan. In L. Finkelstein, D. Truxillo, F. Fraccaroli, & R. Kanfer (Eds.), *Facing the challenges of a multi-age workforce: A use-inspired approach* (pp. 209–229). Routledge.

Zacher, H. (2015). Successful aging at work. *Work, Aging and Retirement, 1*(1), 4–25. https://doi.org/10.1093/workar/wau006

Zacher, H., & Froidevaux, A. (2021). Life stage, lifespan, and life course perspectives on vocational behavior and development: A theoretical framework, review, and research agenda. *Journal of Vocational Behavior, 126*, 103476. https://doi.org/10.1016/j.jvb.2020.103476

17

HEALTHY AGING, ABSENTEEISM, AND PRESENTEEISM

Donald M. Truxillo, Grant M. Brady, David M. Cadiz and Jenn Rineer

As noted throughout this volume, the workforce is aging and becoming more age-diverse, with people working beyond "typical" retirement ages (see Chapter 2). This poses challenges for how to maintain employees' well-being and performance across their working lives, while acknowledging that people may have different needs at different life stages. Two key issues for organizational performance are absenteeism and presenteeism. *Absenteeism*, defined as not being present at the workplace when it is expected (Johns, 2008), is a significant cost for organizations, as is its "flipside", *presenteeism*, or coming to work while ill (Miraglia & Johns, 2016). Not only is absenteeism negatively related to performance (Viswesvaran, 2002), it is also a precursor to other withdrawal behaviors such as turnover (Berry et al., 2012), with significant direct and indirect costs to organizations, teams, and societies (Grinza & Rycx, 2020; Miraglia & Johns, 2021). Although the deleterious effects of presenteeism are less consistently negative (e.g., returning to work while recovering from a noncontagious health issue may not necessarily be a negative event), it can lead to later sickness and absence for the employee as well as for others if a contagious disease (e.g., COVID-19) is involved (Miraglia & Johns, 2016). Moreover, absenteeism and presenteeism that deviate from the norm can be symptoms of not aging successfully at work (Zacher, 2015). That is, absenteeism and presenteeism may serve as barometers for successful aging.

In this chapter, we examine the antecedents of absenteeism and presenteeism and how each is relevant to employees of different ages. We also examine a paradox: Why age, which is associated with declining health, is only weakly associated with absenteeism (see Chapter 5). We conclude with several paths for needed future research.

DOI: 10.4324/9781003089674-21

Absenteeism and Presenteeism: Definitions and Impact

Absenteeism

Absenteeism is a common, foundational behavior studied across disciplines including in the organizational sciences because of its cost to organizations through disrupted work processes and lower productivity (Miraglia & Johns, 2021; Ybema et al., 2010). It may also be an indicator of the early stages of an employee's withdrawal process leading to turnover (Harrison et al., 2006). Absenteeism, whether voluntary (e.g., vacation) or involuntary (e.g., sickness absence), is traditionally defined as not being physically present at work when it is expected (Johns, 2008). However, with recent changes to the nature of work and the fact that those changes have been exacerbated by the COVID-19 pandemic, there are dramatic shifts in how, when, and where work is performed. Thus, the idea of being physically present at work is being challenged and may need to be broadened to also include virtual presence. Although changing conceptualizations of absenteeism will need to be addressed to advance the study of absence behavior, a thorough discussion of changing conceptualizations of absenteeism is beyond the scope of this chapter (see Spreitzer et al., 2017, for a thorough discussion of the changing nature of work). Instead, we will focus on the traditional definition of absenteeism and its relevance to healthy aging.

Presenteeism

Although presenteeism research is in its infancy relative to that of absenteeism, presenteeism research has garnered increased attention over recent decades. *Presenteeism* is most frequently defined in the organizational sciences as attending work while ill. Similar to absenteeism, presenteeism has a negative impact on productivity (Miraglia & Johns, 2016), but it can also have a downstream negative effect on mental and physical health, resulting in future absenteeism (Lu et al., 2013). The COVID-19 pandemic highlighted the relevance of presenteeism in relation to safety concerns about infecting others (Sinclair et al., 2020), and presenteeism can result in exposure to unsafe working conditions due to injuries from errors and distraction (Niven & Ciborowska, 2015). Presenteeism is also an issue in virtual contexts: Some studies suggest that increases in telework have led to increased presenteeism among those working from home (Steidelmüller et al., 2020). However, adding to the complexity of this concept and clouding the waters, presenteeism may reflect some positive factors as well (Johns, 2010). For instance, individuals who see themselves as fully committed to an organization may view attending work while ill as a way of displaying their commitment.

Antecedents of Absenteeism and Presenteeism

Although absenteeism and presenteeism are clearly important, they are complex behaviors that can stem from many causes. Absenteeism's antecedents include individual characteristics like physical and psychological health (Darr & Johns, 2008); work attitudes like job satisfaction (Ybema et al., 2010), job involvement, and organizational commitment (Blau & Boal, 1987); and social and relational factors (which are gaining increased research attention; Miraglia & Johns, 2021) like absence norms (Addae & Johns, 2002) and family-to-work conflict (Johns, 2011). Similar complex antecedents have been identified for presenteeism (Miraglia & Johns, 2016). In the following sections, we describe the antecedents of both variables that are most relevant to aging.

Transition to Retirement

Absenteeism may unfold for different reasons as one transitions to retirement. For example, older workers are generally less likely to engage in absenteeism overall but slightly more likely to engage in sickness-related absenteeism (Ng & Feldman, 2008). Thus, health conditions seem to play a small role in older worker absenteeism, but that is offset by older workers being less likely to engage in absenteeism overall. It may also be that older workers are less absent than working parents, student workers, and those working multiple jobs, all of whom will generally correspond to being younger. This may be partly due to the healthy worker effect, in that the sickest older workers drop out of the workforce completely.

Regarding presenteeism, it seems unlikely that a worker transitioning to retirement would engage in presenteeism because they are more likely to also have financial stability (Beehr et al., 2000) and feel less compelled to come to work when they should not. On the other hand, older workers who want to transition to retirement but cannot may engage in more presenteeism. Thus, there may be several conditional factors that moderate the extent to which life stages or aging influence rates of presenteeism.

Job Type

The requirements of one's job and whether one can meet them are also relevant to the aging workforce (Brady et al., 2020). Employees in jobs with intense demands or requiring full working capacities are likely to experience higher levels of absenteeism, especially if they experience age-related skill and ability losses. This might be found in high-demand occupations, such as manual labor jobs and jobs in which peak performance is frequently required. Even for less physically demanding jobs, people who engage in consistently demanding work may occasionally choose to take a "mental health day."

Regarding presenteeism, Aronsson and colleagues (2000) found that nursing staff and elementary school teachers were among the most likely to engage in presenteeism, whereas traditional office workers (e.g., business professionals) and occupational therapists were least likely to engage in presenteeism. Several explanations could underlie these findings. For example, nurses and teachers are likely exposed to various illnesses (e.g., cold, flu) due to their frequent contact with sick patients or children. However, being absent during each period of illness may prove problematic for these employees, and thus presenteeism may be par for the course in these professions. Other jobs (e.g., occupational therapists who work with vulnerable people such as cancer patients) would lend themselves better to reduced presenteeism—particularly self-reported presenteeism.

Leadership

Workplace cultures shape employee experiences, and leaders play a critical role in shaping those cultures. This is true for workers of all ages. In terms of absenteeism and presenteeism, research has found that cultures for absenteeism and presenteeism are based on experiences and norms in the workplace (Ruhle & Süß, 2020). One way in which leaders influence cultures is through role modeling. Supervisors who encourage taking personal time off for recovery and taking care of oneself may have greater absenteeism utilization rates on their teams but have lower rates of presenteeism. In contrast, supervisors who more strictly enforce attendance policies may have lower absenteeism rates in the short term but higher rates of presenteeism.

Bierla and colleagues (2011) found that manager behaviors influence rates of presenteeism. For example, supervisors may communicate to employees that absences are viewed as "illegitimate" and therefore employees ought to "tough it out" and come to work despite being ill. In the short term, fostering presenteeism may facilitate supervisors meeting performance goals. However, fostering a culture in which absences are punished and presenteeism is increased would seem likely to lead to the spread of illness (e.g., cold, flu) and generally lead to lower employee satisfaction and worse long-term employee and organizational outcomes. Bierla et al. found that age was positively related to presenteeism, perhaps because older workers are more afraid to lose their current job, they want to appear productive, or always being at work is a source of pride and honor for them.

Health

An individual's health is among the most consequential factors for understanding absenteeism and presenteeism. It is also key to successful aging, as individuals tend to accumulate health-related issues over time (e.g., increased blood pressure). In fact, measures of absenteeism often include items such as "hours of work missed due to illness" (Leigh, 1986). Such practices highlight the intertwined nature of health and absenteeism. In their meta-analytic review, Miraglia and Johns (2016) found that healthier workers tend to have lower rates of absenteeism. Although the links between health and absenteeism are at times embedded in the specific measure of absenteeism, researchers have proposed broader definitions of absenteeism, such as failure to report to scheduled work (Johns, 2002) and differentiating voluntary vs involuntary absences. Darr and Johns (2008) found that both physical and psychological illness symptoms influenced absenteeism, and this relationship was found for both voluntary and involuntary absenteeism.

Presenteeism may occur from acute illness (e.g., cold, flu) or from more long-term challenges (e.g., arthritis; Schultz & Edington, 2007). In both cases, working while facing these health challenges may lead to reduced performance. It is also likely to hinder one's recovery, rather than taking time off to recover. Although presenteeism may be avoidable in many cases, it may be difficult to avoid for individuals facing persistent health challenges. In their review, Schultz and Edington found that specific health conditions (e.g., arthritis, allergies) were related to increased presenteeism, and Miraglia and Johns (2016) found that poor health was an antecedent to presenteeism.

Work Ability

Work ability refers to an individual's ability to meet the demands of their job and generally declines with age. Work ability is also an antecedent of absenteeism (Brady et al., 2020; Cadiz et al., 2020; McGonagle et al., 2015). For individuals with low work ability, more time for recovery following work may be needed, and simply coming to work may become increasingly difficult if low levels of work ability persist. Thus, low work ability could lead to absenteeism, or if workers feel compelled to come to work anyway, presenteeism, as we discuss later. For workers in occupations with high levels of intensive, draining demands (e.g., manual labor, nursing, high-stress office occupations), contending with low work ability may prove particularly problematic. On the other hand, employees with high levels of work ability would presumably have little reason to *need* to take sick days or have unplanned absences due to their work capacities. Of course, they may still need to take time off or engage in presenteeism for other reasons, such as for transient health-related illnesses.

Work ability's relationship with presenteeism is less clear as fewer studies have investigated an empirical link between presenteeism and work ability. It is possible that workers with lower work ability feel compelled to work due to potential job insecurity fears, and this may be particularly stressful to aging workers not financially able to retire. In addition, low work ability could serve as a catalyst to experiencing job insecurity, such that those feeling unable to meet the demands of their job—and therefore performing poorly—may also question the security of their job. This is consistent with Miraglia and Johns' (2016) finding that job insecurity is positively related to presenteeism. However, it is also likely that low levels of work ability lead employees to withdraw from the workplace more directly, as work ability is negatively related to absenteeism (Brady et al., 2020; Cadiz et al., 2019; McGonagle et al., 2015). More research is needed to investigate this complex and little-understood relationship among age, work ability, job insecurity, absenteeism, and presenteeism.

Job Attitudes

Not surprisingly, job attitudes such as satisfaction and engagement have been examined for the relationship with absenteeism and presenteeism (e.g., Miraglia & Johns, 2016; Ybema et al., 2010). This is particularly so for absenteeism, and job attitudes have generally been found to relate to absenteeism as a type of withdrawal behavior, such that poor job attitudes are related to increased absenteeism (Miraglia & Johns, 2021). The relationship is more complicated for presenteeism, as more positive job attitudes seem to be associated with greater presenteeism. These relationships with job attitudes are important considerations when thinking about age differences in absenteeism and presenteeism, especially given the increased positivity of job attitudes among older people (Ng & Feldman, 2010). For example, older workers' tendency to have more positive job attitudes may partially explain why absenteeism seems to decrease with age.

The Intersection of Absenteeism, Presenteeism, and Age

Absenteeism

Absenteeism is an important behavior to consider in the context of an aging workforce and healthy aging, as absenteeism may vary by age in terms of levels of absence, types (e.g., voluntary, involuntary), and antecedents. However, the current literature provides more questions than answers. For instance, in their meta-analysis, Ng and Feldman (2008) found a significant negative relationship between chronological age and absenteeism (r = -.26). However, why this relationship exists remains an open question. For example, Ng and Feldman's (2013c) meta-analysis found that older workers self-report fewer physical and mental health issues compared to actual clinical measures of these variables, suggesting that actual health conditions may be less important than perceived health for absenteeism. Alternatively, workers may feel their health is great—relative to others their age. In addition, arguably, lower absenteeism among older workers could reflect a climate/culture of successful aging. However, this could miss some of the causes for low absenteeism among older workers: They may not feel their job is secure, perhaps even leading to presenteeism.

Miraglia and Johns (2021) identify six categories of social and relational work and nonwork factors that lead to absenteeism and the paths through which they operate. The social and relational factors include characteristics of the organization, occupation, family, community, and nation or society. The paths through which they affect individual absenteeism include *ethics* (the influence of moral obligation and social responsibility on work ethic and absenteeism), *emotions* (the influence of emotional regulation and reactions on absenteeism), *attitudes* (the impact of job attitudes on absenteeism), *resources* (the influence of available resources on absenteeism), *economic exchange* (cognitive and rational assessment of one's absence compared to others), and *attendance norms* (shared perceptions of the legitimacy of absence). While Miraglia and Johns' (2021) model recognizes the demographic influence of gender, it does not consider age. However, each of these pathways could theoretically align with lifespan development theory (see Chapter 7). For example, the attitudinal and emotional paths could be influenced by the gains in positive affectivity and emotion regulation observed throughout the lifespan, resulting in the possibility that older workers would be absent less whereas younger workers may be absent more.

Presenteeism

A meta-analysis (Miraglia & Johns, 2016) shed light on antecedents and outcomes of presenteeism that could be relevant to different age groups, finding that older employees were slightly less likely to display presenteeism than younger employees ($\rho = -.03$). However, there was no explanation as to why this might be the case. Here we highlight some of the findings from Miraglia and Johns' (2016) study and specifically how age could influence this relationship. They found that that general health is negatively related to presenteeism, and depression is positively related to presenteeism. These relationships could be influenced by age because physical health generally declines with age while mental health generally improves (Ng & Feldman, 2013b). In terms of contextual influences on presenteeism, Miraglia and Johns observed that restrictive absenteeism policies were positively related to presenteeism, but ease of replacement and job insecurity were significantly related with lower presenteeism. In other words, when people felt like their job would be in jeopardy if they were absent, they were more likely to attend work while ill. Age could influence thoughts of job insecurity and ease of replacement given the difficulty older workers experience when job searching (Wanberg et al., 2016). Emotional exhaustion and felt stress were also significantly and positively correlated with presenteeism. Research supports that emotion regulation management increases with age (Scheibe et al., 2021), meaning that the relationship between presenteeism and exhaustion and stress could be moderated by age. Relational demands including discrimination, harassment, and work–family conflict were positively related to presenteeism. Age could influence the relationship between these demands and presenteeism because these relational demands could fluctuate throughout the lifespan. Finally, Miraglia and Johns observed a positive relationship between presenteeism and job attitudes including satisfaction, commitment, and engagement. Given that Ng and Feldman (2010) found a positive relationship between age and job attitudes, age could potentially enhance the relationship between job attitudes and presenteeism.

On the surface, the meta-analytical finding of a small negative relationship between age and presenteeism implies that age does not play a strong role in presenteeism. However, earlier we highlighted several areas where age could moderate the relationships between established antecedents and presenteeism to either enhance or reduce the likelihood of presenteeism. For instance, we would expect that the relationship between job insecurity and presenteeism could be enhanced by age because an older worker may perceive difficulty in finding reemployment.

A limitation of the presenteeism literature is that most studies are not longitudinal, which means that there could be fluctuations in presenteeism throughout the lifespan. For instance, socioemotional selectivity theory (Carstensen et al., 1999) argues for the increasing importance of relationships throughout the lifespan, which could result in an increasing motivation not to be absent in order to avoid letting down coworkers; therefore, a worker may attend work even when they should not. Finally, although the relationship between absenteeism and presenteeism could both be influenced by life stage or age, the attendance behavior literature rarely examines absenteeism and presenteeism together (Ruhle & Süß, 2020).

The Paradox: Why Age is Weakly Related to Workers' Self-Reported Health (and also Absenteeism and Presenteeism)

One of the most pervasive stereotypes about older workers is that they are less healthy than younger workers (Ng & Feldman, 2012). Yet meta-analyses (Ng & Feldman, 2012, 2013b) suggest that age was either weakly, negatively related or not related to most self-rated health indicators (depression, poor mental health symptoms, psychosomatic complaints, and poor subjective overall health). Age was only found to relate to physical health problems for two indicators: Heightened blood pressure and cholesterol. These weak relationships with age and self-rated health are important for better understanding the relation between age and absenteeism and presenteeism. Below we describe some reasons why workers' self-rated health generally does not appear to change with age.

Age-Related Motivation and Adaptive Strategies

First, it may be that the strategies older workers use to adapt as they age actually help to mitigate the losses associated with aging (see Chapter 7.) Older workers use various selection, optimization, and compensation strategies to cope with changes in their physical and mental health as they age (P. B. Baltes & M. M. Baltes, 1990). *Selection* refers to a person's identification of their most important goals and their choice to focus efforts on those goals. *Optimization* refers to efforts to strengthen the skills and capacities needed to achieve those goals. Finally, *compensation* refers to the utilization of alternate resources (such as technology or other supports) to sustain performance when previously used strategies are no longer effective. Using these strategies, most older workers are able to adapt to remain in the workforce until normal retirement age, after which the likelihood of developing major health issues significantly increases (Ng & Feldman, 2013a).

In addition, socioemotional selectivity theory (Carstentsen et al., 1999) can help explain why older workers on the whole show some declines in physical health—but not mental health—compared to younger workers, thus affecting absenteeism and turnover in unexpected ways. According to this theory, people's perception of time drives goal selection, and emotion-related goals are prioritized when time is perceived as limited. Empirical research has repeatedly found support for this theory. In a recent example, a daily diary study based on socioemotional selectivity and person–job fit theories, Dello Russo and colleagues (2021) showed that age is significantly and positively related to positive emotions and task crafting. Relatedly, in a meta-analysis on the antecedents and outcomes of occupational future time perspective, Rudolph and colleagues (2018) found that those who maintain favorable perceptions of their occupational future seem to be more likely to stay engaged and healthy and to perform well at work. The pursuit of goals and activities that help to maintain optimism and positive affect—often associated with aging—can thus have a positive effect on health—particularly mental health.

Variability Within Age Cohorts

Older workers are not a homogeneous group; there is great variability between individuals in terms of their health and the factors that affect it. For example, a study of older workers by Cho and Chen (2018) examining five waves of longitudinal data from the Health and Retirement Study found that work-to-family conflict was related to higher comorbidity of health problems and greater disability over time, controlling for other known predictors of health. A study of older workers in the Netherlands by Damman and Henkens (2020) showed gender differences in perceived work flexibility, which directly impacts work-family conflict, such that lower work flexibility increases work-family conflict. They found that women on average perceive that they have less workplace flexibility than men in terms of both work schedule and work location (see Chapter 4). This study showed that older women are negatively affected by lack of job flexibility, which was determined by their level of education and the types of jobs they tend to occupy.

Job Quality

Indeed, newer research is beginning to show the effects of job quality on the physical and mental health of older workers. A study by Henseke (2018), which analyzed data from the Survey of Health, Ageing and Retirement in Europe, showed that inequities in health correlate with inequities in job quality as measured across three domains: Intrinsic job quality, job insecurity, and earnings, suggesting protective effects of better jobs on musculoskeletal disorders, mental health, and general health. In this study, job quality was conceptualized comprehensively including working conditions, job characteristics, opportunity to develop new skills, discretion over how to do the work, support, physical work demands, time pressure (Karasek et al., 1998), an effort-reward measure, supplementary data on earnings, occupation, industry, and employment contract type. Importantly, Henseke (2018) showed that there is no indication that negative health effects are permanent or cumulative but that recovery from work-related health problems is possible. Therefore, if workers have the supports and resources to recover from work-related health problems, they can stay in the workforce longer, rather than resorting to retirement or disability. However, lower-wage workers and those in blue-collar jobs are less likely to have access to such resources. Indeed, studies have shown that workers in blue-collar jobs experience more rapid deterioration to their physical health in early old age as compared to workers in professional and managerial jobs (Chandola et al., 2007). Although the organizational sciences have become more inclusive in recent years in terms of different job types, the traditional focus on professional work populations may be one of the reasons that the extant research shows such weak relationships between worker health and age, and this relationship might be greater in more physically demanding jobs.

Social Desirability Bias

In addition to the possible explanations described earlier, it is possible that clinical—but not self-reported—indicators of health show slight declines with age because of social desirability bias and other types of measurement-related bias. Older workers may not feel comfortable honestly reporting health-related issues on a survey because of the stereotype that older workers have poor health and discrimination that can occur because of these stereotypes. In addition, previous research has shown that many different types of measures are used in the self-reporting of health indicators. Lindeboom and Kerkhofs (2009) noted that general health measures (that do not ask about work-related health specifically) are often used in research about the association between health and work status. The use of these "noisy indicators" of health in labor supply and retirement models will generally lead to an underestimate of the effects of health on work.

Inaccurate Assumptions about Age-Related Changes

As noted by Ng and Feldman (2012), negative stereotypes about older people are often based on perceptions of the health of very old people (i.e., those well past retirement). Workers who are still actively employed may not yet be experiencing as many of these age-related health declines, and thus there could be relatively weak age-related effects on absenteeism and presenteeism. Accordingly, Ng and Feldman (2013b) note the distinction between "older adults" and "older workers"; with the former usually referring to people in the general population who are over age 65 or 70. By contrast, the term "older workers" often refers to workers over 40 (perhaps due to age protection legislation in the United States), at least in the organizational sciences literature. This is often used as the cutoff because the full-time active workforce is typically those age 18–65, and 40 is near the midpoint of that range. Given that many people experience relatively good health until after retirement, it is not surprising that "older workers" (between age 40 and retirement age) do not show notable declines in health.

Workforce Withdrawal of Those with Poor Health or Low Work Ability

A key issue that may explain this paradox—and that challenges our ability to detect the relations among age, absenteeism, and presenteeism—is the fact that many of our current datasets are missing a key population: Older people who have already quit working due to poor health and poor work ability. Put differently, many individuals who are the least successful at aging at work (Zacher, 2015) have dropped out of many of our samples. This gap makes it difficult to understand the true role of age. For absenteeism, it may explain why older workers have been observed to have better (or at least as good) attendance than their younger counterparts (Ng & Feldman, 2008) and why older workers, who "ought" to report greater sicknesses appear not to (Ng & Feldman, 2013c). For presenteeism, this gap makes it difficult to understand the meaning of "coming to work while ill" for older workers, if many of the older employees with illnesses that could affect their capacity to work have already dropped out of the sample.

Looking to the Future

As shown throughout this chapter, there are myriad causes of absenteeism and presenteeism. Absenteeism and presenteeism can be indicative of healthy aging— or not, depending on other circumstances. For instance, an older worker may exhibit presenteeism because they are experiencing job insecurity, or it may be a sign that they are highly engaged and generally enjoy their work.

For this reason, we begin by noting that there are great differences among older workers, in what causes absenteeism and presenteeism among older workers, and in what absenteeism and presenteeism even mean for them (e.g., whether it is a positive or negative symptom). In other words, given the paucity of absenteeism and presenteeism research on older workers specifically, it would be hasty to make conclusions about absenteeism and presenteeism among older workers, much less to prescribe specific interventions for different age groups. Thus, our focus in this section is the types of research we need to better understand the implications of absenteeism and presenteeism processes for healthy aging.

Are There Reasons for Absenteeism Particular to Older Workers?

An overemphasis on health as a cause for older worker absenteeism distracts from the true causes for low absenteeism among older workers. Future research should investigate different pathways by which age might affect absenteeism. For instance, Miraglia and Johns (2021) identify five work and nonwork sources of absence behaviors. Work factors include the organization (e.g., climate, culture, support conflict) and the occupation (e.g., expectations about attendance, social demands). Nonwork factors include the family (e.g., work-family interference), the community (e.g., engagement and embeddedness), and the nation/society (e.g., culture). In turn, these multiple factors lead to six causal pathways (ethics, emotions, attitudes, resources, economics, and attendance norms) that can each differentially affect an individual's likelihood of absence. This model implies that many different factors may be operating at the same time within an individual—separately or in concert—to affect their absenteeism, both positively and negatively. These may operate at both a single time point and over time. Such a multifaceted approach to understanding absenteeism is needed to gain traction for what absenteeism means for a given older person (e.g., is it good or bad?) and what should have been done to prevent it (if anything). Similar systematic approaches should be used to investigate the antecedents of presenteeism.

Explicit Integration of Aging and Lifespan Development into Absenteeism and Presenteeism Research

Like many areas of the organizational sciences, the absenteeism and presenteeism literature has largely ignored age as a variable. This is unfortunate, as the aging literature could provide greater depth to this area of study, perhaps identifying underlying processes and suggesting interventions for workers of all ages (see Chapters 11 and 18). For example, the increase in positive affectivity as well as gains in emotional regulation across the lifespan could explain why older workers are absent less and may suggest similar processes among workers of all ages. Similarly, lifespan development theories, which suggest processes such as focusing on social relationships, gains or losses, and compensating for weaknesses, could be used to explain absenteeism and presenteeism not only among older workers but younger workers as well (see Chapter 7). Thus, we call for an explicit integration of aging into the absenteeism and presenteeism literatures.

More Specific/Nuanced Definitions of Absenteeism and Presenteeism

Much of our approach in this chapter has been to look at the downsides of absenteeism and presenteeism given their identified costs to organizations. However, one challenge in these literatures has been a lack of clear definitions of absenteeism and presenteeism, thus hindering our ability to identify their antecedents. Presenteeism is a good example: While coming to work sick with an infectious illness is bad for the employee and for their colleagues and may be a sign of job insecurity, it may also be a sign of employee engagement (albeit misguided). Additionally, depending on the severity and type of illness, engaging in presenteeism could be beneficial, provided the workplace is a positive and supportive one. Similarly, absenteeism may support the recovery process whereby taking time off work, even to simply destress, may facilitate the worker returning to optimal well-being and productivity more quickly. Our point is that it is critical to differentiate these different types of absenteeism (e.g., sickness absence; leave use; simply not showing up) and presenteeism (e.g., based on fear versus enthusiasm for work), as well as their antecedents and outcomes and the different motivations for each. Doing so will help to better explain absenteeism and presenteeism across the lifespan.

A Work Ability Lens Applied to Older Workers' Absenteeism and Presenteeism

Work ability may be a useful lens for examining absenteeism and presenteeism in the late career, especially for workers in highly demanding jobs. While work ability's relationship with absenteeism is fairly clear (Brady et al., 2020), its relationship with presenteeism is less so but has potential for illuminating the presenteeism process. For example, some older employees with lower work ability may feel the need to come to work due to job insecurity. Or low work ability may actually lead to the experience of job insecurity and thus to presenteeism. In short, more research is needed to understand the role of work ability in absenteeism and presenteeism behaviors.

Longitudinal Research Focused on Within-Person Changes Over Time

A number of issues hinder the current literatures on absenteeism and presenteeism: Studies are typically cross-sectional; not focused on how processes unfold within individuals; do not address how absenteeism and presenteeism result for different workers for different reasons; and ignore older employees who have completely quit working due to age-related illness. A shift to longitudinal research, including within-person designs, would address many of these issues (see Chapter 10). For example, such research might identify different trajectories of absenteeism and presenteeism for different workers, at different points in their work lives, depending on personal (e.g., individual differences), work (e.g., job type), life (e.g., family), organizational (e.g., attendance policies), and cultural (e.g., norms about working) circumstances. Similarly, increased absenteeism late in the work life could be a sign of impending disability and retirement if it is due to poor health. On the other hand, for other people it could indicate a developing focus outside of work such as new hobbies or family. Similarly, presenteeism among older workers may indicate job insecurity, or it could indicate work engagement and work-related social connections. Such research is necessary to understand the processes by which age relates to absenteeism and presenteeism and what workers, organizations, and societies can do to address them.

How Do Absenteeism and Presenteeism Relate to Each Other?

Finally, attendance research is limited in its examination of absenteeism and presenteeism together (Ruhle & Süß, 2020). However, there may be a dynamic relationship between absenteeism and presenteeism that could be influenced by one's phase in the lifespan. This issue is particularly important to understanding absenteeism and presenteeism among older workers. For example, does presenteeism lead to increased sickness and absenteeism among older workers more than their younger counterparts?

Conclusion

Absenteeism and presenteeism are two key organizational behaviors with negative consequences for workers, organizations, and society. However, the research on these two variables is complex and multifaceted, and few studies have focused explicitly on their implications for older workers. We call for increased research that examines the antecedents and implications of absenteeism and presenteeism for late-career employees to enrich the absenteeism and presenteeism literatures more broadly and to develop workplace interventions and policies for workers across the lifespan.

References

Addae, H. M., & Johns, G. (2002). National culture and perceptions of absence legitimacy. In M. Koslowsky & M. Krausz (Eds.), *Voluntary employee withdrawal and inattendance: A current perspective* (pp. 21–51). Kluwer/Plenum.

Aronsson, G., Gustafsson, K., & Dallner, M. (2000). Sick but yet at work: An empirical study of sickness presenteeism. *Journal of Epidemiology & Community Health, 54*(7), 502–509. https://doi.org/10.1136/jech.54.7.502

Baltes, P. B., & Baltes, M. M. (Eds.). (1990). *Successful aging: Perspectives from the behavioral sciences.* Cambridge University Press.

Beehr, T. A., Glazer, S., Nielson, N. L., & Farmer, S. J. (2000). Work and nonwork predictors of employees' retirement ages. *Journal of Vocational Behavior, 57*(2), 206–225. https://doi.org/10.1006/jvbe.1999.1736

Berry, C. M., Lelchook, A. M., & Clark, M. A. (2012). A meta-analysis of the interrelationships between employee lateness, absenteeism, and turnover: Implications for models of withdrawal behavior. *Journal of Organizational Behavior*, *33*(5), 678–699. https://doi.org/10.1002/job.778

Bierla, I., Huver, B., & Richard, S. (2011). Presenteeism at work: The influence of managers. *International Journal of Business and Management Studies*, *3*(2), 97–107.

Blau, G. J., & Boal, K. B. (1987). Conceptualizing how job involvement and organizational commitment affect turnover and absenteeism. *Academy of Management Review*, *12*(2), 288–300. https://doi.org/10.5465/amr.1987.4307844

Brady, G. M., Truxillo, D. M., Cadiz, D. M., Rineer, J. R., Caughlin, D. E., & Bodner, T. (2020). Opening the black box: Examining the nomological network of work ability and its role in organizational research. *Journal of Applied Psychology*, *105*(6), 637–670. https://doi.org/10.1037/apl0000454

Cadiz, D. M., Brady, G. M., & Truxillo, D. (2020). Workability: A metric to inform policy for an aging workforce. *Public Policy & Aging Report*, *30*(3), 89–94.

Carstensen, L. L., Isaacowitz, D. M., & Charles, S. T. (1999). Taking time seriously: A theory of socioemotional selectivity. *American Psychologist*, *54*(3), 165–181. https://doi.org/10.1037/0003-066X.54.3.165

Chandola, T., Ferrie, J., Sacker, A., & Marmot, M. (2007). Social inequalities in self reported health in early old age: Follow-up of prospective cohort study. *British Medical Journal*, *334*(7601), 990. https://doi.org/10.1136/bmj.39167.439792.55

Cho, E., & Chen, T.-Y. (2018). The effects of work–family experiences on health among older workers. *Psychology and Aging*, *33*(7), 993–1006. https://doi.org/10.1037/pag0000293

Damman, M., & Henkens, K. (2020). Gender differences in perceived workplace flexibility among older workers in the Netherlands: A brief report. *Journal of Applied Gerontology*, *39*(8), 915–921.

Darr, W., & Johns, G. (2008). Work strain, health, and absenteeism: A meta-analysis. *Journal of Occupational Health Psychology*, *13*(4), 293–318. https://doi.org/10.1037/a0012639

Dello Russo, S., Antino, M., Zaniboni, S., Caetano, A., & Truxillo, D. (2021). The effect of age on daily positive emotions and work behaviors. *Work, Aging and Retirement*, *7*(1), 9–19. https://doi.org/10.1093/workar/waz026

Grinza, E., & Rycx, F. (2020). The impact of sickness absenteeism on firm productivity: New evidence from Belgian matched employer–employee panel data. *Industrial Relations: A Journal of Economy and Society*, *59*(1), 150–194. https://doi.org/10.1111/irel.12252

Harrison, D. A., Newman, D. A., & Roth, P. L. (2006). How important are job attitudes? Meta-analytic comparisons of integrative behavioral outcomes and time sequences. *Academy of Management Journal*, *49*(2), 305–325. https://doi.org/10.5465/amj.2006.20786077

Henseke, G. (2018). Good jobs, good pay, better health? The effects of job quality on health among older European workers. *The European Journal of Health Economics*, *19*(1), 59–73. https://doi.org/10.1007/s10198-017-0867-9

Johns, G. (2002). Absenteeism and mental health. In J. C. Thomas & M. Hersen (Eds.), *Handbook of mental health in the workplace* (pp. 437–455). Sage.

Johns, G. (2008). Absenteeism and presenteeism: Not at work or not working well. In J. Barling & C. L. Cooper (Eds.), *The Sage handbook of organizational behavior*, Vol. 1. *Micro approaches* (pp. 160–177). Sage Publications Ltd.

Johns, G. (2010). Presenteeism in the workplace: A review and research agenda. *Journal of Organizational Behavior*, *31*(4), 519–542. https://doi.org/10.1002/job.630

Johns, G. (2011). Attendance dynamics at work: The antecedents and correlates of presenteeism, absenteeism, and productivity loss. *Journal of Occupational Health Psychology, 16*(4), 483–500. https://doi.org/10.1037/a0025153

Karasek, R., Brisson, C., Kawakami, N., Houtman, I., Bongers, P., & Amick, B. (1998). The Job Content Questionnaire (JCQ): An instrument for internationally comparative assessments of psychosocial job characteristics. *Journal of Occupational Health Psychology, 3*(4), 322–355. https://doi.org/10.1037/1076-8998.3.4.322

Leigh, J. P. (1986). Correlates of absence from work due to illness. *Human Relations, 39*(1), 81–100. https://doi.org/10.1177/001872678603900105

Lindeboom, M., & Kerkhofs, M. (2009). Health and work of the elderly: Subjective health measures, reporting errors and endogeneity in the relationship between health and work. *Journal of Applied Econometrics, 24*(6), 1024–1046.

Lu, L., Lin, H. Y., & Cooper, C. L. (2013). Unhealthy and present: Motives and consequences of the act of presenteeism among Taiwanese employees. *Journal of Occupational Health Psychology, 18*(4), 406–416. https://doi.org/10.1037/a0034331

McGonagle, A. K., Fisher, G. G., Barnes-Farrell, J. L., & Grosch, J. W. (2015). Individual and work factors related to perceived work ability and labor force outcomes. *Journal of Applied Psychology, 100*(2), 376.

Miraglia, M., & Johns, G. (2016). Going to work ill: A meta-analysis of the correlates of presenteeism and a dual-path model. *Journal of Occupational Health Psychology, 21*(3), 261. https://doi.org/10.1037/ocp0000015

Miraglia, M., & Johns, G. (2021). The social and relational dynamics of absenteeism from work: A multilevel review and integration. *Academy of Management Annals, 15*(1), 37–67. https://doi.org/10.5465/annals.2019.0036

Ng, T. W., & Feldman, D. C. (2008). The relationship of age to ten dimensions of job performance. *Journal of Applied Psychology, 93*(2), 392–423. https://doi.org/10.1037/0021-9010.93.2.392

Ng, T. W., & Feldman, D. C. (2010). The relationships of age with job attitudes: A meta-analysis. *Personnel Psychology, 63*(3), 677–718.

Ng, T. W., & Feldman, D. C. (2012). Evaluating six common stereotypes about older workers with meta-analytical data. *Personnel Psychology, 65*(4), 821–858. https://doi.org/10.1111/peps.12003

Ng, T. W., & Feldman, D. C. (2013a). How do within-person changes due to aging affect job performance? *Journal of Vocational Behavior, 83*(3), 500–513. https://doi.org/10.1016/j.jvb.2013.07.007

Ng, T. W., & Feldman, D. C. (2013b). Employee age and health. *Journal of Vocational Behavior, 83*(3), 336–345. https://doi.org/10.1016/j.jvb.2013.06.004

Ng, T. W., & Feldman, D. C. (2013c). A meta-analysis of the relationships of age and tenure with innovation-related behaviour. *Journal of Occupational and Organizational Psychology, 86*(4), 585–616. https://doi.org/10.1111/joop.12031

Niven, K., & Ciborowska, N. (2015). The hidden dangers of attending work while unwell: A survey study of presenteeism among pharmacists. *International Journal of Stress Management, 22*(2), 207–221. https://doi.org/10.1037/a0039131

Rudolph, C. W., Kooij, D. T., Rauvola, R. S., & Zacher, H. (2018). Occupational future time perspective: A meta-analysis of antecedents and outcomes. *Journal of Organizational Behavior, 39*(2), 229–248. https://doi.org/10.1002/job.2264

Ruhle, S. A., & Süß, S. (2020). Presenteeism and absenteeism at work–An analysis of archetypes of sickness attendance cultures. *Journal of Business and Psychology, 35*(2), 241–255. https://doi.org/10.1007/s10869-019-09615-0

Scheibe, S., Walter, F., & Zhan, Y. (2021). Age and emotions in organizations: Main, moderating, and context-specific effects. *Work, Aging and Retirement*, 7(1), 1–8. https://doi.org/10.1093/workar/waaa030

Schultz, A. B., & Edington, D. W. (2007). Employee health and presenteeism: A systematic review. *Journal of Occupational Rehabilitation*, 17(3), 547–579. https://doi.org/10.1007/s10926-007-9096-x

Sinclair, R. R., Allen, T., Barber, L., Bergman, M., Britt, T., Butler, A., . . . Yuan, Z. (2020). Occupational health science in the time of COVID-19: Now more than ever. *Occupational Health Science*, 4(1–2). 1–22. https://doi.org/10.1007/s41542-020-00064-3

Spreitzer, G. M., Cameron, L., & Garrett, L. (2017). Alternative work arrangements: Two images of the new world of work. *Annual Review of Organizational Psychology and Organizational Behavior*, 4, 473–499. https://doi.org/10.1146/annurev-orgpsych-032516-113332

Steidelmüller, C., Meyer, S. C., & Müller, G. (2020). Home-based telework and presenteeism across Europe. *Journal of Occupational and Environmental Medicine*, 62(12), 998–1005. https://doi.org/10.1097/jom.0000000000001992

Viswesvaran, C. (2002). Absenteeism and measures of job performance: A meta-analysis. *International Journal of Selection and Assessment*, 10(1–2), 12–17. https://doi.org/10.1111/1468-2389.00190

Wanberg, C. R., Kanfer, R., Hamann, D. J., & Zhang, Z. (2016). Age and reemployment success after job loss: An integrative model and meta-analysis. *Psychological Bulletin*, 142(4), 400–426. https://doi.org/10.1037/bul0000019

Ybema, J. F., Smulders, P. G., & Bongers, P. M. (2010). Antecedents and consequences of employee absenteeism: A longitudinal perspective on the role of job satisfaction and burnout. *European Journal of Work and Organizational Psychology*, 19(1), 102–124. https://doi.org/10.1080/13594320902793691

Zacher, H. (2015). Successful aging at work. *Work, Aging and Retirement*, 1(1), 4–25. https://doi.org/10.1093/workar/wau006

18

ORGANIZATIONAL METASTRATEGIES FOR YOUNGER AND OLDER WORKERS

Daniela M. Andrei and Sharon K. Parker

The demographic changes happening in most developed countries present complex challenges for managing organizations. Population aging is reflected in a growing mature workforce, as well as a workforce with extended careers. Consequently, organizations need to maintain employee motivation, productivity, and well-being over a significantly longer working lifespan (Bal et al., 2015). Furthermore, an aging workforce requires managing an increasingly age diverse workforce. Higher-level policies (e.g., changes to retirement funding) that promote participation of older workers in response to existing or predicted labor force shortages can further compound these issues (Kunze et al., 2013). How organizations respond to age-related challenges has important implications for their survival and performance (Boehm et al., 2014; Kunze et al., 2013). Research suggests that organizations who do not adapt their strategies to address these demographic trends might face significant negative consequences as age diversity has been linked with reduced team performance (Joshi & Roh, 2009) and organizational level performance (Kunze et al., 2013).

Unfortunately, despite the potential for practical implications, there is a growing consensus that existing research provides an inadequate evidence base to inform organizations as to what management approaches might be most appropriate or under what conditions they are expected to work (Bal et al., 2015; Hertel & Zacher, 2018; Truxillo et al., 2015). While the effects of aging at the individual level are well understood, considerably less research considers aging at the team and organizational level. There is a similar dearth of research focused on organizational and human resource practices used to tackle an aging and age diverse workforce (Bal et al., 2015). Therefore, we know relatively little about what types of work practices and interventions make a positive difference to older workers' experiences and outcomes.

DOI: 10.4324/9781003089674-22

Based on these research gaps as well as our ongoing large-scale research project aimed at guiding organizations to implement interventions to increase participation, productivity, and well-being of older workers,[1] we developed an integrative framework that categorizes various organizational actions (Parker & Andrei, 2020). The framework, "Include, Individualize, Integrate" (or 3i for short), identifies three broad sets of approaches, which we refer to as "metastrategies," that can guide organizational actions aimed at reaping the benefits associated with an increasingly older and age-diverse workforce.

In this chapter, we further elaborate on the original framework and identify key implications for future research and practice.

The 3i Framework

The impetus behind the development of the 3i framework was practical. In 2017, our research team became part of the Centre for Excellence in Population Aging Research (CEPAR), a unique collaboration bringing together several research teams across Australia, as well as government and industry, to address challenges associated with population aging. Our team focuses on the topic of "Organizations and the Mature Workforce" by conducting research with organizations to facilitate and evaluate interventions aimed at improving experiences and outcomes for older workers. When we began to implement this research, it became apparent that the challenges, focus, and areas of interest for possible interventions differed considerably across the organizations. To provide the empirical base for the interventions, we reviewed a large and diverse literature, including: Research on diversity and inclusion (Shore et al., 2011), research on the role of inclusive organizational HR practices and organizational climates for older workers (Boehm et al., 2014), research on work design as a tool for adapting work to the needs of an aging workforce (e.g., Griffiths, 1999), and emerging studies on the implications of age diversity for managing team composition, team processes, and outcomes (Schneid et al., 2016; Wegge et al., 2012). Integration of the evidence across these topics led to the development of a framework that identifies three sets of "metastrategies" or categories of strategies underpinned by distinct theoretical perspectives (Figure 18.1; Table 18.1). We elaborate each next.

"Include" Metastrategies

"Include" brings together organizational strategies, practices, and actions aimed at reducing discrimination and barriers to participation for workers of all ages, as well as creating an environment in which workers are welcomed, valued, accepted for their uniqueness, and fairly treated. In essence, this metastrategy is about the development of inclusive climates not only for older workers but also for other types of diversity (Boehm et al., 2014; Shore et al., 2011). "Include" is relevant to the idea that "in inclusive organizations and societies, people of all identities and

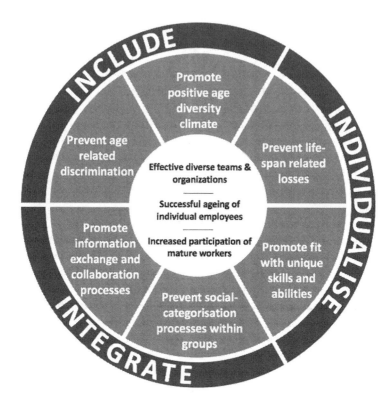

FIGURE 18.1 "Include, Individualize, Integrate" (3i) Framework: Overview of proposed metastrategies and proposed key pathways

many styles can be fully themselves while also contributing to the larger collective, as valued and full members" (Ferdman, 2017, p. 235).

Social identity theory and social categorization theory (Tajfel & Turner, 1986; Tajfel, 1969) underpin the research relevant to this metastrategy. In the context of work, these theories explain how the natural processes that employees use to categorize the social world will likely lead to them perceiving subgroups based on visible and (relatively) stable traits such as gender, race, and age. Since people tend to positively identify with similar others (Tajfel & Turner, 1986) and to favor ingroup members over outgroup members, cooperation and better results are more likely to appear in homogenous groups (Brewer, 1991; Tajfel & Turner, 1986; Tajfel, 1969). This means that cooperation and interaction in heterogenous groups might be hampered because perceiving others as being dissimilar can create difficulties in accepting and treating them equally. When particular traits and abilities are furthermore linked to certain subgroups, stereotype-based discrimination can occur as a result of these processes (Cuddy et al., 2005).

TABLE 18.1 Definition and Examples for the Proposed Metastrategies of the "Include, Individualize, Integrate" (3i) Framework

	Include Metastrategy	Individualize Metastrategy	Integrate Metastrategy
Definition	Organizational strategies to welcome, accept, and fairly treat older workers	Organizational strategies to accommodate and support the changing individual needs and preferences of older workers	Organizational strategies to improve how age-diverse members interact, share knowledge, and learn from each other
Example Strategies/ Interventions— Organizational Level	Vision (e.g., "we are one") Age Diversity and Inclusion strategy Age-Inclusive HRM practices (e.g., nondiscriminatory recruitment or evaluation and reward systems, etc.)	Individualized HRM practices (e.g. maintenance/development practices differentially applied to employees at different ages) Work analysis (to understand specific demands on workers and abilities needed to meet the demands) Implementation of technology/support systems (e.g., robots/computer systems that help compensate for age related changes) Flexible working arrangements (e.g. flex time, job sharing, leave options, diversified pathways to retirement)	Lateral integration mechanisms/organizational designs Collaborative-based HR practices (e.g., practices that support and promote knowledge sharing and collaboration) Reward systems for teamwork, collaboration and information sharing Implementation of team-based work systems Implementation of technology/systems to support knowledge sharing Workforce planning and succession plans
Example Strategies/ Interventions— Workgroup Level	Inclusive leadership training Awareness training for age-related changes and debunking age-related myths (targeted at leaders or team members)	Age differentiated leadership training Top-down work design/redesign Ergonomic interventions Work–life programs	Mentoring/reverse mentoring programs Teambuilding training Team design strategies

TABLE 18.1 (Continued)

	Include Metastrategy	Individualize Metastrategy	Integrate Metastrategy
Example Strategies/ Interventions— Individual Level	Information/training (e.g., aimed at reducing age bias or stereotype threat) Resilience training or employee assistance programs (EAP) for people who experience discrimination Unconscious bias training	Bottom-up work redesign (e.g., job crafting; i-deals; proactive career management) Health promotion interventions (e.g., voluntary preventive health checks; physical exercise) Supporting older workers' individual adjustment to cognitive, physical, and psychosocial life changes (e.g., career management, health promotion, SOC training; coaching) Preretirement and retirement planning initiatives (e.g., midlife planning initiatives, retirement planning, counseling, awareness of retirement pathways)	Training for teamwork skills Perspective taking interventions
Key Outcomes	Attraction and retention of older workers Increased workforce diversity Compliance with regulatory frameworks and equal employment guidelines	Individual performance and occupational well-being Increased participation of older workers in the labor force	Preservation of key organizational knowledge and expertise Optimal team and organizational performance Enhanced innovation

Ample evidence supports the idea that aging employees often face negative outcomes at work such as negative evaluations, limited access to new jobs or advancement opportunities, or limited access to training and networks of information (Bal et al., 2011). These outcomes are likely reflecting negative age stereotypes such as that older workers are less competent, more resistant to change, and have a lower ability to learn compared to younger workers (Cuddy et al., 2005; Posthuma & Campion, 2009).

To counteract these processes, workplaces need to take active steps to reduce or prevent divisions formed around age (as well as other demographic characteristics) through "Include" strategies. A cluster of "Include" strategies focuses on removing age-related exclusions from human resource management processes and other practices, as mandated by antidiscrimination laws and guidelines. For example, it is important to ensure that job advertisements do not use age as a criterion (unless, for some reason, age is essential to job performance) or that, in interviews, older workers are not asked stereotype-based questions (e.g., about technology) that are not asked of younger workers. Likewise, it is important to target more subtle forms of discrimination in which age-related bias is cued indirectly, such as when job advertisements discourage older workers to apply by using images only of young people. As discussed by Finkelstein (2015), at every stage of the employment relationship, there are conditions that serve to amplify or reduce age biases, and these should be actively targeted to enhance inclusion.

Another important cluster of "Include" strategies are those that involve proactively building positive environments for older workers. This means going beyond compliance with existing laws and focusing on building inclusive work environments in which workers can behave authentically, irrespective of their perceived differences (Shore et al., 2018). It is important to note that these strategies are not about "treating everyone as the same" but rather, "appreciating people irrespective of differences." Based on optimal distinctiveness theory (Brewer, 1991), inclusive strategies should ensure diverse members are accepted members of groups (meeting belongingness needs) while at the same time allowing them to maintain a differentiated sense of self (meeting uniqueness needs) (Shore et al., 2011). An example strategy is actively training managers to treat older workers in inclusive ways (e.g., age-inclusive leadership, Kuknor & Bhattacharya, 2020).

Overall, we propose that "Include" strategies will translate into outcomes for individual employees and organizations through two main pathways. One pathway is represented by processes linked to reducing age bias and discrimination at the interaction and process levels, which implicitly or explicitly reduce barriers to employment, promotion, and development opportunities (Toomey & Rudolph, 2018). The second pathway is represented by mechanisms related to the creation of work contexts or climates in which age diversity is viewed positively and valued across the organization and that also reduce the probability of stereotype and metastereotype activation (Finkelstein, 2015).

316 Daniela M. Andrei and Sharon K. Parker

Some research, albeit relatively limited to date, provides evidence for the organizational benefits of inclusive strategies. In a rigorous, multisource study of 93 companies in Germany, Boehm and colleagues (2014) found that the implementation of inclusive human resource management strategies was associated with a more positive age climate that, in turn, predicted increased older workers' retention as well as company level performance indicators. Specific company examples have long been documented. For example, in 1991, as a response to a rapidly decreasing workforce pool, a UK-based do-it-yourself chain trialed a store fully staffed by workers aged 50 and over. Among other activities, their recruitment campaign explicitly communicated the value that the company saw in an older workforce. The initiative was considered an overwhelming success due to significantly reduced turnover and absence rates, as well as similar productivity/staff costs, in this store compared to other stores in the chain (Terence & Barth, 1991).

"Individualize" Metastrategies

The second metastrategy in our framework, "Individualize," focuses on enabling uniqueness by supporting the individual needs and strengths of an aging workforce. While "Include" strategies focus on social and cultural acceptance of people who are different from oneself, "Individualize" strategies target older workers themselves by supporting their adaptation to lifespan changes. They bring together initiatives aimed at supporting the structural changes needed to achieve a better fit with workers' evolving needs and priorities.

This metastrategy is informed by lifespan development theories, such as selective optimization with compensation theory (SOC, Baltes & Baltes, 1990) or the socioemotional selectivity theory (SST, Carstensen et al., 1999). SOC highlights the way people adapt to and compensate for age-related declines such as in their working memory or their physical abilities. SST proposes that some age-related changes are dependent on how people perceive time. With age, people become more present-focused as they switch from an open-ended, future-focused perception of time to viewing time as a limited resource. This results in older employees prioritizing emotion regulation goals, positive work experiences, and targeted social connections, while younger employees prioritize knowledge acquisition goals and expanding social connections. Taken together, these theoretical models point toward the value of compensatory processes that, if supported by the work context, allow people to maintain high levels of performance and to age successfully at work (Zacher, 2015). Empirical evidence supports these theories showing, for example, that for younger workers task variety can lead to more positive results, whilst for older workers skill variety is more positive (Zaniboni et al., 2013). Similarly, job feedback is received differently by employees of different ages, with older workers reacting more positively to positive feedback oriented to social aspects, while for younger workers the utility of the feedback plays a more important role (Wang et al., 2015).

Importantly, however, the "Individualize" metastrategy is also informed by the recognition that there are individual differences in the way people age (Fisher et al., 2017). Thus, whilst, for example, skill variety might on average be more important to older workers than task variety, this will not be so for all older workers. Ignoring such individual differences in how employees age would result in a "one size fits all" approach to adjusting work that is likely to fail. Our use of the term "Individualize" recognizes that interventions are required that accommodate the needs of older workers, albeit in an individualized way.

While interventions can be aimed at supporting the individuals themselves to successfully adapt to age-related changes (see Table 18.1), organizations can *change work designs or work conditions* to better accommodate lifespan changes. Example strategies include ergonomic changes to reduce biomechanical strain on the body; the allocation of more tasks that rely on crystallized intelligence, rather than fluid intelligence, to older workers (that is, tasks that rely on accumulated knowledge rather than tasks that depend on high-level cognitive abilities); and the introduction of flexible work practices that allow workers to meet changing demands on their time outside of work (including, for example, care of parents or grandchildren). Work can also be changed not so much via organizational-led interventions (often referred to as "top-down" work redesign) but by supporting individual employees to change work themselves, for example, through encouraging workers' proactive work behavior (Kooij, 2015), job crafting (see also Chapter 14; Kooij et al., 2015), or negotiating i-deals with their direct supervisors (Bal & Boehm, 2019). Such initiatives allow workers themselves to individualize their work and to align it better to their strengths and needs. As research shows that bottom-up approaches thrive in workplaces where autonomy is high (Slemp et al., 2015) and that top-down approaches benefit from employees' motivation and capability to take advantage of the redesign (Parker & Sprigg, 1999), combining these two approaches might be especially effective (Grant & Parker, 2009).

Overall, we expect that "Individualize" metastrategies will impact on organizational outcomes through maintaining adequate levels of fit or compatibility between employees and their work across the lifespan, which has been shown to relate to positive attitudes toward work (Kim et al., 2020) as well as higher levels of performance and well-being (Rodrigues et al., 2020). Both present and future fit needs to be considered, therefore we expect two possible pathways, one focusing on addressing age-related losses (e.g., reduced physical strength) and a second focused on capitalizing on the different knowledge, skills, and abilities that workers develop during their work-lifespans.

A practical example of a successful "Individualize" intervention is provided by the BMW case (Loch et al., 2010). This intervention involved a participatory work redesign process that resulted in more than 70 different changes being adopted to improve workstations and reduce physical strains for workers of all ages. Most of these were small and not very expensive changes, such as job rotation, installing magnifying glasses, and having wooden floors. Nevertheless, they resulted in a 7% overall increase in line productivity. Other examples include implementing flexibility practices, such as flexible working hours, telecommuting, or working from home solutions. Marriott is recognized for implementing a wide range of flexibility practices alongside fostering a "flexibility mindset" in managers that focuses on identifying innovative solutions for flexibility needs (Roundtree, 2012).

"Integrate" Metastrategies

Workforce aging brings a simultaneous increase in *age diversity*, meaning that there are more interactions among employees of diverse ages. Understanding how to manage these interactions is critical as work becomes more team-based and interdependent, especially as research points to potential negative effects of age diversity (Wegge & Schmidt, 2009; Williams & O'Reilly, 1998; note, however, that some research finds null effects; e.g., Bell et al., 2011; Schneid et al., 2016). While earlier in our framework we discussed differences among employees of different ages (i.e. "diversity as separation"), with "Integrate" we switch focus toward the benefits that can potentially arise from diversity (i.e. "diversity as variety," Harrison & Klein, 2007). Thus, "Integrate" metastrategies focus on improving the way age-diverse members collaborate, exchange knowledge, and produce more innovative solutions. Strategies focused on creating the conditions needed for age diverse teams to thrive (Wegge et al., 2012) or at enhancing knowledge sharing processes (see also Chapter 15) and intergenerational learning (Gerpott et al., 2017) fit this category.

Team diversity theories, especially the information/decision-making perspective (e.g., Van Knippenberg et al., 2004; Williams & O'Reilly, 1998), inform this metastrategy. For example, in team settings, members of different ages can generate a broader pool of resources (e.g., knowledge, skills, abilities, experiences). When dealing with complex tasks or when required to come up with innovative products, a broader pool of resources is expected to generate better outcomes for teams and organizations (Van Knippenberg et al., 2004).

Nevertheless, as noted earlier, the link between age diversity and positive outcomes is not straightforward, mainly because bias and social-categorization processes can be triggered by increased age diversity (Van Knippenberg et al., 2004). Contextual factors in the work environment contribute to the way teams activate these different processes. Creating a work context in which diversity is valued emerges as an important boundary condition for facilitating social integration, performance, and innovation in age diverse teams (Homan et al., 2007). For example, positive effects of diversity can emerge when organizations focus on creating appropriate environments for age-diverse teams to interact effectively (Wegge et al., 2012). Therefore, "Include" strategies might be an important precursor or facilitator for "Integrate" strategies, an idea we return to later.

Other theories, such as social exchange theory (SET, Blau, 1964; Emerson, 1976), inform "Integrate" metastrategies. SET proposes that people's tendency to reciprocate attitudes and behaviors will lead to long-term relationships characterized by trust and commitment. In our model, this theory has implications for the way younger and older workers work together, as their interactions can be seen as a process of exchanging resources that they might not have, yet value in each other. SET suggests the utility of strategies aimed at partnering young and older workers together to build a reciprocal positive exchange, such as mentoring and reverse mentoring. When employees of different ages develop complimentary social ties and interactions, this contributes to increased social capital, allowing the organization to build strong networks of internal and external connections (Li et al., 2021).

In line with existing theories and models, we expect "Integrate" strategies to contribute to enhanced team and organizational effectiveness by, first, weakening the potentially damaging social categorization processes that arise with increased diversity, both within the group itself as well as in the perceptions and behaviors of organizational stakeholders outside the group (Wegge & Schmidt, 2009). Second, these strategies are aimed at stimulating effective group processes and emergent states (e.g., coordination, learning, trust) that contribute to increased effectiveness (Wegge et al., 2012). Both pathways are especially key for offsetting the knowledge losses that can occur when mature workers retire.

A combination of "Integrate" strategies has been implemented by TVA in the United States as part of their knowledge retention program. This program was initiated due to the increased retirement risk in the workforce. It entailed a complex process of monitoring both the retirement risk and the knowledge risk factor for each position to identify areas of potential knowledge loss. These areas were then targeted through tactics such as one-on-one coaching and mentoring, job-shadowing, cross-training, brown-bag lunches, rehiring retirees as consultants, or establishing communities of practice (DeLong, 2004).

Implications for Future Theory, Research and Practice

The "3i" framework provides a foundation to identify needed theoretical, empirical, and practical developments to better support an aging and age-diverse workforce in organizations.

Implications for Theory

Our review identified that the metastrategies are grounded in solid theory, but each approach has tended to develop in a silo. Our emphasis on integration across diverse research fields is a step forward, but there is more to do to understand how the various processes operate together to support individuals and organizations. Similar to other reviews (e.g., Hertel & Zacher, 2018), we call for the need to clarify the mechanisms that carry the effects of organizational strategies and interventions to outcomes. Emerging research points to the idea that the metastrategies might not be independent, and their effects might operate in complementary, synergistic, or sequential ways. For example Li and colleagues (2021) identified that age inclusive management ("Include") is a boundary condition for facilitating the intellectual capital-based processes linked to age diversity ("Integrate"). There is also temporal complexity within each metastrategy to unravel. For example, Fasbender and Gerpott (2020) showed that development practices related to our definition of "Include" affect employees' self-efficacy, with evidence that accommodative HR practices then benefit most people with high levels of self-efficacy (i.e. those who don't experience age discrimination) but harm those with lower levels of occupational self-efficacy (i.e. those who perceive age discrimination). We recommend assessing whether strategies operate independently of each other, simultaneously, or sequentially, as well as theory development regarding the timing of these processes.

Also important is the need for theoretical integration across levels of analysis, which is especially important when the goal is to support practical interventions. While we focused on strategies that operate mainly at the organizational level (e.g., HRM practices), strategies also exist at the team and individual levels (see Table 18.1). Mechanisms and outcomes resulting from the metastrategies can also be expected to operate at different levels. For example, the development of a positive age diversity climate ("Include") might operate particularly at the organizational level, whereas information-elaboration and knowledge exchange processes ("Integrate") likely operate mostly at the work-team level, and person–job fit processes ("Individualize") likely operate mainly at the individual level. Moreover, research suggests that the same mechanism could operate differently across levels. For example, age discrimination as a mechanism based on social categorization is likely to be salient and to have negative effects at the horizontal team level because team members have a similar status and interact frequently. But at the vertical or organizational level the salience and negativity of age discrimination might be reduced due to differences in status associated with age that inhibit social comparisons (Li et al., 2021). We urge attention to such multilevel processes.

Research on aging workers has to date focused primarily on understanding individual outcomes (Wang et al., 2012). But given organizations' interest in achieving organizational-level outcomes, a theoretical jump is needed to understand how individual effects are translated into higher-level effects (see also Chapter 9). Researchers agree that it is not just a matter of "adding up" the individual effects of aging to the team or organizational level, and theory needs to evolve toward a collective approach in examining the value add of aging and age-diverse employees (Boehm et al., 2014; Li et al., 2021). One approach is to link diversity-related strategies to company-level outcomes through dynamic capability frameworks (Roberson et al., 2017). Such approaches move away from seeing diversity as a resource that organizations can use to perform better to instead focus on the company's capacity to activate and use resources to adapt to environmental changes (i.e., their dynamic capability). Different metastrategies might shape different capabilities. For example, building on the model proposed by Roberson and colleagues (2017), we speculate that "Include" strategies will contribute to capabilities such as market access by facilitating a workforce composition that better reflects the demographic that the organization serves. "Integrate" strategies might support dynamic capabilities around research and development, knowledge management, and strategic flexibility, as all these capabilities rely heavily on information-elaboration processes and coordination of knowledge resources. Last but not least, "Individualize" strategies might play a major role for efficiency capabilities, such as the execution of routines and operational processes, by promoting a better fit between the tasks and workers' capabilities. Research investigating how organizations can create different types of capital out of age diversity (Li et al., 2021) shows the potential of this direction.

One further opportunity for theoretical development concerns investigating the role of contextual factors that might shape the implementation and effectiveness of the metastrategies. Such factors might reside again at the organizational level (e.g., organizational characteristics such as size, strategy, functional diversity, culture); work level (e.g., routine vs creative task type); or even the larger context such as national culture.

Methodological Implications

A key methodological implication of the framework is the motivation that stimulated its development in the first place: The scarcity of intervention research (see also Chapter 11). Truxillo et al.'s (2015, see also Söderbacka et al., 2020) conclusions about this lack still ring true: Most aging intervention studies focus on people that are beyond working age, and the few that exist in the context of work rarely consider the processes that explain the effects of an intervention or compare effects across age. Intervention research is critical for understanding what works in practice and why. Ideally, intervention research is accompanied by the use of experimental and quasi-experimental research designs that allow for stronger causal conclusions about outcomes and mechanisms (Hertel & Zacher, 2018; Truxillo et al., 2015).

Of course, there are challenges of experimental/quasi-experimental research (e.g., experimental control is difficult in applied settings; it is hard to isolate mechanisms in the field), which are reflected in an overemphasis of cross-sectional designs in existing studies on aging workers (Hertel & Zacher, 2018). One way forward is to use longitudinal designs to investigate intraindividual change, which might be especially relevant for understanding successful aging at work (see also Chapter 10). Multilevel research designs can also help to assess processes related to interventions around age diversity (see, for example, Nishii et al., 2018). Similar to within-individual change, multilevel and longitudinal designs should assess the time lags of effects (see, for example, Giga et al., 2003 in regard to stress management). Mixed-methods approaches that combine qualitative and quantitative designs are recommended (see also Chapter 12; e.g., Kooij et al., 2014).

There is a need to refine existing measures of organizational-level strategies. HRM practices are increasingly highlighted as important for managing the challenges associated with an aging and age-diverse workforce (Fasbender & Gerpott, 2020; Kooij et al., 2014), but research seems to either solely focus on one area, mostly either "Include" (e.g., Ali & French, 2019) or "Individualize" (e.g., Kooij et al., 2014) or combine items from different metastrategies into a single bundle (e.g., maintenance practices in Fasbender & Gerpott, 2020). In particular, better measures of HRM practices that support "Integrate" strategies are needed.

Implications for Practice

The framework highlights that organizational stakeholders need to do three core things: (1) reduce discrimination in employment processes and develop positive climates in which employees of all ages feel included; (2) support individualized work arrangements/work designs that maximize person–environment fit across the lifespan; and (3) stimulate teamwork and information elaboration processes that capitalize on the unique skills and knowledge of age-diverse employees. While complex dynamics about timing still need more research, it is likely that "Include" strategies are a safe starting point, laying the foundation for the success of "Individualize" and "Integrate" strategies.

Second, the simplicity of the framework helps organizations to move forward in this complex space. We have used the framework in our work with organizations, such as to aid in strategy development and to help communicate insights obtained in the diagnosis phase. As an example, to help organizational stakeholders to understand their challenges, we map the company's policies and practices onto the three metastrategies. We then, with the stakeholders, assess the maturity of each. What results is a high-level overview of where the organization is focusing resources. This approach allows organizations to appraise if their current focus needs realignment, areas that might have been overlooked, and/or where programs exist but need to be better implemented.

Third, we have observed that the framework helps organizations to move beyond reactive, compliance-oriented approaches that seem to dominate practice in this area (that is, the removal of discriminatory practices that is part of "Include") toward a more proactive and strategic focus aimed at capitalizing on the added value of a more mature and diverse workforce ("Individualize" and "Integrate"). By highlighting the full range of interventions areas, as well as the value creation pathways for each, the framework helps stimulate a shift in discourse from dealing with the "problems" of an aging workforce to capitalizing on the benefits of having older workers with diverse experiences and skills.

Conclusions

The development of the integrative "3i" framework was primarily inspired from a practical, use-oriented perspective. As such, the framework delineates the main areas of action for organizations and highlights the underlying processes that enable a positive and strategic use of an age-diverse workforce. While it is not (yet!) a testable theoretical model, we hope that the framework's solid grounding in theory will support diagnosis, intervention, and methodological innovation, enabling practitioners and researchers to achieve an integrative approach to age and age diversity at work.

Note

1 For more details on our research stream, see https://matureworkers.cepar.edu.au/

References

Ali, M., & French, E. (2019). Age diversity management and organisational outcomes: The role of diversity perspectives. *Human Resource Management Journal, 29*(2), 287–307. https://doi.org/10.1111/1748-8583.12225

Bal, A. C., Reiss, A. E. B., Rudolph, C. W., & Baltes, B. B. (2011). Examining positive and negative perceptions of older workers: A meta-analysis. *The Journals of Gerontology Series B: Psychological Sciences and Social Sciences, 66B*(6), 687–698. https://doi.org/10.1093/geronb/gbr056

Bal, P. M., & Boehm, S. A. (2019). How do I-deals influence client satisfaction? The role of exhaustion, collective commitment, and age diversity. *Journal of Management, 45*(4), 1461–1487. https://doi.org/10.1177/0149206317710722

Bal, P. M., Kooij, D. T. A. M., & Rousseau, D. M. (2015). Introduction to aging workers and the employee-employer relationship. In P. M. Bal, D. T. A. M. Kooij, & D. M. Rousseau (Eds.), *Aging workers and the employee-employer relationship* (pp. 1–9). Springer. https://doi.org/10.1007/978-3-319-08007-9

Baltes, P. B., & Baltes, M. M. (1990). Psychological perspectives on successful aging: The model of selective optimization with compensation. In P. B. Baltes & M. M. Baltes (Eds.), *Successful aging: Perspectives from the behavioral sciences* (pp. 1–34). Cambridge University Press.

Bell, S. T., Villado, A. J., Lukasik, M. A., Belau, L., & Briggs, A. L. (2011). Getting specific about demographic diversity variable and team performance relationships: A meta-analysis. *Journal of Management, 37*(3), 709–743. https://doi.org/10.1177/0149206310365001

Blau, P. (1964). *Exchange and power in social life*. John Wiley & Sons.

Boehm, S. A., Kunze, F., & Bruch, H. (2014). Spotlight on age-diversity climate: The impact of age-inclusive HR practices on firm-level outcomes. *Personnel Psychology, 67*(3), 667–704. https://doi.org/10.1111/peps.12047

Brewer, M. B. (1991). The social self: On being the same and different at the same time. *Personality and Social Psychology Bulletin, 17*(5), 475–482. https://doi.org/10.1177/0146167291175001

Carstensen, L. L., Isaacowitz, D. M., & Charles, S. T. (1999). Taking time seriously: A theory of socioemotional selectivity. *American Psychologist, 54*(3), 165–181. https://doi.org/10.1037/0003-066X.54.3.165

Cuddy, A. J. C., Norton, M. I., & Fiske, S. T. (2005). This old stereotype: The pervasiveness and persistence of the elderly stereotype. *Journal of Social Issues, 61*(2), 265–283. https://doi.org/10.1111/j.1540-4560.2005.00405.x

DeLong, D. W. (2004). *Lost knowledge : Confronting the threat of an aging workforce.* Oxford University Press.

Emerson, R. M. (1976). Social exchange theory. *Annual Review of Sociology, 2*, 335–362. https://doi.org/10.1146/annurev.so.02.080176.002003

Fasbender, U., & Gerpott, F. H. (2020). To share or not to share: A social-cognitive internalization model to explain how age discrimination impairs older employees' knowledge sharing with younger colleagues. *European Journal of Work and Organizational Psychology, 30*(1), 125–142. https://doi.org/10.1080/1359432X.2020.1839421

Ferdman, B. M. (2017). Paradoxes of inclusion: Understanding and managing the tensions of diversity and multiculturalism. *The Journal of Applied Behavioral Science, 53*(2), 235–263. https://doi.org/10.1177/0021886317702608

Finkelstein, L. M. (2015). Older workers, stereotypes, and discrimination in the context of the employment relationship. In P. M. Bal, D. T. A. M. Kooij, & D. M. Rousseau (Eds.), *Aging workers and the employee-employer relationship* (pp. 13–32). Springer. https://doi.org/10.1007/978-3-319-08007-9_2

Fisher, G. G., Chaffee, D. S., Tetrick, L. E., Davalos, D. B., & Potter, G. G. (2017). Cognitive functioning, aging, and work: A review and recommendations for research and practice. *Journal of Occupational Health Psychology, 22*, 314–336. https://doi.org/10.1037/ocp0000086

Gerpott, F. H., Lehmann-Willenbrock, N., & Voelpel, S. C. (2017). A phase model of intergenerational learning in organizations. *Academy of Management Learning & Education, 16*(2), 193–216. https://doi.org/10.5465/amle.2015.0185

Giga, S. I., Cooper, C. L., & Faragher, B. (2003). The development of a framework for a comprehensive approach to stress management interventions at work. *International Journal of Stress Management, 10*(4), 280. https://doi.org/10.1037/1072-5245.10.4.280

Grant, A. M., & Parker, S. K. (2009). Redesigning work design theories: The rise of relational and proactive perspectives. *The Academy of Management Annals, 3*(1), 317–375. https://doi.org/10.1080/19416520903047327

Griffiths, A. (1999). Work design and managements–The older worker. *Experimental Aging Research, 25*(4), 411–420. https://doi.org/10.1080/036107399243887

Harrison, D. A., & Klein, K. J. (2007). What's the difference? Diversity constructs as separation, variety, or disparity in organizations. *Academy of Management Review, 32*(4), 1199–1228. https://doi.org/10.5465/AMR.2007.26586096

Hertel, G., & Zacher, H. (2018). Managing the aging workforce. In C. Viswesvaran, N. Anderson, D. S. Ones, & H. K. Sinangil (Eds.), *The SAGE handbook of industrial, work, & organizational psychology* (2nd ed., Vol. 3, pp. 396–428). Sage. https://doi.org/10.1136/jnnp.s1-3.9.65

Homan, A. C., van Knippenberg, D., Van Kleef, G. A., & De Dreu, C. K. W. (2007). Bridging faultlines by valuing diversity: Diversity beliefs, information elaboration, and performance in diverse work groups. *Journal of Applied Psychology, 92*(5), 1189–1199. https://doi.org/10.1037/0021-9010.92.5.1189

Joshi, A., & Roh, H. (2009). The role of context in work team diversity research: A meta-analytic review. *Academy of Management Journal, 52*(3), 599–627. https://doi.org/10.5465/amj.2009.41331491

Kim, T. Y., Schuh, S. C., & Cai, Y. (2020). Person or job? Change in person-job fit and its impact on employee work attitudes over time. *Journal of Management Studies*, *57*(2), 287–313. https://doi.org/10.1111/joms.12433

Kooij, D. T. A. M. (2015). Successful aging at work: The active role of employees. *Work, Aging and Retirement*, *1*(4), 309–319. https://doi.org/10.1093/workar/wav018

Kooij, D. T. A. M., Jansen, P. G. W., Dikkers, J. S. E., & de Lange, A. H. (2014). Managing aging workers: A mixed methods study on bundles of HR practices for aging workers. *The International Journal of Human Resource Management*, *25*(15), 2192–2212. https://doi.org/10.1080/09585192.2013.872169

Kooij, D. T. A. M., Tims, M., & Kanfer, R. (2015). Successful aging at work: The role of job crafting. In P. M. Bal, D. T. A. M. Kooij, & D. M. Rousseau (Eds.), *Aging workers and the employee-employer relationship* (pp. 145–161). Springer. https://doi.org/10.1007/978-3-319-08007-9_9

Kuknor, S. C., & Bhattacharya, S. (2020). Inclusive leadership: New age leadership to foster organizational inclusion. *European Journal of Training and Development*, *ahead-of-p*. https://doi.org/10.1108/EJTD-07-2019-0132

Kunze, F., Boehm, S., & Bruch, H. (2013). Organizational performance consequences of age diversity: Inspecting the role of diversity-friendly HR policies and top managers' negative age stereotypes. *Journal of Management Studies*, *50*(3), 413–442. https://doi.org/10.1111/joms.12016

Li, Y., Gong, Y., Burmeister, A., Wang, M., Alterman, V., Alonso, A., & Robinson, S. (2021). Leveraging age diversity for organizational performance: An intellectual capital perspective. *Journal of Applied Psychology*, *106*(1), 71–91. https://doi.org/10.1037/apl0000497

Loch, C., Sting, F., Bauer, N., & Mauermann, H. (2010). How BMW is defusing the demographic time bomb. *Harvard Business Review*, *88*(3), 99–102.

Nishii, L. H., Khattab, J., Shemla, M., & Paluch, R. M. (2018). A multi-level process model for understanding diversity practice effectiveness. *Academy of Management Annals*, *12*(1), 37–82. https://doi.org/10.5465/annals.2016.0044

Parker, S. K., & Andrei, D. M. (2020). Include, individualize, and integrate: Organizational meta-strategies for mature workers. *Work, Aging and Retirement*, *6*(1), 1–7. https://doi.org/10.1093/workar/waz009

Parker, S. K., & Sprigg, C. A. (1999). Minimizing strain and maximizing learning: The role of job demands, job control and proactive personality. *Journal of Applied Psychology*, *84*(6), 925–939. https://doi.org/10.1037/0021-9010.84.6.925

Posthuma, R. A., & Campion, M. A. (2009). Age stereotypes in the workplace: Common stereotypes, moderators, and future research directions. *Journal of Management*, *35*(1), 158–188. https://doi.org/10.1177/0149206308318617

Roberson, Q., Holmes, O., & Perry, J. L. (2017). Transforming research on diversity and firm performance: A dynamic capabilities perspective. *Academy of Management Annals*, *11*(1), 189–216. https://doi.org/10.5465/annals.2014.0019

Rodrigues, F. R., Pina e Cunha, M., Castanheira, F., Bal, P. M., & Jansen, P. G. W. (2020). Person-job fit across the work lifespan—The case of classical ballet dancers. *Journal of Vocational Behavior*, *118*(February), 103400. https://doi.org/10.1016/j.jvb.2020.103400

Roundtree, L. (2012). Flex strategies to attract, engage and retain older workers. *Innovative Practices*. www.bc.edu/agingandwork

Schneid, M., Isidor, R., Steinmetz, H., & Kabst, R. (2016). Age diversity and team outcomes: A quantitative review. *Journal of Managerial Psychology, 31*(1), 2–17. https://doi.org/10.1108/JMP-07-2012-0228

Shore, L. M., Cleveland, J. N., & Sanchez, D. (2018). Inclusive workplaces: A review and model. *Human Resource Management Review, 28*(2), 176–189. https://doi.org/10.1016/j.hrmr.2017.07.003

Shore, L. M., Randel, A. E., Chung, B. G., Dean, M. A., Ehrhart, K. H., & Singh, G. (2011). Inclusion and diversity in work groups: A review and model for future research. *Journal of Management, 37*(4), 1262–1289. https://doi.org/10.1177/0149206310385943

Slemp, G. R., Kern, M. L., & Vella-Brodrick, D. A. (2015). Workplace well-being: The role of job crafting and autonomy support. *Psychology of Well-Being, 5*, 7. https://doi.org/10.1186/s13612-015-0034-y

Söderbacka, T., Nyholm, L., & Fagerström, L. (2020). Workplace interventions that support older employees' health and work ability–A scoping review. *BMC Health Services Research, 20*(1), 1–9. https://doi.org/10.1186/s12913-020-05323-1

Tajfel, H. (1969). Cognitive aspects of prejudice. *Journal of Biosocial Science, 1*(Suppl. 1), 173–191. https://doi.org/10.1017/S0021932000023336

Tajfel, H., & Turner, J. C. (1986). An integrative theory of intergroup relations. *Psychology of Intergroup Relations*, 7–24.

Terence, H., & Barth, M. C. (1991). Costs and benefits of hiring older workers: A case study of B&Q. *International Journal of Manpower, 12*(8), 5–17. https://doi.org/10.1108/EUM0000000000896

Toomey, E. C., & Rudolph, C. W. (2018). Age-conditional effects in the affective arousal, empathy, and emotional labor linkage: Within-person evidence from an experience sampling study. *Work, Aging and Retirement, 4*(2), 145–160. https://doi.org/10.1093/workar/wax018

Truxillo, D. M., Cadiz, D. M., & Hammer, L. B. (2015). Supporting the aging workforce: A review and recommendations for workplace intervention research. *Annual Review of Organizational Psychology and Organizational Behavior, 2*(2), 351–381. https://doi.org/10.1146/annurev-orgpsych-032414-111435

Van Knippenberg, D., De Dreu, C. K. W. W., & Homan, A. C. (2004). Work group diversity and group performance: An integrative model and research agenda. *Journal of Applied Psychology, 89*(6), 1008–1022. https://doi.org/10.1037/0021-9010.89.6.1008

Wang, M., Burlacu, G., Truxillo, D., James, K., & Yao, X. (2015). Age differences in feedback reactions: The roles of employee feedback orientation on social awareness and utility. *Journal of Applied Psychology, 100*(4), 1296–1308. https://doi.org/10.1037/a0038334

Wang, M., Olson, D. A., & Shultz, K. S. (2012). *Mid and late career issues: An integrative perspective*. Routledge.

Wegge, J., Jungmann, F., Liebermann, S., Shemla, M., Ries, B. C., Diestel, S., & Schmidt, K. H. (2012). What makes age diverse teams effective? Results from a six-year research program. *Work, 41*(Suppl. 1), 5145–5151. https://doi.org/10.3233/WOR-2012-0084-5145

Wegge, J., & Schmidt, K. H. (2009). The impact of age diversity in teams on group performance, innovation and health. In A.-S. G. Antoniou, G. L. Cooper, G. P. Chrousos, C. D. Spielberger, & M. W. Eysenck (Eds.), *Handbook of managerial behavior and occupational health* (pp. 79–94). Edward Elgar.

Williams, K., & O'Reilly, C. (1998). The complexity of diversity: A review of forty years of research. *Research in Organizational Behavior, 21*, 77–140.

Zacher, H. (2015). Successful aging at work. *Work, Aging and Retirement, 1*(1), 4–25. https://doi.org/10.1093/workar/wau006

Zaniboni, S., Truxillo, D. M., & Fraccaroli, F. (2013). Differential effects of task variety and skill variety on burnout and turnover intentions for older and younger workers. *European Journal of Work and Organizational Psychology, 22*(3), 306–317. https://doi.org /10.1080/1359432X.2013.782288

EPILOGUE

Lisa M. Finkelstein

In 2015, I coedited a *Frontiers Series* book on aging, *Facing the Challenges of a Multi-Age Workforce: A Use-Inspired Approach* with Donald Truxillo, Franco Fraccaroli, and Ruth Kanfer (Finkelstein el al., 2015). At the time we were sensing increased energy around aging and work research. It was starting to appear more often at our conferences and in our mainstream journals, and Mo Wang's brainchild, the journal *Work, Aging and Retirement*, was born. Our *Frontiers* volume was designed to be a forward-looking book to present new ideas to keep the momentum going, to explore age and work in new ways, and to be use-inspired to present a clearer path to practical implementation. The introduction of a new *Frontiers* book just seven years later was at first surprising to me, but I soon realized this was reason to celebrate. In just a handful of years there has been so much growth not only in the interest of looking at the aging workforce but also in doing it in more complex and sophisticated ways.

I learned so much while reading this volume, and upon completing it I now see my role as Epilogue writer as being mostly cheerleader but also part harbinger of what might happen if we do not seize the day. In my final commentary in the 2015 book, I wrote a short chapter called "Now that we know what, *how?*" At the risk of being perceived as an old dog with no new tricks, I am taking the same approach here. The current volume has some exciting ideas for methodological advancements, theoretical approaches, and newer work contexts to explore. I think there is content in this book that can truly revolutionize the field of aging and work. I also worry that it will only happen if we as individual researchers, teachers, and practitioners make a clear plan for how we will change our practices based on this book and we as teams of scholars and even as a subfield make coordinated efforts to find ways to support getting some of the bigger ideas in this book off the ground. In the following paragraphs I muse on some of the specific ideas that excited me in this volume and make a few suggestions for things that can and should happen to facilitate maximum impact.

Let's begin with the methodology chapters (Chapters 8–13). I read these first, believing they could be the most broadly instructive and impactful. Here I was struck by the first sentence in Gerpott and Lehmann-Willenbrock's (Chapter 8) abstract: "empirical aging research largely became a science of questionnaires." This is hyperbole, as each of the methods chapters here displays shining examples of its focal method in the aging literature, but the core truth there resonated. And, of course, there is very well-done survey research from which we have learned a lot, and no one is asking we abandon that approach. But could we get out of our methodological comfort zones a bit more?

I was excited by the ideas in each of these chapters—behavioral methods, organization-level foci, diary studies and longitudinal approaches, workplace experiments, interventions, and qualitative and archival methods. There are important research questions in the realm of age and work that could better or more fully be answered using one of more of these approaches. Fortunately, many of these chapters provided us with really assistive tables and/or figures to use as tools as we plan our own work. This is more than we have seen in one volume like this, and I appreciate how these chapter authors were on the whole more specific in their "how-tos" than we typically see in a book like this. I applaud these authors for this. But, in all honesty, I still wanted more. If you could see the copies of the chapters I saved down to my computer, you would see a bunch of comments in the margins that look sort of like this: "I love this. But how?", "Where can I learn this?", "How can I get access to these kinds of samples?", and "What goes on behind the scenes to be able to do this so well?"

The theoretical chapters also open our eyes to some forward-thinking perspectives. In the same habitual ways we may fall back on the comfortable methodology that we know and have relied on, we may have our go-to theoretical frameworks upon which we have built our research models. In this section of the book we find some new light shining on old theories, new integration of classic concepts, and alternatives to ideas that have been debunked. Again, I found this section on the whole to be invigorating, although there are some complexities woven into some of these chapters that may leave some readers, especially those newly exposed to age-and-work research, unsure where to go with these ideas next. Indeed, I found myself wishing for the authors to pop up on my screen so I could ask them for some clarification and specific examples.

The last section of the book looks at particular content areas of work and the workplace, summarizes where we stand, and has ideas for research and practice. These are more traditional-style chapters, but they focus on areas with which a broader audience is probably less familiar. When it comes to practical suggestions, I think they go beyond the typical paragraph or two at the end of the journal article but could perhaps be taken further. How, very literally, can a practitioner take these ideas and use them to improve our workplaces?

This is a fantastic book, and every chapter has the potential to change and improve education, research, and practice. In order to reach this potential, I believe that the authors, the editors, and all of us readers have a job to do. Here is a nonexhaustive list of ideas for what can happen next to take all this great info to the next level.

How about some webinars from the methods authors to walk us through the specifics? Can we develop peer mentoring relationships where we mutually share our expertise to expand our tool kit? How about a podcast where practitioners could learn some science-based actionable tips? Maybe a video series with interviews from researchers who have made some of these ideas work? They could give us the scoop on things like: What went wrong? What were the bloopers? How were these challenges overcome? Detailed strategies for gaining useful, age-diverse working samples, winning over companies to collect data, etc. could go a long way to help move our field forward.

Can those of us who teach offer courses or even one week in a course in graduate school where we get into deep conversations about these theories? Can we do exercises in our lab groups where we think about how we can use some of these theoretical ideas to expand our research? Can we each take our own time to hunker down with a good cup of coffee, turn to a blank page, and reflect on where our own research stands and how we can use some of these ideas to expand or enrich or reinvigorate us?

I'm going to borrow from the Rosing and Zacher chapter on paradoxes (Chapter 5) liberally here. There is a paradox we all face where we are under pressure to do many different things and to do them quickly and efficiently. We have many boxes to tick off. At the same time, we also wish to do impactful, forward-thinking, more complex work that accounts for the messy nuances of our aging and age-diverse workforce. We need to engage in deep work (Newport, 2016), but our circumstances often don't encourage us to do this. How do we deal with this paradox? I'm no finance expert, but I do know that it is basically good practice to balance your portfolio among risky and safe investments. Maybe we balance our research portfolio in the same way? Hard problems are guaranteed not to be solved if we don't give them a good try. Can we continue with some of the type of work we have become comfortable with (as long as it continues to be rigorous and useful, of course) with some of our research time but devote a portion of our time to mastering and engaging in more complex, maybe riskier but more potentially impactful work? Who can we choose to work with who can make that potentially bumpy journey smoother and more enjoyable?

Moreover, I think this is a sweet spot that we are all in right now—the authors and editors as they bask in the excitement of their new book coming out and we as readers as we conclude this volume. One thing I always tell my students is that the couple days after you get back from SIOP (or any conference) are just as important as the days leading up to it or being there. That's when you have to take the time to look over your notes and make a plan as to specifically how you will use them; that's when you send a quick note to those people you met at your poster who you might want to collaborate with; that's when you find those articles someone told you about. You miss your sweet spot, and the momentum and subsequently the potential will vanish.

So, in that spirit, I invite you to stay put right now and stop and have a think. What are some literal and specific actions you can do, and when will you do them, to take something you learned here and join the effort to move us all forward in the quest to understand and improve our aging and age-diverse workplace?

References

Finkelstein, L. M., Truxillo, D. M., Fraccaroli, F., & Kanfer, R. (2015). *Facing the challenges of a multi-age workforce: A use-inspired approach.* Taylor and Francis.

Newport, C. (2016). *Deep work: Rules for focused success in a distracted world.* Grand Central Publishing.

INDEX

Note: Page numbers in *italics* in this index indicate figures; page numbers in **bold type** indicate tables.

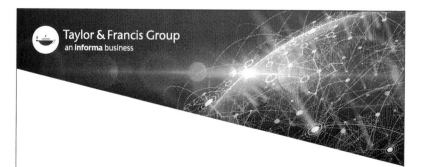